RENEWALS 691-4574
DATE DUE

The Middle East and the Western Alliance

Published under the auspices of the
Center for International and Strategic Affairs,
University of California, Los Angeles.

*A list of other Center publications appears
at the back of this book.*

The Middle East and the Western Alliance

Edited by
Steven L. Spiegel
Professor of Political Science,
Center for International and Strategic Affairs,
University of California, Los Angeles

London
GEORGE ALLEN & UNWIN
Boston   Sydney

George Allen & Unwin (Publishers) Ltd,
40 Museum Street, London WC1A 1LU, UK

George Allen & Unwin (Publishers) Ltd,
Park Lane, Hemel Hempstead, Herts HP2 4TE, UK

Allen & Unwin, Inc.,
9 Winchester Terrace, Winchester, Mass. 01890, USA

George Allen & Unwin Australia Pty Ltd,
8 Napier Street, North Sydney, NSW 2060, Australia

First published in 1982

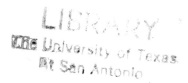
British Library Cataloguing in Publication Data

The Middle East and the Western Alliance.
1. Near East — Foreign relations
2. World politics — 1975-1985
I. Spiegel, Steven L.
327.560171'3   DS63
ISBN 0-04-327067-0

Library of Congress Cataloging in Publication Data

The Middle East and the Western Alliance
Includes index.
1. Near East — Politics and Government — 1945–
I. Spiegel, Steven L.   II. Title.
DS63.1.M4854   956'.04   82-6752
ISBN 0-04-327067-0   AACR2

Set in 10 on 11 point Times by Grove Graphics Tring
and printed in Great Britain
by Mackays of Chatham

Contents

Introduction

STEVEN L. SPIEGEL

The post-World War II Western Alliance has long been heralded by statesmen and scholars alike as a model of diplomacy and international collaboration. As a consequence the alliance has been judged by a standard of cooperation which it has only rarely achieved. In a coalition of democracies – united by common values but a receding sense of external danger and a series of competing domestic interests – controversies were to be anticipated. Indeed, the alliance has never attained the degree of cooperation to which it has often been credited. It was one thing to withstand the perceived threat of a Soviet military thrust into the West German heartland, but it has been more complex to apply principles of cooperation to matters of commerce and to issues affecting regions outside Europe.

Here a singular fallacy has operated. Because the alliance has had major accomplishments in the defense of Europe, many observers have assumed that it has acted elsewhere with similar success. Therefore, the strains which have occurred *vis-à-vis* the Middle East and energy policy since October 1973 have been perceived in some quarters as an indication that the alliance was disintegrating. Yet the conclusion is deceptive. While coalition tensions have indeed existed since 1973, many observers easily ignore that the fact of strain itself is not novel. The conflict between the USA and Europe over issues relating to the colonial empires and their dismantlement were endemic to the postwar period. The American attitude at the time is reflected in a patronizing anti-imperialism, resulting in policy disputes over the future of such areas as Indochina, South Asia and Africa. The Middle East was typical of this approach toward the European imperial tradition. For example, Secretary of State Dulles returned from a fact-finding trip to the area in the spring of 1953 and reported to the president that he believed that the British, French and Israelis were 'millstones around our neck'. According to the official minutes of a meeting during the Suez crisis, 'Secretary Dulles commented that he had been greatly worried for two or three years over our identification with countries pursuing colonial policies not compatible with our own'.

The Middle East, however, was an area of alliance acrimony dating back even to the period before World War II, when the USA sought to displace the supremacy of British oil companies in the area – a process which continued after the war. Meanwhile, in the immediate postwar period the USA eased the French out of Syria and Lebanon and engaged in a tense series of controversies with Britain over the future of Palestine and, later, over the future of the British role in the Suez Canal area. The most distinctive and dramatic alliance crisis since 1945 actually occurred long before 1973 – over the Egyptian nationalization of the Suez Canal in 1956 and many would argue that the Western Alliance has never been the same since.

If alliance conflicts may have eased after Suez, it was more because the Europeans no longer played a dominating role in the region and because alliance differences had been glossed over. In this sense the French switch of clients from Israel to the Arabs in 1967 and the general alliance disarray during the October War and afterward were throwbacks to the original patterns, rather than signs that a break with a cooperative past had occurred.

Alliance problems after 1973 were, however, distinctive for several reasons. First, the roles had been reversed from the 1940s and 1950s. By comparison with American chiding of their European cousins in the 1940s for the perpetuation of their empires, now the Europeans viewed the USA as seeking a Pax Americana over the Middle East and questioned Washington's priorities and judgments. Secondly, alliance disagreements appeared more dramatic, because they occurred after a period of weak European involvement in the Middle East in which the USA was left to operate on the diplomatic scene as the sole representative of the West for practical purposes.

Thirdly, although alliance dissension had indeed occurred in an earlier era, the relative priority of the Middle East for Western decisionmakers by comparison with other domestic and foreign policy questions was much higher in the 1970s. The frequency and priority of Middle Eastern issues also rose as suggested by the issues of price and security of energy supply, the geopolitics of the Persian Gulf, the Arab-Israeli question, the future of Lebanon, the Soviet invasion of Afghanistan, the crisis in Iran, the Iranian-Iraqi war and Russian influence in such disparate countries as South Yemen, Ethiopia and Syria. With such a list and given the high dependence of Europe and Japan on Middle Eastern oil, the salience of Middle Eastern issues inevitably grew – raising concerns and interests which were bound to lead to differences with Washington, where issues were viewed from an alternative perspective.

Fourthly, in previous periods of tension the USA was still regarded as the unquestioned and even rightful leader of the Western Alliance. By the mid-1970s, however, respect in and even trust for American leadership had been seriously eroded after Vietnam, Watergate and the inconsistencies of the Carter era. Diminished faith in the USA coincided with a newly vibrant Europe, creating a foundation for enhanced levels of tension.

Finally, a new condition was created with the active effort on the part of Middle Eastern states themselves to influence individual alliance countries and to sow disagreement within the ranks. After the October 1973 war and again after President Sadat's trip to Jerusalem in November 1977, many Arab states engaged in dynamic policies designed to move individual European states and the Japanese away from identification with US policy. These efforts were new elements in the relationship between the Middle East and the West. Given the dependence of Western Europe and Japan on Middle East oil supplies, the Arab producers had a powerful instrument at their disposal – a power enhanced by the billions gained from the ever-rising cost of OPEC petroleum. These conditions led individual allies to make separate arrangements with specific producers which were often at variance with the policies of other allies – especially the USA. French and Italian nuclear assistance to Iraq in return for preferred oil supplies is a notable case in point. Diplomatic differences between the USA and several of the European allies over the conduct of Arab-Israeli policy also ensued.

Yet, as several of the chapters which follow make clear, the issues at stake within the Western coalition are more complex than might be suggested by the simple explanation that there were differences between the USA and the rest of the alliance over Arab-Israeli policy motivated largely by Japanese and European need for oil supplies. Dominique Moisi, in his essay on Europe and the Middle East, suggests that by the end of the 1970s there had developed in Europe a greater degree of sympathy for the Palestinian cause than was evident in the USA. Moreover, several authors point to the changing nexus of concern by all allies as the Middle East center of attention moved away from the Palestinian issue and toward the problems of the Persian Gulf raised by such events as the overthrow of the shah, the rise to power of a fundamentalist Shi'ite government led by Ayatollah Khomeini, the 1979 uprisings in Saudi Arabia, the Soviet invasion of Afghanistan and the wars between the Yemens and between Iran and Iraq. Janice Stein also points out that when differences have occurred they cannot always be described as a simple distinction between Europe and Japan, on the one hand, and the USA (perhaps backed by Canada), on the other. Not only are there disputes and a variety of views within Europe, but the conflicts over policy – especially at the UN – have often crossed regional and continental lines with several European governments coming closer in their views to the US perspective than to the positions held by some of their neighbors. Several essays – especially those of Janice Gross Stein, Robert Lieber and Joan Garratt – also demonstrate vividly that contact among the allies has not been restricted to conflict, but rather there has indeed been a strong element of cooperation – particularly as the dust settled after the October War. Thus, the International Energy Agency was founded and, through a series of summit meetings, targets for oil consumption and conservation and for actions in emergencies were set. As Janice Stein points out, 'at best, arguments of substantive change in policy and consequent exacerbation of tension within the alliance are considerable exaggerations'. Yet Robert Lieber cautions that, 'The chief pressures toward divisiveness among the NATO and OECD countries stem from the extreme energy and economic vulnerabilities of Europe and Japan'. These basic conditions have not altered during the 1970s and they continue to be confronted in the policy of the allies individually and collectively toward the highly volatile and unstable Middle East.

The chapters in this volume examine the interaction between the allies and the Western Alliance in the wake of the series of crises which have recently emanated from the Middle East – involving energy, the Arab-Israeli dispute, the instability of the Persian Gulf and the Soviet invasion of Afghanistan. Most of the essays were originally presented at a conference held at the UCLA Center for International and Strategic Affairs in

February 1980. They approach the topic of the Middle East and the Western Alliance from a variety of perspectives.

First, three chapters by William Quandt, Dominique Moisi and Masahiro Sasagawa discuss the basic problems confronted and policies pursued in the Middle East by the USA, the Common Market (EEC) countries and Japan, respectively. A second three chapters discuss in broader terms cooperative and conflictual relations among the allies in such areas as Arab-Israeli diplomacy, energy and the Persian Gulf. These essays, written by Janice Stein, Joan Garratt and Robert Lieber, seek to identify the way in which the alliance as a whole has operated in the wake of challenges to individual countries.

Beyond the alliance itself, however, is the superpower confrontation to which we turn in our third section. James R. Kurth examines the role of the USA in the Middle East toward both the Atlantic Alliance and Moscow, and Francis Fukuyama looks at the implications for the alliance of what he calls 'new directions' in Soviet policy toward the area. These two essays serve to remind us of the role of the superpower conflict as background to the interconnection between the Middle East and the Western Alliance.

From the struggle of the Western allies with the Middle East and the superpower conflict over the region, we turn to efforts by the countries of the area to deal with the Western powers. The first series of essays deals with the Arab world's attempt to translate its new-found economic strength into concrete diplomatic achievements. Among others the Saudis, the Egyptians, the Iraqis, the Libyans and the Palestinians have all been confronted with opportunities and frustrations raised by the rush of Western interest in and concern for the region. But Fouad Ajami notes how 'the Arab order that waged the October War had been fragmented' by the end of the 1970s. The essays by Fouad Ajami, Ibrahim Karawan and Tawfic Farah describe how differing factions in the Arab world were dealing with the alliance at that point.

In our final section, we analyze the reaction of the three major non-Arab powers toward the Western Alliance, their Arab neighbors and their own weighty specific problems. In very different ways each of these countries experienced major changes of government and a basic alteration of its role in the region by 1980. In large part, these developments were reactions to the upheavals of the October War and the energy crisis. For Israel, the election of the first Likud government had been followed by an end to her previous isolation with the signing of a peace treaty with Egypt. For Iran, the overthrow of the shah and the rise to power of a revolutionary Shi'ite regime led to a complete transformation of the country's role in the region. For Turkey, internal political tension and economic chaos led eventually to a military coup in 1980 accompanied by many pessimistic assessments of the future of the Turkish polity and economy. The three chapters by Itamar Rabinovitch, Richard Cottam and Ciro Zoppo examine these developments and place their meaning in perspective for the Middle East and the West.

Considered collectively, these essays reflect the inherent complexity of the relationships among the Middle Eastern states and between these states and the Western allies. The clash of cultures, histories, interests and values is staggering. Even within the alliance perspectives vary starkly, but when the Western states confront the fractionalized and divided Middle East, frustrations necessarily arise. In this light, how will future Middle East developments affect the allies? How will the alliance as a unit be able to deal with an area so crucial to its future and yet so distinguished by chaos and instability? Will the alliance be able to develop a coordinated strategy for dealing with these problems, or will it be torn asunder by the fragmented diversity of the region? The chapters which follow may not answer these questions directly, but they do provide the background to a perplexing series of issues which are likely to be paramount throughout the 1980s.

Part One

Policies within the Alliance toward
the Middle East

1 The Western Alliance in the Middle East: Problems for US Foreign Policy

WILLIAM B. QUANDT

The decade of the 1980s promises to be one of continuing difficulty between the United States and her allies in dealing with a wide range of issues in the Middle East. As the USA has struggled to develop a coherent policy for dealing with Middle East realities following the collapse of the imperial regime in Iran, it has anxiously sought European and Japanese support for its efforts. Not surprisingly, cooperation has been far from perfect, resulting in frequent irritation and misunderstanding.

From an American perspective, crises in the Middle East threaten not only US national interests, but those of the entire industrialized world. Therefore, it is almost axiomatic in Washington that a unified allied position should be developed. When this does not happen, suspicions arise that the allies are trying to promote their own narrow concerns at the expense of broader Western interests. In the Middle East the stakes are particularly high and, therefore, the mutual acrimony can become intense. At issue are not only the supply and price of oil, but also Soviet power and developments that could threaten the overall strategic balance. European complacency in the face of such dangers is viewed in Washington as an ominous prelude to 'Finlandization', a process that could be greatly accelerated by Soviet influence over Persian Gulf oil supplies.

That Americans expect allied solidarity in the face of Middle East challenges is hardly surprising, and yet even a glance at the historical record should lead to different expectations. For much of the post-World War II period, the USA has been at odds with its key European allies over Middle Eastern issues. In the early 1950s, the USA frequently took a disdainful attitude toward British and French colonial policies in the region, fearing that too close an association with the former European rulers could damage US interests in the Arab world. The most dramatic breach, of course, came in the Suez war of 1956, which found the USA opposing the British-French-Israeli invasion of Egypt. With the erosion of British and French power in the Middle East, the USA adopted a more assertive position of its own, only to find that allied support for American policies was not automatically forthcoming.

During the Lebanese crisis of 1958 US and British policies were carefully coordinated, but even in this instance the ultimate goals being pursued differed significantly. American troops landed in Beirut with the limited purpose of restoring order in Lebanon, whereas British forces arrived in Jordan not only to shore up King Hussein's regime, but also to move against Iraq if that should prove necessary or feasible. The Americans had no intention of helping to restore British primacy in Iraq, and this last European effort in the Middle East to keep the remnants of an earlier era intact failed for lack of US encouragement, much as the Suez venture had gone awry two years earlier.

Meanwhile the USA was distancing itself from the French effort to keep part of North Africa under colonial rule. In 1957, to the considerable dismay of conventional American diplomats, a young senator from Massachusetts, John F. Kennedy, publicly criticized French policy for not granting independence to Algeria. Shortly thereafter, official, albeit discreet, contacts began between US officials and the Algerian Front de Liberation Nationale (FLN), causing considerable French anger.

Having failed to win US backing for their Middle East ventures, the British and the French were less than enthusiastic in their acceptance of US leadership in the region. Europeans tended to see the Americans as trying to profit – politically and economically – from their misfortunes. The anti-colonial stance of the USA was viewed as a cynical means to curry favor with the Arabs.

The decline of the European political position in the Middle East through the 1950s led to something of a reversal of roles in alliance relations in the region. Once the USA found itself in the 1960s as the predominant military power in the region, it resented the failure of the allies to toe the line and suspected their materialistic motives, much as they had with regard to Washington in the previous decade.

The June 1967 war proved to be a watershed in the history of the Middle East and US-European relations in the region. After some initial hesitation and efforts to develop a common alliance position prior to the war, the USA came down firmly on Israel's side once the conflict erupted, whereas France branded Israel the aggressor and cut off military aid. As a result, for the first time the USA became the primary supplier of arms to Israel.

The diplomacy of the post-June 1967 war period involved an attempt to define the essential terms of an Arab-Israeli peace settlement. The French in particular have seen the UN resolution 242 as calling for full Israeli withdrawal from the occupied territories in return for peace, whereas Washington has gradually diluted its original insistence that Resolution 242 requires withdrawal to the 4 June 1967 lines, with only minor, mutually accepted adjustments. In addition to this difference of interpretation over Israel's obligation to return Arab territory, the Europeans have also pressed the idea that some recognition should be given to the right of the Palestinians to self-determination.

Splits with the allies over the diplomacy of Arab-Israeli peace have caused occasional irritation in Washington, but the sense of betrayal was particularly great when, during the October 1973 Arab-Israeli war, arguments arose over military operations, US-Soviet relations, and oil. The 1973 crisis reminded the USA and its allies of the dangers in the Arab-Israeli arena, but it also demonstrated to Americans that they could not count on European support in confronting the Soviets in the Middle East. American planes airlifting arms to Israel could not refuel in Europe, with the reluctant exception of Portugal.

Crisis diplomacy leaves little time for consultation with allies, and as a result the Europeans and Japanese found themselves on the sidelines when events of enormous importance to them were taking place. They, after all, were more dependent on Middle Eastern oil than the USA and would not have been spared the consequences of a military showdown between Moscow and Washington. But even though their interests were engaged, they were incapable of acting.

The USA emerged from the October war with a sense of irritation toward the allies, disillusionment with US-Soviet détente, and a determination to monopolize the peacemaking efforts. Only on the oil front were efforts made to institutionalize cooperation through the newly formed International Energy Agency (IEA). Japan, which had rarely shown much interest in Middle Eastern affairs, joined the IEA and began the long-overdue task of adjusting its policies to its interests.

If the Arab-Israeli dispute has been the most divisive Middle Eastern issue for the alliance in the past, it will not necessarily remain the only one in the future. Just as likely, and potentially more consequential, will be differences over appropriate policies toward the region of the Persian Gulf and Arabian Peninsula. There the issues of oil and the emerging Soviet threat will come together to create a particularly explosive mixture, one which will place continuing strains on the Western Alliance, and particularly on the USA as it gropes for appropriate policies to meet a multitude of dangers.

In both the Arab-Israeli and Persian Gulf arenas, problems between the USA and its allies arise from several distinct sources. First, there are different assessments of the actual situation in the region. Secondly, there are divergent perceptions of national interest and the appropriate policies to pursue those interests. Thirdly, there are the inevitable problems of co-ordination within an alliance. These involve doubts about the wisdom and the policies of the leader of the alliance – often expressed as irritation over lack of consultation – and a corresponding dissatisfaction on the part of the USA at the independent stances taken by the smaller alliance members, who benefit from the security umbrella of the USA but who refuse to follow Washington's lead.

President Carter reflected this last concern in April 1980, speaking before the American Society of Newspaper Editors:

Nations ask us for leadership. But at the same time, they demand their own independenc of action. They ask us for aid. But they reject any interference. They ask for understanding. Yet they often decline to understand us in return. Some ask for protection, but are wary of the obligations of alliance.

The American assessment of Middle East issues in recent years has diverged significantly from that of many Europeans. The gap has thus far been less profound when dealing with the question of what is at stake in the Persian Gulf region than on the Arab-Israeli conflict. With respect to the Gulf, a consensus can be found that oil is and will remain vital to the Western world for the indefinite future. It is also widely understood that the USSR has both ambitions and significant capabilities in the region. Coupled with internal weaknesses and instability, Soviet pressures on the regimes of the area can have a decisive impact. Agreement on these simple points, however, does not lead to coherence of policy. Instead, the USA finds itself somewhat out of step with its alliance partners when it comes to devising a strategy for dealing with the problems of the region.

The USA has reacted to the fall of the Shah of Iran and to the Soviet invasion of Afghanistan by assigning a new priority in its foreign policy to the Persian Gulf region. This policy, often labeled the 'Carter Doctrine', starts with the recognition of the vital nature of interests in the area of the Persian Gulf, the double threat to those interests stemming from regional instability and Soviet pressures, and the comparative lack of Western power to counterbalance the Soviet threat. This assessment has led to an initial emphasis on building US military strength in the region, starting with relatively modest steps, but possibly leading to more significant developments at a later date. A 'consultative security framework' has now been offered as the response to the demise of the 'Nixon Doctrine'.

The military dimension of the Carter Doctrine has involved a search for access to facilities in a selected number of countries – in the first instance Oman, Somalia, Kenya, and probably Egypt, Israel and possibly Saudi Arabia at a later stage. Arms transfers to some countries will remain a part of US policy, and new emphasis will be placed on prepositioning of equipment which could be wedded to highly mobile US combat forces in crisis situations. The USA is also planning to improve its airlift and sealift capabilities to reach the Persian Gulf region, and is trying to develop understandings with countries in the area to allow access to facilities, airspace and ports. By the mid-1980s the USA hopes to have a Rapid Deployment Force intact, capable of projecting several divisions into the Persian Gulf region and sustaining them, if necessary, over a long period of time.

On the face of it, these developments do not cause the Europeans and Japanese great difficulties, but they do raise questions about the broader strategy of which the Carter Doctrine is only a part. Does the USA, they ask, have a strategy for dealing with Iran? Will American and allied pressures on Iran undermine moderate leaders in Iran and open the way for a leftist government which might turn to the USSR? Would a US-Soviet clash in the Persian Gulf result in the disruption of crucial oil supplies? If so, how would the USA propose to deal with such disruptions?

What if Iraq seizes the opportunity of Iran's weaknesses and its confrontation with the USA to attack the oilproducing areas of Iran? Would the USA stand by, or would the USA try to deter such an Iraqi move? All of these questions touch on political and diplomatic issues which remain ambiguous in the current formulations out of Washington. Many Europeans see the threat to the region as more political than military and, therefore, they are particularly anxious to know Washington's views on such matters, rather than simply focusing on military planning for remote contingencies.

The European allies also appear to be skeptical of the suddenness of the US conversion to a more alert posture in defense of Western interests in the Persian Gulf. President Carter's remarks implying that he was shocked by the Soviet intervention in Afghanistan seemed to many Europeans a remarkable confession of political innocence. With a wordly wise condescension which is not their most attractive feature, many European pundits see new US policy initiatives as simplistic answers to complex problems, long overdue even where sensible, but more often than not premature, inadequate, or misguided. This critique has a certain sting, but would be more convincing if accompanied by alternative strategic concepts. These, most often, are lacking.

Thus, the dialogue that might lead to a stronger alliance posture toward the crucial developments in the Persian Gulf often results in little more than mutual recrimination. At the official level much is said about consultation and coordination, but relatively little seems to take place. It was only when the USA began to threaten military action against Iran in April 1980 over the hostage issue that the European allies and Japan began to offer active support for US diplomatic and economic pressures on Iran as a preferred alternative.

The unsuccessful attempt to rescue the American hostages held in Tehran in late April 1980 further deepened splits in the alliance. The Europeans had agreed to sanctions and diplomatic pressures as an alternative to military action, not as asmokescreen. Their feelings of having been deceived and their irritation at the inevitable lack of advance consultation were frequently expressed. Had the operation succeeded, of course, there would have been unanimous applause, but failure added to the belief that the Americans were not only unreliable partners, but also inept.

The Americans have an understandable desire to see their allies in full support of US policy initiatives. But such unanimity is both unlikely and often unnecessary. What is required, is that the alliance members not work at cross purposes when vital issues are at stake. Identity of views is less important than complementarity. Unified action may be less essential than a coherent division of labor. For example, if the USA finds it necessary to divert some of its naval assets from the Mediterranean and eastern Pacific in order to maintain a permanent presence in the Indian Ocean, it is reasonable to expect the NATO allies to assume more responsibility for security in the Mediterranean, and for the Japanese to do likewise in northeast Asia.

On the political front, some of our European allies have assets which we lack. For example, the French have a political position in Iraq and a military presence in Djibouti, which could be useful to the Western Alliance. The British maintain influence in Oman and in a number of the Gulf sheikdoms. Germany has taken the lead in assisting Turkey ecoomically, and Japan could play a larger role in providing economic aid to Pakistan. European arms supplies are often the only realistic alternative to military dependence on the USSR for countries like Iraq, and possibly Iran in the future. Rather than seeing the Europeans as competitors in these situations, the USA should recognise the importance of precluding the USSR from a dominant position in such strategically located countries, even if this means that European suppliers gain an increasing share of some Middle Eastern markets.

Allied cooperation in the Persian Gulf region could also be enhanced through periodic consultations among British, French, German, Japanese and American experts on political, economic and military trends in the region. Intelligence could be shared to common benefit. Analytical capabilities for tracking Soviet activities in the region need to be strengthened. In these areas, there is much to be gained from cooperation and little cost involved.

Finally, a serious alliance posture toward the Persian Gulf requires an effective energy policy for the alliance as a whole. The USA, as the largest consumer of energy, needs to show the way toward a coherent policy by taking serious steps to reduce consumption of energy.

In the absence of a high degree of alliance solidarity and coordination toward the Persian Gulf region, the Soviets may exploit opportunities to isolate Washington from Europe and Japan. Already seized by doubts about the constancy and wisdom of US leadership, the allies could be induced and pressured toward an independent stance, resulting in deep strains within the alliance. Were this to occur, it could prove to be one of the most substantial gains for Moscow related to the Persian Gulf crisis.

The Arab-Israeli issue is also likely to be a source of disagreement among the allies in the future, but the consequences of disagreement over this issue will be less significant than divergence in policies toward the Gulf. Since the Europeans and Japanese have little real influence over the course of the Arab-Israeli negotiations, there is little reason for Washington to fear the disruptive potential of their adopting an independent stance. By contrast, sharp differences among NATO partners over the Persian Gulf could play into Moscow's hands and greatly complicate the US-led effort to deter Soviet expansion in the vital oil areas of the Persian Gulf.

The USA should be prepared to accept a greater diversity of allied viewpoints with respect to the Arab-Israeli conflict than on Persian Gulf issues. There may even be some benefits from a distinctive European posture toward the Palestine question, particularly if it ensures that countries such as Syria, Iraq, Jordan and the Palestinians themselves feel they have some alternative to heavy dependence on the USSR.

Since President Sadat's bold initiative in traveling to Jerusalem in November 1977, the USA and its allies have generally had a different evaluation of the Arab-Israeli conflict. When faced with the stark question of whether a separate Egyptian-Israeli peace would be better than nothing, the USA answered yes. Among the Europeans, the French clearly thought the answer was no. The question since the Camp David agreements of September 1978 has been whether the Egyptian-Israeli negotiations can lead to a peace settlement that is sufficiently broadly based to enhance stability in the region. The USA has again placed its bets that a comprehensive peace can eventually be achieved through this process, while most Europeans and Japanese are skeptical.

Concerning the specific issue of the Palestinians and their role in the peace negotiations, and specifically the question of contacts with the PLO, US and allied positions have increasingly diverged. The USA has edged away from a belief that the Palestinian issue is central to the prospects for stability in the Middle East and instead is treating it as one of many issues that deserve attention. But it is generally not seen as vital to peace between Egypt and Israel, nor to Saudi stability. The Europeans and Japanese tend to take the Palestinian issue more seriously, seeing the PLO as the legitimate representative of the Palestinians, and believing, perhaps excessively optimistically, that a solution to the Palestinian question will have a significant and positive impact on regional stability and on reliable oil supplies. In their statement issued in Venice in June 1980 the European leaders went so far as to call for the 'association' of the PLO with the peace process, something the USA refuses to countenance unless the PLO accepts UN Resolution 242 and Israel's right to exist.

The US defense of the Camp David process has rested on the belief that negotiations can produce a dynamic influence of their own that will open the way to a gradual resolution of the major issues in contention between Israel and Palestinians. The idea of a transitional period during which Palestinians would have the opportunity to develop institutions of self-government prior to a second phase of negotiations to resolve political and security issues is seen in Washington as reasonable. The lukewarm support of the allies has been resented in some quarters, ignored in others.

Anticipating failure of these talks, the Europeans began in spring 1980 to suggest alternative diplomatic strategies, possibly involving efforts in the United Nations to broaden the principles under which peace talks might take place to include some reference to Palestinian rights or Palestinian self-determination. Washington had toyed with the same idea in August 1979, but had backed away in the face of Israeli and Egyptian disapproval. Europeans have been constrained from pushing aggressively on this point because of their recognition that Carter could do little in an election year, and because of President Sadat's disinclination to force the issue. But differences of this issue cannot be long suppressed, and the USA will have to get used to being isolated in UN Security Council votes and in other international settings when the Palestinian question is raised.

The European critique of US policy on the Arab-Israeli conflict has tended to blame the Americans for not using enough influence with Israel to gain a freeze on settlement activity in occupied territories, to show restraint in Lebanon, to accept the principle of eventual withdrawal as envisaged in UN Resolution 242, and to be a bit more forthcoming on allowing real autonomy for the Palestinians. Washington's allergy toward the PLO has not been shared by the allies.

In reply, the Carter administration has argued that peace cannot be achieved merely through pressure on Israel; that no realistic alternative to Camp David exists; and that the PLO has shown no willingness or ability to take conciliatory steps as the price of its admission to the peace process. On the issue of Israeli settlements, many Americans share the

European view that these are obstacles to peace, but bitter experience has convinced the administration that Prime Minister Begin's government is unyielding on this point.

For the moment, there seems to be little prospect that US and European views will come together on the politically sensitive question of the Palestinians. But does it really matter? From Washington's standpoint, it would of course be preferable to have strong support in the alliance for its policies. This might help to convince skeptical Arabs that the Camp David approach is the only realistic alternative. It might conceivably encourage Egypt and Israel to be more imaginative in the peacemaking, if they felt they had the full support of not only the USA, but also Europe and Japan. But, on balance, it seems unlikely that Middle East peace would be much closer today if the USA and its allies had adopted a common position. The skepticism of the rejectionist Arabs would hardly have been eroded by alliance solidarity, nor would the most intractable of the issues involving the Palestinians melt in the face of a purposeful Western policy. It can be argued, with some plausibility, that the European position has had a modest effect in containing Arab radicalism, leaving hope for the opponents of Camp David that an alternative approach may be available in the future that involves diplomacy rather than a resort to armed force.

Americans are likely to take offense at some European efforts to court Arab favor, particularly when separate oil deals are thrown into the bargain. The 1973 war demonstrated how deep divisions in the alliance can become over Arab-Israeli issues. The allies did not want to be associated with the policy of American support for Israel, whereas Washington saw the issues more in US-Soviet terms and demanded allied support. But the events following the 1973 war also demonstrated that only the USA has significant influence over the diplomacy of peacemaking, and that a European role is neither essential, nor welcomed by all of the parties to the conflict.

The one area where the Europeans rather than the USA may be better placed to play a part is in urging the Palestinians, and perhaps the Syrians, to develop a more moderate posture toward peace negotiations. The USA, unable to deal officially with the leaders of the Palestinian movement, has little ability to influence directly Palestinian perceptions of negotiating opportunities. The Europeans and Japanese, if they take their own role seriously, might turn the PLO's desire for recognition and respectability into a source of leverage over the Palestinian negotiating position. But expectations even here should be limited, and in the end it will probably be the USA, Egypt and Israel who shape the next phase of negotiations involving the Palestinians, not the Europeans.

In summary, the USA, Europe and Japan will face many difficult choices in the Middle East in the 1980s. In the region of the Persian Gulf, a serious effort should be made for complementarity, coordination and some division of labor. The interests at stake are common – oil, containing Soviet influence, and the strategic balance of power – and these shared concerns require a degree of coherence in policies within the alliance. In addition, the allies bring some strength to bear on the situation that the USA lacks and, therefore, coordinated efforts can be mutually beneficial.

On the Arab-Israeli conflict, there is probably no serious alternative to having some disagreements over the most effective means for negotiating the Palestinian question. This need not be a source of great contention, since both the USA and Europe should be able to live with their different positions. The USA will continue to play the lead-role in diplomacy, while the Europeans will explore alternatives, cultivate their Arab relations and hope to be treated well in the event that oil is used as a political weapon. Fortunately, the Arab-Israeli conflict seems unlikely to erupt into war, or even sustained crisis. If it were to do so, as the Europeans fear, allied differences could once again become a serious matter, rather than the relatively minor irritant that they have been in recent years. It is clearly in the interest of all members of the alliance to help ensure that the Arab-Israeli conflict moves toward eventual resolution, and that the danger of another war be minimized. But it is even more essential that the USA, Europe and Japan begin to devise sensible, mutually reinforcing policies to protect their vital interests in the Persian Gulf.

2 Europe and the Middle East

DOMINIQUE MOISI

'She stoops for oil.' In a recent article of the *New Republic*, European policy toward the Middle East was denounced as a perfect symbol of a decadent and coward Europe. 'To an American, Europe's policy seems risky, shortsighted, frantic and amoral. It is a foreign policy based on economics and governed by fear.'[1]

The Middle East, from the Suez crisis to the October War, has been a source of contention between the USA and its European allies and also among the Europeans themselves, at least until 1973. If the present tension does not constitute an exception to a well-established pattern, it still has specific characteristics linked to the fall of the shah and the Soviet invasion of Afghanistan. The Persian Gulf, which until 1979 practically succeeded in escaping direct East–West rivalry has now the dubious honor of being in the front line. Its tensions interact with those of the Middle East and thus aggravate the situation in the region and the potential for division among the allies.

It is now largely with their eyes turned toward the Persian Gulf, the stability of the main oilproducing countries, the security of the Straits of Hormuz, that the Western powers pay such attention to the traditional Arab-Israeli conflict and its key question, the Palestinian problem. There are specific reasons which justify an attempt to understand the role that the Europeans can play today in the Middle East conflict. The mere fact that one can use the expression 'Europe' *vis-à-vis* the Middle East conflict marks a new phenomenon. The numerous joint statements of the Nine on the Middle East conflict since 1973 symbolize their visible rapprochement on the topic, along the lines of France's position in 1973. Can this greater unity of Europe transform itself into a greater influence or a capaacity for action in the region? Or, given the essential military dimension of the conflict, is the role of Europe, a 'civilian power', bound to remain marginal?

Will the USA continue to see the Middle East and its peace process as their own *châsse gardée*? Is there any reality behind the division of labor scheme advanced by the Germans? Can the USA and the Europeans, out of a common vision of their interests favored by the Soviet threat and the domestic instability of the region, really work together in this part of the world? Will, on the contrary, the Middle East constitute the crucial area of tension among the allies? In attending to these questions I shall first analyze the evolution of the positions of the three principal European actors: France, the Federal Republic of Germany and Great Britain.[2]

Then, I look at how a common European policy was shaped on the matter. Finally, I will examine the role Europe can play *vis-à-vis* the new unstable situation created in the Gulf area.

To reflect on the role of the European countries *vis-à-vis* the Middle East conflict, is for someone who wants to believe in Europe a frustrating exercise, a reflection on the role of marginality in history. It is painful to constantly ask oneself not what Europe can do with respect to the Middle East conflict, but what the conflict can do to Western Europe.

NATIONAL EVOLUTIONS

France

In clear contrast to Germany and Britain, France's policy toward the conflict has been characterized since 1967 by a remarkable continuity emphasized by French diplomats to rebuke the accusation that their diplomacy is only motivated by the oil crisis. This continuity arises, in part, from the fact that the Middle East is a region in which France had traditional interests and influence even if one does not need always to recall the alliance between Suleiman and François I, at the beginning of the sixteenth century. For France, the Middle East is also an integral part of a global political project, characterized by the attempt to transcend a purely regional role. In a world divided by blocs, France could see itself as a potential mediator between East and West and, since the concept was coined, between North and South. For France the Middle East could, therefore, represent an ideally suited region for such a dual policy: strategically the Middle East is East–West (or East–South), while economically it can be said to be North–South. France's intervention in Lebanon in May 1978 under the banner of the United Nations, in a country that was formerly under the French mandate, demonstrated both French ambition to play a role and the limits of this ambition. Though it can easily be said that the nature of the Lebanese conflict is such that nothing can really be done by any outside power to 'repair' a country whose inhabitants have ceased to behave as Lebanese. The last significant attempt of France to play the mediator between Arabs and Israelis failed dramatically when, on the eve of the Six Day War, Israel refused to follow French warnings and advice of moderation.

Once liberated from the Algerian albatross, France sought to reestablish its influence in the Arab world, a prerequisite for achieving global influence in the Third World to counterbalance the predominance of the USA and the USSR. This stance implied curtailing the overly close relationship with Israel based on a common anti-Arab position.

There was another element to it especially after 1973: oil. France imports 74 percent of its oil from the Middle East. One of the characteristics of the French approach to trade is its political connotation. The French believe that they can secure economic markets by political declarations and diplomatic stances, an attitude which is just the opposite of the Germans'. This aproach proved quite frustrating in the conquest of markets in general, if one excludes the sales of weapons, a field in which France proved its competitiveness, because it is a political market. The economic links with Iraq, for instance, may also constitute an additional explanation of the French reservations to the Egypt-Israeli peace process.

Neglecting the feeling and sensitivity of public opinion and the majority of the political class, and even some administrative reluctance (translated in the 'Vedettes de Cherbourg' incident), France became, after 1967, the first European country to establish a special relationship with the Arab world providing it with military assistance as part of a globally ambitious arms sale policy, and giving it political and diplomatic support at the United Nations. Defending the principle of Israel's right to exist, France was going as far as possible in the direction of the Arab world. It therefore dissociated itself from the rest of the Europeans, as we shall see, expressing the wish nevertheless that they would follow as long as it retained the leading-edge, sufficient to distinguish France 'from the pack'.

In concrete terms, in the last years, France's attitude has implied two things:

(1) Being the first European country member of the EEC to emphasize the importance of the Palestinian 'national' question, no longer seen as a refugee problem. Already in his presidential campaign, the candidate Giscard d'Estaing was stressing the Palestinian factor as the key to the solution of the conflict, an analysis which he would carry out in actions: the opening in 1975 of a PLO office in Paris; successive meetings between PLO leaders and French officials; visit of Khadumi to Paris; etc.

    The French, however, maintain a dual restriction with respect to the Palestinian question:

    (a) They use the expression *patrie* (homeland, and not the word 'state') when speaking of the rights of the Palestinians.
    (b) They have not yet accepted to receive Arafat in Paris without conditions, though they would like to be the first country in the EEC to receive him, if this visit could be considered by the world as being a positive step toward peace, that is, if Arafat was offering something in exchange that would amount to or be the equivalent of acceptance of the UN Resolution 242, and if his trip did not have purely the symbolic value of gaining him official legitimacy.

(2) *Vis-à-vis* the peace process since 1977, and the Sadat initiative, the French maintain their policy of reservation to a negotiation from which, as in Geneva, they were excluded. They are paying minimal lip-service to US efforts summarizing their reservation by the formula of a need for a 'global solution' and not a separate peace, without offering precise alternative solutions (but presenting itself 'on reserve' for peace). France alone among the Nine has been very reserved in appreciation of Sadat's first trip to Jerusalem, refusing to fully re-cognize the emotional and symbolic value of his gesture, an attitude

that was criticized even in home circles generally favourable to the Middle East policy of France.

Prime Minister Begin's interpretation of the treaty with respect to Jordan can only reinforce its skepticism and serve to justify *a posteriori* its reservations. The French would favor a negotiating formula to which they would be part, preferably in the form of a United Nations Security Council formula. Such a formula is favored by France out of self-interest – it is a permanent member of the Security Council and out of a realism of cynicism such a scheme would not eventually need Israeli support. The French in private give a functional interpretation to the policy, which, though partly true, is mainly an *a posteriori* intellectual rationalization of a political choice, that is, the 'division of labor argument'. It is essential for the West to keep contact with the moderate and extremist Arab regimes. Since the USA is so close to Egypt, France feels it is important to maintain contacts with the countries that refuse the Egypt-Israeli peace process, which happen to be also the oilproducing countries.

Lately, France's ambition of having a global Mediterranean and Middle East policy has given birth to a new 'diplomatic catchword' which corresponds to the declaratory style of French diplomacy, namely, the trilogue. It is a long-term project to link the Euro-Arab dialogue and the Euro-African cooperation, and to consolidate the triangular relation between Europe, Africa and the Middle East and develop their natural solidarity. It is a seducing but still vague intellectual construction which the President himself initiated. This project has not been so far considered very seriously in Europe, nor has it been received very well by the Arab world, which would prefer a reactivation of the Euro-Arab dialogue.

One cannot therefore, as some Americans do, place French policy in the Middle East under the sign of mercantilism alone. For France's economic needs are part of a wider 'real politik' framework, in which prestige and political influence are equally if not more important. French policy is also the fulfilment of a traditional role, whose reactivation seems justified by realities (security and economy) and favored by the Arab actors themselves. President Giscard d'Estaing in his declarations in the various countries of the Gulf went simply further in the same direction that was already that of France. In his first speech the President, for the first time, used the word 'self-determination' as a right for the Palestinians, an expression that had already been used by the Germans as early as 1974, and by the Belgians and the Irish in 1979; but that, coming from the French with Algeria's reminiscence in mind, was equivalent to independence. In Amman, he went further to recognize the right of the PLO to be a party among others to a global negotiation.

The insensitivity of French officials to Israel's concerns and Jewish emotions in France, an attitude that contrasted deeply with the attention given to Arab emotion, was probably unnecessarily accentuated. To start in Kuwait, an outsider country to the conflict and an important oil supplier of France, to proclaim the rights of the Palestinians to self-determination without, at the same time, referring to the rights of all countries of the regions to existence, was probably a tactical error. It could not be compensated by the fuller and more balanced statement of French policy made later on in Amman.

The political consequences of the latest uproar of the Jewish community is not bound to have a serious impact on French foreign policy. There is so far nothing like a Jewish vote in France, and the attitude of the opposition is not clearly more pro-Israeli than the majority is. It still is difficult for France to present itself as a potential mediator while doing everything possible to be rejected by one of the parties, namely, the Israelis.

The Federal Republic of Germany

German policy is still dominated by its exceptional relation to the State of Israel. It is Nazi Germany whose crimes led, in effect, directly to the creation of the State of Israel by giving final justification to the existence of a Jewish State. The Federal Republic's approach to the Middle East seems to be the perfect antithesis of France's. It has less of an historical or geographical tradition in the region. It does not pretend to have a world role, nor does it aim at having a global role in the Middle East. It has succeeded in keeping its political stance and economic interests perfectly separated, an attitude that has proven successful, given the amount of trade between Germany and the Arab world (Syria and Egypt, in particular) and the fact that the Federal Republic does not (officially, at least) [3] sell weapons to the region.

The Federal Republic's policy toward the Middle East has been limited in its capacity to change by the mood of a public opinion that was until recently massively pro-Israeli and that largely remains so. Still, since 1973 and even more since 1977 Germany's evolution away from its previous stance of total support to Israel, an evolution confirmed by Israeli irritation and Arab satisfaction is highly visible. Domestic evolution in the Federal Republic and Israel has favored this change of line. The SPD is freer than the CDU to move away from Israel, given the resistant past of some of its prestigious leaders. The victory of a non-socialist coalition in Israel in 1977, by cutting the links existing inside the Socialist International between government leaders in the two countries, has accelerated that process.

Germany's rationale is precisely the opposite of France's. It is keeping a 'low-profile' policy and takes great care not to appear to be moving ahead of the other Europeans. It is using the political cooperation process as an alibi to move its own position behind the screen of the need for European cohesion. On the peace process, Germany has been more favorable than France to the Sadat initiative and the Camp David agreement, because of its relations with the USA, but also because it has privileged commercial links with Egypt. German ambitions in the region are limited. The Germans do not propose a grandiose global plan for peace, but they are ready to do more than what they are doing now to financially help the Egyptians in the implementation of the peace treaty with Israel, in the same way that they are helping Turkey to remain part of the Western community.

On the Palestinian problem, the Federal Republic was the first country to recognize the rights of the Palestinians, using the word 'self-determination', which evokes the right of the German people to self-determination. In their relation with the PLO, like Britain, they have been much more restrained than France, even if recently there has been officious consultations between the Federal Republic and the PLO about curbing terrorism. In Dublin, in a meeting of the Foreign Ministers of the Nine, the Federal Republic has clearly opposed a political reevaluation of the PLO which France favored.

In the past two years, German diplomacy in the region has been progressively more active, as Germany was slowly gaining a new vision of its international role. This new relation toward itself, which is sometimes described as 'Gaullism in a minor key', has concrete consequences also for Germany's policy in the Middle East. Its diplomacy, especially in the Arab world, has become more dynamic and more open as illustrated by the trip of Foreign Minister Genscher in August 1979 to Syria, Lebanon, Jordan and Egypt, in which he presented himself as a representative of the community as a whole. He declared that the aim of his trip was to reduce the gap between Egypt and the other moderate Arab countries.

This evolution of the German Republic position has had clear consequences in its relations with Israel, which are no longer privileged. Starting from a position that was totally at the opposite pole from France, Germany's evolution on the Middle East conflict has brought it closer to France as Auschwitz faded in the distance and as oil loomed increasingly on the horizon. If a country can be accused of mercantilism, or of 'stooping for oil', it is Germany, much more than France.

Great Britain

Great Britain's diplomacy in the Middle East stands halfway between that of France and Germany. The former mandatory power over Palestine, Great Britain is the inheritor of a colonial past that is still evident in the largely pro-Arab Foreign Office and inside the Conservative Party. This colonial past accounts to a great extent for Britain's satisfactory relations with most of the states of the region, and her commercial successes. France's growing successes in the Gulf and with countries like Jordan appear to be more and more a competition for economic as well as political influence and as such a growing irritation to Britain. The British, even more than the Germans, are largely motivated in their policy in the area by their links to the USA, free as they are because of a crucial new factor, their near total independence from Arab oil.

With regard to the peace process, believing that only the USA could produce a settlement, the British have supported without reservation Sadat's trip to Jerusalem and the Camp David agreement, though underlining the necessity for global peace. On the Palestinian question, the British speak of the Palestinians' right to express their national identity, denouncing therefore the incomplete character of Resolution 242, which does not take into account the legitimate political rights of the Palestinians and their right to a homeland, without using the word self-determination, which, a perfect antithesis of the German position, may negatively evoke in their mind the right of Ulster to self-determination. Like the French, they have denounced Israel's policy of settlement, the decision to allow Israeli citizens to buy land in the occupied territories and also Israel's policy in Lebanon, which undermines the authority of the Lebanese government.

Unlike the French and like the Germans, the British have been much more prudent toward the PLO and for the same dual reason the privileged link with the USA, and even more so, the existence of a terrorist problem in their own territory (the IRA and the Baader–Meinhoff group). Since the coming to power of Mrs Thatcher, the British seem to be willing to exert a greater role in this conflict as in other parts of their former empire, like Zimbabwe. Behind this stance lies the will to awaken the British from the sleepy dreams of the welfare state into the harsh reality of a world dominated by the Soviet threat. The contrast between the 'grand plan' of Mrs Thatcher and the claim of an impoverished Britain inside the EEC is ironic.

The British, with the aim of complementing and supplementing Camp David through the US presidential year, are trying to find ways to transform UN Resolution 242 and seem in the last few months to be competing with France in their common approach to the problem of the Palestinians. That means enlarging the peace process to include the Palestinians, and since the USA cannot do it, the British will. Like the French, they privilege the Security Council, of which they are also a permanent member. Their policy would be to reaffirm 242 but affirm within its context the rights of the Palestinian people.

In fact, one can go as far as to speak of competitive partnership between France and Britain. The two countries in the last few months have been going in the same direction in what sometimes appears as an effort to outbid each other *vis-à-vis* the Palestinian question. The Arab countries, in their officious rating of European countries, would probably place England right after France, though Germany's evolution has permitted it to dispute that position.

THE FORMING OF A EUROPEAN POSITION

Incapable of playing a major and direct political role, Europe has withdrawn into a dual alternative: declaratory policy through political cooperation; economic orientation through the Euro-Arab dialogue. The dual nature of these procedures makes Europe's positions all the more difficult to follow.

Political Cooperation

The coming together of the European countries on the Middle East conflict has coincided with and also been favored by the progress of political cooperation.*

* Decided upon by the Hague conference on European chiefs of state and governments in December 1969 and set to work, in the framework of the Davignon Committee, the process of European Political Cooperation (EPC) is a purely inter-

The process of political cooperation has helped to iron out differences of perceptions among the different European countries. This has come about through the sharing of information and expertise but also because the European partners were willing to compromise on a given position held with sufficient strength by one or more member states. The mechanism proved also to be very important for the information of the smaller European countries that have no part in the important bilateral meetings. This coming together was facilitated by the fact that statements of the Nine were mainly declaratory with little concrete and direct impact on the conflict. European governments, like a Greek chorus, comment upon events and express themselves whenever they judge an important development has occurred.

On the Palestinian issue, there is a steady progression between the November 1973 EEC declaration on the Middle East issued in the wake of the oil crisis, that stressed the fact that 'in the establishment of a just and lasting peace, account must be taken of *the legitimate rights of the Palestinians*', and the June 1977 declaration, 'stressing the need for a *homeland* for the Palestinian people'.

Whatever the importance of French initiatives and pressures made by a country that has found itself very often isolated, at least until recently, in the European sessions, it remains to be said that the essential fact in the June 1977 declaration was the willingness of West Germany, the Netherland and Britain to give in to pressure from within and without the EEC, and to accept wordings that were far from their own previous stances, therefore concretely symbolizing the evolution that was taking place. Its statements on the Middle East peace process since 1977 are also symbolic of the evolution of the EEC.

After Sadat's mission to Jerusalem, the foreign ministers of the EEC who met in Brussels on 22 November 1977 expressed hope and support for 'the bold initiative of President Sadat' and the 'unprecedented dialogue begun in Jerusalem'. But while recognizing that a step had been taken in overcoming 'the mistrust . . . one of the chief obstacles to a peaceful settlement of the Arab-Israeli conflict', they stressed the need for '*comprehensive negotiation* leading to a just and lasting overall settlement' and a 'genuine peace . . . for all the peoples of the area, including the Palestinian people', restating the provision of the June 1977 declaration and the emphasis on 'the legitimate right of the Palestinians including their right to a homeland'. In spite of its rejection of a bilateral solution, the EEC did not want to see at this stage of the negotiations a conflict between the Egypt–Israel rapprochement and a wider peace treaty.

The EEC did not issue another statement until ten months later in September 1978, as the negotiations in progress had led to the Camp David agreement on 17 September 1978. A statement from the foreign

governmental body. It is, therefore, distinct from the community activity that proceeds from the juridical engagement subscribed by the member states in the framework of the Treaty of Rome. In 1970 the EPC chose the Middle East as one of its two political priorities, the other being the CSCE, a choice highly indicative of the importance Europeans attach to this key strategic region.

ministers in Brussels issued on 19 September 1978 gave what was generally regarded as an unreserved welcome.

On 26 March 1979, the EEC issued a statement on the peace treaty itself, insisting that only an overall agreement would bring real peace and
that 'the Israel policy of settlements in the occupied territories had become an obstacle to peace'. Probably due to French pressure, only muted
approval was given to the treaty. The enthusiastic terms used to describe
Sadat's trip to Jerusalem – 'great courage . . . unprecedented . . . historic'
– were no longer employed; moreover, for the first time the EEC clearly
singled out the Israeli policies of settlement as 'being the chief impediment
to peace', a perfect proof of the evolution of the Nine on Israel.

The Declaration of the Nine following the European Council in Venice
on 12–13 June 1980 merely reiterated the previous EEC stance. Its emphasis on the Palestinian national question, its implicit criticism of Camp
David and explicit denunciation of the Israeli policy of settlement were
simply clearer than they used to be. The factfinding mission of the present
President of the Commission, Mr Thorn, which followed the Venice
meeting, brought no spectacular results and proved the limits of the
margin of influence of the EEC in the conflict.

The Euro-Arab Dialogue

Originally, the Euro-Arab dialogue was initiated by the Arab states, who
wanted the Europeans to include the Mediterranean on the Helsinki
agenda.[4] Their pressures were resisted by the Europeans, who felt that
the CSCE should restrict itself to security in Europe and not become involved in peripheral problems. The energy crisis that emerged from the
Yom Kippur War in October 1973 illustrated the linkage that existed
between the political and economic dimension of the Middle East crisis
and reinforced the will of the EEC to develop a Euro-Arab policy outside
the diplomatic confines of the Arab-Israeli conflict from which they were
excluded by the superpowers, as illustrated by the agreement between the
USA and USSR to limit attendance at the Geneva conference to themselves and the parties directly engaged in the conflict. For the Europeans
to establish relations with the Arab world on the basis of a stable long-
term partnership, it was necessary to leave the Arab-Israeli conflict out
of the agenda given the divergent opinions of the Nine on the topic. Such
a desire to dissociate politics and economics could not be accepted
willingly by the Arab side.

The EEC Middle East statement issued on 6 November 1973, clearly
showing an evolution of the European countries as a whole toward the
Arab side, was enough to allow the Euro-Arab dialogue to start even if it
did not really go very far. Inaugurated in July 1974, the Euro-Arab
dialogue included twenty-one members of the Arab League and the
nine members of the EEC. But as for the Arabs, cooperation was to be
based on a comprehensive political agreement, and for the Nine, a
Palestinian representation was to be excluded. This position was finally
accepted by the Arab side, and at the first meeting of experts in Cairo in

June 1973, working groups were constituted for cooperation in certain limited areas, such as agricultural development, industrialization, development of trade, scientific and technical cooperation. Despite successful meetings such as those of Luxembourg (May 1976), Tunis (February 1977) and Brussels (October 1977), the Euro-Arab dialogue produced very modest results.

In fact, it is in the framework of the EEC that the Europeans have expressed themselves collectively toward the Arab-Israeli conflict. Contrary to European hopes, the Euro-Arab dialogue has not so far brought about very positive economic results. One may even say that it was, in fact, mainly used by the Arab side as a rather effective type of collective pressure group whose role is to remind the Europeans of Arab interests and emotions. Because of Egypt's exclusion from the Arab League in 1979, this dialogue has been brought further to a standstill, from which it has been proven difficult to emerge, even if lately new attempts to revive it have been launched.

THE REASONS FOR EUROPEAN COMMON PERCEPTIONS ON THE MIDDLE EAST

European 'unity' on the Middle East took place at Israel's expense. In a new environment dominated by the economic crisis and a realization that prosperity, growth and even the sheer survival of the economy were increasingly dependent on the oil exports, Israel's positive image faded and the Palestinian cause gained ground. The Palestinian problem cased to be considered a refugee problem, becoming instead a nationalist cause, in part thanks to the success of the shrewd Palestinian tactical combination of terrorism and diplomacy.

History will probably judge that in this evolution no event was more decisive and more negative in the long run for the State of Israel's image and interests, than the Six Day War. Less than twenty years after its creation, the small, weak, endangered Israel, whose survival was one of the primary concerns of the Western world, was taking on new boundaries, new responsibilities and a new image. With the best-recognized army in the region, Israel fully became a major regional power whose citizens, for six years, were collectively and individually convinced of their superiority, a state impregnated by *hubris.* The Six Day War also helped reveal to the world the existence of a Palestinian problem that went beyond a refugee issue.

The process of time itself was influential in reinforcing the aloofness of Europe toward Israel, as Auschwitz faded at the very time Israel was gaining strength. These psychological factors, combined with the dictate of economic realities, made themselves fully felt after 1973 and even more after 1977. Realpolitik slowly went unopposed by emotion.

What can be described as the process of isolation of Israel, which is partly self-isolation, increased after Begin's coming to power and Sadat's initiative which made, at least in terms of perception, the contrast between Egyptian goodwill incarnated in Sadat's charisma and warmth, and

Israeli rigidity embodied by Prime Minister Begin, self-evident. Israeli concessions to Egypt, while proving to skeptical outsiders that in face-to-face negotiations Israel is willing to make sacrifices for peace, have not altered the perceptions of a rigid Israel.

Israel's policy toward the occupied territories and the multiplication of settlements, in particular, could only reinforce Europeans, as well as Americans, in their condemnation of Israeli expansionism. The evolution of public opinion, encouraged and preceded by the shift of the left intelligentsia after the 1967 war, was particularly striking in France, where the official French policy toward the Middle East conflict had been a major source of contention between the government and its public. After 1973 this is to a great extent no longer the case, even if the Jewish community in France, followed by a large part of the majority, reacted vigorously to the last trip of President Giscard d'Estaing to the Gulf.

The shift in the position of the USA on the Palestinian problem, accelerated since the coming to power of President Carter, is also a factor that explains the evolution of the Nine. In particular, it has permitted the Germans and the British to move away from a policy of support for Israel. The declaration of the EEC of June 1977 was preceded by a US statement including a vague stand on the Palestinian problem, which may have paved the road of the Nine.

EUROPE, THE USA AND THE SECURITY OF THE GULF

The fall of the shah in early 1979, the Soviet invasion of Afghanistan and the Iraq–Iran war have transformed the strategic environment in the Middle East, increasing the danger of instability in the largest oilproducing area in the world.

By invading Afghanistan, whose absolute control it feared to lose, the USSR has not only enlarged its boundary of security, but also come closer to the Gulf area, giving plausibility to the theory which claims that the USSR's real aim is the control of the oilfield area. Whether or not oil is spurring Soviet moves (indeed the USSR might face a shortage of oil by 1982), the USSR is now in a better strategic position *vis-à-vis* this critical region than a year ago. The fall of the Shah of Iran represents also a benefit for them, by the sheer fact that it is the USA's loss.

The problems at stake in the region are of a very different nature. There are three levels of threats:

(a) *international* – the growth of Soviet influence, coupled with the decline of American power and even more so of US credibility;
(b) *regional* – the confrontation between traditionally rival countries such as Iran and Iraq;
(c) *domestic* – in fact, the most probable and disturbing occurrence linked to the interaction of social, cultural, religious and economic problems leading to potentially unstable situations, of which Saudi Arabia may be the most significant example.

To confront the international threat, there is little more the Europeans can do militarily than what they are doing now. The French in Djibouti, the British in Oman, their respective naval forces in the Indian Ocean, could be considered as a useful complement to the US effort. The British presence in Oman, in particular, represents a significant help to the USA's present attempt to develop facilities there. Division of labor would mean, in fact, much more political support and understanding of the USA's effort in the region and an acceptance on the part of the Europeans of the positioning of military materials on their soil, for use in the case of a Middle East and Red Sea crisis (without repetition of the 1973 precedent of unwelcome pressures). It would also mean a greater conventional effort in Europe on the part of the Europeans in order to compensate for the eventual transfer of US troops frtm Europe to the Middle East and the Gulf.

As for regional conflicts between two states of the area, there is little any outside power can do except to show restraint in selling weapons. French arms sales to Iraq become a highly complex issue in this context. For these sales constitute an integral part of France's close relations to Iraq, a relationship that is appreciated by the USA, which sees it as a guarantee that Iraq will not move too close to the Soviet camp. The sale of nuclear equipment to Iraq is another matter that should raise grave doubts, even more so since the beginning of the war with Iran. The key to the equilibrium of the Gulf, however, lies in its domestic stability. The role of the Europeans there may be more important that it is in the Arab-Israeli conflict. The fall of the shah, far more than the Soviet invasion, preoccupies the leaders of the Gulf region. The Western powers would have given the opposite priority, if it were not for the problem of the hostages.

America failed in Iran on two counts: it was incapable of understanding the religious, cultural, economic and social problems the regime of the shah had to confront, an insensitivity symbolic of US failures elsewhere. Prisoner of the logic of modernization models, badly informed by certain experts in the social sciences, where the advice of historians and anthropologists would have been preferable, the USA was caught largely by surprise by the Iranian revolution. And when it occurred, the USA's abandonment of the shah raised doubts about the credibility of US support elsewhere. Not only was the US not listening to the signals she was receiving, but she was also betraying her most faithful ally, with an inconsistency that was only equaled by the massive support the USA had given the shah beforehand without reservation.

The Europeans in many ways are better equipped than the USA to understand the nature of a revolutionary process and the weight of culture and religion in these societies. Their own history – the French revolution, in particular – and their tradition of presence, commercial first and then colonial, in this region has given them a better preparation simply to 'listen' to these countries. They benefit also from the limitation of their capacity. Because they are not superpowers, the presence of the European countries, their help and advice can be better accepted, even if the countries of the Gulf have no illusion as to their capacity to replace the USA. They would, in fact, wish the USA to be less visible and more credible, so as not to create more instability by its very presence, like in Iran.

Small interventions such as French action in Mecca proved very useful, but may be difficult to repeat and could produce the very result they seek to avoid, if these interventions were to reawaken past colonial frustrations. One can say, ironically, that the Europeans are actually replacing themselves since the USA, in spite of her present capacity, has never really replaced the British in the Gulf.

The 'division of labor' may prove even more important in the case of a country like Turkey. Besides the social and economic problems that are besetting Turkey, there is an essential psychological element. Turkey, the key to NATO's southern flank, is a country whose fate is decisive for the West in general, and Europe in particular. Turkey needs to be reaffirmed, reassured in its choice of the West. The USA has largely incapacitated herself in this country, and Germany's role, though decisive, may not be sufficient. Turkey waits for a symbolic gesture from the Europeans that would make the Turks feel that they are a desired member of the West, and in spite of economic difficulties, a welcome member of Europe.

Still, the role of the Europeans, the British and the French should not be overemphasized. Besides the strict limits of their military capacities, there are structural limitations on their initiatives that constitute precisely objective advantages for the USSR. As *status quo* powers, the Western countries are in an inferior position, at the mercy of any coup that would destabilize the region. Given its evident geostrategic superiority, and as a revolutionary power, the USSR instead can utilize and benefit from the objective factors for instability (economic, social, tribal, religious, and so on).

Whereas they acknowledge with reticence Europe's stance in the Arab-Israeli conflict, the Americans would welcome a growing European presence in the Gulf, to complement or supplement their efforts. They do so without always acknowledging the fact that Europeans are welcomed politically in the oilproducing countries partly because of their support of the Palestinian cause, even if the Arab regimes tend to overemphasize this last point.

Emotionally, and understandably so, dominated by the question of the hostages in Tehran, the USA resented with the utmost irritation Europe's reticence to join them in a policy of toughness against Iran; although Europe had never been consulted about this policy (as it is unfortunately becoming a tradition, even if consultation may prove difficult in a time of crisis). For the Europeans, this tough stance arrives late and has been preceded by an unfortunate lack of decisions. The Europeans wish that the Americans had made earlier a choice between two contradictory and essential objectives, the defense of American honor and the survival of the hostages. These criticisms, though legitimate, should not hide the fact that there was very little the USA could do, and even more, they are essentially justifications of the Europeans for their desire not to cut links with a country that is an important oilproducer, a significant trading partner and, above all, a Third World country. The USA in her part should realize that it is precisely because the European interests at stake in the Gulf area are higher, that the USA has to show prudence and not expect a shift in the European position.

The Europeans do not differ sensibly from the Americans in their interpretation of the Afghan crisis. They agree on the seriousness of the Soviet invasion of the entire region. If Prague was the end of the hope of liberalization of a Soviet-controlled society, an *incident de parcours* according to the apocryphal formula attributed to Michel Debre, Kabul is the beginning of a destabilization. Combined with other preoccupying factors such as the changing balance of force between the two superpowers, it raises grave doubts about the future of détente. The gravity of the crisis is further confirmed for the French by the changing line of the PCF, which returned to a revolutionary message and a policy of isolation. But if Europeans and Americans agree on the diagnosis, they are split according to new lines on the attitude to adopt and the remedy to choose, the French and the Germans giving priority to the preservation of détente, while the British and the Americans are emphasizing the need for a strong answer to the Soviet aggression.

For the Germans, détente means important economic markets with the Eastern bloc and improvement of the human relations between the two Germanys. For the French, the concept of détente whose paternity they claim, is an essential ingredient of their global political project. It is, therefore, easy for the French and the Germans to denounce the indirect, incomplete, overreactive and insufficient nature of American reaction, helped by President Carter's confused mishandling of US foreign policy. There is another factor that contributes to explain the difference between the French and the Germans and the USA. It is the potentially natural inclination toward appeasement policies by the European countries.

A nuisance to the Israelis, who are discovering that Europe is a dubious ally in much the same way that the USA discovered Gaullist France to be in the 1960s, if not an irritation for the Americans and the Egyptians, Europe appears as a helpful but only complementary actor for the Arab and Gulf states which are rejecting the Camp David process. The Europeans are denounced by the Israelis for the very reason they are praised by the Arabs and are used by the rejectionist front in the way Sadat used the Israelis. Sadat's ultimate aim was to link indissolubly Egypt to the USA, the only country that can really help Egypt out of its perennial economic problems. The key to the alliance with the USA is peace with Israel. For the Palestinians, Arafat in particular, the Europeans constitute a welcome pressure-group and a model for the Americans to follow. The Europeans are paving the way for US recognition of the Palestinians by helping the Palestinians in their quest for legitimacy. But the Israelis and the Palestinians alike know that the key country remains the USA, the only one that can exert pressure on Israel, and for a mixture of military and moral reasons also, the only one that is really committed, and not simply in words, to the existence of an Israeli state.

Still, Europe's new role in the Middle East is not to be entirely neglected. The achievement of a European unity of view on the question is, in itself, from a European perspective a welcomed development, even if it is more the result of a return to a 'concert of Europe' diplomacy than a progress of integration. Out of self-interest, declaratory policy and sometimes even in spite of themselves, the Europeans may be playing a useful complementary role, and not only for themselves indirectly by giving new incentives to the Camp David process with the prospect of an alternative solution, but positively by emphasizing the crucial Palestinian problem and helping to stabilize some countries of the Gulf. Paradoxically, it may be when they act separately as in the Gulf that the Europeans may prove most useful.

Discreet diplomacy coupled with real if modest military measures in the Gulf, such as the sending by the French of minesweepers, are significant political and military contributions as exemplified since the beginning of the Iran–Iraq war.

Ultimately, the essential question remains the same as in 1948. Is there an Israeli-Palestinian conflict, an assumption which, in many ways, underlies the intellectual basis of the European policy, or is it an Arab-Israeli conflict, symbolizing the impossibility to reconcile Islam and the West, incarnated by Israel? If the latter proved to be the case, a European presence to protect Western interests in countries where the USA's presence is unwelcomed, may prove to be in vain.* Whatever its inherent legitimacy, the Palestinian problem will have been used by all as a convenient political and intellectual alibi; by the Europeans to get political influence and oil, by the Arabs to further their interests as well as to protect their regimes. There is no answer to this fundamental question, and I deeply believe that without a solution to the Palestinian problem, no peace is possible, even if, with a solution to this problem, peace may not be guaranteed. The Middle East is too dangerous an area to be left to US confusion and European cynicism. The allies should find ways to define a common policy which transcends both.

NOTES: CHAPTER 2

1   *The New Republic,* 26 October 1979.
2   The positions of the other European countries were left out.
3   Private German firms are, in fact, selling weapons to Middle Eastern countries.
4   See the article of Françoise de La Serre, 'Ou en est le dialogue euro-arabe?', *Défense Nationale,* April 1979.

* It is the West and not only the USA that is rejected.

3 Japan and the Middle East

MASAHIRO SASAGAWA

The current situation in the Middle East, particularly the crises in Iran and Afghanistan, has dramatically highlighted Japan's policy dilemma in the region. The nation is caught between two conflicting demands: its allegiance in principle to the Western Alliance and its specific national interests, particularly its dependence on Middle Eastern oil. It is both illuminating and distressing to analyze and appraise the problems facing Japan in its relationship with the Middle East. This chapter will examine the issue from the standpoint of Japan's status *vis-à-vis* various Middle Eastern countries and its understanding of the region in general, as well as in the broader context of Japan's search for a new national and international role that can securely carry it into the next century. The former issue has already preoccupied Japan for some time; but the latter constitutes a new, even revolutionary, departure for a nation whose postwar concern focuses on economic and national interests, rather than on foreign policy. The following discussion will be divided into four parts: (1) Japan's traditional perceptions of the Middle East; (2) problems arising from these perceptions; (3) current problems and constraints; (4) summary and conclusion.

JAPAN'S TRADITIONAL PERCEPTION OF THE MIDDLE EAST

In the conclusion of his 1939 study, *History of Cultural Contacts between Japan and the Islamic World*, Professor Gen Kobayashi, a pioneer in Japanese studies of the Islamic world, writes:

> Before the Meiki Restoration, Japanese knowledge of Islam and the Islamic world had never been systematic, presumably because intellectual contacts between the two sides had been more indirect than direct. Any direct contacts were essentially commercial, while most of the intellectual information was introduced through China. This state of affairs continued until the dawn of the Restoration.[1]

After the Restoration in 1868 Japan launched a modernization program and increasingly modeled itself on Europe, a course that gave it little incentive to improve its understanding of the Islamic world or the Arabs. It may in fact be said that Westernization, which affected Japan's world view, also left the Japanese with European images and biases toward the Middle East. However, there is a fundamental cultural difference between the Western and the Japanese view of the region. Unlike the West, Japan had little cultural contact with the Middle East until modern times. (The exception is the so-called 'Silk Road' that introduced Islamic designs and Persian art-objects to Japan in the eighth century.) Essentially, Japan owed much of its culture to China, its religious heritage to Buddhism, and its Western orientation since the nineteenth century to Europe and the USA. The geographical distance between Japan and the Middle East has, of course, accentuated the general Japanese view of the region as a remote, unknown place.

With a few partial exceptions, this perception has prevailed since the Restoration. Japanese scholars did undertake some Islamic and contemporary Middle Eastern studies before World War II; but these either examined the region from an historical perspective, or within the general framework of international politics. After the war, a ten-year hiatus ensued before interest in the Middle East slowly revived among academic and political circles. Even these later trends did not lead to broader governmental or public interest. It took the shock of the 1973 oil crisis to awaken the whole Japanese nation to the contemporary Middle East.

Another important conditioning-factor concerns the Japanese government's traditional postwar approach to international problems: the 'economy-first policy', pursued under the nuclear umbrella of the USA. In principle, Japan's postwar goal has been the creation of a 'cultural state', a non-military, civilian nation. In practice, this has resulted in a 'New Japan', overconcerned with economic growth and displaying an ostrich-like attitude toward international politics. This approach is clearly reflected in Japanese Middle Eastern policy, which oscillates between cooperation with the Western Alliance, particularly the USA, and sympathetic gestures toward Middle Eastern countries.

PROBLEMS ARISING FROM TRADITIONAL PERCEPTIONS

A brief survey of recent Japanese history suffices to illuminate the basic Japanese orientation toward Western political principles and culture, and its impact on Japanese Middle Eastern policy. The Japanese foreign service was established in 1894 on the Western model, and its most coveted ambassadorial posts are Washington, London, Paris and Moscow. In this connection, it should be noted that Middle Eastern ambassadors who have misjudged political situations in their countries have not in general suffered serious setbacks in prestige or chances of promotion. This state of affairs reflects an intellectual inertia deeply ingrained in the minds of Western-oriented Japanese diplomats – a factor occasionally contributing to serious blunders.

A recent and most pertinent case concerns Iran. Only four months before the shah's downfall, then Prime Minister Fukuda visited Iran, and declared that the occasion marked the beginning of a new era between the two countries. Neither the prime minister nor the local ambassador paid the least attention to the anti-shah demonstrations then raging. In my judgment 'intellectual inertia' is the best explanation.

This intellectual inertia is due in part to the traditional outlook of Japan's highly elite, competitive, and Western-oriented diplomatic corps. According to *Gaimusho Kenkyu*,[2] a study of the Japanese Foreign Ministry, Japan's elite diplomats have five things in common:

(1) Many of them do not find it satisfying to be assigned to the Third World.
(2) Imbued with Western rationalism, they tend to despise various features they deem characteristic of the Third World, including inefficiency and behavior that they attribute to religion.
(3) During their period of apprenticeship, they intentionally avoid the study of Arabic, Spanish and other languages of the Third World, and instead study German, French and Russian. English is also avoided, because a fair knowledge of English may lead to a career in India, Bangladesh, the Middle East, or Africa.
(4) They prefer a career as an administrator to one as an expert. If they choose to become an expert in Middle Eastern or Korean problems, they may end up as respected authorities entirely excluded from the ladder of success.
(5) As ambassadors, their superiority complex often invites hostility from local Japanese, creating a minus diplomatic factor.

Such anachronistic attitudes and behavior die hard. It may be added that Tokyo University, whose history parallels the modernization of Japan, provides the largest portion of the diplomatic elite and has trained many national leaders in political, financial, academic and administrative fields. Tokyo University educated about half of the 245 career diplomats in service between 1965 and 1974, with the rest divided among seventeen other universities. This suggests that traditional elite consciousness at the Foreign Ministry will continue for some time to come. The Middle East is no exception to this trend; as of September 1975, only two ambassadors to the region came from schools other than Tokyo University.[3]

Another more recent, but perhaps more important, factor contributing to intellectual inertia is the inward-looking position that Japan adopted after World War II, and which it now finds very difficult to modify, despite its growing international economic strength and prestige. In the Middle East, Japan steadily followed the US lead, without a single significant conflict or deviation until the 1973 October War.

The 1973 war and the subsequent oil crisis signified a major break in Japan's traditional outlook toward the Middle East. As noted earlier, the war jolted the entire nation into a recognition of the contemporary significance of the Middle East. For example, at a press conference on 10 January 1980, Foreign Minister Saburo Okita confessed that until the 1973 oil crisis, very few Japanese realized where oil came from, and many blindly believed that it came automatically from the major oil companies. The oil crisis created immense problems for Japanese official, political and industrial circles.

Japan responded to the political aspects of the problem in a short statement issued on 22 November 1973. In summary, the statement made three major points. (1) It reaffirmed Japan's desire for urgent implementation of United Nations Security Council Resolution 242, and reiterated support for UN General Assembly resloutions on the Palestinians' right of self-determination. (2) It called for total withdrawal from occupied Arab territories. (3) It alluded to the possibility that events might prompt Japan to reconsider its position toward Israel unless Israel withdrew from the occupied Arab territories.

The reference to Palestinian self-determination and the accompanying hints that Japan might reassess its Israel policy differed from Japan's previous policy of support for Resolution 242 only. The new 'pro-Arab' stance, adopted under pressure from the then International Trade and Industry Minister Nakasone, was obviously motivated by a concern for Japan's oil supply. It remains unchanged.

Similar economic and diplomatic measures were subsequently taken. On 19 December 1973, then Vice Premier Miki visited Kuwait, Qatar, Egypt, Syria, Saudi Arabia, the United Arab Emirates, Iraq and Iran. His official objective was both economic and political, and Mr Miki did discuss peace in the Middle East and Japan's economic and technical role in the region, as well as the oil supply. But his immediate and central concern was oil. For the first time, Japan had 'discovered' the Middle East. Beyond its new economic importance, however, the region still remains a land of medieval romance to much of the Japanese public.

After the oil crisis, the Foreign Ministry strengthened its Middle East and Africa bureaus and increased the number of embassies in the region. This policy was coupled with a new, more pro-Arab position at the United Nations. At a January 1976 Security Council session, Japan's UN Ambassador Saito proposed a direct dialogue between the PLO and Israel.

In the aftermath of the October War, major changes were implemented in various fields. The quadruple oil-price hike made Japan's financial and industrial circles acutely aware of the fragile foundations of the Japanese economy, which had received 77·3 percent of its oil that year from the Middle East. The need for serious study of energy policy was finally recognized. Discussions of how to recycle oil dollars, and reorient Japan's economic interests in the Middle East became routine. Some remarkable successes in these areas were achieved after a period of trial and error. In September 1974 the Economic Research Institute for the Middle East was established in Tokyo under the patronage of Japanese financial and industrial circles. In 1976 the Institute, in cooperation with the National Institute for Research Advancement (NIRA), a national think-tank, issued its first report, *The Economic Survey for the Eighties*.[4] This was followed in 1979 by *Middle East Oil and Global Crisis*.[5] By 1976, a similar organization, the Asia–Pacific Association of Japan, had sufficiently broadened its field of research to issue with NIRA's cooperation, *The Political Situation in the Middle East and Japan's Option*.[6] Many similar projects were undertaken.

In academic circles, the oil crisis played no dramatic role, and Japanese orientalists continued their research as before. No immediate attempt was made to introduce innovations, such as independent area studies programs, into the educational structure. Some extracampus activities, however, must be mentioned. In 1975 the Institute of Developing Economies, a national academic research organization, embarked on the Comprehensive Middle East Research Project,[7] which also included contemporary Middle Eastern literature. In 1976 the first symposium on Middle East–Japan cultural exchange took place in Tokyo. It was sponsored by the Japan Foundation, a semi-governmental cultural exchange organization, and it brought together representatives from Afghanistan, Iran, Iraq and Turkey. In 1978 a second Middle East Cultural Mission was assembled with the public blessing of Prime Minister Fukuda, and it visited Saudi Arabia, Iran, Turkey, Egypt and Morocco. Upon its return, the mission made a number of recommendations; in particular, it urged the immediate establishment of a National Middle East Research Institute for basic research. Since that time, the importance of Japanese cultural exchanges with the Middle East has been increasingly emphasized, but few additional concrete steps have been taken.

CURRENT PROBLEMS AND CONSTRAINTS

The Soviet invasion of Afghanistan, coupled with the latest oil crisis brought on by the Shah of Iran's downfall and the subsequent US hostage issue, have inevitably accentuated Japan's dilemma: how is it to balance its present total dependence on Middle Eastern oil with its commitment to the Western Alliance, particularly its cooperative relationship with the USA? The following discussion of this problem will address both Japan's perceptions and positions with regard to the current Middle East crisis and constraints on Japanese policy.

Japanese Perceptions and Positions

Initially, it may be useful to point out that neither the Japanese public nor government feel responsible for the Middle East crisis. In the Japanese view the current situation has its roots in the regional unrest and conflicts of the late 1940s. During this period, Japan was under US occupation and incapable of playing an independent role in international politics. The end of the occupation in 1951 did not appreciably alter Japan's passive postwar diplomacy, and it displayed no active interest in Middle East affairs. Within two decades, however, the Middle East crisis had assumed global proportions as a result of international skyjackings, terrorism and creeping energy probelms. Japan began gradually to reevaluate its perceptions of the region, a process that was hastened and intensified by the 1973 war and the subsequent oil crisis.

Japan's reassessment of its Middle East policy was accompanied by a broader, more general reappraisal of its overall foreign policy. Early in 1980 Foreign Minister Okita proclaimed an end to Japan's traditional reticence in international affairs and outlined expanded foreign policy goals for the future:

This year marks the dawn of the decade of the 1980s, and the latest events – the taking of hostages at the US embassy in Iran and the Soviet military invasion of Afghanistan – portend a very difficult decade ahead. Today, we can no longer take for granted the existence of an international climate guaranteeing Japan's security and prosperity. Japan can no longer view international relations as external givens but must perceive them as conditions in which Japan should have a major input. The era of so-called passive foreign policy is ended.

In the same speech, Okita set down the following four guiding principles for Japan's foreign policy in the 1980s:

(1) National dedication to peace will continue to form the basis of Japanese foreign policy.
(2) Japan will approach the international situation with the intention of making a positive contribution to world peace and stability.
(3) It will use its economic strength and technological abilities for world development, especially the constructive economic development of the poorer nations.
(4) It will work to eliminate its international image as an economic giant but political dwarf, by playing a constructive global role commensurate with its economic and technological capabilities.

Ohkita elaborated on the Middle Eastern aspects of his policy in a speech before the Diet on 25 January 1980. After expressing concern over the crises in Iran and Afghanistan, he made these points:

(1) Japanese policy toward the Middle East should be one of the important pillars of Japanese foreign policy in the 1980s.
(2) In view of the rapidly growing interdependence between Japan and the Middle East, it is necessary to establish a Japanese presence that will be genuinely welcomed by nations in the region.
(3) Japan must be ready to contribute to nationbuilding and human resources development in the region as well as to deepen mutual understanding in the historical, religious and cultural spheres.
(4) Japan hopes that the Egypt-Israeli peace treaty will lead to a just, lasting and comprehensive peace, and it is ready to cooperate in all measures designed to promote peace in the Middle East.
(5) Japan will continue to strengthen its ongoing dialogue with the PLO.

In its use of such terms and phrases as 'pillar', 'Japanese presence', 'nationbuilding' and 'human resources development', and particularly in its reference to the PLO, the recent Okita statement stands in marked contrast to a similar but less explicit speech delivered a year previously by the then Foreign Minister Sunao Sonoda. Sonoda himself provided further indications of the new trend in Japanese Middle East policy when he was appointed special envoy to the region in January 1980, and said his diplomatic purpose was to create an agreeable climate of mutual interests in which the Middle East nations would perceive a reliable partner and take a sympathetic view of its oil needs. Despite some reservations at the Foreign Ministry, Sonoda also expressed a desire to visit Iran and said that he hoped for the opportunity to act as a liaison between Iran and the West, particularly the USA. In addition, the *Yomiuri Shimbun*[8] quoted government sources as saying that Mr Sonoda was seeking to establish contact with the PLO. This report coincides with the official judgment that contact with the PLO is an indispensable part of the Sonoda objective of establishing a dialogue that will help to stabilize the Middle East situation. Whatever the mission's outcome, it testifies to Japan's current determination to pursue 'positive' Middle Eastern diplomacy.

Although the new policy represents a departure from Japan's stated position of a year ago, both are based on the same fundamental recognition that Japan depends heavily on Middle East oil. It is said that Japan is energy-vulnerable on three counts. The first count is obvious: Japan relies on foreign sources for 88 percent of its energy. A recent government survey shows that oil accounts for 74·5 percent of all imported energy, coal for 11·6 percent and nuclear energy for 2 percent; 80 percent of foreign oil is imported from the Middle East, consequently, the stability of the overall Japanese energy supply is largely determined by events and trends in that region.[9]

Japan's second area of energy vulnerability is its current inability to keep pace with global trends of alternative energy sources development. The nation must also look overseas to obtain primary alternative sources such as coal and nuclear power. In an effort to compensate somewhat for Japan's weakness in this respect, the Western nations at the 1979 Tokyo summit agreed to raise the minimum Japanese oil import target for 1985. Even the revised target, however, presupposes that Japan will meet its energy conservation goals and successfully develop indigenous alternative energy sources. At present, the second assumption remains highly questionable. Power generation from coal, for instance, poses serious difficulties in terms of acquisition, transport, port facilities, maintenance and pollution. Proponents of nuclear energy must come to grips with problems of Japanese capabilities and siting facilities, as well as ingrained national objections to nuclear power in any form. Furthermore, Japanese research and development programs in the areas of solar and geothermal energy and energy conservation have thus far been sadly inadequate. The belated opening of the Organization for Alternative Energy Sources Development will not save Japan from the extremely serious repercussions of another major oil crisis.

Japan is also vulnerable economically. Soaring oil prices will lead to a deterioration of the ordinary revenue and expenditure account and weaken the Japanese foreign exchange position. Japan ended the 1978 fiscal year approximately $11·9 billion in the black, but found itself $11 billion in the red the following year. It is estimated that additional oil-price hikes will leave the country with a balance of payments deficit of $20 billion.

Foreign Minister Okita's Middle East diplomacy thus constitutes an attempt to respond to Japan's critical and potentially crippling energy situation while meeting the new international responsibilities entailed by Japan's growing international status. However, this is more easily said than done. A discussion of Japan's stand on current specific issues such as

Iran, Afghanistan and the PLO will help to clarify its perceptions and position concerning the Middle East.

Within Japan, there is a general consensus that another Middle East war will be a disaster for Japan's livelihood. Most Japanese supported the Egypt-Israeli peace treaty, and any growing sympathy for the PLO also reflects the perception that recognition of the PLO is in the interests of a peaceful solution to the Middle East conflict. In February 1980 Prime Minister Ohira responded to a question posed by a member of the Opposition by saying that his government would accord Yassir Arafat treatment tantamount to that given a chief of state if the PLO leader visited Japan. Foreign Ministry officials have stated that both the prime minister and the foreign minister are ready to grant Mr Arafat's request to meet with them. This decision was taken in recognition of the perceived growing PLO status, of Mr Arafat's successful visits to various European countries, and of the salutary effect that the virtual recognition of the PLO will have on Japan's future diplomacy in the Middle East.[10]

Prime Minister Ohira addressed the issue of Iran in his keynote speech to the Diet on 25 January 1980:

> The seizure of the US embassy in Tehran is an unlawful act that threatens the basic order of the international community, and the taking of the hostages is unacceptable also from the humanitarian viewpoint. I strongly hope that the hostages will be released without loss of time, and the situation resolved in a peaceful manner. To this end, Japan will continue to support actively the international efforts, including those of the United Nations. Also, as the situation requires, Japan will cooperate with the USA, Europe and other countries in efforts to achieve an early release of the hostages.

The guarded language reflects Japan's problems in balancing its basic international beliefs and allegiance to the USA–Japan security treaty with its pursuit of a new cooperative relationship with the Middle East. Some Foreign Ministry officials privately described the hostage issue as an unexpected burden. Parliamentary deliberations on the issue revealed a consensus on the need for continued cooperation with Iran on various projects, if only the giant Iran–Japan petrochemical (IJPC) project. The joint venture was initiated under the shah, but the new Iranian government has expressed a desire to complete it as a 'momentum to the Revolution'. In October 1979 the Japanese government rescued the project from collapse by providing government support as a symbol of friendship between the two peoples.

In mid-January 1980 Iranian Oil Minister Moinfal declared that Iran would suspend oil shipments to any country that supported USA-sponsored economic sanctions. He also warned that if Japan pulled out of the IJPC project, Iran would transfer it to an East European country. In as much as Iranian oil accounts for 11 percent of Japan's total oil imports, abandonment of the project would entail a large loss and inconvenience, including a government payment of Y12,572·9 billion in export insurance. Furthermore, Japan regards the project as both a symbol of friendship, and as a means of keeping Iran in the Western fold. Many officials also feel that the proposed economic sanctions will prove ineffective. Financial leaders are similarly reluctant to take extreme action, because they support the government policy favoring friendship with all countries.

The prime minister's 25 January 1980 speech also made the following reference to Afghanistan:

> The Soviet military intervention in Afghanistan cannot be justified on any account. The internal affairs of Afghanistan must be left to Afghanistan itself. Japan urges the immediate withdrawal of the Soviet forces and strongly supports the resolution adopted for this purpose at the special emergency session of the UN General Assembly.
>
> The government of Japan will continue to make efforts befitting our country in order to contribute to the resolution of this serious situation on the basis of our solidarity with the USA and in cooperation with other friendly countries in Europe and in other parts of the world. As the situation develops, we shall continue to study and implement appropriate measures, including the tightening of the export controls in COCOM, taking into consideration public opinion at home and abroad. I believe that we must not shun these measures even if they involve sacrifices on our part.
>
> To maintain stability of neighboring countries in the area, particularly Pakistan, we would like to give positive consideration, in cooperation with the USA and Western Europe, to their requests for economic assistance.

At the same time, Japan displayed little enthusiasm for USA-sponsored sanctions against the USSR. In a speech three days earlier at the Japan Press Club, Ohira had avoided the use of such terms as 'punishment' and 'retaliation', and preferred to use the word 'displeasure' instead.

Constraints on Japan's Policy

It has already been pointed out that a significant constraint on Japan's efforts to coordinate its Middle Eastern policy with the Western Alliance members emanates from its simultaneous reliance on the West and Middle Eastern oil. However, policy dilemmas most typically occur over issues linked to the USA–Japan security treaty. For example, the so-called Carter Doctrine poses a most serious dilemma with regard to the issue of Persian Gulf defense. On the one hand, the USA feels that the terms of the treaty obligate Japan to extend the maximum possible support for the US military posture in the Persian Gulf. On the other hand, Japan's evolving policy of active but peaceful, non-military cooperation with Persian Gulf countries conflicts with the US position. Japan's new policy is designed to enhance the security of countries facing a Soviet threat, especially the Persian Gulf nations. It offers cooperation in the form of economic and technological aid most acceptable to those countries. Technically, the relevant nations included Pakistan, Thailand, Egypt, the Persian Gulf Arab states, the

Arabian Peninsula countries, African states and Iran, once the hostage issue was resolved. The aid is not profit-centered, as was the case in the past. Rather, it is motivated by Japan's judgment that its security interests will be greatly enhanced by the kind of Middle East peace and stability acceptable to the region's nations themselves. In many respects, of course, Japan's new philosophy of cooperation with the Middle East is still in its embryonic stage, and much friction and many constraints are anticipated.

In 1979, however, a NIRA report[11] entitled 'Comprehensive strategy in the current international environment and the changing Japanese economic and social situation' put forward one of the fundamental assumptions underlying Japan's new policy. A chapter devoted to technological development makes the following point:

> Japan is poor in natural resources and relies on overseas supplies for a large portion of its resources, including oil. This fact constitutes a weak point in Japan's international position. Our most important and effective weapon for overcoming this weakness is our technological capability. Its uses are many, and one of them is bargaining leverage in the course of negotiations with a single state or a group of states. We could induce the other party to increase its dependence on us by offering economic aid, technological aid, or cultural exchanges. Japan's considerable technological skills can be applied as part of its comprehensive national (economic) power to win it a greater voice internationally. This could be done either by increasing the competitive power of our exports or by obtaining a leading position in global trade through the development of higher grade products superior to those of other countries.

The above assessment recognized that Japan, unlike the USA or USSR, is in no position to exercise military control over international affairs. It must, instead, develop a strategy for adaptability and survival in the international system that is commensurate with its own interests, strengths and resources. Some conflict with the USA over the best way to interpret and serve Western defense interests is, therefore, probably inevitable. For example, the USA apparently expects Japan to allow the US Marine forces on Okinawa to be rapidly deployed for military action in the Persian Gulf. The government is trying to make possible military deployment by overcoming public suspicions represented by the Opposition through a legalistic tactic, which may succeed in dodging complex issues, such as the area of the 'Far East' or prior consultation, arising from the application of the Japan–USA security treaty.[12] The Opposition, however, objects to this position, on the ground that it could easily involve Japan in US global military strategy. The debate will continue for some time to come; with the government always acutely aware of the Opposition's readiness to capitalize on public sentiment against any apparently adventurist actions. The Japanese public has yet to fully realize the extent of Japan's new political responsibilities after two complacent decades of the 'GNP-first' mentality.

Japan's continued emphasis on a peaceful security strategy based on economic power and cooperation, and technological-industrial expertise rather than on military strength, is also likely to strain Japanese-US relations in some areas. Japanese resistance to US pressure for economic sanctions against Iran may only signal the beginning of tension over the Middle East, and even elsewhere. Serious economic differences have already strained relations in the past. Without constant coordination and consultation, the combination of political and economic friction may create deeper problems in the future.

Japan, however, is encouraged by the Western European approach to the current Iran and Afghanistan crisis. Although it was most impressed by Europe's ready support in principle for recent US actions, Japan also concurs with Europe's position that it has a major stake in preserving détente and must pursue its own course. Japan finds a great deal to admire as well in Europe's Middle Eastern role: its influence in the region; the intelligent partnership between the Arab nations and the EEC; Europe's ability to respond quickly and knowledgeably to Middle East developments; and last but not least, its extensive channels of communication with Israel. It might be said that European policy imposes few or no constraints on Japan's political relationship with the Middle East; on the contrary, Japan hopes to profit greatly by Europe's example. Japan and Europe have experienced economic friction in the past, however; and these tensions may also surface in the Middle East as Japan expands its role there.

SUMMARY AND CONCLUSION

It is, of course, impossible to reach firm and definite conclusions regarding a policy course that is new, unprecedented, experimental and in a state of flux. Japan stands on the threshold of the unknown as it seeks to forge a viable Middle Eastern policy for the first time in its history. Although it has a long way to go to make up for its past cultural and diplomatic indifference, the first steps have been taken. Recent years have seen increased government interest in cultural exchanges as a kind of peace strategy. Two interesting documents were also recently published. The first is a December 1979 proposal put forward by Japanese ambassadors stationed in the Middle East.[13] It recommends intensified basic Middle East research, increased academic exchanges, and a concerted effort to familiarize the Japanese public with the region's history, culture and religions.

The other document was published in January 1980 by the Kokumin Gaiko Konwakai (Popular Diplomacy Council),[14] whose membership includes such important national leaders as former Foreign Minister Kimura. After analyzing both the international and Middle East situations, it called for recognition of the PLO as the sole representative of the Palestinians not as a mere tactical measure, but as a decisive action. The proposal also recommended that Japan offer all-out cooperation to Middle East countries, not just the oil producers, and encourage their national development as if it were part of their community. Elaboration is certainly required on the last point made by that independent-thinking body. It is significant that some ideas contained in these documents, particularly the first, have already been adopted by the government. It seems that Japan can no longer resist inner pressure for action.

NOTES: CHAPTER 3

This paper was presented at the Conference on the Middle East and the Western Alliance, University of California, Los Angeles, USA, 21–22 February 1980.

1   *History of Cultural Contacts betwen Japan and the Islamic World*, by Professor General Kobayashi was only published by the Chuto Chosakai in 1975, posthumously, after it was written in 1939.
2   *Gaimusho Kenkyu* (A Study of the Foreign Ministry) (Tokyo: Simul Press, 1975).
3   ibid.
4   *The Economic Survey for the Eighties*; a 306-page report comprising five chapters with a 9-page preface. With major research effort concentrated on 1980 and 1985, the report studies economic development prospects in Middle East oilproducing countries and OPEC countries in general and the related outlook for the world economy.
5   *Middle East Oil and Global Crisis* (Tokyo: Mainichi Shimbun Newspapers, 1979); published in bookform the 318-page report is a first attempt in Japan to consider the oil crisis in the context of Middle Eastern politics. Unfortunately, bypassed by developments in Iran.
6   *The Political Situation in the Middle East and Japan's Option* (Tokyo: Asia-Pacific Association of Japan, 1976); a 199-page report placing more emphasis on Middle Eastern politics than on economy and a first serious probe of Japan's role in the Middle East.
7   San-eki Nakaoka, *Gendaiejiputoron* (Study of Modern Egypt), Institute of Developing Economies, 1979.
8   *Yomiuri Shimbun*, 13 February 1980.
9   Sōgō Energy Chōsakai (Comprehensive Energy Sources Research Institute), 28 August 1979, Tokyo.
10   A formal decision was taken on 11 October by the Japan–Palestine Friendship Parliamentarians' Union to see Chairman Yassir Arafat of the PLO in December 1980. The union is a Japanese organization with a supraparty membership of the two Houses, representing all major political parties. It is headed by Toshio Kimura, a former foreign minister. The decision was taken when Mr Kimura accepted an invitation extended to him by Mr Khaled Fanham, Chairman of the Palestine National Council after he met with Mr Abdel Hamid, chief of the PLO bureau in Tokyo, the same day. A Kimura–Arafat meeting would be the first contact between the JPFPU president and the PLO chief. Mr Kimura will head a delegation with a supraparty membership and will also see other PLO high officials (*Asahi Shimbun*, 12 October 1980). It is recalled that Mr Sonada, a former foreign minister and special envoy for the late Prime Minister Ohira, who went on a trip to the Middle East in February 1980, had stopped short of seeing Mr Yassir Arafat during his trip.
11   *Kokusai Kankyo oyobi Wagakuni no Keizai Shakai Henka wofumaeta Sōgōsenryaku no Tenkai* (Japanese original title for quoted report). Sōgō Kenkyū Kaihatsu Kikō (Japanese name for NIRA) 1977.
12   The 'Far East' has never been geographically determined in current Japanese political debates by government officials and, together with the interpretation of 'prior consultation', occasionally creates complex issues.
Article VI of the revised Japan–USA Security Treaty says in part:

For the purpose of contributing to the security of Japan and the maintenance of international peace and security in the Far East, the United States of America is granted the use by its land, air and naval forces of facilities and areas in Japan.

In reference to the foregoing article VI, exchanges of notes took place on the same at the mutual signing of the treaty, 19 January 1960, for an understanding concerning the implementation of the article. The substance of the understanding is as follows:

Major changes in the deployment into Japan of United States armed forces, major changes in their equipment, and the use of facilities and areas in Japan as bases for military combat operations to be undertaken from Japan other than those conducted under Article V of the said Treaty, shall be the subject of prior consultation (between the two countries).

The question is whether the treaty justifies Japan's involvement in possible US military combat operations in the Persian Gulf. The answer is 'no' according to the Japanese official explanations. The reasons follow:

While the range of the 'Far East' covered by the Treaty has been expanded to include 'the Far East and its vicinity,' the latest official statement on whether the latter area includes the Persian Gulf is by Mr Okita (the then Foreign Minister), who said on March 7 in the Diet in response to an Opposition question as follows: 'In response to a question posed by Socialist Tagaya whether the Persian Gulf is included in the vicinity of the Far East, Foreign Minister Okita denied that the Persian Gulf is included in the vicinity of the Far East because "it is unthinkable that any eventuality in the Persian Gulf can pose a menace to the peace and security of the Far East"'. (*Asahi Shimbun*, 8 March)

It may be appropriate to mention here that some vagueness always accompanies the concept of both the Far East and its vicinity.

About the 'Far East', the most elaborate definitions given in the past are still vague. They are:

The area of the Far East of common interest to Japan and the US is an area where the American armed forces in Japan may contribute to the defense of Japan against armed attack by the use of Japanese facilities and areas. Generally it comprises a region north of the Philippines, covering Japan and its vicinity, including South Korea and Nationalist China. (Statement by the then Prime Minister Kishi, 1960)

The area of the Far East is supposed to be north of the Philippines. However, in case an eventuality takes place in its vicinity and that eventuality is considered a menace to the peace and security of the Far East, action to be taken to eliminate this menace may not necessarily be limited to the area of the Far East. Action may be taken in its vicinity to eliminate the menace. (Statement by the then Foreign Minister Shiina, 1965)

About the vicinity of the Far East, Mr Okita in another part of his statement on the same day said:

In case armed attack takes place in the area of the Far East or the security of the Far East is menaced by a development in the vicinity of the Far East, the range of action to be taken by the American armed forces is not necessarily limited to the Far East. The definition of the vicinity of the Far East depends upon the nature of an attack or menace in the Far East. (*Asahi Shimbun*, 8 March)

This vagueness naturally causes suspicions, especially among the Opposition. A case in point is a statement made by Socialist Tagaya in the Diet in which he made these points:

Is not a movement of American armed forces from a Japanese base [Okinawa understood] in contravention of the Japan-US Security Treaty?

By extending the range of American action to the vicinity of the Far East, are not the American armed forces allowed to deploy anywhere in the world by using Japanese facilities and areas? (*Asahi Shimbun*, 31 January)

This is where a question of prior consultation intervenes. The question is: 'Is not American deployment of the Marines or RDF forces the subject of prior consultation?' Again, the government explanation says 'no'. Its argument follows: On 29 January, in his answers to questions posed by the Opposition, including the communists, in the Diet, Mr Ohira (the late then prime minister) said:

> The Japan-US Security Treaty does not anticipate, and it is unrealistic, the use of facilities and areas in Japan as bases for military combat operations to meet any emergency in the Middle East. (*Yomiuri Shimbun*, 30 January)

The next day in another Diet session, Mr Ohira elaborated on his position by saying: 'A movement of American forces which uses our facilities and areas to another region does not constitute an object of prior consultation' (*Asahi Shimbun*, 31 January). On 1 February high officials in the Foreign Ministry explained that a movement of RDF comprising US Marines from Okinawa to the Middle East or elsewhere on non-combat operations creates no problems to the treaty. However, they said, if RDF should depart direct from Okinawa on military combat operations in the Middle East, such as the Persian Gulf, it can become a subject of prior consultation, although current military technology does not allow it. And a reinterpretation of the treaty in favor of such American operations should be avoided (*Yomiuri Shimbun*, 2 February). In other words, while the use of Okinawa as a base for patrol in the Indian Ocean or simply for movement of US armed forces including the Marines creates no problems for the treaty (Mr Ohira's statement on 29 January), the use of Okinawa for direct military action in the Persian Gulf, which shall be the subject of prior consultation, is, according to Foreign Ministry officials, technically unfeasible and so a question of philosophy. If a movement of American armed forces from Okinawa is obviously for military combat operations in the Persian Gulf, what happens? To a similar question posed by a communist in the Diet, Mr Okita on 1 February, answered: 'It is a matter of how to interpret direct military action. If a carrier leaves Okinawa for the Middle East or the Indian Ocean, we do not consider it a direct military action. If a bomber leaves a Japanese base for a direct attack on some target in the Middle East, it is a combat operation' (*Asahi Shimbun*, 2 February). Whatever pitfalls or inadequacies may exist in the government's position in the eyes of the Opposition, it was clear that Mr Ohira was supporting in principle President Carter's 'Persian Gulf Doctrine', as he said in the Diet on 29 January: 'We should reasonably support the position of the United States in its readiness to go to the extreme, if inevitable, of the use of force in order to eliminate an external influence in the Persian Gulf' (*Yomiuri Shimbun*, 30 January). At this writing, the late premier's position still obtains, and that is one major cause of Japan's many constraints.

13 *Showa 54 nendo Chūkintō Taishi Kaigi Teigen* (Proposal made at the 1979 Conference of Middle East Ambassadors), Gaimusho (Foreign Ministry), 1979.
14 *Chūtō Mondai ni kansuru warewareno Teigen* (Our Proposal on the Middle Eastern Problems), Kokumin Gaikoo Konwakai (National Council for Diplomacy), 1980.

Part Two

Alliance Strategies, Cooperation and Conflict

4 Alice in Wonderland: The North Atlantic Alliance and the Arab-Israeli Dispute

JANICE GROSS STEIN

Not for the first time in its history, the Middle East finds itself at the center of the universe. Its contemporary economic, strategic and diplomatic significance needs little elucidation; the Middle East is now the object of sustained attention by developed and underdeveloped societies, by industrialized and agrarian economies and by Eastern and Western polities. The North Atlantic Alliance is no exception. Its members view the Middle East as the nexus of the East–West as well as the North–South conflict and as the source of the world economic crisis which has shaken the industrialized economies in the last several years.

The restored importance of the Middle East has reverberated across policy issues and regimes, or so it is frequently argued. The politics of oil, it is held, has had a strong impact on Western policy toward the Middle East. As the stakes have increased, policy on issues critical to the Middle East has changed substantially and, equally important, divisions within the Western Alliance have grown. The optic of energy-dependent Western Europe is considerably different from that of the superpower and leader of the Western Alliance, and it is not surprising to find exasperation and temper on both sides of the Atlantic.

This chapter disputes both these contentions. At best, arguments of substantive change in policy and consequent exacerbation of tension within the alliance are considerable exaggerations. Using policy toward the Arab-Israeli conflict as the test-case, similarities among alliance members continue to be greater than their differences, this despite the varying degrees of energy dependence on and political involvement in the Middle East. Secondly, policy has evolved considerably on at least one central issue in the Arab-Israeli conflict, but a significant component of the new policy is declaratory and cosmetic, designed to achieve high visibility rather than effective conflict management. The stimulus to this cosmetic approach, moreover, can frequently be traced to rigidities within the Middle East as well as to resistance among alliance members.

If these conclusions are justified by the evidence, they have considerable implications for alliance policy both toward the Arab-Israeli conflict, and the Middle East. They warn of the irrelevance of relevance and dictate judicious consideration of common concerns and careful coordination of policy to enhance shared interests. The record of the last decade shows unilateralism to be a surprisingly ineffective strategy both in the Middle East, and within the alliance. We turn now to a careful tracing of the argument and evidence which generate these rather sobering conclusions.

It is, first, necessary to establish the validity of approaches to the Arab-Israeli conflict as a useful test-case of policy coordination within the alliance. As a policy issue, the Arab-Israeli conflict has in the past and continues in the present to resonate within the Middle East and among Western industrialized states. It has been central to the politics of the Fertile Crescent for the last half-century, if not longer. And members of the alliance bring to it a history of past involvement as well as strong current interests. European participants in the alliance, particularly those who are simultaneously members of the EEC, have a long tradition of involvement in the Middle East. Indeed, their involvement predates the origins of the Arab-Israeli conflict. North Atlantic members – Canada and the USA – as well as Japan are relative newcomers, but they have responded in recent years to the intensity of the conflict in a strategically important but volatile region. Precisely because it has been and continues to be so important, because it is central rather than marginal, policy toward the Arab-Israeli conflict is a suitable object for investigation. In microcosm, it mirrors the strengths and strains within the Western Alliance as it meets the Middle East.

To assess the scope of change in alliance policy toward the Arab-Israeli conflict in the last half-decade, to provide a base-line for comparison, a brief historical retrospective is unavoidable. We begin with an examination of Canadian, European, Japanese and US approaches to conflict management from 1967 to 1973. The roots of the divisions within the alliance, divisions which became apparent after the war in 1973, can be traced to this period. Although 1967 seems a somewhat proximate basis for subsequent comparison, it does mark the exacerbation of the conflict after more than a decade of relative quiescence. Following the crisis over Suez in 1956, a crisis as much for the alliance as for the Middle East, the Arab-Israeli conflict stopped short of all-out war until 1967. The years between 1967 and the outbreak of war again in 1973 can serve as a benchmark, then, for comparison with current approaches to conflict management among the USA, Canada, the EEC and Japan.

What the analysis omits is as important as what it includes. By design, it does not consider the intersecting economic crises which accompanied the last escalation of the Arab-Israeli conflict, nor does it examine changing relationships between the two superpowers. Both these factors, which have had significant impact on the development of the conflict within the Middle East – and on the alliance – are considered elsewhere in this book. Nor does the analysis extend to an examination of alliance policies toward the Middle East generally. Rather, the focus is sharply on the Arab-Israeli dispute, and particularly on differences in approach to its management and resolution and their consequences for cohesion or division within the alliance. Although these limits are adhered to in the body of the analysis, the conclusion does speculate on the consequences of the deteriorating relationship between the superpowers for alliance approaches to the settlement of the Arab-Israeli dispute.

THE ALLIANCE AND THE DISPUTE: THE ROOTS
OF THE DIVISION

In May of 1967, after Egypt requested the withdrawal of the United
Nations' peacekeeping force and blockaded the Straits of Tiran, war
again seemed likely in the Middle East. This time, however, the crisis was
not compounded by serious disagreement among the allies. Britain and
the USA were largely agreed in their approach to the crisis – unlike 1948
or 1956 – and had no need this time of a Canadian 'honest broker'.
President Johnson consulted extensively with members of the alliance in
the weeks preceding the outbreak of war and, although General de Gaulle
differed somewhat in his approach to the management of the conflict, the
scope of the divergence would not become apparent until after the war
had ended. Although the escalation of the Arab-Israeli dispute and the
crisis created by the outbreak of war were severe, consultation and coordination among the allies were effective and free of strain. The contrast
to 1956 could not have been more striking.

Cooperation among the allies continued in the immediate postwar
period through tacit division of responsibility which facilitated the international management of the Arab-Israeli dispute. Under British leadership, with the approval and support of the USA the Security Council
passed the omnibus resolution which would set the parameters of the debate for the next six years. Resolution 242 was a delicate compromise,
arduously achieved through five months of international bargaining. In
its English version, it called for 'withdrawal of Israeli armed forces from
territories occupied in the recent conflict', 'termination of all claims of
belligerency and respect for and acknowledgement of the sovereignty,
territorial integrity, and political independence of every state in the area
and their right to live in peace within secure and recognized boundaries
free from threats or acts of force', and 'a just solution of the refugee
problem'.[1] Deliberately vague in its outline of the terms of a comprehensive settlement of the dispute, it avoided either an explicit demand for
full withdrawal, or for full peace.[2] The resolution was to become the
benchmark of policy for all members of the alliance. Indeed, Japan's first
diplomatic involvement in the Arab-Israeli dispute came when its representative on the UN Security Council expressed support for Resolution
242. Although not then a member of the Council, Canada affirmed the
broad consensus of the Western Alliance when it accepted the resolution
as the official statement of Canadian policy toward the dispute.

With the advent of a new administration in the USA in 1969, President
Nixon began an unprecedented effort to achieve a comprehensive settlement of the dispute. Nixon read the lessons of 1967 differently than did
his predecessor and, repeatedly emphasizing the dangers of renewed
escalation in the 'Balkans of the twentieth century', attached considerable
urgency to a reduction of the conflict.[3] Skeptical of the capacity of the
disputants themselves to reach agreement, the USA began discussions
with the USSR to design the outlines of a general settlement. Simultaneously, parallel four-power negotiations, which included France and
Britain as well, began in New York. The participation of the two Euro-

pean powers in these discussions in 1969 met a longstanding demand for a formal role in the management of the conflict. Indeed, during the war in 1967, President De Gaulle had insisted on an autonomous role in the negotiating process and vigorously opposed a Soviet-US condominium.

The French approach was in striking contrast to that of Canada and, even more so, to that of Japan. Canada was deeply involved in a reassessment of its traditional international role as 'helpful fixer'. The newly elected Prime Minister Trudeau urged a tighter linkage between domestic interest and foreign policy and heightened emphasis on national independence. The relevance of the Arab-Israeli dispute to matters of domestic concern was marginal and the reduced attention to mediation and peacekeeping further decreased the salience of the Arab-Israeli dispute as a foreign policy issue. Japan too had no diplomatic ambitions in the Middle East. Neither Canada nor Japan had been a power in the region in the past and both were content with a passive rather than an activist approach to conflict management. At the end of the 1960s the Western Alliance encompassed both active mediators, struggling to design a comprehensive settlement of the dispute, and passive observers. This divergence in responsibility created little strain within the alliance.

It was not the four-power meetings, however, but the parallel Soviet-US discussions which produced proposals for a comprehensive settlement in December 1969. These proposals were aborted by an escalating war of attrition along the Suez Canal, a war which provoked military intervention by one and diplomatic activism by the other superpower. For the first time in the history of the conflict, the USSR committed its own combat personnel to Egypt's defense and, in so doing, sharpened and polarized its competition with the USA in the region.[4] Responding to Soviet military involvement and its attendant dangers, the USA abandoned its attempt at comprehensive settlement, concentrated on terminating the fighting between Egypt and Israel, and first proposed a partial settlement, achieved incrementally, as an appropriate approach to conflict reduction.[5] The polarization of the Arab-Israeli dispute by the superpowers signalled the eclipse, at least temporarily, of the preferred European approach to the reduction of the conflict; the search for a comprehensive settlement was no longer the basis of American strategy.

Even before President Nixon abandoned the comprehensive approach, however, the European contribution to its development had been more apparent than real. Despite the formality of British and French participation in negotiations in the spring and summer of 1969, it was the bilateral Soviet-US discussions that produced the outline of a package settlement. The limited impact of the two European powers suggested limits to the capacity of Western Europe to influence the development of the conflict. France, at its own initiative, no longer sold sophisticated equipment to Israel and, consequently, was no longer a major supplier of any of the front-line states. Britain withdrew formally and finally from the Persian Gulf in 1971 and thereby ended its long military presence within the region. The old imperialism seemed no more than an historical remnant. Even as their political and military influence in the Middle East declined, however, the economic dependence of Western Europe grew. The two seemed in almost inverse relationship.

In 1970 the production of American oil peaked and the USA entered the international market as an important consumer. That same year, Libya challenged the autonomy of resident oil companies, and in 1971 oilproducers meeting in Tehran first suggested that they would interrupt supply in an effort to improve the terms of trade. As the dynamics of the international oil market began to shift, it is not altogether surprising that the European approach to the management of the Arab-Israeli dispute shifted. Excluded by the superpowers, the foreign ministers of the EEC met to consider a common diplomatic posture.

The shared consensus of the EEC did differ in emphasis from the previously agreed-upon Resolution 242. The Community called for a withdrawal by Israel, with minor adjustments, from all the occupied territories; the preservation of the security and territorial integrity of all states within the region through the creation of demilitarized zones and the stationing of United Nations forces; the internationalization of Jerusalem; and a solution of the refugee problem through repatriation in stages or compensation under the supervision of an international commission.[6] One year later, the EEC announced its intention to implement a Mediterranean policy through a series of bilateral agreements with all Mediterranean states. In these actions, the Community signaled a change in the tone if not the substance of its approach to the management of the Arab-Israeli dispute.

When the failure of the four-power talks and the comprehensive approach became apparent, members of the Community, led by France, preferred a collective posture to national articulation of positions on the issues in dispute. By formulating joint policies through a coordinating process within the Community, the weakness of even the strongest individual member was adumbrated by the weight of the group. The joint document concealed the range of opinion that did exist among members and, even more important, insulated individual states from pressure to modify their position independently of the others. Secondly, the EEC distinguished itself, through its continued emphasis on a comprehensive settlement, from the USA; President Nixon was then pursuing a partial settlement along the Canal to be implemented in phases. Thirdly, the substance of the European position differed marginally from that of the USA. The EEC gave greater priority to international guarantees and, consequently, placed less emphasis on negotiations between the participants both to determine the status of Jerusalem and to secure mutual recognition.[7] Fourthly, the Community paid less attention to Soviet involvement and the ensuing superpower competition than did the USA. Finally, by developing a strategy of bilateral economic arrangements, leaders within the Community attempted to outflank the conflict through commercial and trading relationships with members of the region who were not 'front-line' participants in the dispute. Europe moved from individually to collectively formulated positions, from participation in international negotiations with the superpowers to a regional forum, to a divergence in emphasis and approach from that of the USA, and to a broadening of the instruments of policy.

It is worth noting, first, that this revision in policy antedates the withdrawal of Soviet military personnel from Egypt in 1972 and the consequent reduction in the danger of superpower confrontation. Competition between the USA and the USSR outside of Europe did not invoke alliance solidarity; this interpretation of the limits to the scope of the alliance would bedevil European-US relations in the ensuing decade not only in the Middle East, but throughout the Third World. Secondly, the shift in approach antedated the outbreak of hostilities in the Middle East in 1973 and the accompanying oil embargo. If logic dictates that cause cannot follow consequence, the change in the European approach cannot be traced directly to the intersecting crises of the 1970s; the optic shifted before oil was embargoed. The relationship between energy dependence and policy position is more complicated than their simple equation would suggest. At most, in an explanation of the shift in the European approach, the politics of oil were relevant principally through anticipation. Thirdly, the change that did occur was limited in substance; the Community distinguished itself through approach and technique rather than through content. And what is even more striking, Europe would continue to diverge from its American ally in degree, but not in kind, principally in approach rather than in substance, throughout the traumas of the 1970s.

OCTOBER 1973: THROUGH THE LOOKING GLASS

In 1973 war came to the Middle East unexpectedly and with unprecedented ferocity. Not only the fighting, but also its consequences, were severe. Within three weeks of the Egyptian-Syrian attack, supplies of oil had been curtailed to some members of the alliance, and the USA, locked in fierce competition with its counterpart superpower, had initiated a worldwide nuclear alert in response to a Soviet threat of military intervention. In Europe, Canada and Japan the heightened threat to international security and the international economy provoked concern, if not alarm, and sharply oscillating, poorly coordinated initial responses. Policy varied considerably within the alliance.

Canadian policy was most consistent with its prewar posture. In his first official statement, issued while the fighting still continued, the Minister for External Affairs condemned the resort to force by Egypt and Syria, reaffirmed Canada's support of Resolution 242 and restated Ottawa's longstanding refusal to tamper with the text through addition of subtraction.[8] This initial statement reflected Canada's traditional approach to international conflict management: strong support for the resolutions of the United Nations and peacekeeping and an emphasis on negotiation between the parties to a conflict.

Within the EEC, collective action disintegrated under the pressure of the oil embargo, which accompanied the renewal of fighting. Confronted with intersecting security and economic crises and heavily dependent on imported oil, members scrambled to secure supplies and, in so doing, exacerbated relationships within the Community and within the alliance as a whole. Despite this almost visceral resort to unilateralism and the very dissimilar positions adopted initially by members of the EEC, however, the broad outlines of the collective strategy developed earlier would quickly become apparent.

Initially, divergence of opinion did appear to be considerable. While Holland, like Canada, condemned the use of force by Egypt and Syria, France justified the attack as the repossession of occupied territory. Indeed, disagreement within the EEC was so sharp that Holland and Denmark refused to authorize Britain and France to present a collective position in the Security Council debate at the United Nations. Tension within the Community was compounded by the low priority accorded alliance concerns by critically important European states and their consequent inattention to the competition between the superpowers. Despite the Soviet airlift of equipment to Egypt and Syria, Britain, France and, to a lesser extent, even Germany refused to cooperate with the USA either in the transfer of military equipment to Israel during the war, or in its diplomatic initiatives immediately after the war.[9] There was disagreement not only within Europe, but between Europe and the USA.

Within a month, however, the EEC had coordinated policy sufficiently among its nine members so that it could issue a collective declaration of policy. While the statement issued on 6 November reiterated established policy themes, there was one significant change. The Community renewed its emphasis on the inadmissibility of the acquisition of territory by force; repeated its demand for withdrawal by Israel from all occupied territory; reiterated the right of every state in the Middle East to secure and recognized boundaries; and again urged the creation of demilitarized zones reinforced by international guarantees.[10] What was new was the European treatment of the Palestinian question. The EEC no longer called for a just solution of the refugee problem, as it had in the earlier statement, but for the recognition of the legitimate rights of the Palestinians. Although much remained the same, the new emphasis on Palestinian collective rights would become the leitmotif of European policy. Indeed, it would be the single change of substance for the rest of the decade.

The reaction of Japan, the most heavily dependent on imported oil, was even sharper than that of the EEC. On 22 November 1973 the Chief Cabinet Secretary issued a statement deploring Israel's occupation of Arab territories and calling for total withdrawal, respect for the integrity and security of all countries in the area, accompanied by guarantees, and the recognition and respect of the just rights of the Palestinians. The statement concluded with the warning that Japan would 'continue to observe the situation in the Middle East with grave concern' and, depending on future developments, it might have to 'reconsider' its policy toward Israel.[11] The shift in the tone and substance of Japan's policy, a pronounced shift, brought no immediate reply from the oilproducing states; supply restrictions were not lifted. Very shortly thereafter, Deputy Prime Minister Miki began a seventeen-day visit to eight Arab countries where he pledged US $127 million to restore the Suez Canal and multimillion-dollar commodity and product aid credits. Even before Miki left the Middle East, supply restrictions against Japan were removed.

The thrust of US policy, quickly becoming pivotal in the management of the conflict, was considerably different in its approach. Secretary Kissinger, now seized with the dispute, focused his attention on the process rather than the substance of a settlement. He emphasized a gradualist approach which began with the easier rather than the more difficult issues, built on small successes, and worked through postponement of failure. While Europe and Japan urgently emphasized the solution and elimination of the conflict, the USA concentrated on its management – and transcendence – through incrementalism. Kissinger argued strongly that even the modest objective of management, if it were to be achieved, required the decoupling of economic from political issues and a sharply circumscribed role for the USSR. Moreover, he considered cooperation within the Western alliance an important structural requisite for the effective management of both the Arab-Israeli conflict and the Soviet-US competition.

Europe, to put it mildly, was not overwhelmed by the wisdom of Kissinger's strategy. The difference essentially was one of approach not only to the management of the conflict, but also to a series of political and economic issues which, although not formally part of the Arab-Israeli agenda, nevertheless accompanied the escalation and internationalization of the conflict. The complexities of energy dependence in the 'north' and the terms of technology transfer and the supply of financial and commercial services to the 'south' were difficult enough, but the relationship of this broader set of policy issues to the Arab-Israeli conflict was itself a matter of some dispute. Oilproducers in the Middle East urged and some in Europe accepted a link between the two sets of issues, while the USA led those who insisted on decoupling rather than linking the two agendas. When war in the Middle East pushed the Western Alliance through the looking glass, a division in approach in this new world was an immediate result: some supported linkage and a comprehensive solution, while others suggested decoupling and an incremental, partial approach.

To resolve these differences, members of the alliance tacitly agreed to an initial division of responsibility. The USA would handle the specifics of the dispute in the Middle East and the attendant East–West competition, while Europe concentrated on restructuring and stabilizing relationships with the newly powerful oilproducing states. This initial approach seemed sensible: building on the relative strengths of Europe and the USA, it would utilize American political and military capabilities to deescalate the conflict and, simultaneously, insulate the energy-dependent from the passions of the dispute in the Middle East. This insulation, it was hoped, would facilitate the orderly rearrangement of international energy and financial markets. The approach was more difficult, however, to realize than to conceive. Especially in the immediate postwar period, it was more difficult to decouple economic from political issues than the USA had anticipated. And when the issues were linked, the results of the linkage were far less than Europe and Japan had expected. If linkage seemed to be necessary, it clearly was an insufficient approach to the complex of policy issues which now dominated allied discussion and behavior, public as well as private. A look at the voting record at the United Nations, the public forum *par excellence*, documents the differences and similarities among the allies in their approach to the management of the Arab-Israeli conflict.

THE ARAB-ISRAELI DISPUTE INTERNATIONALIZED: VOTING AT THE UNITED NATIONS

In the years which followed the October War, Arab participants in the conflict expanded the arena and shifted the emphasis of the dispute. Although a solution to the Palestinian problem had always been important, it was to become the overwhelming focus in multilateral meetings. Particularly at the United Nations, Arab leaders insisted that the Palestinian question be approached as a national and political issue, not as a refugee problem. Moreover, they made it clear that they considered voting on resolutions in the General Assembly to be a valid indicator of the policy position of members. A review of the voting records of the EEC, Canada, Japan and the USA is useful, then, to isolate changes in policy as well as differences within the alliance. Examination of the turbulent session of the General Assembly in 1974 can provide the benchmark for subsequent detailed comparison of votes from 1975, the 29th General Assembly to the last meeting of the 34th Assembly in January 1980, and the last session for which valid statistics are currently available.

The first regular meeting of the General Assembly after the October War provided tangible evidence of the changing terms of the Arab-Israeli debate. Two quite distinct issues were at the center of the discussion. Resolutions introduced before the Assembly affirmed the right of Palestinian self-determination and, secondly, asked that the Palestinian Liberation Organization be recognized as the sole legitimate representative of the Palestinians and be invited to participate in the work of the Assembly as well as its committees. Since Resolution 242, the previous embodiment of policy for the Western allies as well as for Arab governments and Israel, made no such provision, submission of these resolutions to a vote created a dilemma for most members of the alliance.

The EEC, Japan and Canada abstained on the resolution, which affirmed the Palestinian right of self-determination, national independence and repatriation, recognized the Palestinians as a principal party in the establishment of peace and requested that the PLO be contacted on all matters relating to Palestine. The USA opposed the resolution.[12] Canada's explanation of the vote is valid for other members of the alliance as well. Ottawa's ambassador to the United Nations noted that the text made no reference to the earlier Resolution 242 as a framework for negotiation and, consequently, ignored the interrelatedness of the complex of issues which constitute the Arab-Israeli dispute. However, Canada considered representation of the Palestinian people to be an essential component of a peaceful settlement of the dispute. Consequently, it abstained.[13] Canada agreed with its European allies: Resolution 242 was a necessary but insufficient basis for discussion of the Arab-Israeli dispute. Specifically, it was incomplete in its failure to make provision for Palestinian participation in the process of negotiations, which must needs follow.

Voting on the second resolution highlighted a different issue and a second, quite distinct trans-Atlantic coalition, which would vote together repeatedly over the next several years. In its opposition to granting the PLO permanent observer status, the USA was joined by Canada and most of the EEC; France and Italy abstained, however, as did Japan.[14] In the debate that followed, Japan made its position explicit. Its representative argued that the Palestinian question was at the heart of the Middle East problem and that PLO participation in the debate was essential.[15] Japan added, however, that it would be helpful if the PLO were 'to work in a constructive spirit for a political settlement through peaceful means'.[16] Opposition to the resolution by members of the alliance stemmed both from general principle, and particular circumstances. Some refused, as a matter of principle, to prejudge the issue of the appropriate representation of the Palestinians.[17] More important, others objected to specific characteristics of the PLO, particularly its unwillingness to forgo the use of terrorism and accept the legitimacy of Israel within the Middle East.[18] Differences in approach to the PLO cut across Europe and created a coalition which spanned the Atlantic. Divergence of opinion on this subject would remain substantial throughout the decade as alliance members moved beyond the issue of representation to consider the suitability of the PLO as a partner in the negotiating process. And in the ongoing debate a core of Europeans would switch their vote to determine a majority either in Europe, or across the ocean.

One additional resolution is worthy of attention. During the 30th General Assembly in 1974, a resolution condemning all forms of racial discrimination *inter alia* declared Zionism to be racist. Introduction of the resolution in this form suggested a deliberate attempt to delegitimize one of the principal parties to the dispute. Members of the Western Alliance were virtually unanimous in their opposition to such a strategy; only Japan abstained. In voting against the resolution, alliance members established the parameters of their approach to conflict resolution: divided on the legitimacy of the PLO as the representative of the Palestinian people and, more to the point, on its suitability as a negotiating partner, they were agreed in their opposition to the delegitimization of Israel.[19]

The pattern of voting in the subsequent five assemblies documents the scope of divergence as well as consensus among the allies in their approach to the dispute. Inspection of the record on some forty-nine resolutions dealing with the Arab-Israeli dispute, all put before the assembly, suggests a rather complicated pattern of voting within the alliance (Table 4.1).[20] Immediately apparent is the low level of consensus in the difficult first years which followed the October War. In 1975, for example, the EEC was deeply divided and voted together on only one of five resolutions, and the USA and a majority of the Community agreed only marginally better than half the time. In a new trend, when the USA and the EEC disagreed in their approach to the Arab-Israeli dispute,

Table 4.1 *Agreement within the Alliance*

	1975 N=5	1976 N=11	1977 N=10	1978 N=14	1979 N=9
EEC	0·20(1)	0·81(9)	0·80(8)	0·78(11)	0·44(4)
The majority of the EEC and USA	0·60(3)	0·45(5)	0·60(6)	0·50(7)	0·66(6)
The majority of the EEC and Canada	0·60(3)	0·90(10)	0·80(8)	0·71(10)	0·77(7)
USA and Canada	0·60(3)	0·45(5)	0·80(8)	0·78(11)	0·88(8)
When USA and a majority of the EEC disagree:	(2)	(6)	(4)	(7)	(3)
Canada and a majority of the EEC	1·00(2)	1·00(6)	0·50(2)	0·43(3)	0·33(1)
Canada and USA	0·00(0)	0·00(0)	0·50(2)	0·57(4)	0·66(2)
Japan and a majority of the EEC	0·20(1)	0·72(8)	0·80(8)	0·50(7)	0·44(4)
Japan and USA	0·00(0)	0·27(3)	0·40(4)	0·21(3)	0·22(2)
Japan and Canada	0·20(1)	0·63(7)	0·60(6)	0·28(4)	0·33(3)
When USA and a majority of the EEC disagree:	(2)	(6)	(4)	(7)	(3)
Japan and a majority of the EEC	0·50(1)	0·66(4)	1·00(4)	0·57(4)	0·66(2)
Japan and USA	0·00(0)	0·00(0)	0·00(0)	0·00(0)	0·00(0)
	% N	% N	% N	% N	% N

Canada voted with the Community; one year later, Canada was even more strongly in agreement with a majority of the EEC.[21] These data suggest a considerable reorientation of Canada's policy, but inspection of the record for the subsequent three years shows a return to Canada's more usual position of balance between allies in disagreement. Although Canada no longer considers itself an 'honest broker' within the alliance, although it abjures its activist role of the 1950s, it continues to distribute its vote even-handedly, if not within the Middle East, at least within the alliance.

Japan, on the other hand, never voted with the USA when America disagreed with the EEC. Indeed, Japan's disagreement with the EEC, when it occurred, can be explained largely by its approval, along with a large part of the Third World, of resolutions which the Community, much less the USA, could not support or opposed. The level of agreement between Japan and other members of the alliance is significantly lower than that among all other allies. On issues relating to the Arab-Israeli dispute, Japan is singular in its failure to do as the others do.

During these five years, what did vary was the level of cohesion within the EEC and the shifting coalitions which resulted. After 1975 cohesion improved markedly and only in this past assembly did division reappear. In the United Nations, EEC members demonstrated the capacity to follow a collective policy on the Arab-Israeli dispute. Closely associated with improved policy coordination within the EEC, was disagreement with the USA. When the EEC did not vote together, however, a trans-Atlantic coalition was almost always present, a coalition which included at a minimum the USA, Canada, Belgium, Germany, the Netherlands, Britain and Denmark. In this last assembly, for example, this was the dominant coalition within alliance voting on Arab-Israeli issues. The evidence of the last five years does not support an argument of intensifying trans-Atlantic division. On the contrary, almost as often as not, a majority of Europeans voted with the USA. Divisions within the alliance were not only between the USA and Europe, but also within Europe itself. A suggestion of a European and a US perspective on the Arab-Israeli dispute appears a considerable oversimplification of the complexities of alliance policies in the Middle East. Examination of the substance of policy as well as the pattern of voting should uncover trans-Atlantic consensus as well as difference.

THE ARAB-ISRAELI CONFLICT: THE TERMS OF A SETTLEMENT

For the past thirty years, a settlement of the Arab-Israeli conflict has been of international concern and, in the last five years, it has had priority on the international agenda. A canvass of the substance of allied positions on the appropriate terms of a settlement shows surprising consensus within the alliance. There is little disagreement within Europe or between Europe and the USA on the broad parameters of a resolution to the conflict. The problem lies elsewhere.

The USA, Canada, the EEC and Japan, all support the security, territorial integrity and political independence of all the states in the Middle East. In so doing, they explicitly uphold Israel's right to exist within the region. Indeed, Prime Minister Miki of Japan, in one of the earliest criticisms of Resolution 242, suggested in 1975 that the resolution was deficient in its failure to refer explicitly by name to the state of Israel.[22] And the EEC, in its most recent declaration issued in Venice, affirmed Israel's right to existence within the region as essential to a settlement.[23]

Secondly, although there are minor differences in language, the EEC as well as Japan, the USA and Canada support the withdrawal of Israel from the occupied territories. Japan, in its statements at the United Nations, has demanded total withdrawal from all the territories captured in 1967, as have Italy, France and Germany.[24] In Venice the Community used somewhat more circumspect language; it called on Israel 'to put an end to the territorial occupation . . . as it has done for part of Sinai'.[25] The analogue of Sinai, of course, is to a total withdrawal. The position of the USA is little different. As long as a decade ago, the USA called for a return to the 1967 borders with only 'minor' rectifications. Canada's position is most open-ended: it argues that final borders must be settled through a process of negotiation. Although these differences in language suggest shadings in policy, there is overwhelming consensus for virtually complete withdrawal.

From this shared consensus, springs common opposition to any unilateral change in the status of the occupied territories which would prejudice the outcome of negotiation between the parties to the conflict. There is unanimous opposition, for example, to the establishment of settlements by Israel, expressed frequently at the United Nations and most recently in the Venice declaration of the EEC. Equally, there is widespread opposition to intemperate and one-sided criticism of Israel, criticism which has dominated debate at the UN this last half-decade.[26] This opposition to unbalanced attack is reflected in the trans-Atlantic coalition which appears persistently during the last five years.

Finally, there is widespread consensus within the alliance that the Palestinian problem requires a political and territorial solution. A textual analysis of the vocabulary of Western leaders would isolate differences in language which, however, indicate only minor differences in substance. Addressing a town meeting in Clinton, Massachusetts after only two months in office, President Carter spoke of the need of a 'homeland' for the Palestinian refugees.[27] Canada's statements have been models of linguistic acrobatics, arguing that the future of the Palestinian people was a central element in the Middle East conflict and an enduring solution must provide 'a territorial foundation for political self-expression by the Palestinian people consistent with the principle of self-determination'.[28] Most recently, a report prepared for Prime Minister Clark, now no longer in office, urged Canada to lend its support to the Palestinian right to a 'homeland'.[29]

Opinion in Europe is little different. Germany, strongly committed to the unification of its own people, speaks of the right to self-determination of the Palestinians.[30] At the conclusion of a tour of the Persian Gulf, President Giscard d'Estaing of France, in an official communiqué issued in March 1980, similarly endorsed the right of the Palestinian people to self-determination.[31] Britain refers formally to the 'national identity' or 'personality' of the Palestinian people. European leaders, however, have not supported the creation of an independent Palestinian state; indeed, Britain and France abstained recently when this proposal was put to the Security Council.[32] France's foreign minister explained that the political form of self-determination was beyond the competence of outside powers to determine.[33]

Collectively, the position of Europe is little different from that of its individual members. Indeed, a review of the series of formal statements issued by the EEC points to a steady evolution of Community thinking. In November 1973 the EEC spoke of the 'legitimate rights' of the Palestinians. Four years later, in June 1977, Community leaders explained that the right to a 'homeland' was a component of these legitimate rights;[34] in so doing, they joined their colleagues across the Atlantic. Most recently at their meeting in Venice, leaders of the EEC reiterated that the Palestinian people must be given an opportunity to fully exercise its rights to self-determination.[35]

This examination of opinion on both sides of the Atlantic points to a surprisingly broad consensus within the alliance on the terms of a settlement of the Arab-Israeli dispute. In its recent meeting in Venice, the EEC argued that a settlement must be based on two principles: the right to existence and security of all states in the region, including Israel, and justice for all peoples, which implies recognition of the legitimate rights of the Palestinian people.[36] No member of the Western Alliance would quarrel with this statement. The broad consensus on ends – the security of Israel and a political solution to the Palestinian problem – does not extend, however, to the means to reconcile and achieve these objectives.

Disagreement within the alliance stems not from the components of a comprehensive settlement of the dispute, but from important differences over negotiating methods and participants. Europe and the USA differ, not for the first or only time in the last decade, in their assessments of the most effective approach to the management and resolution of the conflict. Two issues are central to these divergent assessments: the first, a disagreement over the practicability of an immediate and comprehensive settlement, has been institutionalized in the codewords 'Camp David' and 'Geneva'; the second raises the suitability of the PLO as a participant in the negotiating process. These two issues were present, in one form or another, in all the resolutions which provoked different votes on the two sides of the Atlantic. Beneath this disagreement over strategy and tactics, moreover, lies a difference in appreciation of the independent role of Europe as a conflict mediator. As on so many other issues, the Middle East is again a harbinger of things to come.

A STEP-BY-STEP APPROACH TO CAMP DAVID

After the October War, Europe, Canada and Japan accepted the preeminent role of the USA in engineering a settlement of the Arab-Israeli dispute. Britain and France, participants in the negotiations in New York in 1969, had shown neither capacity to, nor interest in, defining a new role for themselves following the failure of the four-power talks. The outbreak of war, accompanied by a near-confrontation between the two superpowers, underlined the special resources needed to mediate the Arab-Israeli dispute. Cognizant of their limited capabilities, the allies almost seemed to prefer an allocation of responsibility which provided some distance from the enveloping and dangerous dispute. Unrestrained by the need to set and meet concrete negotiating objectives, Europe and Japan were free to outline their view of a comprehensive settlement with little attention to the obstacles to its immediate achievement or to the required negotiating procedures. Canada was more restrained: it emphasized its role as peacekeeper rather than peacemaker and focused some attention on the process of negotiations as well as the substance.

It was the USA who assumed principal responsibility for the deescalation of the conflict. Kissinger opted for a partial, incremental approach whose objective was a reduction in the probability of renewed warfare and its attendant dislocations and dilemmas. Very much preoccupied with the possible rather than the desirable, US diplomacy succeeded in disengaging the military forces of the combatants and engineered a series of partial agreements between Egypt and Israel, the two most forthcoming participants in the negotiating process. Although the pace was often painfully slow, the approach was designed to build the basis over time for a series of interrelated agreements. Given the real obstacles to agreement and the slow progress toward even modest objectives, the USA was not terribly sympathetic to demands for an immediate and comprehensive settlement; it considered such an approach irresponsible and a recipe for failure. Only after the second round of agreements between Egypt and Israel, in 1975, did Secretary Kissinger consider that the process had indeed been cumulative in its results, creating a basis for broader agreement. Preliminary exploration of the outlines of such an agreement ended with the electoral defeat of President Ford.

Under President Carter, the USA shifted completely to the preferred strategy of the Community and Japan and concentrated on the negotiating dynamics of a comprehensive settlement. It consciously strengthened its relations with front-line confrontation states and indirectly offered incentives to the PLO to encourage it to modify its position and join the negotiating process. The Carter administration also reopened discussions with the USSR in an effort to ensure its cooperation should the Geneva Conference be resumed; superpower consensus is a structural requisite of a comprehensive settlement. For a brief period of time, from January to November 1977, there was agreement between the USA and Europe not only on the substance, but also on the strategy and tactics of settlement.

A comprehensive approach to conflict resolution, tried again for the first time since 1969, was similarly disappointing in its outcome. It produced consensus among the allies but no progress in the negotiations. American overtures to the PLO were not reciprocated, the reintroduction of the USSR antagonized two of the principals in the negotiating process and, in frustration, President Sadat launched his unilateral initiative. He did so not only to deprive his more militant Arab allies of their veto, but also to exclude the USSR from the peacemaking process. The president of Egypt considered the USSR obstructive, a hindrance rather than a help.

After some initial confusion, the USA adjusted its approach and returned to the vigorous pursuit of an agreement between Egypt and Israel which would simultaneously provide at least a framework for progress on other fronts. The ensuing Camp David accords and peace treaty between Egypt and Israel exchanged full withdrawal from the Sinai for some demilitarization of the desert area, limited force zones and normalization of relations. The agreements were comprehensive – all outstanding bilateral issues between the two signatories were resolved – and partial – in their creation of a loosely defined framework for further open-ended negotiation with other participants who had not yet joined the process. It was a signal moment in the long and tortured history of the Arab-Israeli conflict.

APPROACHES TO CONFLICT MANAGEMENT:
PROCEDURES AND PARTICIPANTS

Contrary to US expectations, Camp David got mixed notices from some
members of the alliance. The dilemma of the allies in 1978 was similar to
that of 1973 with, however, one important exception. The agreement between Egypt and Israel did significantly reduce the probability of major
war in the Middle East, at least in the short term, and consequently
virtually eliminated the possibility of an oil embargo. In engineering the
agreement, therefore, the USA met one of the principal demands of
energy-dependent Western Europe and Japan. Strong Arab skepticism
and opposition to the proposals for Palestinian autonomy, however, again
created a policy problem for Western leaders, who could not simultaneously support the USA's attempt at conflict reduction and meet Arab
criticism. Particularly strong opposition came from the PLO, which was
given no formal role in the forthcoming series of negotiations. Again, a
partial and evolutionary approach was grossly insufficient to satisfy Arab
and particularly PLO demands. Yet an evolutionary approach seemed the
only possible alternative to comprehensive policies which could not
succeed.

Reaction to this dilemma was considerably different on each side of the
Atlantic. Canada, as well as the USA of course, was strongly supportive
of Camp David and the ensuing treaty. Officials in Ottawa considered the
treaty to be the most significant development in the thirty-year history of
the conflict.[37] Canada was careful to add that a comprehensive peace
treaty between all Arab participants in the conflict and Israel was essential, if peace were to be permanent and stable, but insisted that the
settlement between Egypt and Israel was a valuable first step and deserving of international support. Even after almost a year of frustrating
deadlock in the autonomy discussions, a special report prepared for
Ottawa reaffirmed the importance of negotiations between the parties;
Arab opposition to Camp David, it concluded, must go beyond general
statements to concrete alternatives.[38] In its analysis of the peacemaking
process, Canada placed as much emphasis on the evolutionary component
of the negotiating process as on the substantive content of the agreement.

In Europe, however, the general reaction was guarded. Even before the
peace treaty was concluded, Europe's leaders were reserved in the support
they extended to President Sadat. After his visit to Jerusalem in November
1977, the EEC, meeting in Brussels, issued a statement commending the
initiative but reiterating the importance of an 'overall' settlement which
would meet the 'rights and concerns of all the parties involved'.[39] Ten
months later, after the meeting at Camp David in September 1978, the
foreign ministers of the EEC commended President Carter as well as the
leaders of Egypt and Israel but again reiterated their hope that the
conference was a major step toward a comprehensive peace.[40] Com-
menting on the peace treaty which grew out of Camp David, the EEC
underscored the urgency of a comprehensive settlement, a settlement
which would require Palestinian participation and international endorse-

ment.[41] The flush of enthusiasm was considerably less on this side of the Atlantic.

Within the boundaries of their collective response, there were shadings of difference among members of the EEC. Britain was supportive of US mediation, as was Germany, who had special obligations to Israel and strong commercial interests in Egypt. France, generally less well-disposed toward the USA, and a heavy importer and exporter to the Gulf states, not surprisingly was critical. Unhappy with the USA's dominance of the peacemaking process, France supported an enlarged Geneva Conference or an international conference at the United Nations, where it would be better able to exercise independent influence. In his perspective, President Giscard d'Estaing differed little from his predecessor a decade earlier; De Gaulle too had protested superpower domination and demanded four-power talks which would recognize the role of France in the international community. At the 34th General Assembly, in December 1979, France alone among members of the EEC abstained on two resolutions, which declared Camp David illegal, condemned all partial agreements and separate treaties which violate the rights of the Palestinian people and contradict the principle of comprehensive settlement, and called for the reconvening of the Geneva Conference.[42] A seasoned observer of the North Atlantic alliance in the Middle East could not help but experience a sense of *déjà vu*.

France was the principal exponent of a new European initiative which could provide a 'third way', an alternative to US or Soviet mediation in the Middle East. Touring the Persian Gulf in the spring of 1980 the president of France urged Arab states to look to Europe as a military and diplomatic alternative to either superpower. At French prodding, the EEC considered introducing an amendment to UN Resolution 242 in the Security Council which would recognise the legitimate rights of the Palestinians and provide formally for their self-determination; the French foreign minister argued that passage of such an amended resolution would help to break the impasse in the autonomy negotiations.[43] President Carter was vehement in his opposition to a European *démarche* which would compromise the Camp David process. Indeed, the alliance was treated to the rather unusual spectacle of one ally threatening to veto a resolution introduced by the others.[44] Deterrence of an ally is apparently easier than deterring an adversary, for under threat of an American veto, the EEC abandoned its project of a revision to Resolution 242 and decided instead to issue a collective statement at its summit meeting in Venice in June 1980.

Members of the Community were not agreed on the thrust of the proposed statement. West Germany, Holland and Denmark pressed for a limited intiative which would complement, rather than challenge, negotiations going on under US auspices. Deliberately, they sought to reduce division within the alliance. France, on the other hand, supported a strongly worded statement, insisting that an independent diplomatic role for Europe was more important than smoothly equilibrated relations with the USA. At stake in the debate were not only European relations with the Middle East, or even the future of the US effort at mediation, but more important, divergent perspectives on the international role of members of the alliance.

The statement finally agreed to at Venice was a compromise. Its treatment of Palestinian participation in the negotiating process, an issue we shall examine in a moment, was designed to avoid explicit challenge to the USA. The EEC was unequivocal, however, in its emphasis on an independent European role in the mediation of the conflict. Citing traditional ties and common interests, the EEC offered to participate in a system of concrete and binding international guarantees within the framework of a comprehensive settlement. In addition, the EEC decided to launch an independent effort at mediation, quite distinct from the negotiations going on between Egypt and Israel. The statement concluded with the announcement that a mission would be dispatched to the Middle East to establish contact with all the parties to the dispute, with a view to determining the form of a subsequent European initiative.[45]

This difference in perspective is not new to the alliance. Not for the first time Europe urged a comprehensive settlement, while the USA insisted on the value of gradual and limited progress over time which would have cumulative consequence. Again, not for the first time, Europe offered to guarantee a settlement reached under international auspices. And again, Europe rebelled against American domination of the diplomacy of conflict resolution in the Middle East. Indeed, careful reading of the record at the beginning and end of the decade of the 1970s would find much in common and little difference. True, in 1969, Britain and France participated with the USA, while in 1980, Europe collectively demanded an independent and direct role in mediating the dispute. This demand had to do as much, however, with shifting dynamics within the alliance as it did with the contours of the Arab-Israeli dispute. The decade-old difference in perspective, temporarily submerged during active periods of mediation under Kissinger and Carter, reemerged as a continuing disagreement both over the appropriate process of conflict resolution, and the proper role for Europe in that process.

A final issue, which arises directly from these competing perspectives, is the role of the Palestine Liberation Organization in the negotiating process. On this issue, unlike the others, there has been significant change in policy, which has created distinct differences within the alliance. Alone among the Western allies, the USA has undertaken a formal commitment to refrain from recognition of and negotiation with the PLO until it recognizes Israel's right to exist and accepts Resolutions 242 and 338.[46] Early in the Carter administration, officials did suggest informally that acceptance of the UN resolutions would be sufficient to initiate a dialogue with the USA. This effort to encourage discussion met with no success, however, and ended when the Egypt–Israel dialogue accelerated. Current US policy, working within the framework of the autonomy negotiations, makes no provision under present circumstances for the participation of the PLO.

Canadian policy, flowing from a similar set of premises, is also somewhat reserved. Traditionally, Ottawa has been unwilling to pronounce formally on the issue of the appropriate representation of the Palestinians, but argues strongly that the Palestinians must be represented in the negotiations. It views the policies of the PLO, however, as unhelpful to the peace process; indeed, until the PLO is prepared to accept Resolution 242 and the legitimacy of Israel, Canada cannot envisage its constructive participation in negotiations.[47] Unlike the USA, however, the recent re-evaluation of Canadian policy toward the conflict recommended a broadening of contacts with the PLO to encourage 'moderation and realism and . . . open acceptance of the legitimacy of the State of Israel'.[48] Here the criterion of policy is encouragement of constructive participation in the negotiating process.

Given their emphasis on the urgency of an immediate and comprehensive solution, policy is considerably different within Europe and Japan. Although Japan has not officially recognized the PLO, nor given its office in Tokyo diplomatic status, as early as 1976 it urged a direct Israel–PLO dialogue.[49] Most members of the EEC similarly have withheld formal diplomatic recognition from the PLO, although they acknowledge its receipt of observer status at the United Nations. Most, however, have authorized the establishment of PLO information facilities, if not the opening of offices in their capitals.[50] Individually, moreover, some of Western Europe's leaders have talked informally and formally with representatives of the PLO. Among the first to do so was the former French Foreign Minister, Jean Sauvagnargues, who met with Yassir Arafat in Beirut in 1976. German policy was more reserved: it established as the criteria of recognition renunciation by the PLO of terrorism and acceptance of the existence of Israel.

In the wake of the Camp David accords, Arafat led the PLO in a major attempt to secure official recognition from Western Europe. From the perspective of the PLO, such recognition is important, if the USA is to be outflanked, the autonomy negotiations discredited and the validity of a comprehensive strategy reestablished. Responding to this initiative in the summer of 1979, former German Chancellor Willy Brandt, and the current Chancellor of Austria, Bruno Kreisky, met with Arafat in Vienna under the auspices of the Socialist International in an effort to mediate the Israel-Palestinian dispute. Although the mediators were not present in their capacity as governmental representatives, it was the first semi-official attempt by West Europeans to resume an active and direct role in the management and resolution of the conflict. Despite the cordial tone, however, the meeting ended with no change in the official position of the PLO.

Although no progress had been made in these initial diplomatic contacts, the quasi-official discussions presaged a change first in French and then in EEC policy toward the PLO. In March 1980 the French Cabinet issued a communiqué at the end of President Giscard d'Estaing's tour of the Persian Gulf. Arguing that a settlement must be based on the two principles of security and self-determination, the communiqué called for the participation of the Palestine Liberation Organization in negotiations on this basis.[51] The Venice declaration of the EEC, issued three months later, followed this outline closely: with only slight modification of language, modification designed to avoid provocation of the USA, it insisted that the PLO be 'associated' with the negotiations.[52] This new demand for 'association' is a considerable change in policy: Europe now does not insist on acceptance by the PLO of Resolution 242, or the existence of Israel as a condition of participation in negotiation of a settlement. The USA responded that the PLO is not a suitable participant in the negotiating process until it meets both these conditions.[53]

So matters rest, at least temporarily. To decade-old differences between the USA and Europe on procedures appropriate to the management of the Arab-Israeli dispute, have been added new differences on suitable participants in the process of conflicting management. Paradoxically, although the incendiary potential of the Arab-Israeli dispute is somewhat less than it was a decade ago, differences among the allies persist. These differences in approach to conflict resolution take on added importance, however, because of the substantially greater involvement of the USA in the peacemaking process and the consequent implications for alliance cohesion.

THE ARAB-ISRAELI DISPUTE IN ALLIANCE POLITICS

The scope of present US involvement in the management of the Arab-Israeli dispute is unprecedented. For the first time in the history of the conflict, the USA is not only patron or mediator, but a visible 'partner' in the ongoing negotiations. Inevitably, the USA becomes the target of those who are opposed to its strategy of conflict resolution, and disagreement within the alliance, while long-standing and not substantially different in scope, acquires new significance. Old disagreements on processes and new differences over participants translate directly into divergent assessments of the roles of Europe and the USA within the alliance. These differences have significantly greater consequences for the alliance than they do for the Middle East. Indeed, with only mild exaggeration, European approaches to the resolution of the Arab-Israeli dispute can better be explained by the dynamics of the alliance than by the dynamics of the dispute.

At the core of the European approach are the two concepts of comprehensive participation and comprehensive settlement. Both are flawed either in concept, or in practice. Comprehensive participation through 'association' of the PLO with future negotiations can, Europeans suggest, serve three distinct purposes. First, meeting the Arab demand for PLO participation is as important, if not more important, than the negotiations themselves; it can prevent an Arab turn to the Soviet Union should US mediation fail. President Giscard d'Estaing of France argues that Europe can serve as a diplomatic alternative and a substitute military supplier to the Arab world.[54] The argument has some credibility at the margin. France, Britain and Germany may be able to supply some of the military needs of some of the Arab states. Egypt, Iraq and Saudi Arabia, for example, recently have diversified their military suppliers. The scope of arms purchases in the Middle East is of such magnitude, however, that on a longer-term basis, Europe does not have the military resources to substitute for the USSR and the USA. Europe can complement but not supplant the superpowers. The 'third way' seems unlikely in theory or in practice.

A second, more modest objective of the European initiative, is moderation of the position of the PLO to create a framework for negotiation with Israel. Such an objective is attractive and important as a strategy of conflict resolutions,[55] but its timing and use by the EEC cast serious doubt on its effectiveness. European leaders met in Venice directly after the congress of *al-Fatah* in Damascus, the first to be held in nine years. Far from moderating its position, *al Fatah* the central constituent unit of the PLO, declared in its final communiqué: 'Fatah is an independent national movement, whose aim is to liberate Palestine completely and to liquidate the Zionist entity politically, economically, militarily, culturally and ideologically.'[56] Although the closing statement suggested unrelenting militancy, the EEC pressed for the inclusion of the PLO with no accompanying demand that it moderate its policies. Given the rigid, public position of the PLO it is not likely that unconditional acceptance of the PLO as a suitable participant will advance the process of conflict resolution. More important, nor will it encourage the PLO to take the steps necessary to alter its position, privately and then publicly. Both the timing and the form of the EEC demand for broadened participation suggest that the target of the Venice declaration was neither the PLO, nor a settlement of the Arab-Israeli dispute. Indeed, Yassir Arafat concurs with this analysis.[57]

If the first two purposes are either ill-conceived, or badly executed, a third objective is still more modest. The EEC, recognizing the limits both to its capabilities and its influence, designed its initiative principally to press the USA to bring pressure on Israel to make concessions in the stalemated negotiations. Some members of the US State Department have informally put forward such a hypothesis.[58] Such a strategy is unlikely to succeed, however, either in the USA, or in Israel. Israel's reaction to the Venice declaration was as vitriolic as that of Arafat, and the sense of outrage provoked by the statement is not likely to create the climate of security needed for diplomatic concession.[59]

A review of the reaction to the Venice declaration suggests that for some in the Middle East it went too far, while for others it did not go far enough. Nor would an amendment to Resolution 242, the original project of the EEC, have met with a better reception. Two months before the Venice meeting, at the fourth summit of the Arab Steadfastness and Confrontation Front in Tripoli, its five members rejected even a revised or amended Resolution 242 as an adequate basis for a solution to the conflict.[60] The cosmetics of the European strategy were clear in the Middle East.[61] It is difficult to escape the conclusion that far more important than the stated objectives of conflict resolution was a desire by the Community to distance itself from the USA. The European emphasis on broadened participation through 'association' of the PLO with the negotiations, while contributing little immediately to the resolution of the conflict, nevertheless clearly distinguished Europe from the USA.

The second, older and well-rehearsed difference within the alliance pits a comprehensive settlement against a gradual and partial approach. Two factors are relevant here. First, the practicality of each approach must be considered, and secondly, the current differences between the two may be somewhat exaggerated. To succeed, a comprehensive solution to the Arab-Israeli dispute requires a minimum coalition within the Arab world in favor of compromise and normalization, a willingness by Israel to return all the territory captured in 1967, and superpower consensus on the terms and implementation of a solution. None of these three prerequisite conditions exist presently, nor for that matter have the first two existed in the past.

Most immediately relevant is the striking deterioration of relations between the USA and the USSR in the last year. Indeed, this is a serious obstacle to a global settlement which has as a central constitutive element Soviet-US consensus on its substance and enforcement. Such a consensus implies considerable cooperation between the two superpowers and, indeed, only twice in the last decade – in late 1969, and in the autumn of 1977 – did the rudiments of such a consensus appear to exist. In retrospect, moreover, this past decade may appear as one of relative harmony between the two great powers; in the immediate future, Soviet-US cooperation is likely to be considerably more difficult. The Middle East, more so than most other regions, cannot escape the consequences of renewed superpower competition. In such a context, the Arab-Israeli conflict will become less amenable to comprehensive solution.

If this analysis is correct, the European concentration on an immediate comprehensive solution is conceptually unsound. And, if the emphasis on comprehensive solution through comprehensive participation is impractical as well as conceptually flawed, it appears that the EEC designed its strategy with too little attention to the Arab-Israeli dispute and too much attention to the attractiveness of an independent European role in the Middle East and in the international arena. Europe's approach to the Middle East responds as much to its own need for independence from the USA as it does to the realities within the region. Its strategy reflects serious doubt about the quality of current US leadership as well as US capabilities and a resurgent and restless community which seeks international outlets for its growing aspirations. Not for the first time in its history, the Arab-Israeli dispute is once again the pawn in great-power politics.

If the prospects of a comprehensive solution are not good, the difficulties with current American strategy are painfully obvious. The ongoing deadlock in negotiations, the failure of other Arab states to join the discussions and the inadequate representation of the Palestinians threaten not only the current negotiations, but also the relationship between Egypt and Israel. The current process is dangerously slow, dangerously partial and dangerously isolated. Moreover, despite the enormous investment of US effort and prestige, it is far from obvious how the pace can be quickened and the process broadened.

The Arab-Israeli dispute has shown itself remarkably resistant to national and international solution for most of this century. It is not surprising, therefore, that a complex and intractable conflict of such major proportions defies both incremental and comprehensive solution;

the obstacles to agreement are real. Precisely because the answers are not obvious, because both of the principal approaches are flawed, alliance coordination and cooperation are especially important. When the obstacles to comprehensive solution and the dangers of incremental and partial strategies are acknowledged, moreover, differences between the USA and Europe narrow considerably in practice. Members of the alliance must adjust their strategy, if they are to advance their collective interest as well as those of the participants in the dispute.

An alliance strategy toward the Arab-Israeli dispute must build on the strengths and resources of its members to encourage the belligerents to compromise. Europe has historic economic and cultural ties to important states in the Middle East, who themselves exercise influence on front-line Arab participants in the dispute. Abjuring declaratory politics and public posturing, Europe can insist on moderation, acceptance of the legitimacy of Israel as well as the other parties to the dispute, and a commitment to formal peace; its insistence could greatly improve the prospects of successful conflict resolution. Particularly with respect to the Palestine Liberation Organization, Europe can use its diplomatic resources directly and indirectly with Arab patrons of the PLO to encourage the change in position which is prerequisite to a break in the current logjam. Europe's diplomatic recognition must be recognized as the valuable resource it is; it must be deployed rather than expended. The USA similarly can use its unique access to Israel to encourage necessary concession, both on the process and the substance of negotiations.

Equally important, the USA must acknowledge the strong European interest in and ties to the Middle East as well as its determination to participate actively in the mediation of the conflict. The foreign minister of France on a visit to Washington, underscored the new assertiveness of Europe even as he acknowledged the inadequacy of existing mechanisms of consultation and cooperation.[62] Indeed, the activism of the EEC toward the Arab-Israeli conflict is symptomatic of a determination to expand Europe's role throughout the international system. The USA, in cooperation with its allies, must design mechanisms to consider, consult and coordinate joint strategy and tactics to resolve the Arab-Israeli conflict and, of course, other issues as well. A joint strategy offers the best prospect of moving the Arab-Israeli dispute beyond the current impasse in negotiation. Through cooperation rather than competition, consultation rather than declaration, through division and sharing of responsibility, the Western allies can use their resources collectively to reward concession and encourage moderation.

Coordination of strategy toward the Arab-Israeli dispute would serve the interests of the alliance as well as the interests of the participants in the conflict. Europe would respond favorably to an acknowledgment of its interest and expertise and to a sharing of responsibility, while the USA would benefit from the commitment of European resources to specific objectives necessary to an effective process of conflict resolution. Moreover, a joint approach on process and participants as well as substance, would consolidate the unique position of the Western Alliance as peacemakers as well as powdermonkeys. Finally, it would better insulate members of the alliance from the vicissitudes of politics in the Middle East.

Common sense and common interest dictate a strategy which builds on the differential strengths of members, deliberately emphasizes consensus rather than difference, pays heed to what is common rather than what distinguishes, shares responsibility rather than foments competition, and harmonizes rather than declares policy. Although the common good through cooperation would be greater than the individual benefit through competition, history is replete with examples of the pursuit of individual interest at the expense of common benefit. And just as common interest is frequently difficult to realize, common sense often does not distinguish the conduct of foreign policy. Notwithstanding these realities, a sense of the possible as well as the desirable and explicit attention to common interest would well serve both the Middle East and the North Atlantic alliance in the difficult years ahead.

APPENDIX

Year	Resolution	
1975	3375	Invitation to the PLO to participate in the efforts for peace in the Middle East.
	3376	Question of Palestine.
	3379	Elimination of all forms of racial discrimination (Zionism as racism).
	3414	The situation in the Middle East.
	3419C	UNRWA: population and refugees displaced since 1967.
1976	15D	UNRWA: population and refugees displaced since 1967.
	15E	UNRWA: Palestine refugees in the Gaza Strip.
	20	Question of Palestine.
	61	The situation in the Middle East.
	62	Peace conference on the Middle East.
	106A	Report of the Special Committee to Investigate Israeli Practices Affecting the Human Rights of the Population of the Occupied Territories – measures by Israel in occupied territories to alter demographic composition or geographical nature.
	106B	Compliance with Geneva Convention relative to the protection of civilian persons in time of war.
	106C	Israeli policies and practices in the occupied territories.
	106D	Destruction of Quneitra.
	110	Living conditions of the Palestinian people.
	186	Permanent sovereignty over national resources in the occupied Arab territories.

1977	5	Recent illegal Israeli measures in the occupied Arab territories designed to change the legal status, geographical nature and demographic composition of those territories in contravention on the principles of the Charter of the United Nations, of Israeli's international obligations under the 4th Geneva Convention of 1949 and UN resolutions, and obstruction of efforts aimed at achieving a just and lasting peace in the Middle East.
1977	20	The situation in the Middle East.
	40A	Question of Palestine: report and recommendations of the Committee on the Exercise of the Inalienable Rights of the Palestinian People.
	40B	Question of Palestine: etablishment of UN special units on Palestinian rights.
	90A	UNRWA: assistance to Palestinian refugees.
	90C	UNRWA: Palestine refugees in the Gaza Strip.
	90E	UNRWA: population and refugees displaced since 1967.
	91A	Report of the Special Committee to Investigate Israeli Practices Affecting the Human Rights of the Population of the Occupied Territories: application of the Geneva Convention relative to the protection of civilian persons in time of war.
	91B	Compensation to Syrian Arab Republic for destruction in Quneitra.
	91C	Report and activities of the Special Committee to Investigate Israeli Practices Affecting the Human Rights of the Population of the Occupied Territories.
1978	28A	Question of Palestine: implementation of prior recommendations of the Committee on the Exercise of the Inalienable Rights of the Palestinian People.
	28B	Question of Palestine: report and activities of the Committee on the Exercise of the Inalienable Rights of the Palestinian People.
	28C	Question of Palestine: establishment of a UN special unit on Palestinian rights.
	29	The situation in the Middle East.
	110	Living conditions of the Palestinian people.
	112A	UNRWA: assistance to Palestine refugees.

	112C	UNRWA: offers by member states of grants and scholarships for higher education, including vocational training, for the Palestine refugees.
	112E	Palestine refugees in the Gaza Strip.
1978	112F	UNRWA: population and refugees displaced since 1967.
	113A	Report of the Special Committee to Investigate Israeli Practices Affecting the Human Rights of the Population of the Occupied Territories: application of the Geneva Convention relative to the protection of civilian persons in time of war to the Arab territories occupied by Israel since 1967.
	113B	Measures by Israel to change the legal status, geographical nature and demographic composition of the Arab territories occupied since June 1967.
	113C	Activities of the Special Committee to Investigate Israeli Practices Affecting the Human Rights of the Population of the Occupied Territories.
	147	Assistance to the Palestinian people.
	183D	Relations between Israel and South Africa.
1979	3465A	Report of the Committee on the Exercise of the Inalienable Rights of the Palestinian People: call for participation of the PLO in UN-sponsored negotiations on the Middle East.
	3465B	Declares Camp David accords invalid with respect to the Palestinian people and territories occupied since 1967.
	3465C	Report of the Committee on the Exercise of the Inalienable Rights of the Palestinian People.
	3465D	Requests closer cooperation between United Nations facilities and the Committee on the Exercise of the Inalienable Rights of the Palestinian People.
	3470	The situation in the Middle East: condemns partial agreements and separate treaties which contradict the principles of a just and comprehensive settlement; calls for the convening of a peace conference under the auspices of the United Nations and the co-chairmanship of the USA and the USSR with the participation of all parties, including the PLO.

	3490A	Report of the Special Committee to Investigate Israeli Practices Affecting the Human Rights of the Population of the Occupied Territories: condemns annexation, establishment of settlements; reaffirms that all measures taken by Israel to change the *status quo* are null and void.
1979	3490B	Condemns Israel for failure to observe the Geneva Convention relative to the protection of civilian persons; calls on Israel to acknowledge the applicability of the Geneva Convention.
	3490C	Calls on Israel to desist from all action which would result in changing the legal status, geographic nature, or demographic composition of Arab territories occupied since 1967, including Jerusalem.
	34133	Assistance to the Palestinian people.

NOTES: CHAPTER 4

1 United Nations Resolution 242 was passed by the Security Council on 22 November 1967. In addition to the three clauses cited, the resolution also called for guarantees of freedom of navigation through international waterways in the area and guarantees of territorial inviolability and political independence of every state in the area. For a full text of the resloution, see United Nations, Security Council Documents (UN.S/), 30 November 1967, p. 8.

2 The French translation of Resolution 242 used the article 'the' before the word 'territories' – withdrawal from *the* territories – thereby requiring a total withdrawal by Israel from the territories captured in 1967. This difference between the French and English version subsequently engendered considerable controversy.

3 This phrase would recur frequently in President Nixon's speeches. During the war of attrition of 1970, for example, the president painted a grim portrait: 'I think the Middle East now is terribly dangerous. It is like the Balkans before World War I – where two superpowers, the United States and the Soviet Union, could be drawn into confrontation that neither of them wants because of the differences there.' See Interview of President Richard Nixon on television, 1 July 1970, *Department of State Bulletin*, 27 July 1970, pp. 112–13. William Quandt, subsequently deputy and then head of the Middle East office of the National Security Council, attests to the intense US interest in engineering a settlement during this period. See William B. Quandt, *Decade of Decisions* (Berkeley, Calif.: University of California Press, 1977), pp. 72–104.

4 Estimates of the Soviet commitment vary, but it is generally agreed that the USSR sent SA-3 missiles with combat crews to man the sites while Egyptian crews were undergoing training. In addition, Soviet air combat units, equipped with MIG-21J fighters, provided air cover for Egypt's heartland. Soviet personnel, both in advisory and combat roles, numbered about 20,000. More important than the size of the Soviet presence was the commitment of combat forces beyond the Warsaw Pact area, the first time the USSR had so deployed forces since World War II.

5 For a detailed examination of superpower attempts to end the wars in the Middle East, see my 'Proxy wars – how superpowers end them: the diplomacy of war termination in the Middle East', *International Journal*, vol. XXXV, no. 3 (September 1980), pp. 478–519.

6 For a detailed discussion of the working paper prepared by the foreign ministers of the then six members, see Hans Maull, 'The strategy of avoidance: Europe's Middle East policies after the October war', in J. C. Hurewitz (ed.) *Oil, the Arab-Israel Dispute, and the Industrial World* (Boulder, Colo: Westview Press, 1976, 110–37), p. 118. The statement was not officially a document of the EEC, but rather of the European Political Cooperation, or EPC. Created in 1970 following the Davignon Report the EPC was designed as a political instrument of negotiation for members of the EEC which, nevertheless, would be institutionally separate. The foreign ministers of member-states meet four times annually and their agenda is prepared by the political directors of participating foreign ministries. It was at such a meeting in May 1971 that the foreign ministers approved the working document prepared by their political directors in committee.

7 The Rogers formulation, the result of Soviet-US discussions and known as the Rogers Plan A, differed in its emphasis on a formal end to the state of war and negotiation through indirect talks using the Rhodes formula. The role of the four powers – Britian and France as well as the USA and the USSR – was restricted to their promise 'to exert their efforts to help the two sides adhere to the provisions of the agreement'. See *Arab Report and Record*, 1–15 December 1969, pp. 521–2. Differences were largely those of modalities rather than substance. For a full text of the proposals, see the speech by Secretary of State William Rogers, *New York Times*, 11 December 1969.

8 See the statement by the Minister for External Affairs, Mitchell Sharp, to the House of Commons, 16 October 1973, *Statements and Speeches,* Department of External Affairs, Information Division, Ottawa.

9 Britain, for example, refused to permit the USA to use its bases in Cyprus for the airlift of supplies to Israel during the fighting. Germany, with considerably stronger security ties to the USA, permitted the use of its facilities as long as cooperation was not made public.

10 For the text of the resolution, see *Bulletin of the European Community*, vol. 6, no. 10 (1973), p. 2502.

11 The statement by the Chief Cabinet Secretary of Japan was reported in the *New York Times* on 24 November 1973. For a complete text, see *Keesing's Contemporary Archives,* 26 November – 2 December 1973, p. 26228.

12 Resolution 3236 was approved by the General Assembly by a vote of 89(Y) – 8(N) – 37(A).

13 Statement on Resolutions 3236 and 3237 by Ambassador Saul Rae, Press Release No. 35, Canadian Delegation to the United Nations, 22 November 1974.

14 Resolution 3237 was approved by the General Assembly by a vote of 95(Y) – 17 (N) – 19 (A).

15 See the statement by Shizuo Sato, Permanent Representative to the United Nations General Assembly, *United Nations Monthly Chronicle,* vol. XI, no. 11 (December 1974), pp. 105–6.

16 ibid.

17 See, for example, the reply by the Minister for External Affairs to a question in the House of Commons, House of Commons Debates, *Hansard,* 12 November 1974, p. 1260, Ottawa, Canada.

18 This was the thrust of the USA's objection. The USA subsequently undertook formally to engage in no negotiation with the PLO until it accepted Resolutions 242 and 338 and the legitimacy of Israel. See the text of the Memorandum of Understanding between the United States and Israel, 4 September 1975, in *New York Times*, 17 September 1975.

19 Resolution 3379 was approved by the General Assembly by a vote of 72(Y) – 35(N) – 32(A). In 1979 the same issue arose again with somewhat different results. A resolution put before the General Assembly declared 'hegemonism' unacceptable and again condemned 'racism including zionism'. An attempt to delete the reference to Zionism was defeated by a vote of 79–26 with 33 abstentions; the EEC, Japan, Canada and the USA, all voted in support of deletion. When the amendment was lost, however, only Canada and the USA, along with Australia and Israel, opposed the resolution; Europe and Japan

abstained. Members of their delegation explained subsequently that they were reluctant to stand against a general condemnation of discrimination. Their abstention should not be construed, therefore, as acceptance of the equation of Zionism with racism.

20 A list of these resolutions is found in the accompanying Appendix. The list was constructed by examining all resolutions put before the General Assembly and selecting only those dealing specifically with the Arab–Israel dispute. Selection of these resolutions is however, by no means obvious; there is often considerable discrepancy among analysts. Proposals to establish a nuclear-free zone in the Middle East, for example, were omitted since they do not touch directly on the conflict while resolutions dealing with the United Nations Relief Works Agency (UNRWA) and its responsibilities to the Palestinians are included. To calculate agreement, votes on each of the resolutions are compared annually and the percentage of agreement calculated. When the EEC is divided, the position of the majority of its members provides the point of comparison. Of particular interest is voting by Canada and Japan on resolutions where the EEC and the USA vote differently. Such resolutions are a subset of the larger number in any given year.

21 A somewhat different analysis compares Canadian voting on sixteen resolutions from 1967 to 1972 with its pattern from 1973 to 1976 on twenty-eight resolutions. While the number of resolutions included in the comparison differs from this analysis, the findings are similar for the years 1975–6. While Canada voted with the USA 81·2 percent of the time before 1973, it did so only 33·3 percent after the October War. Similarly, Ottawa voted with the EEC only 37·5 percent in 1967–73 but 88·8 percent of the time during 1973–6. See Lawrence Grossman, 'The shifting Canadian vote on Mideast questions at the United Nations', *International Perspectives* (Ottawa: Department of External Affairs, May–June 1978).

22 Prime Minister Miki made this point in his maiden address to the Diet of Japan in January 1975. For a partial text of the speech, see Kazushige Hirasawa, 'Japan's tilting neutrality', in J. C. Hurewitz, op. cit., p. 144.

23 The text of the Venice Declaration is reprinted in full in the *New York Times,* 14 June 1980; see article 4.

24 See, for example, the statement of Shizuo Saito Japan's Permanent Representative to the General Assembly, on 18 Novmber 1974 in *UN Monthly Chronicle,* vol. XI, no. 11 (December 1974), pp. 105–6; his statement explaining Japan's position on the draft resolution before the Security Council on 26 January 1976, in *UN Monthly Chronicle,* vol. XIII, no. 2 (February 1976), p. 11; and the address by Iichiro Hatoyama, Minister for Foreign Affairs to the General Assembly, 27 September 1977, in *UN Monthly Chronicle,* vol. XIV, no. 10 (New York: United Nations Office of Public Information, November 1977), pp. 75–6.

25 See the text of the Venice Declaration, op. cit. article 9.

26 See the Venice Declaration, op. cit., article 9 and the text of the report prepared by R. L. Stanfield, the Special Representative of the Government of Canada and Ambassador-at-Large, submitted to the government of Canada on 20 February 1980. Hereafter, this document is referred to as the Stanfield Report. Stanfield was explicit in his criticism of one-sided resolutions which are counter-productive in their consequences; see p. 14 of the report.

27 Comment of President Carter to a town meeting in Clinton, Massachusetts, 16 March 1977. See the *New York Times,* 17 March 1977.

28 See, for example, M. Fernand Leblanc, Parliamentary Secretary to the Minister for External Affairs, 'Canada and the United Nations' resolutions concerning Israel and the Middle East', *Statements and Speeches,* No. 77/12, Department of External Affairs, Information Division, Ottawa.

29 See the Stanfield Report p. 7.

30 West Germany's Foreign Minister, Hans Deitrich Genscher, spoke of the right of self-determination of the Palestinian people as early as 1974. Most recently, in an interview with *Frankfeuter Allgemeine Zeitung* on 12 March 1980, he applauded French recognition of that right and urged other states to follow suit. In June 1978, during a visit of Crown Prince Fahd of Saudi Arabia to Bonn,

Chancellor Schmidt referred to the need for a 'stäätliche Organization' for the Palestinians. The phrase has been translated both as a 'statelike organization' and as the right 'to organize as a state'. The text of the statement, made on 23 June 1978, is available in *Deutschland-Berichte,* vol. 14, no. 7/8 (July–August 1978).

31 The government of France issued an official communiqué on 11 March 1980 at the conclusion of the visit of President Valéry Giscard d'Estaing to the Middle East. The communiqué called on all the parties to the dispute to recognize that a lasting settlement 'must be based on two universal and complementary principles which are for each state the right to security and for each people the right to self-determination. Each state in the region, in particular the state of Israel whose preoccupations in this field are legitimate, should be able to live in peace within secure, recognized and guaranteed frontiers, which implies a withdrawal by Israel from the territories occupied since 1967. The Palestinian people, whose aspiration is to exist and organize itself as such, should be able to exercise its right to self-determination within the framework of a peaceful settlement'. See *Le Monde,* 12 March 1980; translation by the author.

32 The draft resolution before the Security Council on 30 April 1980 affirmed that 'the Palestinian people should be enabled to exercise its inalienable national right of self-determination, including the right to establish an independent state in Palestine'. Other articles in the draft resolution called for guarantees of the sovereignty and territorial integrity of all states in the Middle East and withdrawal by Israel from all the territories occupied in 1967. The draft resloution also affirmed the right of the Palestinians to return to their homes or receive compensation. See the *New York Times,* 1 May 1980. The USA vetoed the resolution.

33 Interview with Foreign Minister Jean François-Poncet, *Washington Post,* 30 May 1980. The Foreign Minister added that 'we do not exclude a Palestinian state if the Palestinians want a state'.

34 Statement by the EEC, 6 November 1973, *Bulletin of the European Community,* vol. 6, no. 10 (1973), 2502. Statement of 29 June 1977, in *Bulletin of the European Community,* vol. 10, no. 6, 1977, p. 62.

35 See the Venice Declaration, op. cit., article 6. Two months earlier, the larger Council of Europe had issued a statement supporting the Palestinian right to self-determination. Their statement differed, however, from that of the Nine in the accompanying demand that Resolution 242 be amended to incorporate explicit recognition of the right to self-determination. For a partial text of the resolution approved by the Council of Europe on 23 April 1980 in Strasbourg, France, see *Le Monde,* 25 April 1980.

36 Venice Declaration, op. cit., article 4.

37 Interview with senior officer of the Department of External Affairs, Middle East Division, December 1979.

38 See the Stanfield Report, op. cit., p. 8.

39 Statement by the Ministers of Foreign Affairs of the European Economic Community, 22 November 1977, Brussels, in *Bulletin of the European Community,* vol. 10, no. 11 (1977), p. 52: 2.2.4.

40 Statement by the Foreign Ministers of the European Economic Community, 19 September 1978, in *Bulletin of the European Community* vol. 11, no. 9 (1978), pp. 53–4: 2.2.8.

41 Statement by the Ministers of Foreign Affairs of the European Economic Community, 26 March 1979, Paris, in *Bulletin of the European Community,* vol. 12, no. 3 (1979), p. 86: 2.2.74.

42 See the text of Resolutions 3465B and 3470, put before the General Assembly in December 1979, in *Resolutions and Decisions Adopted by the General Assembly During Its 34th Session* (New York: United Nations Department of Public Information, 1980), pp. 15, 20–21. Japan also abstained while all other members of the EEC, as well as the USA and Canada, opposed the two resolutions. In both cases, the trans-Atlantic consensus was greater than the cohesion within Europe.

43 See the statement by the Foreign Minsiter of France, Jean François-Poncet, on 29 May 1980, in the *New York Times*, 30 May 1980.

44 The President was explicit in his threat to veto European action in the UN: 'We will not permit in the United Nations any action that would destroy the sanctity of and the present form of UN 242. We have a veto power that we can exercise if necessary to prevent this Camp David process from being destroyed or subverted and I would not hesitate to use it if necessary . . . To summarize, we have a good basis, the issues are clearly defined, Israel and Egypt both want a peace settlement. We are asking the European allies not to get involved in it for the time being' (the *New York Times*, 31 May 1980).

45 See the Venice Declaration, op. cit., articles 2, 5 and 11. The tone of the declaration was much less provocative of the USA than the statement issued, for example, by the Council of Europe six weeks earlier. Members of the EEC, also members of the Council, had approved or abstained on a resolution which termed Resolution 242 inadequate in its treatment of the Palestinians as refugees, condemned Israel's settlements as a violation of international law, and argued that the Camp David accords could not serve as the basis for a comprehensive settlement in the Middle East. Simultaneously, however, the Council of Europe explicitly called upon the PLO to acknowledge Israel's right to existence, security and independence. In all respects, then, the Council statement was considerably stronger than the declaration issued at Venice six weeks later. For a partial text of the statement issued by the Council of Europe, see *Le Monde*, 25 April 1980.

46 This undertaking was given to Israel in a Memorandum of Understanding on 4 September 1975 as an inducement to sign the second disengagement agreement with Egypt. For the text of the Memorandum, see the *New York Times*, 17 September 1975.

47 Interview with senior officer, Middle East Division, Department of External Affairs, Ottawa, January 1980.

48 See the Stanfield Report, op. cit., p. 10. Prime Minister Clark who commissioned the report but was defeated at the polls before its final submission, argued that Canada would be prepared to recognize the PLO only if it were prepared to renounce terrorism and recognize the right of Israel to exist. See the interview of Prime Minister Clark by the Canadian Broadcast Corporation on 9 October 1979, reported in the *Globe and Mail*, 10 October 1979. Prime Minister Trudeau has not repeated these conditions, however, but has reverted to the earlier Canadian position that representation of the Palestinians is a matter for the Palestinians themselves to decide.

49 More recently, it was reported that Japan had considered a meeting between a special government envoy, former Foreign Minister Sunao Sonoda, and Yassir Arafat during a twenty-five-day tour by Mr Sonoda to oilsuppliers in the Middle East. The purpose of the meeting was to prepare for a visit by the leader of the PLO to Tokyo later in 1980. The proposed meeting was strongly supported by the Ministry of International Trade and Industry but vigorously opposed by the Foreign Ministry. The dispute was ultimately resolved by then Prime Minister Ohira, who ruled against the meeting and for continued delay in recognition of the PLO. A detailed discussion of the policy debate within Japan is found in the *New York Times*, 28 February 1980, citing 'official sources'.

50 The PLO is represented officially, for example, in Bonn and London and has established information offices in Brussels, Paris and Luxembourg. No such official representation exists in North America. Austria recently went one step further and extended special diplomatic status to the PLO on 10 March 1980.

51 For the text of the communiqué, see *Le Monde*, 12 March 1980.

52 See the Venice Declaration, op. cit., article 7.

53 See the statement by Secretary of State Edmund Muskie in the *New York Times*, 14 June 1980.

54 See statement by President Giscard d'Estaing, *Le Monde*, 6 March 1980. In his discussions with the Sultan of Kuwait, the president urged the Gulf States to pursue a policy of non-alignment with the superpowers and turn to Europe as a dependable alternative. In an effort to expand French influence in the Gulf,

France has increased its sale of tanks to Saudi Arabia and is currently negotiating the sale of approximately eighty Mirage F-1 planes to Qatar. It is already an established supplier of Libya.

55   In his report to the government of Canada, Stanfield explicitly set the moderation of the policy of the PLO as the principal objective of communication with its leaders: 'In my view, Canada should broaden contacts with the PLO on issues affecting negotiations and the peace process, with a view to encouraging that Organization towards greater moderation and realism and towards open acceptance of the legitimacy of the State of Israel. This will require frank communication and discussion.' See the Stanfield Report, op. cit., p. 10. The Council of Europe, in its resolution of 23 April 1980, made a similar demand of the PLO. See n. 45 above.

56   See the communiqué of the 4th Congress of Al-Fatah, issued on 2 June 1980 in Damascus. The statement continues: 'It [al-Fatah] also aims at establishing a Palestinian democratic state on all the Palestinian soil . . . This struggle will not stop until the Zionist entity is liquidated and Palestine is liberated.' The full text of the communiqué is found in *Al-Liwa*, 2 June 1980, Beirut.

57   In an interview on the French radio station, Europe 1, on 18 May 1980, Arafat alleged that President Giscard d'Estaing was using the Palestinians to improve relations with the oilproducing states and not concerned with Palestinian interests. The radio interview is reported in *Le Monde*, 20 May 1980. In his initial reaction to the Venice Declaration, Arafat levelled a similar charge: 'The Europeans are seeking to find a piece of bone that they could throw to us and keep us busy.' See the *New York Times*, 15 June 1980.

58   Interview with a 'senior official', *New York Times*, 18 June 1980. A diplomat from Western Europe similarly explained: 'We are trying to hold the Arab moderates together while we wait for the US'. See the *New York Times*, 13 July 1980.

59   Following a Cabinet meeting, Prime Minister Begin issued a long statement. Responding to the European demand for 'association' of the PLO with the negotiations, the prime minister argued: 'For the peace that would be achieved with the participation of that organisation . . . a number of European countries are willing to give guarantees – even military ones and knowing the results of such guarantees given to Czechoslovakia in 1938, after Sudetenland was torn from it . . . Israel asks for no security guarantees from any European countries . . . Any man of good will who studies that document will see in it a Munich surrender . . . and an encouragement to all those elements who seek to undermine the Camp David agreements and bring about the failure of the peace process in the Middle East.' For a partial text of the statement issued on 15 June 1980, see *Jerusalem Post*, international edition, 15–21 June, no. 1,024.

The reaction by frontline Arab participants to the Venice Declaration was harsh as well. Damascus Radio, for example, alleged that reactionary forces within the Arab world favored collaboration with Western Europe. The daily newspaper *Tichrin*, in an editorial on 24 June, said that Syria would not stand by idly while Arab leaders broke solidarity and cooperated with Western Europe. Consequently, Syria would expand its ties with the USSR.

The official PLO reaction was one of strong condemnation. In a statement issued in Damascus on 15 June, it denounced the Venice Declaration as the product of US blackmail: 'The European position fell short of our expectations because the European countries are still on the American line and still on the line of Camp David. This position will not be a contribution to a just and lasting peace in the Middle East.' The text of the PLO statement is in the *New York Times*, 16 June 1980.

60   See the communiqué issued by the Arab Steadfastness and Confrontation Front, 15 April 1980, after their meeting in Tripoli, Libya, in *Arab Record and Report* 16–30 April 1980. The five members of the Front are Algeria, Libya, the PLO, South Yemen and Syria.

61   They were clear in Europe as well. The respected French political sociologist and commentator, Raymond Aron, writing in *L'Express* after the visit of President Giscard d'Estaing to the Gulf and the communiqué which followed,

argued: 'Either this is "declamatory" diplomacy to assure France leadership among the Europeans and the gratitude of the Arab states, or it is an attempt to launch negotiations and reach an effective overall settlement, in which case I doubt its efficacy.' See *L'Express,* 15 March 1980; translation by the author.

62 During a visit to Washington in May 1980, French Foreign Minister Jean François-Poncet explained: 'Europe has grown into a partner, which is economically, scientifically, industrially, equal to the United States and wishes to be treated so. And I think this is one of our problems, how do we organize our relations between equals, how does consultation develop in a way that is satisfactory for both parties? I think a lot of ground has to be covered in that respect.' See interview of Poncet published in the *New York Times* 22 June 1980.

5 Euro-American Energy Diplomacy in the Middle East, 1970–80: The Pervasive Crisis

JOAN GARRATT

INTRODUCTION

The 1970s may best be remembered for the metamorphosis which occurred in the realm of international oil politics. The structural changes have been so profound that energy has ceased to be primarily an economic issue. Energy security has been catapulted from the confines of economics to the realm of national security and has consequently been politicized at the highest levels of governments.

Trans-Atlantic energy cooperation has been visibly lacking throughout much of the past decade. More often than not, it has been plagued by competitive behavior owing to resource asymmetries, divergent national interests and fierce commercial competition. Moreover, US global interests have often conflicted with European regional concerns, which has been an additional source of trans-Atlantic tension. The 1973 oil crisis high-lighted these differences and became the catalyst for a new international organization designed to bridge the trans-Atlantic gap. The challenges before the Atlantic Alliance have not ceased, however. Not only does the energy security dilemma still exist, but the contours of the problem are constantly taking new form as a direct result of structural changes in international oil politics and trade.

Our focus here is on Euro-American policy toward the energy security dilemma of the 1970s and its implications for trans-Atlantic relations. The purpose is to delineate periods of trans-Atlantic cooperation and conflict and explain those factors most responsible.

THE ATLANTIC ALLIANCE AND THE 1973 OIL CRISIS

The 1973 oil crisis could not have come at a worse time for the Atlantic alliance. The alliance was already plagued by a cornucopia of conflicting interests and orientations. Trans-Atlantic competition was particularly fierce as a result of divergent trade and monetary policies. Politically, the alliance was divided over a host of foreign policy issues, ranging from East–West relations to Vietnam. Europe's quest for its own role in world affairs, commensurate with that of its economic power, sought not to emulate the USA, but to assert its own identity and independence. Since European independence is usually measured by the gap separating US and European policy, this portended even further erosion of trans-Atlantic solidarity. The tenor of trans-Atlantic relations became so acrimonious that the necessity for remedial measures as well as a redefinition of alliance principles became a high priority in the USA. Only six months before the crisis, Secretary of State Henry Kissinger proclaimed 1973 as the 'Year of Europe'. The theme underlying Kissinger's call for a new Atlantic Charter was that trans-Atlantic rivalries and 'disputes must be ended and be replaced by a determined commitment on both sides of the Atlantic to find cooperative solutions'.[1]

The Year of Europe, however, was dealt a fatal blow as the crescendo of alliance strains culminated in the 1973 oil crisis. The crisis precipitated intraalliance schisms immediately and whether one was a contemporary observer in 1973 or a retrospective analyst in 1980, the impression that the Atlantic alliance was on the brink of disintegration was hard to avoid.

The immediate impact of the crisis was its elucidation of the fundamental differences between US 'global' interests and European 'regional' interests. In contrast to Europe, the USA tended to view the Middle East through global lenses, emphasizing the central role of the USSR, while inadvertently subordinating the relevance of regional developments as well as relegating European regional concerns to a subordinate rank of priorities. The US global approach conflicted sharply with European interests, which were more narrowly defined as a direct result of their disproportionate dependence on Middle Eastern oil. Europe's conspicuous vulnerability stemmed from the fact that Middle East oil was the lifeline of European economic activity. Consequently, energy security became an issue of national security and was politicized at the highest levels of government. In addition to oil, there were other less conspicuous indicators of European vulnerability. Europe had substantial trading arrangements in the Middle East, which it sought to protect. Foreign trade accounts for a much higher percentage of Europe's total gross national product (GNP) than it does for a country like the USA. Trade was not only profit-oriented, but essential in light of the burden which increasing oil imports placed on European balance of payments. In short, oil supply interruptions and foreign trade disruptions portended serious political and economic consequences for Europe, whereas the USA was less susceptible to both.

The political side-effects of European vulnerability made neutrality with a pro-Arab tilt a perceived necessity. Neutrality, however, required that Europe dissociate itself from US policy and support for Israel. At no time during the crisis did Europe ever explicitly state that its policy was to separate itself from the USA, but it didn't have to. Actions spoke louder than words. Britain refused Kissinger's request to sponsor a ceasefire in the United Nations, because Sadat objected. France continued arms sales to Libya and Saudi Arabia, despite Saudi participation on the Syrian front against Israel. The North Atlantic Treaty Organization (NATO) with the reluctant exception of Portugal (which incidentally imported most of its oil from Angola and Iran) denied the USA access to NATO bases and facilities. Spain refused to allow the USA use of a $500 million chain of military bases just built and paid for by the USA. Germany forbade the further use of its ports when a highly publicized report appeared in the German press, showing an Israeli vessel loading arms at Bremenhaven. British Prime Minister Heath even rejected a personal request from President Nixon for landing rights at the British base in Akrotiri, Cyprus. Greece and Turkey were especially culpable, however. Only one year earlier, Nixon defended US military aid to Greece and Turkey against criticisms by presidential contender George McGovern by noting that 'without aid to Greece and aid to Turkey you have no viable policy to save Israel'.[2] Yet Turkey and Greece not only denied the USA access to military bases, but Turkey did not even object to overflights by Soviet transport jets carrying war material en route to Egypt and Syria.

Alliance disunity was also reinforced by divergent perceptions of the Soviet threat. Again this was indicative of the differences dividing Europe and the USA. In Europe the primacy of economic issues superseded traditional concern over the Soviet threat. Illustrative of the dilemma was the Anglo-French refusal to support the USA in its opposition to Egyptian President Anwar el Sadat's proposal for a joint Soviet-US force to maintain the fragile ceasefire in the Sinai. Neither the British nor the French were willing to challenge Sadat and possibly risk economic reprisal. Nor were they averse to halting the Israeli offensive in the Sinai which Kissinger had thus far been unable to do. Kissinger, however, saw a joint US-Soviet force as a potential 'trip-wire' which could escalate into a superpower confrontation. Moreover, deployment of Soviet troops would not only be destabilizing, but would convey to the Arab world that what Kissinger was trying to deliver through diplomatic channels could only be accomplished through military means. This would bolster Soviet prestige at the expense of the USA, but more importantly, it threatened to jeopardize Kissinger's diplomatic role. Lacking allied support and faced with the prospect of unilateral Soviet intervention, the USA declared and implemented a world-wide alert on 25 October (DefCon 3) which was undertaken without even the pretense of consultation. This provoked a storm of European protest, particularly by those countries in which US military bases were situated. There was considerable resentment over what Europe saw as its 'right to be consulted about policies crucial to their survival'.[3]

Prominent European leaders were outraged at their subordinate status. French Foreign Minister Michel Jobert chastised both the USA and USSR for treating Europe like a 'non-person in the Middle East crisis', 'humiliated in its non-existence' even though the oil embargo made Europe 'the target of the second front in the Middle East War'.[4] Even West German Chancellor Willy Brandt demanded that the USA 'treat Europe as an equal partner', noting that 'partnership cannot mean subordination' and that 'what goes on in the Middle East affects Europe directly'.[5] When Kissinger had earlier expressed his 'disgust with NATO for the lack of European support', the prominent French newspaper *Le Monde* wrote, 'American criticism has apparently dealt a fatal blow to the Year of Europe'.[6]

The collapse of alliance solidarity extended to within Europe as well. The crisis triggered a series of 'sauve qui peut' policies in Europe, which threatened not only regional (EEC) economies, but international (OECD) trading arrangements as well. At the regional level the crisis exposed the mythical character of European unity. As Robert Lieber observed: 'the energy crisis was considered a matter of national survival: oil supplies were crucial for industry, agriculture, heating, electricity, and transportation and narrow conceptions of national self-interest received priority over European solidarity.'[7]

Even the sacred Treaty of Rome was desecrated as autarkic policies temporarily superseded the treaty's provision for free circulation of commodities within the Common Market. Belgium, Holland, Italy, Spain and Britain, all of which were major exporters of refined products, imposed export controls to cushion their domestic economies from the disruptive forces of interdependence. This proved futile, however, because governments had no control over the importation of oil. The oil companies simply rerouted their oil deliveries to countries that had not imposed such controls.

The Organization of Arab Petroleum Exporting Countries' (OAPEC) strategy of dividing nations into categories – 'friendly' (Britain, France, Belgium), 'neutral' (Germany), or 'embargoed' (Holland) – was no doubt instrumental in eroding whatever semblance of solidarity was left. When Holland's defiant support for Israel caused it to be victimized by a total OAPEC embargo, Holland found itself deserted by its Community partners. When Holland formally requested on 30 October, that the European oilsharing system within the OECD be activated, a request that required unanimity by participating countries, Britain and France stymied the effort by blocking implementation of the International Industry Advisory Board (IIAB)[8], which would have equitably allocated oil to Holland. Anglo-French reticence to aid the Dutch was predicated on their common fear lest they antagonize OAPEC and jeopardize their privileged (that is, friendly) positions. For France, this was a predictable outcome. It was more than a mere continuation of its pro-Arab policy launched under the presidency of Charles De Gaulle, although France certainly expected to capitalize on its compliance later. But it was also an opportunity to strike at the Dutch with whom the French had long been at odds. As the parent government of one of the international majors (Royal Dutch Shell), Holland has been a common target for French condemnation and competition. One needs only remind a Frenchman that while France concentrated on the eastern front in World War I, Royal Dutch Shell moved in to gain control of French concessions. Whatever was left was divided among the other Anglo-Saxon companies. Resentful at having lost its 'place in the sun' to the perfidy of 'les trusts', France has consistently sought to undermine the position of the majors while advancing its own designs. But even at the Community level France and Holland have been natural adversaries in respect to a Community energy policy and Euro-American relations. French attempts to regulate the Community's oil market along the lines of French *dirigisme* have met stiff resistance from the Dutch, who prefer the laissez-faire approach. Holland's 'Atlanticist' orientation toward the USA has also led to deep disagreements.

British behavior, while hardly commendable, was at least more easily justified. By a rather unfortunate coincidence of events, the Conservative British government found itself confronted by the National Union of Mineworkers, which began a partial coal strike in early November, culminating in an all-out strike in February 1974. The twofold threat posed by both OAPEC and the coalminers acutely sensitized British leaders to the importance of secure oil supplies. Evidently, the costs of betraying the Dutch, who were the most enthusiastic supporters of British entry into the Common Market, were considered less damaging than forfeiting scarce energy supplies. In short, due to a combination of political machinations, national self-interest and the pervasive sense of uncertainty, Holland was left to fend for itself. Only when the Dutch decided to play by the same rules of the game and threatened to curtail exports of natural gas to France, Belgium and Germany, did resolution of the Dutch predicament take place.[9]

In Europe the perceived threat to national security clearly superseded the willingness of individual nations to cooperate in accordance with the Common Market (EEC) principles. This was a sad commentary for the state of European unity, particularly since at no time during or after the crisis was there ever a real shortage of oil. The cutbacks imposed by OAPEC reduced the availability of Arab oil from 20·8 million barrels a day in October 1973 to 15·8 million barrels a day in December.[10] But the loss of approximately 5 million barrels a day from Arab sources was partially offset by increased production in Iran, Indonesia, Nigeria, Canada and communist countries which brought the total loss of oil to only about 4·4 million barrels a day.[11] The availablity of oil for Britain, France, Germany, Italy and Holland was only about 5 percent below what it had been a year earlier. Moreover, stockpiles in Europe never descended below the eighty-day equivalent of consumption. In fact, reserves in Italy actually increased by 23 percent and Dutch reserves increased by a third of its preembargo level. While these figures definitively show that there was no actual shortage of oil, they do tend to underestimate the real economic impact of the cutbacks because world oil consumption was growing by 7·5 percent annually and international oil trade by about 11 percent yearly.[12] None the less, the availability of oil as well as adequate stockpiles suggest that the panic experienced during the initial phase of the crisis was largely self-induced as a result of uncertainty and insecurity and not the result of actual oil shortages.

European behavior during the crisis portended serious complications for Kissinger's diplomacy. Kissinger deliberately sought to 'delink' the oil weapon from the Arab-Israeli context in order to maintain diplomatic maneuverability by insulating the USA from exposure to Arab political pressure. While the costs were tolerable for the USA, for Europe they were not. European behavior, by its dissociation from the US politically and militarily, and by its rivalrous economic nationalism, all but officially validated the linkage. Following the cessation of hostilities, European diplomacy conveyed the same impression.

European diplomatic initiatives, ostensibly undertaken for the purpose of demonstrating 'their capacity to contribute to the settlement of world problems',[13] proved futile and become another source of trans-Atlantic strain. The unveiling of the 6 November 1973 'Statement on the situation in the Middle East', which essentially supported the Arab interpretation

of Resolution 242 and stressed formal recognition of Palestinian rights contributed 'little for the European reputation or Middle East peace' and
has been repeatedly referred to as European 'self-abasement'.[14] What the
document did do, however, was embarrass Sadat and anger Kissinger by
demanding even more Israeli concessions than Sadat had called for.[15]

The subsequent Copenhagen summit that December, referred to by one
author as 'the ultimate fawning at the feet of the Arabs',[16] was met with
equal US vituperation when five Arab foreign ministers from OAPEC
states were allowed to participate. This was a privilege long sought and
denied to Henry Kissinger. For Europe, however, the results of the summit
defied the very purpose for which it was convened by unequivocally
exposing the depths of European weakness and its inability to deal collectively with the energy crisis. The nine heads of state failed to reach consensus on any of the issues for which they were summoned to adjudicate.
The tradeoffs involved in each issue were too risky. For example, should
the Community support the Dutch or placate the Arabs? Should Community preference be given to bilateral oil diplomacy or a coordinated
regional response? Should stress be placed on security of supply or price
reduction? To what extent should the Community seek cooperation with
the USA or OECD? The summit not only conveyed a sense of European
impotency, but exacerbated differences among the Nine once the domestic
costs surfaced and intensified. Faced with the intractable problems of unemployment, inflation, fiscal and monetary policies, and in juxtaposition
with the politicization of energy issues which translated into polarization
among political parties, interest groups and public opinion, the Nine's
concern for a broader Community policy dissipated as the exigencies for
domestic safeguards proliferated.

ORIGINS OF EURO-AMERICAN POLITICAL DIFFERENCES

European defection from the USA dramatically illustrated the divergence
between US and European interests and their perspectives on the Arab-
Israeli conflict. Prior to the 1973 war, Europe was quite content to allow
the USA to bear the onus of 'crisis management' and 'conflict resolution'
in the Middle East. European leaders were cognizant that they possessed
neither the capabilities, nor the influence, required to play a major role
or usurp US responsibilities in the region. Britain was already in the process
of terminating its steady decline in the region. In 1967 British forces withdrew from Aden (presently South Yemen), and finally from the Gulf in
1971. As one article stressed, 'their withdrawal was a striking affirmation
of the decline of Europe's influence in that part of the world'.[17] Nor was
there any compelling desire, with the possible and limited exception of
France, to inherit this role.

Yet by 1971 much to the consternation of Europe, the USA was disengaging itself from an active diplomatic role. In large measure this was
due to Nixon's and Kissinger's tendency to view the Middle East through
global lenses, emphasizing the central role of the Soviets, while in-

advertently subordinating the relevance of regional developments conducive to diplomatic progress. This was not always the case. Prior to 1971, US Secretary of State Rogers was actively engaged in the diplomatic process and quite able and assertive in applying pressure on Israel when deemed necessary. There was little cooperation from the Soviets, however, who concentrated on increasing Egyptian military capabilities while simultaneously encouraging 'maximal' demands of total Israeli withdrawal before negotiating. The central and destabilizing role of the Soviets illustrated by their intransigence to the Rogers plans, their refusal to limit arms to the area, their active combat participation during the 1970 war of attrition, their collusion in the Egyptian ceasefire violations soon afterward and their alleged involvement in the 1970 Syrian invasion of Jordan led to a reappraisal of US policy. Not coincidentally, the reappraisal corresponded with Kissinger's usurpation of Middle East decisionmaking from Rogers in the State Department. The dramatic turning-point came during the Jordanian crisis, ostensibly precipitated by Egypt's acceptance of the Rogers Plan, but which culminated in a Syrian military invasion threatening Jordan's King Hussein's moderate regime. Although Israeli force was never used, Israel's military deterrent proved decisive in helping Hussein repel the invading armies. Israel proved without question its reliability as an ally which not only defended the Jordanian regime directly, but other friendly Arab states (Saudi Arabia) indirectly.[18]

President Nixon, who had taken personal control of the crisis and had called it 'the gravest threat to world peace – Vietnam not excluded',[19] was deeply impressed with Israel's determination and performance. Israel's role was all the more appreciated in light of the behavior of the European allies. Britain refused a personal request from Hussein for military support, while France absolved itself of any responsibility by publicly denying that it had ever been consulted about the Rogers Plan and by reaffirming the efficacy of the Four-Power Accord.[20]

The end-result was a virtual metamorphosis in US-Israeli relations. Nixon and Kissinger were no longer disposed to pressure Israel for concessions while the Soviets played the role of spoiler and exploiter. Consequently, Israel became the recipient of unprecedented amounts of US arms to maintain a favorable balance in the region. The message was clear: if the Soviets did not refrain from encouraging intransigent diplomacy and an arms race, Israeli military superiority would be guaranteed for the purpose of denying the Soviets and their clients a victory on the battlefield.

It is an irony of history that during the very month the US-Israeli relations were solidified, Anwar Sadat assumed the presidency in Egypt. He wasted no time in demonstrating his propensity for moderation but his efforts fell on deaf ears. He was less intransigent and more pragmatic than etiher his predecessor, Nasser, or his military patron, the USSR. He conceded his interest in signing a peace treaty with Israel as early as February 1971 and even went so far as to call Resolution 242 an 'embryonic peace treaty'.[21] Rather than insist on unrealistic demands such as total Israeli withdrawal, he concurred to an interim approach as a first step toward a comprehensive settlement.[22]

Moreover, he sent a host of signals to Washington, indicating his dissatisfaction with the Soviets as well as his interests in opening a dialogue with the USA. Sadat realized that the Soviets were more a liability than an asset. They provided neither the arms nor the diplomatic leverage necessary to retrieve lost territory. Close association with the Soviets only drove the USA closer to Israel and precluded a more even-handed approach. Sadat's expulsion of the Soviets in July 1972 was a signal of extraordinary significance, yet it failed to elicit a response commensurate with the magnitude of his decision, despite frequent hints from Secretary Rogers and Kissinger that the USA would be forthcoming, if the Soviet presence were reduced. Not even the formation of the Cairo–Riyadh axis in May 1973 produced any notable shift in US willingness to engage itself at that time. Rather than reacting to these developments based on their own intrinsic significance, Kissinger preferred the dividends that might be gained through his strategy of linkage. His immersion in the Vietnam peace talks and Israel's ability to contain the situation militarily obviated the sense of urgency. The Middle East became a pawn in which concessions were linked to Soviet behavior elsewhere. Kissinger wrote in his memoirs for example, 'After the start of Hanoi's Easter offensive on March 30, I interrupted the private Middle East talks with Dobrynin as a sign of displeasure with the Soviet arms shipments that have made the North Vietnamese offensive possible'.[23] The Soviets also used linkage and at one point offered Soviet withdrawal from Egypt in return for the withdrawal of US advisers from Iran and a comprehensive peace treaty.[24]

For Europe, these missed opportunities were cold comfort to a continent which since the mid-1950s had ben transformed from a self-sufficient, coal-based economy to one which by 1973 imported 85 percent of its energy needs from the Middle East. Having already experienced two Arab embargoes in 1956–7 and 1967, Europe did not dispute the linkage between the Arab-Israeli conflict and the oil weapon. The empirical evidence mattered less, however, than the structural changes in international oil politics, beginning with the Tripoli–Tehran agreements in early 1971 and followed by the trend toward nationalization and participation, which enhanced the potential to use oil as a weapon as the host governments accrued more power. Libya, under the leadership of Muamar Qadaffi, was taking great pride in demonstrating just how much oil and politics mixed. Qadaffi nationalized British Petroleum's assets in 1972 for the somewhat unconvincing excuse that Britain allowed the Iranians to occupy two small islands in the Gulf. In June 1973 he nationalized a US independent, Bunker Hunt, and boasted that 'it was a strong slap on the cool arrogant face of the US'.[25] Qadaffi made no secret of the fact that his aim was to pressure the 'moderate' Arab regimes to adopt a hardline approach in the name of 'Arab unity' for the purpose of forcing the USA to revise its Middle Eastern policy. Saudi Arabia was his chief target. It more than any other oilproducing state possessed the applicable leverage with which to affect the USA, or to negate any unilateral Libyan embargo by simply increasing production. Feisal had stated as late as August 1973 that oil should not be used as a weapon, but as James E. Akins (an Arabist, US energy expert and later US ambassador to Saudi Arabia) noted: 'on this issue it seems all too likely that his is an isolated voice. In 1972, other Arabs in responsible or influential positions made no less than 15 different threats to use oil as a weapon agaist their enemies.'[26]

In any event, the short-lived embargoes in 1956 and 1967 proved rather clearly that Saudi Arabia was indeed very susceptible to radical pressures in the Arab world. But more significant, however, the Cairo–Riyadh axis of May 1973 was widely interpreted to have strengthened the linkage between the Arab-Israeli conflict and the oil weapon.

American disengagement from an active diplomatic role in light of the heightened potential to use oil as a weapon and moderate developments in the Middle East generated considerable resentment within Europe. Europe resented the subordination of its regional interests to the global calculus of Kissinger and Nixon, particularly since by 1972 Europe increasingly began to feel hostage to US policy. Proponents of the 'Europe as hostage' scenario pointed out that an embargo specifically directed at the USA would be insufficient to create an energy deficit in the USA, since the USA imported only approximately 17 percent of its oil from the Arab world. Europe might, therefore, be forced to share the burden of an embargo as a means of pressuring the USA indirectly. Moreover, even if Europe were not selectively targeted, OECD calculations in 1973 estimated that should world oil production fall 20 percent, the USA would lose only 1·5–3 percent of its energy needs, while Europe stood to lose between 12–15 percent, and its key economic sectors would be hardest hit in contrast to the USA whose transportation sector stood the most to lose.[27] Consequently, Europe felt, in effect, hostage to US policy, because whether they were selectively targeted or not, they stood the most to lose either way. As one European diplomat put it, 'There would be some impatience with the US if the Europeans were asked to pay the bill for American policy'.[28]

Attempts at the Community[29] level to formulate an independent policy toward the Arab-Israeli dispute is illustrative of Europe's sensitivity to developments in international oil politics. In 1970 an intergovernmental body known as the European Political Cooperation (EPC), created at the Hague conference by the then six members of the Common Market for the purpose of expediting progress toward greater harmonization of foreign policy, chose the Middle East as one of its two priorities, the other being the Conference on Security and Cooperation in Europe (CSCE). The EPC was juridically distinct from the Community institutions but its significance was not. The choice of the Middle East was indicative of the salience Europe attached to the Middle East, even though substantive progress never really followed. By 1971 the Arab-Israeli conflict was elevated to the level of the highest deliberative body in the EEC, the Council of Ministers, which usually refrains from dealing with 'high-policy' issues where the prospects for the required unanimity are low. The six members agreed unanimously however on a position paper which was never published, but whose contents were leaked to the press.[30] Persistent differences existed within Europe regarding the proper interpretation of the report, but when West Germany's Foreign Minister Walter Scheel visited Israel in 1971, he refused to renounce the principle of withdrawal from *all* territories when pressed by Isreal. The EEC never succeeded in formulating an official policy, but it can safely be said that the 1973 crisis only catalyzed a lethargic Europe into formally proclaiming what it had unofficially been saying since 1970.

Yet despite attempts to formulate an independent policy, distinct from the USA and which might spare Europe the agony of an embargo, Europe was hardly in a position to effect the course of events in the Middle East. France was the most ardent supporter of an independent policy but evidently unaware of the contradictions inherent in its own position which precluded an active and meaningful role. French guarantees of security and territorial integrity were virtually meaningless to Israel in light of France's conspicuous pro-Arab policy and ambitions in the Arab world. Rather than reassuring Israel, French policy tended to alienate Israel which prevented France from playing a viable role either independently, or within the context of the Big Four diplomacy. Nor was Britain in a position to play a major role. British reticence to participate in the international flotilla to open the Straits of Tiran in 1967, and its withdrawal from the Persian Gulf by the early 1970s, testified to the demise of British power and influence in the area. Moreover, if there is any truth to the dictum that 'history repeats itself', Israel had already learned in 1967 that international guarantees could be abrogated. A vulnerable Europe was hardly more comforting where Israeli security was concerned. Lacking influence over the political enigma in the Middle East, one might have imagined more prodigious efforts toward a viable consumer energy policy. Euro-American as well as intra-European differences inhibited progress on that front, too.

FAILURE OF MULTILATERAL ENERGY DIPLOMACY

The idea of a multilateral energy approach was first suggested in 1969 by the USA while addressing its OECD partners. The rationale underlying the approach was that through a combination of stockpiling, emergency allocation schemes and consumer solidarity, the use of the oil weapon could be deterred, or failing that, it could at least cushion the impact of selective targeting by providing some form of protection to importing nations. In the absence of such an approach, it was feared that energy shortages would precipitate a scrambling for bilateral deals, leading to higher prices and protective trade wars which would weaken economies and create general economic chaos. Yet, prior to 1972, Europe evinced little interest in the multilateral approach. The French vehemently opposed this approach, interpreting it as a US attempt to reexert its waning hegemony over the European continent. Other European nations saw multilateralism as an attempt by the USA to maintain the preeminent position of the US majors, while the host governments were successfully supplanting their role. There was little incentive for non-parent governments like Germany or Italy to align themselves with the USA, just for the purpose of protecting corporate interests in which they had no stake.

There was also some doubt as to how efficacious multilateralism would be. After all, the USA warned the OECD Oil Committee in 1969 that, in the event of a future crisis, the USA would not divert domestic sources of energy to Europe as it had done during the 1956 and 1967 crises. This position was reiterated at an OECD meeting in 1972, when the USA insisted that emergency sharing should be based on water-borne imports rather than on total energy requirements. This view was unacceptable to Europe, however, due to the disproportionate percentage of water-borne imports destined for Europe and the USA. For example, water-borne imports to the USA were approximately 14 percent, compared with approximately 70 percent to Europe. Sharing in accordance with this formula, meant a disproportionate burden for Europe. The French however, followed by Germany, argued that oil be shared in accordance with the requirements of key sectors of the economy. Since the French relegated transportation as a low priority, the USA stood the most to lose in this case, since a higher percentage of imports were destined for transportation use in the USA.

American diplomacy in the Middle East also mitigated Europe's enthusiasm to align itself squarely on the side of the USA. The belief in Europe was that an embargo would probably come at the instigation of the USA and that European interests were better served by remaining aloof from the USA. Moreover, there was clearly a disinclination to overtly antagonize the Arabs by entering into anything synonymous with a consumer cartel. Yamani made it a point to warn the West in early 1973 that, should a countercartel be established, the West would find its interests jeopardized rather than served.

Despite substantive differences with the USA over energy sharing, rhetorical threats of reprisal by OAPEC and divergent Euro-American interests, multilateralism was finally endorsed at the October 1972 Paris summit under the 'Guidelines and priorities for a Community energy policy'. Yet the fate of multilateral diplomacy fell to the French when the issue went before the Council of Ministers in May 1973. Equipped with the power of the veto, France single-handedly prevented the other eight EEC members from participating in multilateral negotiations with either the USA, or the OECD. The French argued that Europe's first priority was to formulate its own energy policy and unify its oil market before negotiating with outsiders.

But the French argument was unrealistic to anyone familiar with EEC energy policy. Europe had no coherent oil or energy policy. The Community institutions which did exist were inadequate mechanisms for the energy dilemma of the 1970s. Euratom and the European Coal and Steel Community (ECSC) did have a mandate for regulating and coordinating the Community's energy policy but their respective jurisdictions were confined to nuclear research and coal development. No Community institution existed which was equipped to deal with oil, since at the time the other institutions were created oil represented only 10 percent of Europe's energy needs.[31] Faith in the future of nuclear technology coupled with the low level of oil use obviated the need for a common oil policy. Oil was left as a prerogative of national governments and the policies chosen varied from country to country. As Europe's appetite for oil grew during the 1960s, so did the differences among individual countries. Britain and

Holland, for example, are homes of two of the international majors (Royal Dutch Shell and British Petroleum) and, together with Germany, have followed laissez-faire policies in connection with the European oil market. Conversely, France and Italy as energy-poor states have regulated their oil markets through direct state intervention, with France giving preferential treatment to French companies and oil from the franc zone. As energy-poor states, Italy and France have traditionally sought to break the hold of the international majors which they viewed as impediments to their own interests. The result has been a series of provocative challenges against the parent governments (Britain, Holland and the USA). The Italian state-owned company, Ente Nazionale Idrocarburi (ENI), first challenged the majors by offering producer states a 75/25 profit-sharing formula, thereby shattering the attractiveness of the conventional fifty-fifty formula. Since 1958 ENI had advocated the creation of a 'Community Oil Corporation' to challenge the dominance of the majors. By the mid-1960s ENI had the strong support of the French, who were actively pursuing such a course. In 1967 the French state-owned company, Compagnie Française des Pétroles (CFP), took over confiscated concessions from the majors in Iraq, provoking a storm of protest from industry and government officials alike. The culmination of efforts directed against the majors materialized in the 1971 'Zurich group', whose ostensible purpose was to 'decolonize the oil industry' and buy into the existing concessions at the expense of the majors.[32] Even in times of crisis, France and Italy have avoided close association with the majors. In 1967, for example, France refused to give any public sign that it was cooperating with other Western states which were establishing emergency energy procedures.[33] In 1970 after the showdown between the Libyan government and the oil industry, twenty-three independent and major oil companies collectively formed a negotiating bloc known as the London Policy Group. ENI and its subsidiary, Azienda Generale Italiana Petrole (AGIP), refused to join, thereby forfeiting assistance from the Libyan Producers Agreement (LPA) which pledged each company to aid any other in the event that its assets or supplies were jeopardized. Italy's policy paid poor dividends, however, when 51 percent of AGIP's assets were nationalized in 1972. Italy was, of course, ineligible for LPA assistance.

Although the other eight members of the EEC favored some form of multilateral dialogue with the USA within the OECD framework, the French alternative of establishing bilateral oil deals was not without support. For example, the 'Guidelines and priorities for a Community energy policy' endorsed two very different courses of action. On the one hand, the EEC members endorsed the principle of multilateral negotiations with the USA, yet direct negotiations with the oil-producers was also advocated. In other words, Europe was merely supplementing its position with additional guarantees rather than adopting a new policy as urged by the USA.

In fact, developments during 1970–73 generated considerable incentives to reach accommodation with Arab oilproducers directly. The consummation of the Tripoli–Tehran agreements in early 1971, for example, signaled the beginning of the end of the oligopolistic role of the international majors as control over production and pricing shifted from their jurisdiction to the sovereign prerogative of the oilproducers. Henri Simonet (EEC commissioner in charge of energy and vice-president of the European Commission) noted the implications by pointing out, 'The producer countries now determine prices and quantities produced . . . It is now necessary for consumer states to find ways of negotiating directly with producing states'.[34] Meanwhile, as nationalization and participation came to dominate much of OPEC's agenda, European 'have-not' energy states perceived new opportunities as well as new necessities to negotiate directly with oilproducers as a means of enhancing security of supply.

Equally significant was the regularity of price increases during this period, which provided an added incentive to negotiate bilaterally. Higher prices negatively impacted European balance of payments due to the large quantities of oil imported. Conversely, higher prices meant greater profits for both the international majors, and the oilproducers. Since five of the majors were American, this created an asymmetrical advantage for the USA, since higher profits would be recycled back to the parent government via the majors in the form of profits and taxes. The oilproducers conveyed the same message inadvertently. Witness, for example, Iran's burgeoning military purchases from the USA and the 1972 Yamani proposal in which Saudi Arabia offered the USA a stable supply of oil and downstream investments in return for US technology and developmental assistance. The French state-owned oil company, Enterprise de Recherches et d'Activités Pétrolieres (ERAP), was quick to point out and condemn the disadvantages of such a relationship, noting:

> What an inducement to the raising of crude oil prices if the money paid by Europe should be invested through the producing state in the country of origin of these companies strengthening their power. Who would still be able to maintain that the companies which produce in Arabia are impartial intermediaries between these countries and the European consumer?[35]

In fact, during 1970–73 Europe became increasingly suspicious over what they perceived to be US approval for higher prices. To place events in their proper perspective, it should be recalled that this was a period when trans-Atlantic economic competition was particularly fierce as a result of divergent trade and monetary policies. The US economy was suffering balance of payment problems which were partially attributable to financial commitments to NATO and EEC discriminatory trade policies. The USA was attempting to readjust the inequities in the Western trade and military spheres through political channels, but often acted unilaterally. The Nixon shocks of 1971, in which the USA unilaterally suspended the convertibility of dollars into gold and imposed a 10 percent surcharge on all dutiable imports, injected a heavy dose of acrimony into trans-Atlantic economic relations. Moreover, the US soybean embargo of June 1973 exacerbated tensions and raised doubts in Europe as to whether US economic policy took account of their needs. The unilateral and relatively self-serving nature of US economic policy led to speculation that the

USA was equally anxious to reduce the competitive price advantage Europe enjoyed in energy, which the USA inadvertently created by its enactment of the 1959 Mandatory Import Quota Program.

A series of events in 1970–73 lent credence to the view that the USA was actually encouraging higher oil prices as one panacea for trans-Atlantic competition. For example, in 1970, when confronted with a series of challenges from Middle Eastern oilproducers, the oil industry collectively formed the London Policy Group (LPC), comprised of twenty-three oil companies, for the purpose of enhancing their bargaining position. The dilemma before the oil industry was how to negotiate new contracts which would obviate 'price ratcheting' (whereby gains achieved by one state precipitated imitative demands by others), which ultimately threatened price stability as various states sought to outdo one another. The strategy of the LPG was, therefore, to negotiate with both the Persian Gulf and Mediterranean producers simultaneously, in order to obviate price ratcheting by consummating *one* all-encompassing agreement. On the eve of the negotiations, however, the LPG strategy was virtually sabotaged by the Irwin mission, sent to the Persian Gulf by President Nixon. The ostensible purpose of the Irwin mission was to explain why the US government permitted the industry to negotiate jointly; prevent an imminent impasse in the negotiations; and seek assurances from the Gulf producers that oil would be available for the free world.[36] Yet the deeds of the mission belied its purpose, when Under-Secretary John Irwin recommended separate negotiations. The result was not one broad agreement as envisioned by the oil industry, but two separate agreements (the Tehran agreement of February 1971, and the Tripoli agreement of April 1971), in which price ratcheting continued with the concomitant result of higher prices.

A second incident occurred in the summer of 1972, when James E. Akins delivered a speech at the Eighth Petroleum Congress of the Arab League. Akins was only invited as an observer, yet explains that he felt compelled to make an impromptu speech in order to halt the trend toward nationalization, when near to the end of the conference Iraq nationalized the Iraqi Petroleum Co. Akins did not actually recommend higher prices, but stated that this was 'an unavoidable trend' and that oil prices should be 'expected to go up sharply due to the lack of short-term alternatives to Arab oil'.[37] The speech was interpreted by Western observers and OPEC officials alike as US approval for higher prices. A Canadian observer noted that Akins's speech amounted to 'advocating that the Arabs raise the price of oil to $5 per barrel', while the oil minister of the United Arab Emirates cited Akins as proof that the 'world will be ready to accept considerable increases in prices'.[38]

By mid-1973 a new US policy emerged which all but confirmed Europe's worst suspicions. The new policy deliberately sought to increase US-Saudi interdependence. *Platt's Oilgram* reported that 'under the direction of the new Secretary of State [Kissinger] the US is reversing its position of eschewing special relations with oil producing states, especially Saudi Arabia'.[39] Akins was also cited as a key figure in the policy of 'tying the Saudi Arabian economy to the US through massive investment in Saudi Arabia and Saudi Arabian investments in the US'.[40] The State Department was instructed to encourage private businesses to invest in the export-industry sector as a means of increasing their ties to the US economy. The State Department was to set up a 'clearinghouse', in order to 'evaluate firms on the basis of long-term commitment to Saudi Arabia, stability and capacity for contribution to the Saudi economy'.[41] Firms which passed inspection could 'expect a good deal of help from Akins' embassy . . . further than simply helping them set up shop'.[42] This policy was not merely new, it was a reversal of previous policy. In 1972 the State Department rejected the Yamani proposal, ostensibly because it would jeopardize US energy diplomacy with its allies. One year later, however, it was the State Department which reversed its objections and proposed a similar initiative despite the stalemate in trans-Atlantic energy diplomacy.

The ramifications of increased US-Saudi interdependence and what appeared as US approval for higher prices, were interpreted differently by the states directly affected. Saudi Arabia and Iran saw this as a mutually beneficial arrangement, whereby increased oil revenues would be recycled back to the USA in the form of investment or arms purchases. Europe interpreted US policy in a very different light, however, and suspected that this was a unilateral attempt to gain economic advantage. This view was difficult to refute, particularly when the White House Council on International Economic Policy (CIEP) reported in 1973 that 'the US stood to gain from higher prices and the resulting surplus of OPEC's funds', because it will 'receive a large share of these funds'.[43]

While European suspicions were logically deducted from US policy, the economic windfalls emanating from higher prices before 1973 were 'side-effects', rather than motivating factors of US policy. Higher prices were a means of serving political objectives espoused by central decisionmakers where other means were unavailable. It should be recalled that Iran's role was gradually being transformed during this period. This was not due to oil alone, but rather to the British decision to evacuate its forces from the Gulf by 1971, and Iranian willingness to fill the vacuum by acting as a regional superpower under the aegis of the Nixon Doctrine. One of the Shah of Iran's conditions for accepting the role was a US pledge to sell as much and as high a quality of arms as the shah requested. Yet the shah, plagued with substantial balance of payments deficits, required additional revenue to finance these purchases. Kissinger knew he could not persuade Congress to tax Americans for that purpose. Congress was already using the power of the purse-strings to expedite the USA's withdrawal from Vietnam. Acrimonious Congressional–executive relations typical of the period worried Kissinger lest the Soviets misinterpret US resolve and attempt exploitation of regional tension. The lack of confidence in the foreign aid appropriations process, therefore, led policymakers to favor disguised vehicles to extend financial assistance deemed important in US foreign policy calculus. For Kissinger, higher prices financed the shah's military role, obviated Congressional constraints and moderated Saudi behavior by giving it a stake in the liberal economic order. Moreover, higher prices posed less of a threat than did the prospects of an embargo. Iran which was consistently a hardliner on price escalation was a more reliable source of oil than the Saudis, who were less concerned with exorbitant prices but more susceptible to radical pressures within the Arab world.

Thus on the eve of the first oil crisis, fruitful multilateral diplomacy failed to materialize despite increased vulnerability of the West. The energy stalemate in Europe was matched by bureaucratic inertia in the USA. The policy process in the USA was dominated by low-ranking officials who were committed to multilateralism in principle, but biased in their perception that Europe would be unable to sway US policy in the event of a crisis. This stifled the sense of urgency and produced few bold initiatives which would have been necessary to break the energy stalemate at home or in Europe.

BRIDGING THE TRANS-ATLANTIC GAP: THE CREATION OF THE INTERNATIONAL ENERGY AGENCY

The ultimate success of the Washington energy conference in February 1974, which established the Energy Coordinating Group, and later became the International Energy Agency (IEA) in November 1975, was not a foregone conclusion at the time of its convening. The Europeans were, as before the crisis, divided over the efficacy of two divergent courses. The French, for example, vehemently opposed Kissinger's approach and offered the 'Euro-Arab dialogue' as an alternative. Kissinger's strategy, therefore, aimed at forcing the Europeans to either demonstrate their 'independence', or alternatively, force their recognition that they needed the USA for sustained alliance leadership. He did this by taking the issue outside the confines of the OECD oil committee and by offering the key European states (Britain, Germany, France, Italy, Norway and Holland) a 'separate' invitation, which would force them to either accept or reject an alliance approach. Kissinger was, in effect, forcing Europe to reconcile what he distastefully perceived as the 'inconsistency between establishing a European identity and a close working relationship with the US'. The invitation was accepted with the qualification that all EEC members attend.

Europe's concurrence to formally join the IEA (with the exception of France) was due to a combination of American strengths and European weaknesses which the crisis manifested. Europe had already demonstrated its inability to deal collectively with the energy crisis at the Copenhagen summit when confronted with risk-ridden tradeoffs, mounting domestic pressures and dissension among the Nine over the degree to which Europe should align itself with the USA. The energy stalemate at the Community level thus enabled the USA to exploit differences and exert pressure where European vulnerabilities were most conspicuous. Linkage politics, for example, was a major instrument and employed by the highest government officials. On the eve of the Washington conference, Nixon asserted that 'security and economic considerations are inevitably linked and energy cannot be separated from either'.[44] Kissinger, Nixon and Defense Secretary Schlesinger, all warned that unless Europe complied with US policy, US troops might be withdrawn from Europe. For Germany, the staunchest supporter of NATO in Europe due to security considerations peculiar to its own environment, this type of political blackmail, however repugnant, was quite effective though probably unnecessary.

Linkage was supplemented with bait. Kissinger spoke confidently of the rewards which would emanate from a cooperative approach. 'The USA', Kissinger declared, 'is prepared to make a very major financial and intellectual contribution to the objective of solving the energy problem on a common basis . . . The energy crisis can become the economic equivalent of the Sputnik challenge of 1957'.[45] American science and technology were offered as long-term solutions for developing alternative sources of energy in addition to incentives such as the Minimum Safeguard Price. These were mere appetizers however, compared with the $25 billion financial safety-net which Europe both wanted and needed as short-term insurance, when by mid-1974, the economic consequences of the crisis forced Western economies on a steep slide downward.

Meanwhile, by the time that the IEA was officially consecrated in the OECD in November 1974, Kissinger had already successfully negotiated one Egyptian-Israeli disengagement accord and shortly thereafter one with Syria and another with Egypt. Kissinger had, thus, diffused the crisis by personally undertaking an active diplomatic role which restored European confidence in US leadership to a considerable degree.

A final tool employed by Kissinger was compromise. Under the IEA, the USA reversed its previous opposition and committed itself to share its domestically produced oil in the event of an energy shortage. Moreover, Kissinger reached a compromise with French President Giscard d'Estaing, at the December 1974 Martinique summit, by withdrawing his objections to the convening of a producer–consumer dialogue. Kissinger's concurrence to a multilateral North–South forum set the stage for a new phase of US energy diplomacy, beginning with the abortive Paris preparatory conference in April 1975 and followed by the Conference on International Economic Cooperation (CIEC) in December 1975. Particularly noticeable about this phase was the convergence of North–South issues with energy diplomacy. Kissinger's acceptance of a broader approach was motivated by the need to accommodate Europe, which was already moving unilaterally, as evidenced by the 1975 Lome Convention which liberalized European trade relations with a number of Third World countries. Kissinger felt some conciliatory gesture toward the Third World was necessary in order to maintain a semblance of moral leadership, but more compelling was the need to maintain alliance solidarity. 'The realities of European politics', according to one State Department official, 'forced the USA to accept a linkage between energy and North–South issues'.

The IEA was, thus, an example of a confluence of Euro-American interests. The IEA satisfied European regional interests through its emphasis on an emergency allocation plan, stockpiling, conservation and long-term development of alternative energy resources. The IEA, thus, assuaged European concerns by providing both short- and long-term relief. Even the French, while abstaining from formal membership in the IEA, have joined the IEA-related $25 billion financial safety-net for short-term alleviation of their oil deficits. The IEA has also satisfied US global interests by reinforcing the Atlantic Alliance and preserving the liberal economic order within a multilateral context.

THE BALANCE-SHEET: EURO-AMERICAN RELATIONS AND THE IEA

Despite the success of the IEA, trans-Atlantic tension has not entirely dissipated. The USA, for example, has adamantly opposed the 'Euro-Arab dialogue' but has been unable to prevent Europe from participating. Nor have the USA or the IEA been successful in reducing the level of bilateral agreements. Europe, on the other hand, has become increasingly alienated by the style as well as the substance of US energy policy. As concerns style, US energy policy has lost much of its earlier foreign policy thrust as the crisis receded and the State Department's role progressively diminished. Institutional reorganization in the USA was continual after 1975, until it finally culminated in the creation of the Department of Energy. The implication is simply that the State Department and Treasury which were the most sensitive to European concerns were over-shadowed by a new bureaucratic organization, equipped with its own domestic constituency, whose views are not always congruent with those of Europe. This is in sharp contrast to the 1974–5 period, when Kissinger, and to a lesser extent former Treasury Secretary William Simon, dominated much of the policy process and whose objectives were specifically geared toward reassuring and meeting Europe's needs.

As concerns substance, US has fallen short of European expectations. President Carter's energy package, which consisted of deregulation of oil and natural gas, greater conservation and the stimulation of alternative energy resources, was hostage to a coalition of divergent interest groups, fragmented congressional parochialism and a suspicious public opinion. The energy stalemate in the USA not only nurtures resentment, but precludes confidence in US leadership. Bold US commitments, such as those enunciated at the 1979 Tokyo summit, pledging greater conservation and freezing imports at the 1979 level until 1985 appear more rhetorical than substantive steps forward. Domestic price controls, for example, were hardly conducive to generating greater conservation and partially explain why US imports actually increased by 25 percent during 1973–9.[46] In May 1979 European faith in US policy was severely shaken, when the discovery was made that US imports of heating fuel from the Caribbean (amounting to 100,000 barrels a day) were subsidized by $5 a barrel. This provoked a storm of European protest and charges of the USA's bad faith even though mitigating circumstances existed. The subsidy, for example, was part of the 1974 Entitlement Program, in which US refiners using cheap oil, not the US government, compensated refiners using expensive imported oil. None the less, progress on the US energy front has been slow. It was not until 1979 that the USA actually registered its first decrease in oil consumption by 2·2 percent.[47] Moreover, implementation of the phased decontrol program did not begin until June 1979 and was not completed until September 1981. In short, domestication of energy policy in the USA has stymied progress on the energy front by precluding coherence of policy with energy realities and inhibiting progress toward goals consistent with the alliance approach.

The 1978–9 Iranian crisis was less dramatic than the 1973 crisis but highly significant in so far as it illuminated some of the shortcomings in multilateral oil diplomacy. Since no country suffered a shortage exceeding 7 percent of total energy needs, IEA mechanisms designed to alleviate an energy crunch were not invoked. Instead, what occurred was a flurry of competitive bidding on the spot markets where oil prices rose from the then current price of $12·70 a barrel to as high as $40 in some cases. Once the spot market prices rose, it was only a matter of time before OPEC officially readjusted its price scales. This was particularly damaging to consuming nations, since OPEC prices are not freely fluctuating market prices, and once raised, do not come down. The market is manipulated in a manner to deliberately maintain high prices. In times where ordinary market conditions of supply and demand would decrease the price, OPEC can simply cut back production to prevent such a possibility. In any event, the importing nations did themselves a great disservice by frenzied competitive bidding and lent substance to the charge that 'most of the wounds of 1979 were self-inflicted'.[48] In fact, in a rather startling turnabout from Carter's routine anti-OPEC statements, a senior State Department official reported as late as August 1980 that 'it would be a mistake and scapegoating to say the events of 1979 were due to OPEC. Prices in 1979 were driven up by . . . the scramble for oil'.[49] The result was a virtual doubling of price in 1978–9 which, in turn, meant the oil import bill as a share of GDP rose from 2·3 to 2·8 percent for IEA members.[50] In an attempt to grapple with this problem IEA members agreed, in May 1980, to urge private and public bodies to refrain from abnormal purchases on the spot market, but it remains to be seen whether in times of crisis this problem will not surface again.

In fact, many of the potential challenges ahead may be beyond the control of the IEA as a result of the structural changes in international oil trade since the early 1970s. The three major problems confronting Europe, and the West in general, are security of supply, price stability and economic arrangements which ensure a modicum of equitable recycling. Is the IEA better equipped to cope with these problems than state-to-state bilateral arrangements? Some think not. The demise of the international majors as impartial intermediaries, for example, could handicap IEA allocation programs. The share of the majors' oil trade has declined from 78 percent in 1974 to approximately 44 percent in 1979, and will decline even further. What this means simply is that in times of crisis an international allocation program would be considerably more difficult to implement, since producer governments now occupy much of the role once assumed by the majors. This reduces the flexibility of the market considerably and precludes a repeat performance of the majors' role in the 1973 oil crisis. Moreover, should only a few nations be reticent in complying with IEA energysharing arrangements, the spillover effects could paralyze IEA consumer solidarity.

Secondly, because oil prices are curently the major problem confronting Europe, many have come to believe in the aftermath of the Iranian crisis that bilateral arrangements may be more fiscally sound than conventional sources. Guaranteeing the terms of trade through contractual agreements in advance is seen as less destabilizing then when confronted with spiraling spot market prices in times of temporary or prolonged energy shortages. Consequently, traditional importers of spot market products (Sweden, Belgium and Ireland) have switched to long-term bilateral contracts, citing price as the major reason.[51] Likewise, traditional state oil buyers (France, Italy, Spain and Greece) were particularly active during 1979.[52] Not surprisingly, 'the big upswing in direct government deals' was cited as the most 'significant market change in 1979'.[53] The result was the further erosion of the majors' position. Equally significant, however, is the potential danger this poses for importing nations, who may find themselves considerably more susceptible to economic and political pressures emanating from individual OPEC countries.

Finally, European economies have a vested interest in ensuring adequate recycling. European economies derive a substantial percentage of their respective GNPs from Middle Eastern trade. Europe has kept a steady eye on seeing that it gets its fair share of trade as petrodollars filter out in search of technology, arms, investments and consumer goods. Protecting these links could, though not necessarily, supersede consumer solidarity. European reticence to join the USA in a full and retroactive embargo against Iran after the taking of the hostages is illustrative of the salience European leaders attach to Middle Eastern trade. But to conclude on this point, due to the strong interest Europe has in security of supply, price stability and trade, one has to wonder whether or not Europe might not be torn between pledging its allegiance to the IEA or bilateral agreements, in light of both the structural changes and the empirical evidence accompanying them.

The trials and tribulations before the Atlantic Alliance are far from over. The energy-security dilemma is not a static problem subject to a quick solution. On the contrary, it is constantly evolving due to a variety of factors, which in turn poses new challenges and constraints for the West. What has remained constant, however, is the primacy of European regional interests versus US global interests and the tendency of energy issues to spill over into the political realm. This portends even greater complexity for a cooperative alliance approach. Yet alliance solidarity as embodied in the IEA is essential as a deterrent to excessive and reckless OPEC demands as well as a form of insurance, however limited, for Western consuming nations.

NOTES: CHAPTER 5

1   Address by Henry Kissinger to the Associated Press, New York, 23 April 1973.
2   *New York Times*, 25 October 1973, p. 1.
3   *New York Times*, 31 October 1973, p. 44.
4   Jobert speech to French Parliament, 12 November 1973.
5   Brandt speech to European Parliament, Strasbourg, 13 November 1973.

6   *Le Monde,* 30 October 1973, p. 1.
7   Robert J. Lieber, *Oil and the Middle East War: Europe in the Energy Crisis,* No. 35 Harvard University Center for International Affairs, 1976.
8   This is an *ad hoc* group of industry officials located within the OECD. It was set up after the 1956 Suez crisis, and following the 1967 war it received a mandate to develop an emergency allocation programme.
9   *The Economist,* 24 November 1973.
10 Robert B. Stobaugh, 'The oil companies in crisis', in Raymond Vernon (ed.), *The Oil Crisis* (New York: Norton 1976), pp. 179–202.
11 ibid.
12 BP, *Statistical Review of the World Oil Industry* (London: British Petroleum, 1973), p. 21.
13 Quote is from President Pompidou, *Le Monde,* 2 November 1973, p. 1.
14 James O. Goldsborough, 'France, the European crisis and the alliance', *Foreign Affairs,* vol. 52, no. 3 (April 1974), p. 538.
15 Walter Laquer, *New York Times Magazine,* 20 January 1974.
16 Werner J. Feld, 'West European foreign policies: impact of the energy crisis', *Orbis,* vol. 22 no. 1 (Spring 1978), p. 69.
17 Romano Prodi and Alberto Clo, 'Europe', in Raymond Vernon (ed.), *The Oil Crisis* (New York: Norton, 1976), p. 98.
18 Nadav Safran, *The Embattled Ally* (Cambridge, Mass./London: Belknap Press of Harvard University, 1978), pp. 455–6.
19 President's report to Congress, 1971, p. 127.
20 *Le Monde,* 26 September 1970, p. 1.
21 *Newsweek,* 15 February 1971.
22 Anwar El Sadat, 'Where Egypt stands', *Foreign Affairs,* vol. 51, no. 1 (1971).
23 Henry Kissinger *White House Years* (Boston, Mass./Toronto: Little, Brown, 1979), p. 1291.
24 ibid., p. 1288.
25 *New York Times,* 14 August 1973.
26 Akins, 'The oil crisis: this time the wolf is here', *Foreign Affairs,* vol. 51, no. 3 (April 1973), p. 467.
27 Organization for Economic Cooperation and Development, *Energy Prospects to 1985* (Paris: OECD, 1973).
28 'Worldwide oil politics', *National Journal Reports,* 13 October 1973, p. 1540.
29 Community refers to the Common Market (EEC) countries. The original six members were France, Germany, Italy, Belgium, Luxembourg and Holland. By 1972 the Community was enlarged to nine with the entry of Britain, Denmark and Ireland. In 1980 Greece became the tenth member.
30 Hans Maull, 'The strategy of avoidance: Europe's Middle East policies after the October war' in J. C. Hurewitz (ed.), *Oil, the Arab-Israeli Dispute and the Industrial World* (Boulder, Colo: Westview Press, 1976), p. 118 for details.
31 Frans A. M. Alting Von Geusau (ed.), *Energy in the European Communities* (Leyden: Sytnoff, 1975), p. 3.
32 See Louis Turner, 'Oil companies in the international system', Royal Institute of International Affairs (London: Allen & Unwin Billing), p. 170.
33 Senate Subcommittee Hearings on US Foreign Policy and Multinational Corporations, pt 8, p. 549.
34 Reproduced from 'US-Europe Relations and the 1973 War'. Hearings before the Subcommittees on Europe and on the Near East and South Asia of 93rd Congress of the Committee on Foreign Affairs, p. 76.
35 Walter J. Levy, 'Euro-Japanese energy policy', *Foreign Policy,* no. 7 (Summer 1972), p. 173.
36 See Senate Hearings, pt V, p. 147; se also Forbes, 'Don't blame the oil companies: blame the State Department', 15 April 1976, pp. 69–85.
37 *Platt's Oilgram,* 49th edn., 6 June 1972; see also *Platt's Oilgram,* 12 June 1972.
38 See V. H. Oppenheim, 'The past: we pushed them', *Foreign Policy,* no. 25 (Winter 1976–7), pp. 31–2.
39 *Platt's Oilgram,* vol. 51, no. 188 (27 September 1973), p. 1.

40   ibid.
41   ibid.
42   ibid.
43   *Platt's Oilgram,* 50th edn., 23 March 1973.
44   *Department of State Bulletin,* 4 March 1974; see also *New York Times,* 15 February 1974   1.
45   Address to the Pilgrims of Great Britain, London, 12 December 1973.
46   Joseph S. Nye, 'Energy nightmares', *Foreign Policy,* no. 40 (Fall 1980).
47   Department of Energy, *US Energy Policy: Development and Performance,* 16 October 1980, p. 5.
48   Walter J. Levy, 'Oil and the decline of the West', *Foreign Affairs,* vol. 58, no. 5 (Summer 1980), p. 1000.
49   *Platt's Oilgram,* vol. 58, no. 165 (25 August 1980), p. 4.
50   International Energy Agency, *Outlook for the Eighties* (Paris: OECD, 1980), p. 13.
51   'More European nations buying oil in state deals', *Petroleum Intelligence Weekly,* 15 October 1979, p. 3.
52   ibid.
53   *Petroleum Intelligence Weekly,* 1 October 1978, p. 2.

6 Energy and the Western Alliance

ROBERT J. LIEBER

INTRODUCTION

Energy, in its availability and price and its political consequences, deeply affects relationships within the Western Alliance system. From the watershed of the October 1973 Yom Kippur War and international energy crisis, through a decisive (to some) lull of several years, to a second crisis triggered by the Iranian revolution, energy has come to occupy a crucial position on security and foreign policy agendas.

The energy crisis has affected relations within the alliance and contributed to a new set of tensions within it. One interpretation of this pattern sees energy as particularly prone to exacerbate alliance difficulties, due to inherent differences of interest, vulnerability and geography. Thus Europe's overwhelming dependence on imported energy (read OPEC and Arab oil), its location atop the Mediterranean, and its historical, cultural and commercial ties with many of the oilproducing states, may be seen as giving it a very different perspective from that of the USA, with its vast continental energy resources, infrastructure based on seemingly limitless and cheap energy, and its special relationship with Israel.

In fact, such a depiction may mislead as much as it clarifies, for relationships are far more complex, as are policy choices and consequences. In the relationship of the USA to Western Europe over energy policy, the role of the Arab-Israeli conflict is much more indirect and the pressures toward alliance disruption are at least as likely to be countered by imperatives toward greater cohesion as to prevail themselves. Illustratively, if Israel and its Arab antagonists were miraculously to conclude a stable peace agreement tomorrow, the major outlines, problems and dangers of the international energy problem would continue to exist in only slightly altered form. In no fundamental way would there be solved such problems as political instability and risks to oil production levels – in Iran and elsewhere, production decisions in Saudi Arabia, burdens of petrodollar recycling, impacts on the non-oil, less-developed countries and long-term uncertainties of oil supply and price. Indeed, it is at least arguable that without the pressence of the Arab-Israeli conflict, intra-Arab rivalries and regional instability could even intensify. From this perspective, events such as the October 1973 war, and the Iranian revolution are more usefully understood as catalysts of successive energy crises than as causes. Thus a 'solution' to one of these intractable problems desirable as it may be – will not perforce produce the international results which are sometimes heralded as the fruits of or justification for a policy such as US arm-twisting of the Israelis.

In order, therefore, better to appreciate the consequences of the energy problem for the Alliance, this chapter examines the lessons of the 1970s during periods of crisis and lull, the factors conducive to both conflict and cooperation, and some of the experiences and risks which the Europeans and the USA face in coping – or failing to cope – with the energy crisis.

LESSONS OF THE 1970s: THE FIRST CRISIS

The October 1973 war created real difficulties not only for Atlantic relationships, but for the European Community as well. During the initial stage of the crisis, as a result of the partial Arab oil embargo, anxieties over the physical availability of oil supplies predominated. Caught without prior preparation or effective institutional means of cooperation, the individual European states scrambled for scarce energy supplies on an individual basis. Countries such as Germany and Holland, which were inclined to seek cooperative European and Atlantic solutions, found themselves without wide support. Indeed, for a brief moment the governments of Britain and France were willing to comply with the Arab oil embargo of The Netherlands.[1] At one point, the Nine gave unprecedented access to Arab representatives at their December 1973 Copenhagen summit meeting – a privilege which the USA had sought unsuccessfully for itself in prior years.

The initial *supply* phase of the crisis was thus marked by security anxieties, lack of intra-European or intra-alliance cohesion, efforts at bilateral deals between individual consumer and producer states, a wild scramble for scarce oil, and considerable insecurity. By early 1974, however, the picture had begun to change in important respects. The international oil supply shortfall was found to be manageable at a level – albeit painful – of roughly 7 percent. Thus, instead of the actual supply of oil being the chief difficulty, attention now began to focus on the problem of paying for a resource whose price was in the process of increasing approximately 400 percent in the space of a few months.

During this second, *price,* phase of the crisis, the USA was able to reassert an important measure of alliance leadership, particularly at and after the February 1974 Washington energy conference. Cooperative measures were organized at a multilateral level (which moved away from the European Community by transcending it, just as the earlier phase had also seen countries bypass the EEC on an individual level). During this period the International Energy Agency (IEA) and its standby emergency oilsharing program were established, and those unreceptive to such approaches (particularly France under President Georges Pompidou and Foreign Minister Michel Jobert) found themselves isolated.

Increasingly, attention focused on the means for recycling vast petroleum revenue surpluses generated by OPEC price increases and on financing balance of payments deficits of both the advanced industrial oilimporting states, and the non-oil, less-developed countries. Here, multilateral bodies such as the OECD and IMF, as well as the major international banks, became key actors.[2] Further, despite a period of intense activity in which countries such as France initialed enormous state-to-state deals and in which huge commitments for Western industrial goods, technology and sometimes armaments were envisaged in exchange for specified amounts of petroleum, many of these preferential and bilateral agreements were never fully consummated. On the one hand, the oil-producing countries were willing and able to purchase goods and services on an international competitive basis; on the other hand, the oilconsuming states found that individual negotiations and special relationships conveyed no price advantages and, for the most part, no additional supplies of oil. In view of these and other factors, cooperative behavior among countries of the Western Alliance became less difficult than it had been during the height of the initial crisis.

THE INTERLUDE

From late 1974 to late 1978, there ensued a period in which, for many, the immediacy of the energy crisis seemed to recede. Consuming states managed to cope with the price and balance of payments effects of the oil price rise albeit at a significant cost in reduced economic growth and heightened inflation and both the supply and price of OPEC oil seemed to diminish as urgent problems. Thus, despite official OPEC increases, the real oil import price (deflated by the prices of OECD manufactured exports) which increased from a 1973 index level of 100 to a 1974 figure of 248, actually declined by 13 percent from 249 in 1976 to 216 in 1978.[3] In the same period, the overall OPEC balance of payments surplus, which had been at a seemingly enormous and unmanageable level of $60 billion in 1974, had almost disappeared by 1978.

National responses to these developments diverged significantly, however, on opposite sides of the Atlantic. The Europeans (and Japanese) tended to remain acutely aware of their dangerous resource and economic vulnerability. As a result of several factors (conservation, pricing policies, slower economic growth, efforts to substitute other energy sources), total oil requirements of OECD countries other than the USA actually declined by 2·3 percent during 1973–8.[4] By contrast, the USA experienced five years of near-stalemate in energy policy with a lack of consensus over the likelihood of impending oil scarcity or energy glut. Indeed, as late as March 1979, two-thirds of the US public believed the oil crisis was a hoax. During this five-year period, total US oil requirements actually increased 11·8 percent. Even more damaging, however, were oil import figures. While the other OECD countries (excluding Britain and Norway, as oil-producers) experienced a 2·2 percent decrease in net oil imports in 1973–8, US imports had soared by 28·5 percent, as a result not only of increased consumption, but of declining domestic production. Together with a sharp decrease in US oil imports from Canada, this resulted in seriously increased US dependence on Middle Eastern oil imports.

Given the fact that the USA accounted for one-third of total OECD oil imports, the increase in US demand was of major significance. In particular, it stimulated growing resentment that the USA's failure to conserve and to exploit its indigenous energy supplies more extensively were seriously jeopardizing Europe's resource and economic security. In a complex series of interrelationships, such factors as potential pressure on the international supply and demand balance for OPEC oil, the inflationary and internationally destabilizing consequences of huge US balance of payments deficits, and the increased vulnerability of the international oil supply situation to unforeseen shocks were all linked. Their consequence was to make cooperation within various Western groupings more difficult, as well as to strengthen the hand of those Europeans advocating a *modus vivendi* with Arab oilproducers. They also contributed to a focus on increased export sales to all parties and promotion of virtually everything saleable (weapons, high technology and nuclear facilities) on a *tous azimuts* basis.

THE SECOND CRISIS

It was against this background, with previous experience suggesting that the oil crisis could better be faced on the basis of consumer cooperation than by a *sauve qui peut* scramble, tempered by the limited achievements of the intercrisis period and resentment at US energy performance, that the Western Alliance countries faced the Iranian crisis in late 1978. Events in Iran first reduced, then halted, oil production there. Production resumed in the early spring of 1979 at a level approximately half the precrisis figure of 6 million barrels of oil per day.

Although the lessons of 1973–4 seemed to suggest the practical utility of greater cooperation among Western oilconsuming countries, and the existence of the IEA as well as the experience of a prior crisis provided some basis for facing renewed energy difficulties, significant obstacles to cooperation existed as well. The most important of these was the eruption of frenzied competitive bidding for oil on spot markets, particularly in Rotterdam. Although spot market trading had previously amounted to no more than a few percent of international oil sales, based on oil not already moving under long-term contract, the rapid run-up in price into the \$30–\$40 per barrel range – and beyond – quickly outdistanced the official OPEC figure, which had been \$12·70 in December 1978. Bidding for oil on the spot market to offset Iranian production shortfalls touched off a chain-reaction process, whereby rising prices tempted some OPEC producers to divert oil (which had previously been under contract) to the spot market in order to reap the benefit of sharply higher prices. In turn, this forced international oil companies either to turn to the spot market themselves in an effort to make good their additional shortfalls, or more often – to reduce deliveries to their own customers. These customers, in turn, whether private or government-related companies, then entered the spot market in search of additional supplies, thus further bidding up prices. Although the USA sought to discourage spot market purchases in order to damp down some of these pressures, and France advocated restraints on the spot market, IEA and EEC countries were unable to agree on such measures. The Germans and Japanese were particularly active as spot market buyers of highpriced oil, in part due to their then buoyant currencies, strong balance of payments positions and competitive economic strength, and in part – at least in the German case – as a reflection of a devotion to market-oriented conceptions of economic policy and a skepticism toward regulation.

IEA mechanisms proved irrelevant, because shortfalls were below the 7 percent threshold figure for invoking emergency oilsharing measures. While the IEA secretariat had obtained assurances from its member-countries, plus France, that they were willing to honor their commitments should this become necessary, the stage was never reached. Indeed, the overall oil supply gap was rather modest. According to IEA calculations, the shortfall (between OPEC supply and demand) during the first quarter of 1979 was approximately 4 percent and virtually all of this was accounted for by stockbuilding.[5] In short, other producers, both OPEC and non-OPEC, had made up most of the Iranian shortfall on a temporary basis, but political and economic anxieties, coupled with sporadic distributional disruptions, caused governments, international oil companies, businesses and even individuals to seek to build up their own oil reserves. Had an effective system or agreement existed, under IEA auspices or elsewhere, much of this problem, particularly the immediate pressures which gave rise to an approximate doubling of OPEC prices over a twelve-month period, might have been limited.

The problems of alliance cooperation are, however, complex. Japan and Germany were by no means the only countries less disposed toward effective practical measures of cooperation. Thus, in one vivid instance – in May 1979 the USA suddenly appeared to have given its oil importers a $5 a barrel import subsidy. In fact, the 'subsidy' was quite limited, applying only as a temporary measure to heating and diesel oil imports from Caribbean refineries, covering less than 1 percent of net US petroleum imports, and involving no actual government subsidy but an adjustment through the complex Entitlement Program. None the less, before it was accurately explained, it provoked an explosive European reaction and newspaper headlines heralding a new 'oil war'.[6] While the uproar was disproportionate to the cause, it reflected both the extreme sensitivity and vulnerability of the Europeans over international energy issues and the maladroitness of US energy policymakers in failing to consult with their IEA partners on a sensitive matter.

Cooperative efforts did, nevertheless, take place. The most important of them occurring at the two summit meetings in June 1979. The first of these, at Strasbourg, brought together the nine heads of state and government of the European Community. They undertook to have the Community hold overall petroleum imports during the years 1980–5 at a level not to exceed that of 1978. At the subsequent Tokyo summit, the seven leading industrial powers (the USA, Japan, Germany, France, Britain, Italy and Canada) adopted oil import goals for 1985. However, the Americans and Europeans disagreed over whether the EEC would be committed to an overall figure (thus allowing it to benefit from projected increases in Britain's North Sea oil), or to individual country targets. Resentment also arose among some of the five smaller EEC member-states not present at Tokyo over decisionmaking proceedings in their absence.

Not until early December did the Nine reach agreement among themselves on individual national import goals within the Community's overall Tokyo target. Five of these national figures (for Belgium, Ireland, Italy, Luxembourg and The Netherlands) actually involved *increases* during 1980–5, which were counterbalanced by net reductions elsewhere, particularly via increased British oil production. This difficult process made the Common Market members reluctant to consider any further changes or reductions at the subsequent IEA ministerial meeting. On 10 December the nineteen IEA member-states (including all of the Nine, except France) agreed on their 1980 import 'ceilings' and 1985 'goals'. Additional measures were also begun to gain better information about the spot market, to discourage unnecessary spot market purchases by government-related and private companies, to develop a 'code of conduct' for market participants, to seek greater governmental influence over stock levels, and to develop plans for adjusting oil import ceilings and goals in response to tightening of market patterns in the future.[7] Most of these measures, while representing constructive steps, remained limited or qualified. And US efforts to gain approval for an additional reduction in 1980 ceilings and for sanctions to enforce these failed. They did so in substantial part because of the legacy of energy-related conflicts and differences of interest between the USA and Europe over the previous six years, because of a perception that the USA's past energy performance had made it disproportionately responsible for common energy difficulties, and because of problems in partial overlap and incomplete membership among the various available forums (the IEA, the EEC, and seven-power summits).

THE ALLIANCE, THE MIDDLE EAST AND ENERGY

Do the pressures engendered by the energy crisis and Middle East conflict imply increased difficulties within the Atlantic Alliance and among the developed countries of the non-communist world, or may they actually result in greater cohesion? This crucial question does not lead to a simple answer. Instead, a careful analysis suggests that conflictual and co-operative tendencies exist simultaneously.

Pressures toward Disruption

The chief pressures toward divisiveness among the NATO and OECD countries stem from the extreme energy and economic vulnerabilities of Europe and Japan. In particular, these areas are so desperately dependent on imported oil that a major interruption of supply threatens to leave them exposed to grave hardships and potential economic and political disruption. These fears were evident in the early weeks of the 1973–4 crisis and again (to a lesser extent) during the 1978–9 Iranian upheavals. Thus, for example, the reluctance of Japan in December 1979 to support the USA's measures during the Iranian hostage crisis reflected a concern that alternative oil supplies would not be readily available.

In a less dramatic way, the disposition of the European Community countries – individually and sometimes collectively – toward Middle East issues, including terrorism, UN anti-Zionism resolutions, weapons sales and efforts at establishing privileged relationships with Arab oilproducing countries reflect a form of response to this vulnerability. So does the cautious nature of their reaction to events in Iran and Afghanistan. Additionally, the increased efforts of oilproducing states in bypassing the major oil companies in order to market a larger proportion of their own petroleum production results in a greater number of deals between government-related oil companies as buyers and sellers. This makes it harder to diffuse the political linkages which are often otherwise obscured by the role of the oil majors. Potentially, with the percentage of direct deals having grown to approximately 30 percent of total crude oil sales volume, this may make it more difficult to redistribute and conceal – oil supply flows in the event of a crisis. As a result, operation of the IEA emergency-sharing scheme faces greater obstacles and individual consuming states become more exposed to direct pressures from producers.

Finally, pressures toward divisiveness will tend to grow to the extent that no one state convincingly provides effective and legitimate leadership. The maintenance of cooperation among major oilconsuming states poses questions of international regime maintenance and a collective goods problem. A detailed discussion of this lies outside the scope of the present chapter, but just as in the monetary and trade fields, there is reason to judge that in the absence or incapability of a hegemonic power (comparable to Britain until the 1930s, and the USA in the 1950s and 1960s) willing to exercise leadership and pay certain costs, there is a growing likelihood of disruption among the countries concerned.

Factors for Cooperation

External threats or challenges do not automatically result in one or the other type of response. Europe and the USA failed to react cooperatively and effectively to the economic difficulties of the 1930s and were particularly slow in responding to the menace of fascism. On the other hand, under US leadership, the Western countries organized themselves with considerable success in the late 1940s and early 1950s in dealing with economic and security challenges. More recently, the European Community proved utterly unable to deal with the 1973–4 energy crisis and its aftermath and was only somewhat more active during the 1978–9 crisis.

In essence, much depends on the substance of the problem(s) involved. One of the chief reasons why the Community could not effectively respond to the first energy crisis was that the short-term (supply) consequences tended to find states responding at a sub-Community (that is, national) level, and over the longer term, efforts were most likely to prove effective at a level above the Community (that is, on a broader multi-lateral basis).

The international problems of energy, particularly oil, are so complex and far-reaching that only longer-term measures involving cooperation among all major consumer states hold out the possibility of effectiveness. Even a potential producer–consumer dialogue or negotiation would almost necessarily prove more fruitful, if not confined to individual consuming nations or regions. (For example, the Europeans would have difficulty in going-it-alone without the Americans and Japanese.) This point is not merely conjectural: during the six years following the 1973–4 crisis, a series of more limited efforts (European-Arab dialogue, bilateral under-standings, European-African-Arab 'trialogue') either failed to get off the ground, or produced little tangible result. While it may be the case that no further or truly effective consumer response will succeed beyond existing measures (such as the IEA), less inclusive efforts are even more likely to fail.

In sum, the gravity of the situation, the essence of both supply and price problems, and the potential nature of producer–consumer bargaining, all create a propensity to seek solutions at a multilateral level in which Europe, Japan and the USA will find themselves necessarily in-volved.

Lessons of the French Experience

If the above discussion appears rather general, a brief consideration of the French experience will suggest why it is that the energy problem creates at least a propensity to seek multilateral, cooperative solutions.[8] Of all the principal oilconsuming states, France has traditionally pursued the most independent course of action. Coupled with the capacities of a strong, historically centralized and dirigiste state apparatus, the impera-tives of Gaullism have driven France to act at both national and inter-national levels to safeguard or promote a maximum degree of national autonomy.

Domestically, France has pursued the most ambitious nuclear power program of any Western country, is overall the most advanced at all stages of the nuclear fuel cycle, and has been most able to override environmentalist opposition to nuclear power. France has also carried out Europe's most extensive energy conservation program (albeit one which remains underfinanced and which has by no means exhausted cost-effective opportunities for greater energy efficiency) and has priced gaso-line at over $3·00 a gallon. Yet despite these and other efforts, by 1985 France will still remain dependent on external supplies (mainly imported Middle East oil) for about 67 percent of its primary energy requirements, and even by 1990 the level of dependence will remain at 60 percent.

Nor did the external measures of Presidents Pompidou and Giscard d'Estaing bring France any profound respite from the energy problem. Despite forceful promotion of the European-Arab dialogue within the EEC, aggressive pursuit of bilateral deals with individual oilproducers, a coldly calculated pro-Arab stance toward the Israeli-Arab conflict, the blocking of a more favorable EEC response to the Israeli-Egyptian peace agreement, intense efforts at building a special relationship with Iraq, virtually unrestrained (except *vis-à-vis* Israel) weapons sales programs, a willingness to export sensitive nuclear facilities, the avoidance of too firm a position on terrorism (despite a number of incidents in France), and the provision of unusually generous terms of temporary residence for Ayatollah Khomeini, the ultimate payoffs for France have been meager. In fact, France's active international energy diplomacy has not gained it any advantage in price, nor any significant provision of additional supplies (although certain understandings with Iraq have been achieved). Even commercial links have not benefited to the extent that might have been anticipated. Thus, France's share of OECD exports to the OPEC countries, which stood at 10·3 percent in 1972–3, actually declined to 7·9 percent in 1978. By contrast, the share held by The Netherlands, ostensibly more sympathetic to Israel, declined only from 3·5 to 3·1 percent, and that of the USA was reduced only modestly, from 22·8 to 21·1 percent.[9] Even French hospitality for the Ayatollah conveyed no tangible advantages and did not protect France from cancellation of major industrial and nuclear contracts, nor insulate her from the impact of steeply higher OPEC oil prices in the year following the Iranian revolution. In sum, despite determined domestic and international energy policies, France has experienced the limits of what it can achieve on a national or independent basis. As a result, the French government took a substantially more cooperative posture in addressing the second energy crisis than during the 1973–4 events. Within the European Community and at Western summit levels, the French proved far more willing to consider and even promote measures aimed at conservation, spot market controls and other collective agreements meant to alleviate the effects of the crisis.

CONCLUSIONS

While this chapter has sought to analyze certain of the givens of the international energy picture, it would be a mistake to approach the situation in excessively static terms. To be sure, some elements are relatively fixed in the medium term and dictate the serious constraints and risks which the consuming states face over the next decade. In particular, the serious even worsening – relationship between international petroleum supply and demand suggests the likelihood of periodic disruption and crises in response to 'unexpected' events during the 1980s. These may well occur despite even the best efforts at cooperation among the major oilconsuming states. None the less, important elements of this system remain dynamic. Effective cooperation may at least mitigate some of the most harmful international and domestic effects. It is here that opportunities exist for the US leadership in organizing and promoting a coherent response. A skilled and effective policy (and one which recognizes the imperatives for the USA to *reduce* significantly its oil consumption and imports rather than conduct energy policy largely by exhortation), will be crucial. In the absence of such efforts, the disarray and potential conflict among OECD and NATO countries could well jeopardize their existing economic and security relationships.

NOTES: CHAPTER 6

This paper was presented at the Conference on the Middle East and the Western Alliance, University of California, Los Angeles, USA 21–22 February 1980.

1 For a detailed analysis of this period, see Robert J. Lieber, *Oil and the Middle East War: Europe in the Energy Crisis* (Cambridge, Mass.: Harvard Center for International Affairs, 1976), esp. pp. 11–29.
2 The role of private bank financing of LDC debt in the years following the 1973–4 crisis is analyzed in an excellent study by Benjamin J. Cohen with Fabio Basagni, for the Atlantic Institute for International Affairs (Paris: forthcoming).
3 My percentage calculations from figures in *OECD Economic Outlook* (Paris), no. 25 (July 1979) p. 57.
4 Unless otherwise noted, these are my percentage calculations, based on OECD data, particularly from *Economic Outlook*, no. 25 (July 1979), table 32, p. 63, and table 61, p. 140. Figures exclude marine bunkers. Note that overall oil consumption and import figures sometimes differ among commonly used sources and even occasionally *within* them (for example, US Department of Energy), in part due to different statistical base periods, definitions and assumptions (for instance, treatment of marine bunkers, US possessions including Guam and Puerto Rico, natural gas liquids and refinery gain). None the less, overall percentage shifts are relatively consistent.
5 Information based on interviews by the author at International Energy Agency and OECD, Paris, 19–21 December 1979.
6 See, for example, *Le Matin* (Paris) 1 June 1979. The incident is discussed in detail in Robert J. Lieber, 'Energy, economics and security in alliance perspective', *International Security* (Spring 1980), pp. 156–7.
7 IEA communiqué, Meeting of Governing Board at Ministerial Level, IEA/Press (79) 28 (Paris), 10 December 1979.
8 For an extended discussion of French responses to the energy problem, see Robert J. Lieber, 'Energy policies of the Fifth Republic: autonomy versus constraint, in William G. Andrews and Stanley Hoffmann (eds), *The Impact of the Fifth Republic on France* (New York: State University of New York Press, 1981), pp. 179–96. Aspects of French policies on export of nuclear facilities to Iran, on weapons exports and terrorism are treated in Lieber, *International Security*, op. cit.
9 *OECD Economic Outlook* (Paris), no. 25 (July 1979) table 62, p. 141.

Part Three

The Superpower Connection

7 American Leadership The Western Alliance and the Old Regime in the Persian Gulf

JAMES R. KURTH

FROM THE WESTERN ALLIANCE TO THE PERSIAN GULF:
IRAN, AFGHANISTAN AND THE END OF THE OLD REGIME

In the years after World War II, the USA achieved greater foreign policy
successes in its relations with Western Europe than with any other region
of the world. The economic prosperity brought about by the Marshall
Plan and an open international economy and the military security brought
about by NATO and the US troops in Europe were solid accomplishments which endured for thirty years, until the end of the 1970s.

In contrast, the relations of the USA with the Middle East seemed to
show little solid achievement. Indeed, each US administration confronted
at least one major Middle East crisis, usually involving an Arab-Israeli
war, which undid much of its previous efforts. Yet for a quarter-century,
from the late 1940s to the early 1970s, there was one element of stability in
US relations with the region, a steady flow of cheap oil from the Middle
East to Western Europe. And this was a major contributor to the economic
recovery and prosperity of the USA's industrial allies.

The events in the Middle East of the past few years, and especially of
the past two years, have greatly altered the old equilibrium, that of a
secure and prosperous Western Alliance fueled by secure and cheap Middle
East oil. The quadrupling of world oil prices in 1973-4, their doubling
again in 1979-80, and the consequent volatility in international financial
flows both diminished the economic prosperity of the USA and Western
Europe, and produced sharp economic conflicts of interest between them
which were much greater than those that had existed before. The occupation of the US embassy in Iran and the holding of American hostages in
November 1979 produced new conflicts between the USA and its allies
over what should be the appropriate and coordinated response. The Soviet
invasion of Afghanistan in December 1979 not only produced its own new
conflicts over response, but for the first time brought the USSR into a
position where it could pose a direct threat to that central component of
the old equilibrium, the Persian Gulf oilfields and the Straits of Hormuz.
And, finally, the war between Iran and Iraq brought about the actual
destruction of major portions of the oil facilities of the region.

In this chapter, we shall suggest that these doleful events were a
natural-enough development, given the realities of Middle East countries
and given the factors shaping US policies toward the region since World

War II. We shall also consider possible alternative US policies for the future which might bring about a new equilibrium between the USA, Western Europe and the Middle East. But, in the end, we conclude that such alternative policies are unlikely to be adopted and that rather the US will continue to recycle its old policies with greater and greater costs, risks and dangers.

THE SPECIAL US RELATIONSHIP WITH AUTHORITARIAN MONARCHIES: FROM SAUDI ARABIA TO THE SHAH'S IRAN

Since its first appearance as a major actor in the Middle East at the end of World War II, the USA has pursued a policy of close association, a 'special relationship', with the authoritarian monarchies of the region. The original calculations giving rise to this policy were reasonable enough. Authoritarian monarchy was the normal, and seemed to be the natural, mode of government for the countries of the Middle East, especially the oilproducing states. The British, whose great recessional from the Middle East provided both the opportunity and the necessity for the USA's presence, had for several generations pursued a similar policy of supporting authoritarian monarchs, their 'most loyal ally'. And, perhaps most importantly, the authoritarian monarchies, which were traditional in their legitimacy but modernizing in their policies, provided the ideal regimes for the newly arriving US oil corporations; an authoritarian monarchy provided relative ease and simplicity in negotiating agreements and concessions and also provided a high degree of political stability to ensure that the concessions would last. The prototype of this new US policy, this opening to the kings, was the USA's and particularly the Aramco special relationship with King Saud in the Arabian peninsula; never before had the USA developed a close association with a traditional monarchy.[1]

Yet it also would have been reasonable to calculate that the authoritarian monarchies of the Middle East were unstable equilibria. The recent history (1910s–1940s) of monarchy in the modernizing societies of Eastern and Southern Europe suggested that the institution was really only a transitional phenomenon, doomed to disappear in a political upheaval after a few generations of economic growth and social modernization had brought into being new groups, classes and conflicts. Given their position on the near-periphery of industrial Europe and given the income from their growing oil production, the Middle Eastern states would undergo economic growth and social modernization and, therefore, political stress and strain comparable to that which had occurred on that earlier periphery on the eastern and southern fringes of Europe, including countries such as Greece and Turkey which obviously had much in common with the states of the Middle East.[2] Indeed, the oil wealth and the new means of mass communications would accelerate and accentuate the process in the Middle East compared to Europe. And here too there was a prototype, the military nationalist revolution that overthrew the Egyptian monarchy in 1952.

The issue, then, was a matter of timing. A US special relationship with a Middle East authoritarian monarchy would for a period clearly bring benefits to the US national interest, or at least to the USA's oil corporations' interests. On the oher hand, the inevitable modernization of the country, accelerated and accentuated by the very US government presence and US oil corporation royalties, would in turn bring the monarchy and probably the entire *ancien régime* to an end, and the special relationship along with it. It would, therefore, have been wise for US foreign policy officials, and in particular for the State Department and the Central Intelligence Agency, to anticipate that there would be this inevitable turn of the wheel of fate and to prepare for a less-special but still mutually beneficial relationship with the new revolutionary regime. Another great 'transnational' institution, the Roman Catholic Church, has often faced this problem with authoritarian regimes in the twentieth century and has developed some highly sophisticated modes of negotiating the transition.[3]

Indeed, the US did try, if rather fitfully, to work out good arrangements with the new revolutionary regime in Egypt after 1952 (but it had been the British, not the Americans, that had had a special relationship with the Egyptian monarchy). But in 1953 the USA also acted decisively in Iran to bring about a second coming of a authoritarian monarchy, that of the shah, which would last for another twenty-five years. And it was the Iranian, rather than the Egyptian, model that the USA would follow in later years.

It was probably too much to expect the State Department and the Central Intelligence Agency, wholly human institutions and relatively inexperienced ones at that, to develop an historical consciousness comparable to that of the Roman Catholic Church. And even if they had, the immediate interests of the oil corporations would have been sufficient to return their minds to the comfortable grooves of the special relationships.[4]

Thus, over the twenty-five years after 1953, US foreign policy officials developed a close association with and support of a number of Middle East monarchies. Among these were a special relationship with the Iraqi monarchy of King Faisal II in the 1950s, the Libyan monarchy of King Idris in the 1960s and the Iranian monarchy of the shah from the 1950s until 1978. (A similar special relationship existed, outside the Middle East proper but within close geographic proximity, with the Ethiopian monarchy of Emperor Haile Sellasie from the 1950s until 1974.) In each case, US foreign policy officials looked upon the monarchy as conservative in its domestic policy, pro-American and anti-Soviet in its foreign policy, and enduring in its political prospects. In each case, these officials assured skeptics and critics in Congress and in the public that the relationship was a fundamental and durable asset to the USA. And in each case, these officials were utterly surprised when a radical military coup or a popular revolution, a sudden storm out of the desert, swept away the old regime and replaced it with something like its opposite. Such was the case with Iraq in 1958, Libya in 1969, Ethiopia in 1974 and, of course, Iran in 1978. In the first three cases, the country changed almost overnight from being one of the most pro-American countries in the region into being one of the most pro-Soviet. And in the last case, Iran, it merely changed into being one of the most anti-American.

The surprise of US foreign policy officials was least excusable in the case of Iran. In 1971 Henry Kissinger, then the National Security Assistant to President Nixon, had encouraged the shah to raise oil prices substantially in the Tehran agreements of that year. Kissinger imagined that a shah rich with oil revenues and armed with US weapons would be able to play the role of a most loyal ally, a pillar or policeman of the Persian Gulf. And in any event, high oil prices were to the advantage of the USA's greatest economic interests: the oil corporations which would also receive higher profits at the same time that the OPEC governments were receiving higher royalties; the international banks which would receive the petrodollar deposits from OPEC governments; and the aerospace corporations which would receive new arms contracts from the shah and the Saudis to compensate for the ones disappearing with the winding down of the USA's combat role in Indochina.[5]

The sharp rise in oil revenues in Iran, however, brought about the very political instability that it was supposed to prevent. The conjunction of rapid economic change, great social strain and a narrow-minded, corrupt and arbitrary imperial regime made political turmoil highly likely. Iran in the late 1970s was a timebomb ticking away, an accident waiting to happen.[6] Yet President Carter visited the shah on 31 December 1977 and declared that the shah was an island of stability. And his National Security Assistant, the facile and superficial Zbigniew Brzezinski, tried until the very end to bring about more repression by the Iranian military in order to keep the Shah of Iran in power.[7]

THE FUTURE OF THE PERSIAN GULF MONARCHIES: FROM SAUDI ARABIA TO QADDAFI ARABIA

Given this doleful history of authoritarian monarchies in the Middle East, the political prospects for the Saudi royal family or for the sheiks of the Persian Gulf would seem to be rather bleak. And similarly, a US foreign policy and an oil dependency based upon the continuation of the Saudi monarchy or the Gulf sheikdoms for more than a half-dozen years would seem to be rather reckless.

Historical comparisons are not the only reason to be dubious about the future of the Saudis and the sheiks, however; the present internal conditions of the countries suggest that they are even more prone to political instability now than were Iraq, Libya, Ethiopia, or Iran in an earlier day. For under the impact of the explosion of oil revenues and the consequent rapid economic expansion and urban growth, these monarchies have become polarized, even pulverized societies. Each now contains large foreign minorities (and in some urban centers, large foreign majorities), composed of Palestinians and Yemenis, who perform crucial tasks in the economies, but who are not well integrated into the societies, and who have little or no loyalty to the traditional polities. At minimum, these Palestinian and Yemeni minorities advocate policies which inevitably will be opposed from time to time to policies of the USA. But these minorities also form the potential base for a radical coup or popular uprising which could sweep away the monarchies and install yet another anti-American or even pro-Soviet regime.

Rapid economic expansion and urban growth does not only generate political threats from foreign minorities, however. As the case of Iran (and earlier the case of Libya) demonstrates, massive oil revenues and the social and economic disruptions they produce can also generate political threats from the traditional local population.

These internal conditions provide additional reasons why a US foreign policy and an oil dependency based upon the continuation of the Saudi monarchy or the Gulf sheikdoms is reckless. Indeed, by the mid-1980s it is more likely that there will be a 'Qaddafi Arabia' than there will be a Saudi Arabia.[8]

Even if these monarchies should continue to survive, however, it is not at all obvious that they will continue to be pro-American. The increasing vulnerability of the Saudis and the sheiks to these various political threats, be they from Palestinian nationalists, Islamic revivalists, or radical military officers, will cause the monarchies to search for ways to revive their waning political legitimacy. And this will cause them to employ 'the oil weapon' against the USA in order to achieve foreign policies aims, such as those in the Arab-Israeli conflict, and to employ this weapon even more frequently in the future than in the past. And they might add to the oil weapon, 'the money weapon' based upon their enormous holdings of dollars, which can be withdrawn quickly from US financial institutions.[9]

The Arab oilproducers, and even especially the conservative Arab monarchies, have already employed an oil embargo against particular Western countries during each of the last three Arab-Israeli wars. The first two efforts, in 1956 and 1967, are little remembered in the West, because they were totally ineffective. But by 1973 conditions in the world oil market had greatly changed, and the embargo of 1973–4 is very well remembered indeed.

Since 1974, US foreign policy officials have tried to cultivate the largest producer of all, the Saudis, with a variety of extraordinary policies: these have included the sales of advanced weapons systems, beginning with F-5E fighter-bombers and Maverick air-to-ground missiles in 1976 and culminating with F-15s, the 'top-of-the-line' fighter, in 1978. They have also included military aid in support of dubious Saudi foreign policy enterprises in Yemen and a number of statements in support of this or that Saudi position in the Arab-Israeli conflict. Each time, US policymakers defended these unusual or, in the case of the advanced weapons sales, even radical foreign policy departures as the means by which the Saudis would be brought to cooperate with the USA on oil prices and on the Egyptian-Israeli peace efforts.

However, these pro-Saudi policies and the 'special relationship' seem to have been of no use at all during the oil crisis of 1979. Where were the Saudis when we really needed them? Rather, the Saudis employed the oil weapon again. Opposed to the new peace arrangements between Egypt and Israel, and to the USA role in them, the Saudis cut back their oil production by about 15 percent in March 1979 at a time when the world oil market was already extraordinarily tight, in part because of the earlier drop in Iranian oil production. As Saudi Finance Minister Abalkhail explained it,

The question of a comprehensive peace treaty that recognizes Palestinian rights and returns the Moslem holy places in East Jerusalem is so important to us, so emotionally felt by us, that other problems disappear. Obviously, we would give you more oil.[10]

It is likely that the Arab oilproducers, including Saudi Arabia, will use the oil weapon even more frequently and under more normal circumstances in the future than they have in the past. As the Saudi behavior in 1979 demonstrates, they will uses the oil weapon not only in an Arab-Israeli war, but also against an Arab-Israeli peace. And although the peace agreements between Egypt and the Israelis may do much to reduce the probability of a fifth Arab-Israeli war, Egypt too is subject to much of the same political instability that we have observed elsewhere in the Middle East. A post-Sadat regime may calculate its interests rather differently. And if those calculations or if some other conjunction of circumstances should issue in yet another Arab-Israeli war, it is a virtual certainty that the USA would be the object of yet another Arab oil embargo, as it has been in the past.

THE SOVIET SPHERE OF INFLUENCE AND AN AUTHORITARIAN MONARCHY: FROM ZAHIR'S AFGHANISTAN TO SOVIET AFGHANISTAN

It was also in the early 1950s, about the time of the restoration of the Shah of Iran, that a process began in yet another authoritarian monarchy, Afghanistan, that would reach full development in the late 1970s and would alter the geopolitical landscape in the Middle East. For more than a century the British and the Russians had contested each other in 'the great game', vying for influence in Afghanistan, the commanding heights of the subcontinent. With the withdrawal of British influence from the region, the Americans stepped into their place. But the USA, like the British before them, of course never developed a special relationship with King Zahir, but rather shared influence with the USSR.

Internationally, the Afghanistan of King Zahir was a buffer state of a rather curious sort, one in which the Soviets, by virtue of geographical proximity, had roughly two-thirds the foreign presence and the Americans had roughly one-third. Internally, Afghanistan was one of the least developed countries in the world. But it, too, was undergoing modernization. The king, like every centralizing and modernizing monarchy in other countries before him, needed an expanded cadre of bureaucrats, which meant that he needed educated persons. But, as has been often pointed out, the natural ideology of newly educated men in newly developing countries, is Marxism.[11] Had Afghanistan been a few hundred miles further away from the USSR, and had the Soviet presence in the country been less prominent, the king and his officials might have met the problem of Marxist youths with sustained repression. But given Afghanistan's Soviet connection, this was not feasible. Thus it was inevitable that the Afghan monarchy, like other authoritarian monarchies, would be overthrown (as happened in 1973), and thus it was inevitable that there would be a substantial urban Marxist movement which would bid for complete power (as happened in 1978). From the mid-1950s, Afghanistan and its delicate international position was another timebomb ticking away, an accident waiting to happen.

Given the nature of the Soviet and American foreign aid (centered in the cities), however, it was also natural that Afghanistan would become an extreme case of 'uneven development', with a great chasm between urban Marxist revolutionaries and rural Islamic revivalists. And so the Marxists would seize power in the cities long before they had developed the strength with which to exercise it effectively in the countryside.[12] The Marxist regimes of Taraki and Amin (1978–9), then, were by themselves doomed to defeat and collapse, and the only issue was what would be the response to this of the USSR?

An argument can be made that the USSR was bound to undertake military intervention to preserve a Marxist regime in Afghanistan. The power and legitimacy of the communist regime in the USSR itself is threatened when a communist government is overthrown by a popular revolt or movement in a Soviet ally. Thus, the Soviet military interventions in East Germany in June 1953, Hungary in November 1956 and Czechoslovakia in August 1968.

These earlier interventions suggest something about the particular timing of the Afghan intervention in December 1979, however. In each case, the Soviet 'problem' with its ally had been growing for some time, yet the moment that the Soviets invaded was one when the West was diverted and engaged elsewhere (concluding the armistice negotiations in the Korean War in 1953; the Suez crisis in 1956; the turmoil surrounding the anti-war protests and the Democratic National Convention in 1968). Similarly, the Soviets invaded Afghanistan when the relationships between the USA and Iran and Pakistan, the two countries most immediately threatened by the Afghan intervention, had never been worse (the occupation of the US embassy in Tehran and the burning of the US embassy in Islamabad both having occurred in November 1979).

Conversely, an argument can be made that the USSR only undertook this first direct military intervention outside its own alliance system (the Warsaw Pact), because the policies of the Carter administration, such as the Soviet brigade in Cuba affair of September 1979 and the NATO missile-buildup decision of December 1979, had already convinced the Soviets that détente was defunct and that they had nothing left to lose by alienating the West.

Whatever the Soviet calculations before undertaking the Afghan intervention, the potential consequences for the future of the Middle East are momentous. By occupying Afghanistan, the Soviets for the first time pose a threat to the oil states and the vital straits of the Persian Gulf. The threat is double; first, after the Soviets consolidate their hold on Afghanistan, they will be able to launch (or more practically seem to threaten to launch) a *blitzkrieg* attack and occupation of the oilfields and the straits. Secondly, the Soviets can employ the Baluchis in Afghanistan to bring about subversion and turmoil in the Baluchi regions of Iran and Pakistan, which overlook the straits and the Arabian Sea.

If there were ever to develop again a severe diplomatic and military confrontation between the USA and the USSR, analogous to the Berlin crises of 1948, 1958 and 1961, or to the Cuban missile crisis of 1962, the Soviets would not necessarily have to undertake some variety of nuclear action or a conventional attack on Western Europe in order to impose a great cost on the USA and its allies. Given the existing structure of oil dependency, merely an attack on the oiltankers going through the narrow straits of the Persian Gulf would be quite enough to throw the economies of the USA, Europe, and Japan into turmoil and, in some cases, into collapse.

America's industrial allies will begin to assimilate this new fact of economic life, indeed 'internalize' it in the sense that it will become a factor in the internal politics of some West European states, in particular France and West Germany. The new 'brooding omnipresence' of Soviet military power over Western Europe's oil supply will reinforce the established network of West European trade and loans with the Soviet bloc. But while the existing trade and loans make coexistence, or appeasement if you will, of the USSR a convenience, the new power configuration in the Persian Gulf may make it a necessity. It would be an odd while ominous twist of history, if the path to Findlandization should turn out to lead through the hot sands of the Persian Gulf.

US POLICY RESPONSES TO IRAN AND AFGHANISTAN

Can the USA respond to the new conditions created by the recent events in Iran and Afghanistan with positive foreign policies which will lead the Western Alliance to a new equilibrium? Let us consider briefly policies in three dimensions: diplomatic, military and economic.

The Diplomatic Dimension: an Opening to Revolutionary Iran

American policymakers have never found it easy to deal with revolutionary regimes. This has been most obviously true of communist ones, where it has sometimes taken fifteen years (Russia) or even thirty years (China) to even establish diplomatic relations with the no-longer-new communist government. But it has even been true of non-communist revolutionary regimes, such as those in Mexico and China in the 1910s and 1920s and in Egypt and Indonesia in the 1950s and early 1960s. Under the best of circumstances, then, it probably would have been difficult for US policymakers to deal with the Islamic revolutionaries in Iran. In any event, the Iranian taking of the American hostages and the holding of them for more than a year, and the reciprocal US freezing of Iranian assets have placed massive impediments in the way of any establishment of normal relations between the USA and Iran, perhaps for years to come.

Yet a useful perspective on revolutionary Iran might be gained, if we look back on those earlier cases of revolutionary regimes and of US opposition to them. In most of the cases, the revolutionaries naturally tried for a time to export their revoluion (the Soviets through the Comintern in the 1910s–1920s, the Chinese Kuomintang in Indochina in the 1920s–1930s, the Chinese communists in Indochina in the 1950s–1970s, the Egyptians in the Arab world in the 1950s–1960s, the Indonesians in Malaysia in the 1960s, as did the Iranians in Iraq in 1979–80). But in most of the cases, these export efforts or revolutions from abroad failed, and the revolution ended up contained within the country where it began. Even the Chinese communist 'success' in Indochina ended by creating a formidable Vietnamese communist enemy of China. The only real successes were those of the USSR, but these were the result not of its revolutionary momentum in the 1920s, when its efforts failed everywhere except in Mongolia, but of its military force as a traditional great power at the end of World War II. These earlier cases suggest, then, that the Islamic revolution of Iran will end up contained within Iran itself, or that at most, its appeal will be limited to Shi'ite minorities within neighboring countries.

In addition, in these earlier cases, the revolutionary momentum ebbed away after the death of the original revolutionary leader, if not earlier, and indeed in the non-communist cases the revolutionary regime was replaced by a conservative military one (Mexico, Kuomintang China, Egypt and Indonesia). This suggests that after death of Ayatollah Khomeini, the Islamic revolutionaries are likely to lose power to military figures. This is even more likely to happen as the Iranian-Iraqi war produces young, battle-proven officers with their own ideas about what Iranian salvation means and their own supporters to bring it about.

Finally, in all but one of the earlier cases, US policymakers eventually came to the realization that there was no fundamental conflict of interest between the USA and the once-revolutionary country and, indeed, that the USA had a major and substantial interest in the territorial integrity of the country and in a strong and stable central government within it. The exception is the USSR, but here the continuing conflict again results from the fact that the USSR is a great power deploying great military forces. (And, of course, no US policymakers complained in 1941–5 about the presence of a strong and stable central government in Moscow or its efforts to maintain its territorial integrity.)

These considerations suggest that a few years hence political analysts will probably agree that there is then no fundamental conflict of interest between the USA and Iran and indeed that, without the holding of the hostages and the freezing of the assets, there need not have been a fundamental conflict in 1979–81. Washington and Tehran each have and will continue to have a substantial interest in an Iran that is unified under a strong and stable central government and is exporting a steady flow of oil of the order of 4–6 million barrels a day. America's European allies recognized these realities about Iran very early. In part, of course, this was because they had no occupied embassy or captured hostages at stake; in part, it was because they are usually more sage and seasoned in dealing with the ebbs and flows of revolutionary enthusiasms; and in part, it was because their economic self-interests were more dependent upon Iranian good will.

The Military Dimension: an Off-Shore Military Capacity

There seems to be general agreement in the USA at present on the need to build up the US military presence in the Persian Gulf region. But it is not yet clear what concretely that presence should be. As we have noted, the political instability of Middle Eastern countries earlier issued in the overthrow of the Iraqi monarchy in 1958 (with the Baghdad Pact being expelled from Baghdad), the overthrow of the Libyan monarchy in 1969 (with the USA being expelled from a prime airbase) and the overthrow of the Iranian monarchy in 1978 (with 20,000 US military advisers and technicians being expelled). A similar fate is likely to strike Somalia or Oman or Saudi Arabia, which now appear to be the most promising hosts for US military bases (or 'service facilities' as they are now politely called), sometime in the next half-decade or so. Accordingly, if such US military bases are to be established, they should also be expendable, perhaps seen as interchangeable parts for each other.

There might be a significantly lower probability of expulsion of certain West European military forces than of US ones. The French, for example, still maintain a base in Djibouti (the former French Somaliland). The British might regain one in Kenya or even in the sheikdoms of the Persian Gulf, and the Italians one in Somalia. As for the USA, it would be wiser for it to pursue a policy of off-shore military facilities. This would take the form of the establishment of a permanent Fifth Fleet, operating in the Arabian Sea and based in the British Indian Ocean Territory (Diego Garcia), a place distinguished by little land and less local population.

The Economic Dimension: A Policy of Oil Proliferation

In the longer run and in the more fundamental sense, the USA should move decisively in leading the Western Alliance away from its extreme dependence upon Persian Gulf oil. The topic of alternative sources of energy has, of course, generated a vast literature in the last decade, and I shall not discuss it here.[13] There is, however, some value in a brief examination of a policy of *oil proliferation*, that is, the US government encouraging exploration and exploitation of new sources of oil outside the Persian Gulf or outside the Middle East more generally, with these new sources to be not only in the USA, but in other countries as well.[14]

The five largest US international oil corporations, the 'majors', are Exxon, Mobil, Socal, Texaco and Gulf. The first four also form Aramco, which draws oil from Saudi Arabia; Gulf draws much of its oil from Kuwait. These five majors have little incentive to bring on line new sources of oil outside the Middle East which would undercut their present highly profitable structure of limited production and high price. Rather, US government policy should be to encourage oil companies other than the majors to undertake exploration and exploitation for oil within countries which are outside the Middle East.

Mexico, with massive oil reserves and its own state oil company, Pemex, offers a model for a policy of oil proliferation. Mexican political leaders will find it in their interest within a couple of years to export 3 million or more barrels a day. Mexico's large and rapidly growing population and its need for massive capital for economic development will probably propel Mexican policymakers toward maximum sustainable oil exports, despite their current hesitations.

American imports of this Mexican oil, for both ongoing consumption and for filling the Strategic Petroleum Reserve in Louisiana and Texas, would go far toward reducing US dependence upon Middle East oil. Indeed, it would probably be feasible for US policymakers to offer Pemex the opportunity to distribute and retail within the USA, in return for long-term supply contracts and perhaps significant price reductions.

Other likely countries for new oil exploration and exploitation include Argentina, Columbia, Peru, Zaire, Namibia, Bangladesh, Burma and China. And likely companies could include large US oil firms other than the majors, perhaps for example Arco, Phillips, Union and Getty, as well as certain state oil companies, such as that of Argentina. The US government could offer a variety of financial incentives and guarantees in support of agreements between such countries and companies, such as loans, enhanced expropriation insurance, and long-term purchase contracts (for example, for oil for the Strategic Petroleum Reserve). And it could offer these directly through its own institutions, such as the Export-Import Bank or the foreign aid program, or indirectly through the World Bank and various regional development banks.

The probability of US policymakers adopting a policy of oil proliferation is low, however. Indeed, in early 1979 Exxon and other majors succeeded in persuading Treasury Secretary Michael Blumenthal to oppose a World Bank proposal for a special fund which would finance exploration and exploitation of new sources of oil in less-developed countries.[15]

If there is to be significant development of new oil sources outside the Middle East, the leadership may have to be taken by the national oil corporations of the West European nations. But here, too, the probability of adopting a policy of oil proliferation is rather low. The British, French and Western German governments each have an interest in preserving high oil prices: the British because of their North Sea oil, the French because of their massive investments in nuclear power and the Germans because of their massive investments in both nuclear power and in coal.

The most likely outcome, then, is that the Western Alliance will remain greatly dependent upon Persian Gulf oil, and thus upon the fates of the Islamic world and the will of the USSR. The revolutions to come against the monarchies of the Persian Gulf will periodically disrupt the flow of oil to the West and aggravate the disorder in its economies. The 'brooding omnipresence' of the Soviet military over the Persian Gulf will gradually deflect the course of West European internal politics and foreign policies. And the potential conjunction of the two, of Middle East revolutions and Soviet military power, of the legacies of Iran and of Afghanistan, could mean one day a Soviet military intervention in a Persian Gulf state to preserve a Marxist revolutionary regime. And the perennial Middle East crises of our own time would come more and more to resemble those perennial Near Eastern, that is, Balkan, crises in the last years before 1914.[16]

NOTES: CHAPTER 7

1 On the origins of the American relationship with King Saud, see: J. B. Kelly, *Arabia, the Gulf and the West* (New York Basic Books, 1980), ch. V; John M. Blair, *The Control of Oil* (New York: Panther Books, 1976), ch. 2; and US Senate Subcommittee on Multinational Corporations, Committee on Foreign Relations, *Multinational Oil Corporations and US Foreign Policy* (Washington, DC: US Government Printing Office, 1975).

2 On the political vulnerability of authoritarian monarchies in modernizing societies, see Samuel P. Huntington, *Political Order in Changing Societies* (New Haven, Conn.: Yale University Press, 1968), ch. 3. I have discussed the authoritarian monarchies of Eastern and Southern Europe in the 1910s–1940s in my 'Industrial change and political change: a European perspective', in David Collier (ed.) *The New Authoritarianism in Latin America* (Princeton, NJ: Princeton University Press, 1979), pp. 319–62.

3 On the Roman Catholic Church as a transnational organization, see Samuel P. Huntington, 'Transnational organizations and world politics', *World Politics*, vol. XXV, no. 3 (April 1973), pp. 333–68.

4 On the American oil corporations in the Middle East, see Kelly, *Arabia, the Gulf and the West*, op. cit., chs V–VIII; Blair, *The Control of Oil*, chs 2–5, 11–13; US Senate Subcommittee on Multinational Corporations *Multinational Oil Corporations and US Foreign Policy*, op. cit.; and Anthony Sampson, *The Seven Sisters: The Great Oil Companies and the World They Shaped* (New York: Viking, 1975).

5 V. H. Oppenheim, 'Why oil prices go up. The past: we pushed them', *Foreign Policy*, no. 25 (Winter 1976–7), pp. 24–57.

6 Kelly, *Arabia, the Gulf and the West*, op. cit., ch. VI. A summary statement is his 'Of valuable oil and worthless policies', *Encounter*, vol. LII no. 6 (June 1979), pp. 14–80.

7 William H. Sullivan, 'Dateline Iran: the road not taken', *Foreign Policy*, no. 40 (Fall 1980), pp. 175–86.

8 On the prospects for the Saudi monarchy, see Kelly, *Arabia, the Gulf and the West*, op. cit., and 'Of valuable oil and worthless policies', op. cit.

9 The potential financial and consequent political power of Arab oilproducers is analysed in 'Arab banks grow: a tool to control the world's capital', *Business Week*, 6 October 1980, pp. 70–84.

10 Quoted in 'OPEC: the cartel's deadly new sting', *Business Week*, 9 April 1979, p. 98.

11 Adam B. Ulam, *The Unfinished Revolution: An Essay on the Sources of Influence of Marxism and Communism* (New York: Vintage Books, 1964).

12 On the conflict between city and countryside in revolutions, see Huntington, *Political Order in Changing Societies*, op. cit., ch. 5.

13 A useful analysis of alternative sources of energy is presented in Barry Commoner, *The Politics of Energy* (New York: Knopf, 1979); I have discussed the topic in my testimony in 'Hearings on Alternatives to Dealing with OPEC', US House of Representatives Subcommittee on Environment, Energy and Natural Resources, Committee on Government Operation, US House of Representatives, 96th Congress, 20 June 1979 (Washington, DC: US Government Printing Office, 1979) pp. 70–90.

14 On the possibilities of oil proliferation, see Arnold E. Safer, *International Oil Policy* (Lexington, Mass.: D. C. Heath (Lexington Books), 1979), chs 3 and 9; and World Bank, *A Program to Accelerate Petroleum Production in the Developing Countries* (Washington DC: January 1979).

15 This incident is described in a report of the US General Accounting Office, 'Issues related to foreign oil supply diversification' (Washington, DC: 31 May 1979), esp. appendix I. Documentation is given in 'Capping third world gushers', *Nation*, vol. 229, no. 3 (28 July–4 August 1979), pp. 68–9.

16 An excellent comparative analysis of the period before World War I and the contemporary period is Miles Kahler, 'Rumors of war: the 1914 analogy', *Foreign Affairs*, vol. 58, no. 2 (Winter 1979–80) pp. 374–96.

8 New Directions for Soviet Middle East Policy in the 1980s: Implications for the Atlantic Alliance

FRANCIS FUKUYAMA

INTRODUCTION

In the decade of the 1970s Soviet policy in the Middle East has had to contend with the central fact that during 1972–4 Moscow was closed out of the Middle Eastern heartland. Cairo's defection to the US camp was a substantial blow to Soviet prestige, and became a seminal event affecting much of subsequent Soviet policy. Since that time the Soviets have had to face two different sorts of problem. The first concerned what one might call the short-term quantitative problem of either restoring earlier Soviet influence in Egypt, or else finding compensation with new positions elsewhere. The second was a longer-term difficulty that had to do with the 'quality' of influence, namely, how secure and make permanent Moscow's presence such that the expulsion from Egypt was not repeated elsewhere and, generally, how to increase the degree of control over clients such that the allies Moscow had could be of greater use to its foreign policy.

The Soviets' attempted solution to the first of these problems has been reasonably straightforward and generally recognized by most observers. After Henry Kissinger's intent to exclude Moscow through step-by-step diplomacy became clear with the initial disengagement agreements in January and May of 1974, the Soviets attempted to block the bilateral diplomacy by throwing greater support to the radical Arab camp whose interests were also threatened by Kissinger's approach. In 1974–5 Moscow greatly upgraded its commitment to Syria and the PLO, and to yet more radical rejectionists like Libya and Iraq. By calling for a return to a comprehensive Geneva peace conference that would include both the Syrians and Palestinians, Moscow hoped to force Cairo to abandon its efforts to seek a settlement through the USA, and to demonstrate to the other Arab parties that its support was crucial to their objectives. At best, Moscow might hope to be restored to its previous role in Egypt; at worst, it could expect to hold onto existing positions in Syria and with the PLO. The loss of Egypt substantially increased Moscow's incentive to increase the visibility of its presence in what had formerly been rather marginal countries like South Yemen, and to seize upon opportunities to obtain new clients even further afield (as in Africa) where they arose. Soviet success in solving the tactical problems raised by Egypt's defection have been limited; while

Syria and the Palestinians were prevented from following Sadat down the path to a US-mediated piecemeal solution, the Soviets were unable either to prevent the final conclusion of an Egypt-Israeli peace treaty, or to force a return to Geneva.

But the most important shift in Soviet strategy, and the one with the greatest implication for the future, has come in response to the second problem regarding the 'quality' of Soviet influence. Since 1975 a shift in Soviet Middle East policy has been evident, making use of local communist parties and direct force projection as a means of increasing Moscow's political control over the internal politics of its clients, and to ensure the greater permanence of its influence. This shift does not represent a new strategy in the traditional geopolitical sense as much as a different mode of operations designed to take better advantage of existing opportunities. This chapter will begin with an overview of the traditional mode of Soviet behavior in the Middle East as it evolved in the two decades between 1955 and 1975, with special reference to its difficult experience in Egypt and Iraq. It will then analyze the steps that the Soviets have taken over the past half-decade to ensure that their expulsion from Egypt would not be repeated elsewhere, and will conclude with a discussion of the implications of this shift for the Western Alliance. Seen in this light, Moscow's intervention in Afghanistan was not as precedent-breaking as Western commentaries made it seem at the time, but rather came as the logical culmination of a broader trend that has been visible for the preceding four or five years.

THE SOVIET EXPERIENCE IN EGYPT AND IRAQ

Up until the late 1970s, one could make several generalizations about the nature of the Soviet presence in the Middle East. In the first place, Moscow's regional influence was anchored among left-wing nationalist regimes which, while often virulently anti-Western in temperament, sought to steer genuinely independent courses in foreign and domestic policy. Countries like Egypt, Iraq, Syria, Libya and Algeria could by no means be regarded as simple Soviet pawns or proxies, despite the fact that they frequently served Soviet purposes. All of them, for example, have shown an extreme reluctance to grant Moscow anything that could be regarded as basing rights on their territory.

Secondly, the Soviets have generally taken an arms-length approach to the internal politics of these countries. After a brief period in the late 1950s when Khrushchev tried to enhance the position of a number of Arab communist parties, and was badly burned in the process, the Soviets have learned to work with existing nationalist regimes, whatever their particular ideological complexion. The friendship and cooperation treaties signed with countries like Egypt and Iraq, all feature clauses prominently abjuring 'interference in each other's internal affairs'.

Thirdly, the primary vehicle for Soviet influence has been arms transfers. The one commodity in which the USSR possessed a significant comparative advantage over the West was in the export of technologically advanced weapons, which it was willing to trade in a hard-nosed fashion for political influence. But arms transfers proved to be an extremely clumsy instrument of leverage either because they tended to embroil Moscow in dangerous confrontations with the USA, or because the threat to withhold weapons was an ineffective source of control.

Finally, it proved that the Soviet position, even among its most long-standing clients, could be undermined totally by competitive outbidding by either the USA, or its European allies. This is, of course, what happened in Egypt between 1972 and 1975; but in Iraq as well, French efforts to establish a privileged position for themselves have resulted in an increased margin of maneuver for Baghdad *vis-à-vis* Moscow.

THE PROBLEM OF SOVIET INFLUENCE: THE CASE OF EGYPT

It is common for observers of the Middle East to remark in a tone of bemused irony the apparent paradox that, whereas the disastrous Arab defeat in 1967 led to a sudden and dramatic increase in the Soviet presence in Egypt, the relative Arab success in the October War resulted in their complete exclusion. The truth of the matter, however, is that there was no paradox: the Egyptian reversal of alliances after 1974 was a delayed reaction to the June War, which if anything, proves the validity of the traditional influence game. The Soviets undermined their own position initially by failing to prevent the 1967 defeat. They delayed their departure and even increased their presence by promising to make good the Arabs' territorial losses, but were unable to deliver on that promise six years and two wars later. The USA could outbid the USSR for Egypt's allegiance by, on the one hand, successfully blocking any attempt to win back the occupied territories through force of arms and, on the other, by offering to mediate their return in a negotiated settlement that excluded the USSR. The case of Egypt prior to 1974 demonstrated the genuine differences that emerged between Moscow and its leading left-wing nationalist client, and the relatively weak leverage the Soviets could exercise as a result of their arms-length attitude.

Soviet problems in Egypt revolved around Moscow's unwillingness to confront the USA on Egypt's behalf. While the June War created insistent Arab demands that prompt military action be taken, the same conflict had a sobering effect on the USSR, which all but guaranteed that nothing of the sort would occur. Not only did Moscow carefully avoid incitements of the sort that had led to the June War, but they took active measures to prevent the outbreak of a new conflict as well. The Soviets gingerly pushed Nasser toward a negotiated solution of the conflict through manipulation of arms supplies: they gave Egypt and Syria enough weapons to plausibly bargain for a favorable settlement, but not enough that Nasser would be tempted to go to war. This proved an impossible balance to strike. In January 1970 Nasser frankly threatened to defect to the US camp unless the USSR gave him greater support; the result was a substantial but grudging Soviet combat involvement during the 1970 war of attrition.

Moscow's participation observed very strict limits and was not sufficient to intimidate Israel or the USA into substantial concessions. The same drama played itself out again after the August 1970 ceasefire. The Soviets delayed on arms shipments and pressed for political negotiations, leading Anwar Sadat to finally expel the Soviet advisers in July 1972, and in effect threaten that if they did not allow him to go to war, he would turn directly to the Americans.[1]

The October War was the Soviets' last big chance to redeem themselves. Whatever gloomy connotations that conflict has for many Israelis, and whatever ancillary benefits the Soviets might have derived, it was not a success for Soviet arms. Despite the fact that Soviet military assistance prior to and during the war was quite generous in absolute amounts, militarily their efforts did little more than forestall another 1967-style defeat. The Soviets, after having pressed the Egyptians continuously to accept a ceasefire from the sixth hour of the war, failed to threaten to intervene until 24 October, by which time the fighting had all but died down and the USA had committed itself to a ceasefire by two votes in the UN. According to Sadat, it was not the Soviet threat to intervene that saved the trapped Egyptian Third Army, but Henry Kissinger. The USA had proved that it was, in his words, 'the world's greatest power', and the only one capable of extracting Israel from the rest of the Sinai. Egypt's radical shift of alliances after 1974 was a direct result of this judgment.[2]

Thus the Soviets were able to control neither the timing of Egypt's conflict with Israel, nor its ultimate outcome. It should be noted, however, that the weakness of the Soviet position was intimately related to the strength of the USA's commitments in the Middle East, and the strength of the USA's regional allies. Among the wrong or misleading conclusions being currently drawn from the Soviet failure in Egypt is the notion that the forces of nationalism will of themselves somehow rise up and drive out the USSR. This is often used as a justification for a more relaxed attitude toward Soviet Third World activities. In fact, precisely the opposite conclusion is warranted. While nationalist resentment against the prominent Soviet adviser presence in Egypt facilitated their departure, this was hardly the precipitating cause. The Soviet position was ultimately undermined, because the level of military support the Russians made available to the Arabs was simply insufficient to achieve their national purposes, given the fact that Moscow was unwilling to risk serious confrontation with the USA.

There is no automaticity to this process. The Soviets had to be persuaded not to risk confrontation, and had to be prevented from achieving any successes through means short of confrontation. Had the rapid Soviet rearmament of Egypt and Syria after 1967 managed to soften the US-Israeli position substantially, had the USA not actively resisted every Soviet escalation with an escalation of its own, Egypt might today still be a Soviet client. Weaning it away from the Soviet orbit was a drawn-out and costly process which absorbed the attention of US policymakers for prolonged periods and drew the USA into indirect participation in several wars. Future generations of Americans may decide that it is not worth paying such a price, but they should be careful not to delude themselves into thinking that the same result could be had for less.

THE PROBLEM OF SOVIET INFLUENCE: THE CASE OF IRAQ

The problems in Moscow's relationship with Baghdad have not been as visible as those with Egypt, but are quite significant none the less. They promise to loom even larger as Iraq grows in political importance and comes to take on the premier role among Arab states. While the Iraqi Ba'th has acted contrary to Moscow's wishes on numerous occasions since coming to power in 1968, the most serious differences have coincided with a period after 1975, when Iraq's relationship with France improved considerably. Paris has not yet supplanted Moscow as an armourer and out-side political patron, but has succeeded in eroding the Soviet position considerably around the edges.

France, of course, sought a special relationship with the oilproducing Arab states ever since the June War. Her first foothold in Iraq came in the late 1960s, when the Iraqi Ba'th was seeking foreign oildrilling technology to break the monopoly of the British-owned Iraq Petroleum Co. (IPC). The state-owned Iraqi National Oil Co. (INOC) used some French equipment to supplement an ongoing Soviet project to develop the large North Rumaila oilfield. When this was completed in 1972, the extra capacity allowed Baghdad to survive any possible retaliation by the Western oil companies when it nationalized the IPC's holdings in June of that year. The French contribution at that point was rather minor, and it was the Russians who walked off with the lion's share of the political benefits, in the form of the 1972 Iraqi-Soviet Friendship and Cooperation Treaty. But the French did prove their willingness to compete head-on with the Soviets for influence in Iraq by helping Baghdad to do things that were decidedly harmful to the interests of France's North Atlantic neighbors.

The real opening for the French did not come until 1975, however, when Soviet-Iraqi relations took a sudden turn for the worse. By then, the 1973–4 revolution in world oil prices had ended Iraq's status as an economic pariah and allowed it to begin accumulating substantial hard-currency reserves. These were used to make large purchases of capital equipment from the West; as one Iraqi explained, 'We have the money and so we can afford to buy the best'. Iraq's trade patterns shifted completely in the space of a year or two from heavy dependence on the Soviet bloc to an equally heavy dependence on the West. This apparent ingratitude rankled the Soviets, who were particularly defensive about the quality of their technology. But the most important development came when the Iraqis settled the war in Kurdistan by signing the Algiers Agreement with the Shah of Iran in April 1975. This seemed to be a cynical sellout of Iraq's anti-imperialist pretensions and drastically reduced Baghdad's need for Soviet weapons and spare parts. It foreshadowed a prolonged period of independent Iraqi foreign policy.

To forestall such a development, the Soviets in effect embargoed arms shipments to Iraq in late June and early July 1975, as they had done to Egypt the previous year.[3] The Iraqis, profiting from the Egyptian example, refused to give in to Soviet pressure and sought instead to diversify their sources of arms by offering to buy from the French. In September 1975 Saddam Hussein and the Chief of Staff Abd al-Jabber Shanshal paid a major state visit to France and negotiated an arms deal that was as large in its dollar volume as any of the agreements previously reached with the USSR. When deliveries began in 1978, the order included forty Mirage F-1s, forty SA-330L Puma and sixty SA-342K Gazelle helicopters, AMX-20P and AMX-30 armored vehicles, air-to-air, air-to-surface, anti-tank and surface-to-air missiles.[4]

The first round of arms agreements was supplemented by a second one in 1979, which included other European arms producers besides France. In May the Iraqi Defense Minister Adnan Khairallah toured the French and Spanish arms industries and indicated an interest in a volume of business that would enable Paris to supplant the USSR as Iraq's primary arms supplier by the early 1980s. While in France, he placed firm orders for $250 million worth of weapons· discussions initiated at that time could lead to total sales as high as $1·5–$1·6 billion in 1979 dollars. In Spain he held talks that reportedly envisaged a five-year purchase of weapons and warships worth some $900 million.[5] Soviet arms sales to Iraq, by contrast, have averaged $800 billion 1976 dollars a year over the last several years:[6]

	1973	1974	1975	1976	1977
US $billion (1976)	790	750	606	825	1043

Orders placed with France included a second squadron of forty Mirage F-1s, two 3,200-ton anti-submarine frigates, six Cherbourg-class fast patrol boats, Super-Frelon helicopters and a large number of AMX-30 main battle tanks. The Spanish were said to be negotiating the sale of factories to be set up in Iraq to manufacture small arms.[7]

There is no question but that Iraqi purchases of French weapons have brought them increased freedom of maneuver *vis-à-vis* Moscow. This was most evident in Baghdad's policy toward the Arab-Israeli conflict. Iraq has the distinction of being at the same time more extreme and, in a way, more moderate than Moscow in its posture toward Israel. On a rhetorical level, Baghdad's fanatical anti-Zionism has been an established feature of its own national identity ever since its failure to sign an armistice with Israel in 1948. Iraq's unconditional opposition to any sort of negotiations with Israel has run afoul of Moscow's efforts over the past decade to promote a comprehensive Geneva conference to settle the Arab-Israeli conflict. On the other hand, the Iraqi Ba'th has consistently used the very radicalness of its anti-Zionism as an excuse not to take concrete measures to aid the other Arab states in their confrontation with Israel. The Soviets have been urging the creation of a single Syrian-Iraqi-Palestinian 'Northern Front' for many years to little avail. The problem became the most acute following Sadat's trip to Jerusalem in November 1977. The 'Steadfastness and Confrontation Front' which was assembled in Tripoli, Libya, to block a bilateral Egypt-Israeli peace was disrupted by the Iraqis, who, as the only 'pure' anti-Zionists, demanded the impossible condition that Syria explicitly retract its acceptance of UN resolutions 242 and 338. The Soviets, who had strongly supported the activities of the Tripoli summit, were visibly angered by Iraq's behavior but found that they had very limited leverage with which to affect it. The Iraqis' French connection insulated them from further Soviet attempts to manipulate the arms pipeline, and in any case they had built up substantial stocks of Soviet spare-parts.[8] When Baghdad made an abrupt aboutface on the issue of cooperation with Syria in October 1978, following the signing of the Camp David agreements, it did so for reasons having to do with its relationship with Iran and not as a result of Soviet pressure.

French motives in pursuing their aggressive arms sale policy were not hard to discover. Proceeds from the transactions helped the French balance of payments situation and offset the sharply increased cost of oil coming from the Middle East. The French also increased the security of oil supplies in an overall 'package' deal with Baghdad: In March 1979 the Iraqis promised to supply France with an additional 100,000 barrels a day of oil, followed by a pledge for an additional 100,000 barrels a day in July.[9] Arms transfers on this scale permit the French to maintain and even expand their domestic weapons industry.

In building a priviledged relationship with Iraq, the French have arguably performed a useful service for the USA and for the rest of the Atlantic Alliance. France had done with regard to Iraq what the USA did in Egypt, albeit less dramatically: reduced its dependence on the USSR by satisfying certain of its needs and thereby undercut Moscow's ability to manipulate its foreign policy. This was a task the USA might have attempted to undertake itself (and might yet in the future), but which for a variety of reasons the French were better suited to carry out. After De Gaulle dropped France's ties to Israel in 1967, the French were free of any embarrassing connections which would have made the Iraqis less willing to collaborate with them. Moreover, to this day the French political system remains relatively free of those moral restraints that would have stood in the way of any US effort to woo the Iraqis out of the Soviet camp. The French, it can be argued, allow the USA to enjoy the best of all possible worlds, benefiting from Iraqi independence from the Soviet camp without, at the same time, having to alter their own commitment to Israel. Since the Soviets would have been willing to subsidize Iraqi behavior detrimental to Western interests anyway, why not have the subsidy come from a country which at times has been known to cooperate with the USA?

It is questionable whether France is fully capable of supplanting the USSR as the patron of a country like Iraq, however, even though the dollar value of its arms transactions may exceed those of the Soviets in certain years. Baghdad remains dependent on Moscow not only for the greater part of its arsenal, but for other vital aspects of its national security as well. As we saw in our analysis of the Soviet experience in Egypt, great power patronage and its resulting influence depends on much more than the routine provision of weapons. Moscow's standing in Egypt and Syria was related to its ability to mount massive and resupply efforts out of its own inventories, paid for either by long-term credits or given gratis. At other times it has had to bring its own military forces to bear directly on the Middle East, or else threaten more drastic countermeasures against the opposing superpower. France lacks the airlift, sealift, or logistics capability to perform any of these functions, and cannot afford to give away its weapons. A European power like France may hope to erode the influence of a superpower around the edges, but not actually occupy its place. In the end, France's real role may be to pave the way for an eventual replacement of Soviet influence in Iraq with that of the USA.

NEW MODES AND ORDERS OF SOVIET STRATEGY

The fact that the USA and France have been able to undercut the Soviet position in the Middle East has led many US observers to the conclusion that Soviet influence in the Third World is not much of a threat to Western interests, because it is everywhere weak and impermanent. Regardless of the specific countries in which the Soviets had influence, and the sorts of short-term diplomatic adjustments they could make to shove up their position, all such gains and losses would be in some sense fundamentally illusory, if the Russians could not improve the degree of control they exercised over their clients. For example, the Russians have for long been suspected of wanting to control the sources of oil in the Persian Gulf. However accurate this might be as a description of their intentions, it is hard to know how these designs could be implemented, if such 'control' were based on traditional clients like Egypt and Iraq. The inability of outside powers to control Third World nationalism is in accord with the general Western experience since World War II – it was a lesson learned by Britain and France at the time of Suez, and by the USA in Vietnam. The American reaction to its own difficulties has been chiefly to abjure further attempts to attain the degree of influence to which it once aspired, and to hope that other powers will do the same. But while the USSR has clearly undergone a similar rethinking of its Third World strategy in recent years, it is a mistake to assume that the conclusions it has reached are at all comparable to Western ones. While Moscow's objectives in areas like the Middle East have not changed, the tactics on operational style employed to achieve them have undergone a number of pronounced changes. These include:

An increased reliance on local communist parties rather than bourgeois nationalists. Since 1975, pro-Soviet Marxist-Leninist regimes have come to power in Angola, Ethiopia, Afghanistan and South Yemen, and there is evidence of an attempted communist takeover in Iraq. Under Stalin the USSR of course, relied almost entirely on local communists for influence in the then colonial or recently ex-colonial world. The use of 'non-aligned' bourgeois nationalists was an innovation that came about only with Khrushchev's rise to power. In retrospect it is doubtful that the Russians ever believed in the principle of non-alignment, but in the 1950s and 1960s they had little choice but to accommodate themselves to it for lack of power and alternatives. Certainly, their experience not only in Egypt and Iraq, but with countries like Syria, Algeria, Indonesia and Ghana, must have confirmed their distrust of bourgeois nationalists and reinforced their natural ideological proclivities in favor of orthodox Marxist-Leninists. Despite considerable differences that exist within the world Communist movement, the coming to power of a local communist party remains the best guarantee of that country's continuing loyalty and alignment. Such an emphasis on the part of the USSR does not, of course, signal an increased interest in ideology as such, but in the use of ideology for the pragmatic purposes of the Soviet state. The difference between the positions of these Marxist-Leninist groups and the bourgeois nationalists they replaced reflects a narrowing of the band of permissible deviation from Moscow's foreign policy objectives.

A much greater willingness to interfere in the affairs of client-states in order to achieve objectives of political control. A major, though largely unrecognized, instrument to achieve this end has been the East German *Ministerium für Staatsicherheit* (MfS), or state security service. The East Germans have been busy refurbishing the security apparatus of a number of African and Middle Eastern countries, including Angola, Mozambique, Guinea-Bissau, the PDRY and Sudan. MfS operations not only contribute to the consolidation of centralized Marxist-Leninist states, but provide the Soviets with up-to-date intelligence and a degree of previously unattainable political control.[10] The importance of direct police controls over local party apparatis should not be underestimated. One wonders, for example, whether Sadat would have been able to expel the Soviet advisers as he did in July 1972 had the East Germans been active in restructuring the Egyptian security service.

A vastly increased military infrastructure with which to influence regional and internal developments in the Third World. Instead of simply bartering arms for influence, the Soviets have acquired the means of applying direct military pressure. Such capabilities have existed for some years as potentialities, with the deployment of naval squadrons in the Mediterranean and Indian Ocean, and the creation of mobile airborne units with substantial airlift capacity. Their acutalization has undergone a continuous evolution over the past decade, beginning with the selective transfer of pilots and air-defense crews, continuing through the use of Cuban and East European proxies and culminating in the deployment of regular Soviet combat forces. The novel aspect of recent Soviet force projection has been its use against ostensible allies and clients. The first example of this was the staging of Cuban troops through South Yemen to Ethiopia, where they were used to fight the Somalis and Eritreans. Then in the summer of 1978 the Cubans were brought back from Ethiopia to help Abd al-Fattah Ismail suppress army factions loyal to Selim Rubia Ali in the PDRY. More recently, Soviet airborne divisions secured Kabul and toppled Hafizullah Amin in Afghanistan.

This new set of Soviet tactics has been visible here and there, as opportunities for their application arose, since 1975. The very problems we saw emerging between Moscow and the Iraqi Ba'th seem to have prompted Soviet encouragement of stepped-up activities by the Iraqi Communist Party in the winter of 1977–8. It is not clear whether the ICP was actually planning a putsch, or whether it was merely broadening its base in a routine fashion, but in any case the regime in Baghdad behaved as if a communist takeover was imminent. The ferocity and duration of the ensuing purge of ICP cadres in the army and elsewhere is difficult to explain, given Iraq's dependence on the USSR except as a response to what it believed was a genuine threat.[11] Indeed, a series of articles appeared in the Iraqi Ba'th Party newspaper *ath-Thawra* in January 1980 following the Soviet intervention of Afghanistan, which followed a line of analysis of Soviet foreign policy similar to the one presented above. The article took note of Moscow's difficulties with its bourgeois nationalist clients:

> There is speculation, and we hope that it will not prove true, that the Soviet Union is now seeking partners in a relationship to insure ideological and political expansion in the region, a method that it has found to be preferable to relations of superficial friendship with other parties. For these relations though based on friendship, progressiveness and a frank, sincere hostility to imperialism – do not guarantee the desired expansion.

The article went on to emphasize that recent Soviet involvement in Ethiopia, Afghanistan and the PDRY suggested a preference for local communists over the earlier class of allies:

> However, it appears that the Soviets have become interested and we hope that speculations to this effect also prove to be unfounded – not only in a party that is more sincere in its hostility to imperialism, a socialist and national party that is sincere in its respect for relations of friendship with the Soviet Union (i.e., the Iraqi Ba'th party or the UPONF under Rubai Ali), but in alternative parties that are inclined toward the USSR's short- and long-term strategy (i.e., Communists).[12]

While the ICP was not mentioned, the thrust of the paper's analysis clearly reflected the Ba'th Party's suspicions of Moscow's intentions toward itself.

The Case of Afghanistan

The most fully developed case in which the Soviets have sought to qualitatively alter the nature of their influence has been Afghanistan. While much of the world's attention has understandably been focused on the Soviet intervention of December 1979, the most revealing period from the standpoint of evaluating Soviet intentions was in fact the two or three years preceding the coup against Daud in April 1978.

Afghanistan first became a Soviet client in 1956 when, rebuffed by the USA, it signed an arms transfer agreement with the USSR. Since that time, its armed forces have been exclusively equipped by Moscow, and many of its officers indoctrinated in Marxist-Leninist ideology during their training in the USSR. That relationship continued after the monarchy of Zahir Shah was overthrown by his kinsman Mohammed Daud in 1973. Daud may be characterized as a left-wing nationalist of a sort common in the Arab world. He came to power with the help of one of the Afghan communist parties, Percham, whose services he quickly dispensed with once he consolidated his rule. (Among the leaders of Percham at the time was Babrak Karmal, the present president of Afghanistan installed by the Soviets.) Daud declared a socialist ideology for Afghanistan and undertook a number of half-hearted modernizing measures, most of which soon bogged down amidst inefficient administration and growing economic difficulties.[13]

It was in the field of foreign policy that Daud demonstrated his genuine independence of Moscow. Ever since the formation of Pakistan in 1947, governments in Kabul have contested the Durand line separating the two countries, because it left many of their kindred Pushtuns across the border in Pakistan's North West Frontier Province. A subsidiary issue was the Afghan demand to establish an independent Baluchistan out of parts of Pakistan and Iran. The Soviets found these irredenta useful for their own purposes, because they put pressure on two of the USA's regional clients. Daud himself during his first tenure as prime minister in 1953–63 stressed these nationalist claims, and raised them once again when he returned to power in 1973. But after a number of serious border incidents and mutual threats of war, Daud came to an understanding with Zulfikar Ali Bhutto of Pakistan in 1976 and agreed to respect Pakistan's territorial integrity. At the same time, Daud responded favorably to overtures from the Shah of Iran to improve relations between their two countries. The latter extended economic aid to Kabul, agreed to several joint agricultural projects, and began to construct a railroad link from Bandar Abbas to several important Afghan cities. In addition, the Iranian Savak was reported to have given Daud assistance in suppressing the two Afghan communist parties, Percham and Khalq. Daud went on to establish friendly relations with other pro-American Middle Eastern states, paying visits to both Egypt and Saudi Arabia in 1977.

These developments hurt Soviet interests in two ways, by removing an important source of leverage over Iran and Pakistan, and by reducing Kabul's overall economic dependence on the USSR. The rail-link to the Persian Gulf in particular was expressly designed to end Afghanistan's reliance on land routes through the USSR for its external trade. But what is noteworthy here is the fact that both of these developments can at best be described as inconveniences for Soviet foreign policy, rather than serious setbacks. They were within the range of the sort of dissidence that the USSR had previously tolerated among its Third World clients. For example, both Egypt under Nasser and Iraq under Saddam Hussein sought reconciliations with major ideological opponents, and both tried to broaden their economic base by seeking ties with pro-Western neighbors. There is no way that Daud's turn to the right in foreign policy could be construed as a serious threat to Soviet security: He did not, for example, attempt to arm his military with US weapons in place of Soviet ones, or enter into a military agreement with his pro-Western neighbors. The fact that Moscow was none the less unwilling to tolerate his actions indicates the more demanding standards that the Soviets now seem to apply to their Third World clients.

Daud was overthrown by Percham and Khalq in a coup on 27–8 April 1978, in which Perchami influence over the Soviet-trained officer corps was crucial. A Soviet role in the coup has been denied altogether by some, but it seems clear from the circumstantial evidence that, while Moscow played no part in the planning in a tactical sense, its overall support was instrumental in bringing it about. The takeover was precipitated by the murder of a prominent leftist, Mir Akbar Khyber, which led to massive demonstrations by sympathizers at his funeral on 19 April. Daud's ensuing crackdown on leftist leaders prompted the Khalq strongman, Hafizullah Amin, to order his friends in the armed forces to act. The coup itself was, therefore, hastily planned and executed. The fact that this particular sequence of events was not foreseen by either Moscow, or the Afghan communists, has been taken by some as proof that the Soviets neither planned, nor desired it.[14] Yet to conclude this is to misunderstand the nature of the relationship between the CPSU leadership in Moscow and its allied parties in the Third World. The Soviets do not have the power to order takeovers at particular times and places; what they can do is to encourage local communists with advice and promises of future support once they come to power. By some accounts, Moscow pressured Khalq and Percham to form a united front with the help of the Communist Party of India and the Iraqi Communist Party in May 1977, after the rightist trend of Daud's foreign policy became evident. There is also some speculation that Soviet pilots flew the planes used to bomb the presidential palace during the takeover itself.[15] In any case, the sequence of events following the coup is more revealing of the USSR's prior intentions: Moscow recognized the new government of Nur Mohammed Taraki instantly, Soviet military and economic advisers entered the country in large numbers, and in November 1978 Taraki signed a Friendship and Cooperation Treaty with the USSR.

The difficulties that Moscow encountered with the regime in Kabul after April 1978 were of a totally different order than what it had faced before. The disagreements were not on the level of ideology or substantive policy, but over tactics and implementation. Shortly after coming to power the Khalqis began purging the Perchamis, and many prominent leftists, including the Vice-President Babrak Karmal, were forced to flee the country. Khalq strongman Hafizullah Amin pushed through what the Russians regarded as an '.nfantile' left-wing communist program in the context of Afghanistan, declaring a radical land reform program, abolition of dowries and the education of women. By the fall of 1978, this had already led to substantial unrest among tribal groups and conservative Muslim elements. A major uprising in the western city of Herat in March 1979 was followed by serious deterioration in the 100,000-man Afghan army over the summer. This prompted the Soviets to prod Taraki and Amin to broaden their base of support in August, by some reports even advising them to take members of the old royal family into a coalition government.[16] When this proved unavailing, Moscow appears to have attempted to play off Taraki against the hardline Amin. Taraki seems to have been on the verge of purging Amin, when the latter preemptively purged him in a shootout in the presidential palace. Amin subsequently demanded the recall of the Soviet ambassador, Alexander Pusanov, whom he accused of complicity in the plot to unseat him.

In many respects, the Soviet intervention of December 1979 was much easier to explain in terms of traditional defensive concerns than was Moscow's involvement in the April 1978 coup that brought Taraki and Amin to power. Had the tribal rebellion succeeded in overthrowing the Khalqi regime, Soviet interests would have been affected in several fairly serious ways. In the first place, the Soviets had invested considerable prestige in the existence and survival of a Red Afghanistan. The Khalqis were a virtually unknown faction in April 1978 and their suppression by Daud would have passed unnoticed and unmourned by most of the world, whereas by late 1979 they had been elevated to the status of a major Third World client. The Soviets would have looked very weak if they could not protect a socialist regime on their southern border from a revolt by primitive tribesmen. Secondly, were Taraki and Amin to be overthrown, any Islamic regime established in their place would most likely be fanatically anti-Soviet and hostile, probably for decades. Such a state would probably turn to the West for arms and economic aid, and might go so far as to seek a formal defense agreement with the USA. Were that to happen, the American sphere of influence, and with it perhaps basing rights, would be extended all the way up to the frontiers of the USSR. For all of Daud's overtures to pro-American regimes like Pakistan and Iran, he never threatened Afghanistan's basic status as a Soviet client, or sought to buy weapons from the USA. Finally, the victory of a fundamentalist Islamic regime in Afghanistan might well lead to a resurgence of Islam throughout Central Asia. This would be a dangerous development from a Soviet perspective not so much because of any direct spillover effects in Soviet Central Asia, but because of its possible anti-communist implications for countries in the northern tier and possibly beyond.

The fact that the Russians were forced to intervene as they did in December 1979 and physically replace Amin with their own candidate, the ex-Perchami leader Babrak Karmal, indicates that ideological orthodoxy is not enough to guarantee that Moscow's interests will be well served in a particular client-state. On the other hand, one could not ask for a more dramatic demonstration of the new turn in Soviet Third World strategy. The Russians showed they were not interested merely in the largest possible quantity of influence, but in its *quality* as well. They hoped to be able to dictate not only the major lines of Afghan foreign policy, but its day-to-day management: hence Daud's replacement with Taraki/Amin, and then their subsequent replacement with Karmal. The Russians were about to be expelled from Afghanistan, not as in Egypt by the established leadership of the country, but by a popular rebellion, and they showed quite convincingly that they were no longer prepared to accept such an outcome passively. The massive troop intervention was no more than the culmination, under unexpectedly adverse circumstances, of a turn in overall policy that had begun more than a year and a half earlier.

IMPLICATIONS FOR THE ATLANTIC ALLIANCE

In evaluating the threat posed to the interests of the Western allies by these recent changes in Soviet tactics, it must be borne in mind that they have all arisen as a response to the basic *weakness* of the previous Soviet position. Since 1974 the Russians have had to deal with the central fact that they were closed out of the Middle Eastern heartland, and their subsequent choice of targets around the periphery – Ethiopia, South Yemen and Afghanistan – was a necessity imposed on them. Soviet-style Marxism-Leninism is a doctrine with very little inherent appeal anywhere in the Middle East, and where it has become the ruling ideology, it has had to be applied from the outside – often at great cost to the Soviets. Moscow's influence remains tenuous among its traditional clients like Syria and Iraq, and even in those countries where it has consolidated the rule of an ideologically sympathetic regime, its control has not been optimal (as its problems with Hafizullah Amin have shown).

Moreover, as the Soviet intention to have puppets rather than allies becomes clearer, new opportunities will arise for the West to wean older 'non-aligned' clients out of the Soviet orbit. Countries like Iraq and Somalia have already been seriously alienated by what they regard as communist machinations against them, and it is significant that both voted in favor of the UN General Assembly resolution demanding a withdrawal of Soviet troops from Afghanistan. It is now possible for Western diplomats to argue rather persuasively to Third World countries receiving or seeking Soviet military assistance that such programs are potential fifth columns; that, in the words of the Kennedy inaugural, 'those who foolishly sought power by riding the back of the tiger ended up inside'.

On the other hand, to the extent that the new Russian strategy is a successful adaptation to these weaknesses, the consequences could be far-reaching indeed. One of the notable features of the old international regime in the Middle East was the reluctance of most left-wing nationalists to cooperate overtly with the USSR on military matters. The memory of European colonialism made leaders like Nasser and Boumedienne extremely sensitive to the presence of foreign bases, no matter what their origin, on their territory. While the Russians gained access to some facilities through the 1950s and 1960s, this occurred haphazardly and in response to specific political developments. The new crop of Soviet clients, by contrast, have given Moscow direct military assistance from the outset. Aden became a major Soviet-Cuban logistics facility during Ethiopia's war with *Muslim* Somalis and Eritreans and Ethiopia, in turn, was used as a staging base for operations against Rubai Ali. The Karmal regime in Kabul has collaborated in the occupation of Afghanistan by a Soviet army.

A second problem is that these regimes will be much harder to dislodge either from power, or from the Soviet orbit. Politics in the Middle East often resembled a gigantic bazaar in which the Western powers could, as the examples of Egypt and Iran showed, purchase the favors of a given country for the right political-military price. The new crop of Soviet clients are less likely to succumb to such blandishments on ideological grounds; moreover, the extreme narrowness of their domestic bases makes them much more dependent on Soviet-bloc support.

The Western allies must also reach some agreement on the specific meaning of recent events in Afghanistan. The Carter administration has chosen to interpret the intervention as part of a larger strategy aimed at securing a warm-water port or control over oil in the Persian Gulf. Such an assertion contains elements of truth but is somewhat misleading, if one concludes that these objectives were the *primary* motivation. The timing and circumstances of the Soviet action do not suggest that Moscow had planned beforehand to send 100,000 men into Afghanistan in order to bring pressure to bear on Iran and Palestine. More generally, it is doubtful that the Soviets have had up till now a terribly precise or well-thought-out geopolitical strategy in the Middle East. While a warm-water port or control over oil probably exists as an aspiration or long-range objective in the minds of Soviet planners, it is doubtful that they have the route from here to there blocked out in the manner of, say, Hitler's 1938 Hossbach memorandum. In the past Moscow's major success in the region – the arms deal with Nasser in 1955, the 1958 overthrow of the Hashemite monarchy in Iraq, or the revolution against the shah – was the result of largely local developments over which the Russians had very little control, but which they were able to exploit aggressively after the fact. To plan to do more than this, is a rather difficult proposition in as politically unpredictable and unstable an area as the Middle East.

The real significance of the Soviet intervention in Afghanistan is somewhat different. It does not concern the nature or direction of Soviet objectives, which have remained constant throughout the postwar period, but the potential success with which those objectives can be achieved. The Western Alliance presently faces a critical problem in the Middle East as a result of the vulnerability of European oil supplies to political instability arising from purely regional factors. The problem will worsen by an order of magnitude should the quality of Soviet influence over the sources of oil evolve into something approaching control. At the present moment, Moscow cannot order the Iraqi Ba'th to turn off the tap to Western Europe and Japan; indeed, many of the difficulties in the Soviet-Iraqi relationship have arisen over Baghdad's willingness to deal with the West on purely commercial terms. What politicization there has been in the overall economic relationship between Iraq and the West, has revolved chiefly around issues of regional concern, such as the Arab-Israeli dispute. We have already seen in the past decade the corrosive effects that such control can have on the cohesion of the Western Alliance with respect to this particular issue. European and Japanese dependence on Persian Gulf oil is such that these countries have felt they had no choice but to accommodate to the political demands made of them. But this type of alliance disunity was tolerable as long as it did not seriously jeopardize NATO's purpose as an anti-Soviet organization. Imagine, then, what would happen to the alliance should Ba'thist Iraq, to take one example, be replaced by a communist one. The greater degree of political control this would bestow upon the Soviets would in all probability spell the end of the alliance as we know it. It would mean that the oil weapon could be coupled to a whole host of East–West issues that are currently isolated from one another, such as theater nuclear modernization. It would be ironic indeed if the unity of the Atlantic Alliance, which has held together under the pressure of hundreds of thousands of Soviet troops armed with nuclear weapons for over three decades, should suddenly be undone by a communist coup d'état in a faraway Persian Gulf country.

NOTES: CHAPTER 8

1   A rather extensive inside account of Soviet-Egyptian dealings during the period
    1967–73 has now been provided by Mohammed Heikal in *The Road to
    Ramadan* (New York: Ballantine, 1975) and *The Sphinx and the Commissar*
    (New York: Harper & Row, 1978), and in Anwar El Sadat, *In Search of
    Identity* (New York: Harper & Row, 1977). See also Abd al-Majid Farid's
    The Secret Conversations of Abd al-Nasir (Washington, DC: Joint Publications
    Research Service, 72223, Translations on the Middle East and North Africa,
    14 November 1978).
2   See Sadat, *In Search of Identity*, op. cit. pp. 146–7.
3   See William Beecher in the *Boston Globe*, 10 July 1975.
4   SIPRI, *World Armaments and Disarmament Yearbook 1979*, pp. 218–20.
5   *The Middle East*, no. 101, 8 June 1979, p. 20, and no. 102, 22 June 1979.
6   US Arms Control and Disarmament Agency, *World Military Expenditures and
    Arms Transfers*, 1979.
7   *Washington Post*, 13 July 1979.
8   *New York Times*, 2 July 1978.
9   *Washington Post*, 13 July 1979.
10 There is a discussion of MFS activities in Brian Crozier, 'The surrogate forces
    of the Soviet Union', *Conflict Studies*, no. 92 pp. 9–10.
11 There is no direct evidence of Soviet involvement in a coup attempt by the
    ICP; on the other hand, we should not expect to have any. The strongest
    argument that the Iraqi communists were positioning themselves for a take-
    over is the strength of the Ba'thist reaction. The purge, which began in
    May 1978, continued unabated for over a year and netted, by some accounts,
    several thousand communists (probably a majority of the ICP's total member-
    ship). The Iraqi leadership has made direct accusations that the ICP (and
    behind it, the USSR) was plotting a takeover. In May 1979 the Iraqis walked
    out of the Arab People's Congress on the ground that the Sudanese Communist
    Party was being drawn into the leadership – the Sudanese communists, it will
    be remembered, attempted to overthrow Jaafar Numeiry in 1971. All of this
    occurred in a period when Sadat's peace moves and the Iranian revolution
    required, if anything, a greater degree of cooperation with the USSR. The
    purge was too serious to be a merely symbolic gesture. In the Ba'th Party's first
    tensure of office in 1963, they had undertaken a similar purge and were severely
    hurt as a result. It is not the sort of action they would undertake for frivolous
    reasons.
12 *FBIS MEA*, 7 January 1980, p. E1.
13 See Hannah Negaran, 'The Afghan coup of April 1978: revolution and inter-
    national security', *ORBIS*, vol. 23 no. 1 (Spring 1979), pp. 94–9; Theodore L.
    Eliot, Jr, 'Afghanistan after the 1978 revolution', *Strategic Review*, vol. 7, no. 2
    (Spring 1979), pp. 59–60.
14 See, for example, Louis Duprée, 'Afghanistan under the Khalq', *Problems of
    Communism*, vol. 28, no. 4 (July–August 1979), p. 34.
15 *Mideast Events*, 16 June 1978; Selig S. Harrison, 'The shah, not Kremlin
    touched off Afghan coup', *Washington Post*, 13 May 1979, p. 159.
16 *New York Times*, 2 August 1979, p. 297.

Part Four

The Arab World and the Western Alliance

9 Geopolitical Illusions

FOUAD AJAMI

It is now essential that the United States should manifest through joint action of the President and the Congress our determination to assist those nations of the Mid East area, which desire that assistance.

The action which I propose would have the following features. It would, first of all, authorize the United States to cooperate with and assist any nation or group of nations in the general area of the Middle East in the development of economic strength dedicated to the maintenance of national independence.

It would, in the second place, authorize the Executive to undertake in the same region programs of military assistance and cooperation with any nation or group of nations which desires such aid.

It would, in the third place, authorize such assistance and cooperation to include the employment of the armed forces of the United States to secure and protect the territorial integrity and political independence of such nations, requesting such aid, against overt armed aggression from any nation controlled by International Communism. President Eisenhower, 5 January 1957

Let our position be absolutely clear. Any attempt by any outside force to gain control of the Persian Gulf region will be regarded as an assault on the vital interests of the United States of America. And such an assault will be repelled by any means necessary, including military force. President Carter, 23 January 1980

We need a deployment in threatened areas which makes it plausible that we have the intention to intervene, to assist threatened countries . . . We urgently need greater capacity for action in that so-called arc of crisis. Henry Kissinger, 21 January 1980

INTRODUCTION

'Hegel remarks that all great world historical facts and personages occur, as it were, twice. He has forgotten to add: the first time as tragedy, the second time as farce.' These are the opening lines to Marx's classic *Eighteenth Brumaire*. They aptly capture what we have been offered lately by way of insights into the so-called 'arc of crisis'. We enter the 1980s with the things that tragically failed us in the 1950s. Are we witnessing, then, mere farce and shadows?

The most interesting aspect of the current drama in the 'arc of crisis' is not so much the spectacular action that we race to catch up with, but the failure it conceals. Indeed the drama thickens, its pace intensifies, as the men on stage realize that they have no script to follow. Frantic action must go on, if catastrophe is to be averted. The men on stage intuit that they can ride it out by appealing to nostalgia, or repeating lines and scenes that worked in the past. But there is a danger: the audience is different; there have been great changes in its tastes and expectations. The old act is no longer gripping or even adequate.

We are repeatedly told of Islam's resurgence and return – the old lines, the old dogma reappearing after the failure of the secularists. The language of politics is oddly ancient; from Iran, politics is the realm of God and Satan; the world is a duel between Islam and paganism. But there are other forms of 'return' in other places. There has been a reincarnation of John Foster Dulles in Washington; his language and his strategy are back. The world would be a safer place if only others were to allow military bases in the area, if Pakistan, Turkey and the 'northern tier' are shored up against Soviet aggression. Never mind the lessons of the last quarter-century about the failure of military bases, the fact that foreign bases compromise the regimes that offer them, the fact that the funds that hardpressed governments seek in return for the bases do nothing to solve basic questions of political order and viability. Worse yet, they enable regimes to conceal and run away from their troubles. What in Dr Kissinger's theocracy is called the 'geopolitical design' and offers rulers a way out, of sorts; Zia ul Haq of Pakistan taunts the USA about her reliability as an ally, her toughness. Presumably toughness will be proven, if his military dictatorship is sustained – as though powers from afar can spare regimes the agonies and troubles of home. Mr Sadat and Mr Begin recently concluded a meeting by agreeing on the 'geopolitical situation' in Afghanistan, on the need for toughness against the USSR. There was little said about the Palestinian question; there the failure would have to be faced up to. So in the absence of an agreement on Palestinian autonomy, Egypt and Israel did the usual things; they fed the fires of the cold war; they offered the USA military bases that were wisely declined, because a base in Israel would be politically unusable and one in Egypt perhaps deadly dangerous to the stability of the Egyptian regime; they pushed their case as the USA's reliable allies and hence their claims to economic aid.

Moscow's behavior, too, though outwardly decisive, on the surface of things an embarrassing contrast to the seeming ineptness of US power, may conceal more frustration than those who play up Soviet might would lead us to believe. In one analysis put forth by historian Firuz Kazemzadeh, the Soviet occupation of Afghanistan is the 'fulfillment of the old imperial dream . . . a logical extension of traditional politics, another move in the Great Game' that once engaged Britain and Russia and now pits the USA against the USSR. In another interpretation put forth by Robert W. Tucker the Soviet invasion of Afghanistan was a 'flash of lightning that suddenly illuminated the political landscape'. It 'laid bare as never before the vulnerability of the American position in a region of vital interests'. The Soviet leaders knew they would get away with it, that Afghanistan would not stand in the way of another détente.

Other interpretations proceed from a different reading of the situation. Instead of seeing a Soviet blueprint at work, they see the usual predicament of a great power drawn into a quagmire: stakes that escalate beyond original intentions, troublesome allies who get out of hand. Thus, as Selig Harrison put it, the move against Hafizullah Amin in December 1979 may have been motivated by the fact that: Amin, who still commanded strong loyalty among the army and security forces at the time of his ouster, had increasingly come to be viewed by Moscow as a potential Tito'.

While some see the move as a Soviet attack against détente, there is a more compelling line of reasoning advanced by Stanley Hoffmann in a brilliant set of 'reflections': 'Did the Soviets act because they thought that the Western stake in détente would lead us to minimize their violation of it, or because they believed that the USA, in recent months had emptied détente of any real substance?' It was more or less conceded that SALT was dead, that the Carter administration had failed to discipline the New Right and to put the Soviet-American relation beyond local squabbles and grievances. From Kissinger's Middle Eastern shuttle in 1974, which shut out the USSR, through Angola in 1975, to Kabul in 1980, détente had faltered and become an empty shell.

Great powers shut out of respectable deals and denied the prerogatives of power are tempted to play revisionist games. And when they do, their behavior faces us with a basic question: do they play the way they do because they want to be taken seriously, to warn that they cannot be frozen out of critical areas, or because they are bent on challenging the pecking-order of the world and wrecking the stability of world order?

Afghanistan may have provided the Soviets an opportunity to reenter an area from which they were expelled. As always, ambition and fears converged. Afghanistan was never really important in the USA's scheme of things. It assumed such great importance because it became living proof of the ghosts that the New Right in the USA had been conjuring up for some time – ghosts that Mr Carter had unsuccessfully tried to exorcise when he came to power with a pledge to go beyond the USA's 'inordinate fear of communism'. The fear has returned, making the world again a duel between the two powers: small countries are again pawns; social realities are to be ignored in favor of geostrategic doctrines. The gap between the doctrines we came up with and the ailments we have to address is turning into an abyss.

Since October 1973, we have been witnessing the unraveling of a civilizational and cultural order in the Middle East. The categories and weapons we have come up with have turned out to be either blunt, or counterproductive. Since more trouble is in the offing, we had better know the Middle East 'as it really is', and we had better shed the illusion that alien civilizations can be shaped to our liking, that awesome psychological and cultural problems can be swept under some great geostrategic rug. If there are more questions than answers in this analysis, if some of it seems skeptical of all claims, and some of it a bit

elusive, the effect is intentional. We have not fared so well with our
'precise' policy analysis, with our grand doctrines. This much the Middle
East (particularly after Iran's eruption) has recently done: it has drama-
tized the shallowness of geostrategic doctrines, the illusions of rulers, the
importance of outsiders.

It is the illusion of power that it can command, that power lost to one
camp is the gain of the other. Some predicaments are deeper and more
complex than that: they engulf all players. The   players may effect great
decisiveness and skill. But behind their action can be discerned frustration and futility. Such may be the case with the two superpowers in our
drama, for the world is increasingly less amenable to their control. Such
may be the case with both President Sadat and his Arab rivals. For it is
true that the Egyptian president has no solution to the Palestinian question, and it is equally true that his Arab rivals are stalemated, that the
best they can do is wait him out and continue to hope that Egypt – a
country they hardly know – will finally draw the line for him. Such, too,
may be the case with Israel – a country which has enough power to hang
onto the West Bank but is really swimming against the currents of history.
'Do not look for solutions in this book – there are none; in general modern
man has no solutions', wrote the profound Russian populist Alexander
Herzen in an introduction to one of his books. There are no solutions
here. And there may be no solutions to the problems of men and societies
slugging it out in that increasingly troubled region of the world.

THE AMERICAN MOVEMENT

History is the best kind of fiction. No futurologist could have predicted
the fate of the dreams – both Arab and Iranian dreams – entertained in
the post-October 1973 period. As the decade drew to a close, the shah's
dreams lay in ruin, the Arab order that waged the October War had
fragmented. In the scheme of things both the local dreams and the
'American moment in the Middle East – the extension of Pax Americana
into the Middle East – proved to be short-lived.

The American ascendancy in the region emerged out of a fundamental
and interesting contradiction in the October War – a contradiction noted
by John C. Campbell in a perceptive essay aptly entitled 'The burden of
empire in the Middle East': 'The October War spawned an American-
backed structure with Jerusalem, Cairo, Riyadh, and Teheran as its nodal
points.' Campbell might have added the more 'discreet' Damascus to his
list, for even that once-militant capital was far more interested in the
gains of the new order than in staying out. The regime of Hafiz Asad sat
on the fence; its noise was radical but there was a conservative substance
to its policies.

It was 'strange', observed Campbell, 'that the moment of crisis for the
United States which revealed this vulnerability to the new economic
power of OPEC also left it in a stronger position than ever before, as it
gained new influence in the Arab world without losing its special re-

lationship with Israel, and as it stepped forward as the principal partner in the security and economic development of the oil producing states of the Gulf'. And for a while the post-October 1973 US structure looked awesome indeed. It suggested the possibility of taming the region's passions, containing the USSR (even 'expelling' it, to use Mr Kissinger's terminology) and keeping 'castrated' Europe dependent on the USA. What Mr Kissinger proudly called 'the reversal of alliances' in the Arab world took place with remarkable ease. The Middle East was to be what southeast Asia, after so much blood and treasure, turned out not to be: a place where US will and resources make a difference. This was to be Pax Americana's new frontier at a time when the Nixon–Kissinger design, battered in southeast Asia, needed a show of its competence.

But this structure too – like so much of the Nixon–Kissinger handiwork – stood on flimsier ground than was assumed from afar. As the decade ended, of the entire structure there remained an Egyptian-Israeli accord. The Iranian pillar was in shambles and the regional Arab order had crumbled, making pale by comparison the 'Arab cold war' that dominated the politics of the 1950s and 1960s.

For some who are taken in by shadows, Iran's collapse was a triumph of Islamic 'fanaticism', the story of a 'society being dragged back into the Middle Ages'. For Henry A. Kissinger, Joseph Kraft and Irving Kristol, the shah is just another casualty of the USA's 'geopolitical decline', of Mr Carter's naïve Wilsonian advocacy of human rights, of the non-Western revolt against 'civilization'. In Kissinger's words, the shah was overthrown not only for what he did wrong, but also for what he did right – 'his friendship for the USA, his support for Middle East peace, his rapid modernization, his land reform, his support for public education and women's rights, in short his effort to bring Iran into the twentieth century as an ally of the free world'.

Less ideological and more sophisticated interpretations see Iran's upheaval as the upheaval of a bourgeois society against an *ancien régime*. The triumph of Khomeini was not so much due to the primacy of religion, but to the failure of the bourgeoisie to pull off its own revolution. Whatever the correct interpretation, that pillar of Western interests is gone. In a highly nationalistic age, outright foreign collaboration is a liability: the embrace of powers from afar can kill.

The prime geopolitical casualty of the Iranian revolution was the Nixon Doctrine. One could anoint regional powers (in Brzezinski jargon, regional influentials), one could give them unlimited access to military hardware, but they turn out to have feet of clay. They strut on the world stage and both we and their rulers forget the material with which such rulers have to work, the constraints on their ambitions.

So much for the Iranian outcome. Our central domain is the Arab world. There, to, we can witness elements of the Iranian theme: men strutting on the world stage, previous limits ignored and the difficulty of juggling one's claim to self and authenticity with the pervasive US presence.

In recent Arab history the essence of the October War was the triumph of the dominant order against the radicalism unleashed by the 1967 defeat. Far more important, the 'victory' against Israel was the capacity of the dominant order – vulnerable since 1967 – to hold its own against men like George Habash from the Left and radical fundamentalists like Qaddafi from the Right. The 1967 defeat had shattered the world of the elders, punctured its claims, displayed its historical inadequacy. A frightening generation gap developed in its aftermath that issued in a deep and bitter kind of radicalism. The two wars of the period – Nasser's war of attrition and the October War served as effective sponges. They absorbed the wrath and the frustrations. The October War promised, and for a while succeeded in delivering, a brighter world. Patriotism and the new wealth combined to dramatize the futility of radical politics.

The 'deep structure' of that development was a reaffirmation of the old order. The Arab world seemed to enter what was labeled *al Higba al Saudia* (the Saudi era). The victory of the men of the desert was a victory for authenticity, for those who had (supposedly) remained themselves. For more than a generation, radical nationalists in Egypt and the Fertile Crescent had been saying that the past must be shed and the 'feudalists' destroyed, if the Arab order is to stand up to the outside world. But this was not to be, for the 1967 defeat had given the conservative states a new lease on life.

Thus from the era of nationalism the Arab world had moved to the era of the commissions and the middlemen. In the mood that prevailed in 1974–5 the recovery of the West Bank and Gaza was just around the corner. After all, the Arab armies had vindicated themselves and Arab oil had 'cornered' the USA, the power that holds '99 percent of the cards'. If the Israeli policies were a mere echo of US wishes, then an American-sponsored settlement would enable the guardians of the Arab order to claim that they saw an historic fight to some honourable conclusion: halfway between the utopia of eradicating Israel from the region and the hell of the post-1967 *status quo*.

That was Saudi Arabia's view of things; and that too was the view of Mr Sadat, who would claim as late as April 1977 that he had successfully convinced President Carter of establishing a Palestinian state. Mr Sadat's dramatic deed – his journey to Jerusalem – showed his impatience with his own dictum. By then Israel had successfully withstood US pressure and dashed the expectation that the Carter administration had come to power – with the promise of a comprehensive settlement. Frustrated by the incapacity of the superpower to get them off the hook, the Arab states went their separate ways. Egypt was pushed further down the road of isolation than its president had assumed it would be, Syria scurried to solidify its position and claim its place as the 'principal confrontation state'. This was not exactly what the Saudis had in mind when they set out to de-radicalize Arab politics in the aftermath of October 1973. Egyptian and Syrian policies taught them that allies, even financially dependent ones, can be unwieldy and troublesome. The turn that Islamic fundamentalism took in Iran showed the Saudis, who always insisted that Islam was their weapon, that the weapon one brandishes takes on a life of its own, that one can die at the gallows one sets up for others.

For all its wealth, Saudi Arabia – the other US pillar – was an under-populated, weak country in a region seething with unrest and schemes of all kinds. In its post-October 1973 exuberance, Saudi Arabia could enter-tain all sorts of possibilities. It was even convinced, back in 1976, that it must combat Eurocommunism in France and Italy. By 1979 the Saudi-organized Arab order had come apart and Saudi Arabia's battle was at home. The attack on the Grand Mosque in November 1979 was not exactly Iranian-scale upheaval, but it was a warning of things to come.

Of all the weapons in the Saudi arsenal, none proved as problematic as the US connection. The great ally was busy on too many fronts and, besides, the Saudis knew their own history. In their defeat of the Hashem-ites half a century ago, they played up the foreign collaboration of the Hashemites – the British connection of that dynasty – and stressed their own fidelity to tradition. That is why the Saudis seem to alternate between a Kissingerian kind of doom about the decline of the USA's power and a reluctance to associate themselves with the USA whenever the USA sought open displays of friendship. Subtlety is not exactly an American virtue. The more Saudi Arabia was called upon to 'stop ducking', to stop being 'skittish', the more the Saudis felt compelled to show their distance from their patron. Iran had demonstrated the rage felt against the USA in the region; Sadat's Egypt had deeply 'embarrassed' the Saudis by the zeal with which it embraced America and things American. 'Tradition-mongering' had been Saudi Arabia's game and now the Saudis had to live with it.

The 'special relationship' with the USA could be justified, perhaps even proudly displayed, so long as the mighty superpower was said to be cap-able of delivering a comprehensive Middle Eastern settlement. Denied the cover of the comprehensive peace, the USA's Arab friends would have to face the deeper reasons for their embrace of the USA – reasons that go beyond diplomacy into the realm of culture and cultural preferences. America's presumed diplomatic prowess enabled those in the Arab world who were politically, culturally, psychologically inclined toward the USA to hide – partly from themselves, partly from others – the deeper motiva-tions for their embrace of the USA, to claim that the US connection was a price that had to be paid for a resolution of the Palestinian question. If the road to Palestine went through Washington, so to speak, then America's friends should forgive their exuberance for things American. But what if it did not? What if such hopes were the product of wishful thinking on the part of the Arabs, *hubris* on the part of the mighty super-power? Then the fundamental Arab ambivalence about the USA's pre-sence would have to be faced.

It follows from what has just been stated that the US crisis in the Arab world cannot be solely explained as a 'credibility problem' due to the USA's failure to do something on the Palestinian question. There was a deeper cultural drama at work here. The success of October 1973 had enabled the Arab elites to indulge their taste – in technology, in alli-ances, in models of development – and the USA's advantage was there for all to see. Americanization and anti-Americanism are two sides of the same coin. The anti-Americanism displayed in the Arab states (and in Iran) as the 1970s came to an end was but an expression of that region aimed at itself. It was a display of its own agony over its cultural surrender. Muslim fundamentalism, reassertion, call it what you will, was then summoned as a psychological device, a defense of self. In a climate of this kind, rulers ran for cover. The Arab state most instrumental in inviting the USA into the region – Saudi Arabia – was most vulnerable, most anxious to display its independence. The collapse of the seemingly awesome Pahlavi dynasty was a local trauma, perhaps a crystal ball in which the Saudis and others could see their own future.

Incoherent and idiosyncratic as it was, the message of Khomeinism was plain and simple wrath. Its appeal to mass opinion throughout the Arab world, across the deep divide between the Sunni Islam of the majority of Arabs and the Shi'a Islam of Iran, across the historical split between Arabs and Persians, underlined the vulnerability of the Arab order, the lack of a single charismatic leader or of a credible order that would give people some belief in the quality of their leadership and its commitment. The failure of the dominant political system to keep the outside world at bay, to show a serious commitment to a public project of some kind, to show tangible gains on the Palestinian question, left it vulnerable to messianic messages and to the wrath of tradition. The dominant order's dialogue with the outside world was seen to have turned into an embrace and then a cultural surrender, but there was very little to show for it by way of concrete gains.

For men and women in the Arab world witnessing Iran's upheaval, the interesting thing about it was the spectacle of Iranians in the streets making and remaking their own history. Win or lose, they were out there demanding to be counted and listened to. All the Arab elites' attempts to show that Iran's troubles were peculiar to that society, to point out the legitimate differences between their own situation and Iran's, were in a way beside the point. The half-hearted attempts at democratization reported in the aftermath of the Iranian revolution in Kuwait, Saudi Arabia and Iraq showed that the Arab rulers were running for cover. But these measures could only be cosmetic. At stake was nothing less than the dominant style of authority. The habits of mind, the institutions, needed to allow the citizenry to become more than sheer spectators, were nowhere to be seen in the Arab order.

Short of that drastic changing of their soul, the Arab regimes could change their skin. They could keep a safe distance away from the USA and that is why Saudi Arabia has systematically resisted the USA's request for military bases on Saudi soil. They could try to close the gap between state and society that plagues such regimes as Syria and Iraq, where a war of sorts goes on between minority-based regimes – the Alawis in the former, the Sunnis in the latter – and the popular culture below. Only Sadat seems defiant: sustained by a Pharaonic tradition that gives the ruler a great latitude, by a patient peasant culture that waits a long time for promises made to be redeemed and by Egypt's resentment of what it saw as an unfair distribution of burdens and gains in the Arab world.

A QUESTION OF EGYPT

No other issue, not even the Palestinian question, has loomed as large in recent Arab politics as the question of Egypt's place in the Arab system, Egypt's wounds and choices, that painful gap between her cultural pre-eminence and her wretched economic conditions. Whether pushed by the 'lure of primacy' or by the isolationist temptation – what I called else-where the push of the desert and the pull of the Mediterranean – Egyptian choices pretty much dominated Arab politics. Whether it was Egyptian armor crossing the Suez Canal in October 1973 or the psychohistorical shock of Sadat's solitary journey to Jerusalem, Egypt's preeminence was time and again driven home to other Arabs.

Where others – Saudis, Iraqis and Syrians – once feared Egypt's reach beyond her boundaries, the Sadat diplomacy presented them with an unequally unsettling situation: Egypt's indifference to the Arab system, her separate diplomacy with Israel, her turn to the West. This has been the main question for Arab summits and diplomatic conferences – for the ones held in Tripoli, in Algiers, in Damascus, in Baghdad and Tunis – and it will be for future ones as well. More importantly still, it is a pro-found cultural and psychohistorical dilemma.

All the tensions that lay beneath the surface between Egypt and the Arab states – tensions that go back to the way other Arabs treated Egypt and Egyptians in the aftermath of the 1967 defeat, anger over the milit-ancy of those who lecture Egyptians from the safety of Tripoli and Riyadh – were exploded by Sadat's statecraft: the gap between Egypt and her former Nasserite allies, whom Sadat had patiently tolerated prior to October 1973 turned into an abyss. But there were troubles ahead be-tween Egypt and her new allies – the 'moderate' Arab states. The patience with which Sadat had constructed his alliance with Syria and Saudi Arabia would come to fail him; he made his decision to go on his own. His path began with the first disengagement accord in early 1974, then with the Sinai Accord; it took him on his solitary trip to Jerusalem in November 1977, then all the way to a 'separate peace' with Israel.

We simply do not know whether his path was 'inevitable' – a futile but always an inviting intellectual territory. Were we to follow the analysis of Mohamed Heikal, the entire Egyptian path becomes a leader's choice: the Egyptian 'decisionmaker' wanted it this way; there were other choices to make but Mr Sadat chose to break with the pan-Arab alliance at a moment in Arab history when there was an opportunity to put together a viable Arab order against Israel and a more effective bargaining-unit vis-à-vis the USA and the West. Were we to follow more 'ideological' analyses, we would root the new policies in the recent ascendancy of the bourgeois Right. The defeat of Nasser and Nasserism brought back to Egypt – both physically and psychologically – the bourgeois Right and its view of the world. Men who were in prison or exile – influential journal-ists like Ali and Mustapha Amin, Ahmud Abu al Fath, a lawyer like Mahid Rifaat, who had been in Kuwait working for its ruling family, a former politician and Pasha like Fuad Serrag al Din, who came back and actually became an active force in Egyptian politics – returned after

October 1973 with a spirit of defiance. The world has proven them right: the oppressive, 'uncouth' elements who played havoc with the world and 'imported' heretical doctrines were defeated; their defeat was proof that old Egypt – the men who matter and own should run the world – was correct all along, that the Egyptian excursion into pan-Arab politics was a total disaster.

But both explanations are frustrating and incomplete: they leave out some richer and more structural things. They seem too mechanistic, because they do not tell us enough about Egypt as a nation-state, and thus fail to impart the drama, the complexity, as well as the imperatives of national behavior. Moreover, they say nothing about the cluster of emotions in the popular culture that leaders tap, arouse and often become captives of. Leaders may interpret national wounds, grievances and ambitions in a particular way, but we cannot fully comprehend why they get away with what they do, if we only focus on the leader. The leader may be, as Mr Sadat put it, 'a solo performer on a stage' – but a meaningful evaluation of the theater must also understand the audience's state of mind. It is here where gifted actors are made or where they collapse: the audience must appreciate and applaud, if the act is to last.

If the leader as performer is insufficient, so too is a straitjacketed ideological analysis. Class analysis has a way of seeming sterile, or secondary at best when powerful currents push nations forward – or backward for that matter – into grave decisions. The discord between Egypt and her Arab allies seemed independent of ideology. The allies may have been radical – the Arab Left, the Palestinians, Qaddafi – or centrist, conservative actors – Assad's of Syria, Saudi Arabia – but the results were the same. If Egypt could not afford to live with the Arab *thawra* (revolution), she found it equally difficult to live with the Arab *tharwa* (fortune). In both cases, she insisted on her right to pursue her own independent paths; in both ruptures, the popular emotions were there that made hitherto unimaginable events and choices materialize.

As they ponder the exchange of embassies between Egypt and Israel, Arab choices must not be particularly happy or bright. Sadat has baffled his Arab rivals as they continue to convince themselves that each new 'violation' by him will prove to be his undoing, that he is destined to falter in the face of both massive economic troubles, and Israel's determination to remain on the West Bank. The assumption (unwarranted, it would seem to me) is that the 'Egyptian problem' is a strictly personal problem due to Sadat's idiosyncrasy, that some other leader or set of leaders would change the substance of Sadat's policies.

The reasons for the weakness of the anti-Sadat camp are many. The first had to do with the very nature of the task at hand – namely, the confrontation with Israel. It being a military task, there simply is no way that another war could be waged without Egypt. In one metaphor, recent Egyptian policies are a 'gladiator's revolt': the Arab state that did most of the fighting decided to change its profession. Sadat's search for a way out took on the moral quality of a rejection on the part of the relatively dispossessed of a dangerous pan-Arab assignment.

A second reason has to do with the cultural centrality of Egypt and, thus, with the difficulty of isolating Egypt. Impoverished as it is, Egypt remains the cultural center of the Arab world, its capital the pre-eminent Arab Muslim city. Qaddafi's Tripoli can hardly serve as a base for his own ambitions, let alone as a Berlin for the would be Arab Bismarck. Beirut, once an intellectual and cultural rival to Cairo, is a divided city, broken by war, ravaged by its passions. Tunis may serve as a base for the Arab League, but Tunis is a provincial North African city. Not much of the memories of the Arab world are evoked by Tunis. Politics is not solely about strategic matters. Memories, emotions and cultural artefacts are a material force in their own right.

A third reason operating to Sadat's advantage has to do with the drift of things – political, economic and cultural – in the Arab world since October 1973. If Egypt seems 'compromised', 'uncommitted', do its rivals fare any better? To disgrace 'surrender' and corruption, one would have to put forth principled projects. Rifaat al Asad (President Asad's brother, the most controversial man in Syria) would have a hard time posing an alternative to Sadat's policies. He is free to attack Sadat's policies, as he indeed does, but an audience has to listen and to believe. Far more important than Rifaat al Asad's sermons against Sadat is his own corruption and abuse of power. People living in glasshouses cannot go about hurling rocks at others. There is a bleakness to contemporary Arab politics that has to do with the scale of corruption, with the realities of everyday life that men and women experience. Men denouncing Egyptian 'cowardice' have themselves to exhibit some commitment. The sight of Arabic newspapers based in Paris and London – newspapers which cater to affluent Arabs – has a pathology all its own that has not been lost on Egyptians and other Arabs.

The outward militancy of Sadat's rivals is at blatant variance with the way they live, with the drift of things in their own societies. This is understood and masterfully manipulated by Sadat, first, in his attacks against 'nightclub revolutionaries', then in his recent denunciation of Saudi Arabia.

A fourth reason why Sadat's rivals seem unable to put together a viable option has to do with the rivalries and suspicions within their own ranks. Syria and Iraq may both have quarrels with Sadat but they have more deadly quarrels with each other. Saudi Arabia and Libya share a certain cultural disdain of Sadat's ways, but can the two of them work together? Algeria enjoys some prestige, but it is far away, with priorities all its own. Among those posing as Palestine's defenders – some of them more royalist than the king – rhetoric is one thing, conduct is another. Iraq's attempts to dominate the Palestinian movement, even through liquidating Palestinians, has more to do with old Iraq's hegemonic claims in the Fertile Crescent than in radical pretensions. For Libya's Qaddafi, the Palestinians are never quite militant enough. He wishes them to play out the despair and radicalism shunned by his own population. The Palestinians are to do what Libya's affluent population shows no interest in whatsoever; live by Qaddafi's third theory, abide by the utterances of his Green Book. Syria was once the Palestinians' self-appointed protector, but the cruelty of Syrian armor in 1976 against the Palestinians has already become part of Palestinian memory and folklore. Sadat's rivals are held together by the power of a myth – pan-Arabism – and like all myths this one does not fare so well when tested.

The fifth and final Egyptian advantage is a unique and important one. By classical strictures, Egypt may be the only *nation-state* in the Arab world. By contrast, Sadat's rivals are of two kinds; they are either isolated sectarian-based regimes, or vulnerable dynasties. For all the mumbo-jumbo of the Ba'th Party in Syria and Iraq, for all of Michel Aflaq's metaphysics, the politics in both remains communal at heart and the gap between state and society almost paralyzing.

We have recently been treated to a flurry of writings on Iraq as a regional power (we never give up on 'regional powers', when some collapse we anoint others). It is in this light that a piece in *Foreign Affairs* (Winter 1979–80) by the journalist Claudia Wright has to be viewed. Like the analyses we were treated to on the shah's Iran, this one too is replete with awesome statistics, with endless references to the regime's 'pragmatism' and 'self-confidence', and conveys the requisite fascinations with the man at the helm. And like so many of the Iranian analyses of yesterday, it shows no understanding of the realities on the ground of the vast gulf between the Sunni ruling elite running a brittle, repressive state and the society below. Disconnected from their social base, brittle states are never really powerful. They rest on glamor and terror and those commodities that only go so far. 'Iraq', said President Sadat to an interviewer, 'wants to be the architect of the Greater Palestine. But mark my word and mark it well. Iraq is, and will continue to be, a country of no weight in the Arab world'. Once again, there is the vintage Sadat contempt for his rivals mixed with a great deal of insight.

The disarray of Sadat's rivals, then, is a complex phenomenon that can not be pushed away or exorcised by summit conferences. This has given him room for maneuver. But he has problems of his own. What are the goals in pursuit of which his tactical skills are deployed? What kind of society does he seek to build? What does he intend to do about the 'real' question in Egyptian politics – the mounting gap between the rich and the poor?

About Sadat, I have a final query: could it be that the self-professed admirer of Sa'd Zaghlul dismantled the legacy of Abdul Nasser (the pan-Arabist idea) in pursuit of Sa'd's Egyptian nationalism, only to become a modern-day Khedive Ismael? In other words, has his propensity toward extremism pushed him to a scale of dependency and Western mimicry that is sure to offend some young Abdul Nasser, or young Sadat for that matter, who sees in Sadat's embrace of the West an injury to national pride?

BETWEEN PAX AMERICANA AND THE EUROPEAN PREDICAMENT

We now come to our last set of concerns: what kinds of question does all this pose to the 'trilateral community' of the USA, Western Europe and

Japan? Is there a single trilateral policy, or are we dealing here with different and often competing national interests? Can a Pax Americana protect European interests, or are we faced with yet another illustration of the European predicament in its relation to the USA –a predicament brilliantly depicted by the French Foreign Minister Michel Jobert, when he observed that 'the [American] protection no longer exists but the tutelage remains'? Conversely, does the Arab world have a European card, so to speak, in its relation with the USA? And, finally, what are the ramifications of the mix of Arab, European and American choices for the quality of international order?

The Middle East provides a fascinating arena where larger currents of world politics converge. Perhaps no other part of the world provides such a clear mirror of not only the 'objective' changes in the world, but also of subjective perceptions – the way men see reality and the extent to which later developments sustain or crush their expectation. First and foremost, the most dramatic thing that the Middle East reflects is the exhaustion and eclipse of Europe after the world wars. Once the center of international society, Europe ceased to be so at the end of World War II. Europeans tried to ignore the deeper changes, the outflanking of Europe from the east and the west by Russia and the USA, the revolt of the colonies. Suez was the last European throw of the dice, but it failed. Algeria was another bloody and doomed episode. After World War II, Europe shrinks and power slips away to former colonies and to the superpowers.

The second phase is dominated by the politics of the cold war. Middle Eastern countries are enlisted in a global crusade: some (Iraq under the Hashemites, Saudi Arabia) succumb, others opt for non-alignment. The USSR feeds off US mistakes and is introduced to the area by Egypt. This is a time of European recovery, European struggle with the 'tutelage'. Locally, the tone of the period is dominated by the more romantic, intangible strand of nationalism. The masses in the Arab world enter the political arena, superseding the more restrictive nationalism of the Arab liberals. This is as Nasser's era, just as it was the era of Nkrumah, Sukarno, and Nehru elsewhere. Locally, the era is brought to a close with the June 1967 defeat.

The third phase spans 1967–73. Loccally there is the anguish of a defeated civilization. Globally the politics of détente (particularly under the Nixon–Kissinger balance of power of 1969–73) 'freezes' the Middle East conflict and marginalizes the area. Quite interestingly, for the purposes of our analysis here, Europe and the USA begin to move in opposite directions on Middle Eastern questions: this phase witnesses what Nadar Safran aptly called the 'prevailing of the US-Israeli relationship' at the same time that De Gaulle moves in a pro-Arab direction. This is also a phase of great turmoil in US-European relations.

The fourth phase (1973–7) is a mixed bag. It opens with the revolt of the non-West and the launching of the so-called 'new international economic order'. The oil embargo, nuclear proliferation and the revolt of the 'new majority' at the United Nations, challenge the rule of the game. There are increasing cracks in the edifice of superpower détente and growing US conviction that détente had been oversold, that its 'code' had been repeatedly violated. Locally this phase marks the extension of Pax Americana into the Middle East and the ascendancy of the conservative oil states in inter-Arab politics. This phase witnesses Egypt's (steady) diplomatic defection and the fragmentation of the dominant Arab center.

The fifth phase (1977–?) is in full swing. Its real substance is the inability of the managers of order to keep things from falling apart. Objectively speaking, both superpowers are stalemated, both are incapable of keeping clients in power (witness Iran, witness Afghanistan), of setting jectively speaking, both superpowers are stalemated, both are incapable of keeping clients in power (witness Iran, witness Afghanistan) of setting their way. From the perspectives of the *status quo* power, there is a perceived decline in power. From the revisionist power's viewpoint, there is a sense of being hemmed in, of being driven out of favored positions. The incapacity of the Carter administration to stand behind the joint USA–USSR declaration of October 1977 on the Middle East seals the fate of a 'global' settlement. The initiative against the global settlement is seized by Sadat, whose journey to Jerusalem was a vote of protest against the reintroduction of the USSR into the negotiations. To use Sadat's jargon, the USA becomes a 'full partner' in the search for a settlement. Mr Carter begins with the blueprint of the Brookings Report favoring a comprehensive peace and ends up sponsoring a separate Egypt-Israeli accord.

This last phase witnesses an attempt to reduce things onec again into stark cold war terms, that is, to offer the recipes of the second phase. The prospects for such an attempt are not particularly promising, because the objective troubles and trends identified in the fourth phase (the demographic explosion, nuclear proliferation, the diffusion of economic power, the growing assertiveness of almost everybody) still persist.

Any assessment of Europe's chances and possibilities in the Arab world would have to proceed from a wager on the nature of the international system. According to what Stanley Hoffmann has labeled the 'tough guy' approach to international politics, a kind of 'High Noon' version of international diplomacy, Europe would have an insignificant role to play in the Middle East. She would have to toe the US line, for the Middle East remains a 'war system' and the advantage belongs to the power that possesses the capacity to play on the geostrategic chessboard.

This, for example, is the view of someone like Walter Laqueur. For him one idea of closer Arab-European cooperation does not have

> that much to recommend it. A weak and divided Europe would be of no great help to the Arabs either politically or militarily; a strong and united Europe, on the other hand, would be a potential danger to the Arabs for it would be in a position to assert forcefully its interests in the Eastern Mediterranean and the Persian Gulf.

Laqueur's analysis is, in my view, flawed and inadequate. It places too much emphasis on the traditional conception of world politics as a state of war; it pays insufficient attention to non-security issues. Its reductionism marginalizes Europe, because it believes that the only 'weapons' that count in the international system are military clubs.

Whenever European and American interests differ, the High Noon version of international politics is quick to see 'cravenness' on the part of Europe, the cynicism of the 'free rider'. Or it is quick to berate Europe for its 'parochialism' – what Kissinger refers to in his memoirs as Europe's 'narrowing horizons'. In this view of things, the wider horizons of the USA should be binding on Europeans. From the High Noon view of the world, it is a short journey to an unrestrained advocacy of Pax Americana.

The traditional view of statecraft has very little tolerance for pluralism and diversity. Challenges to the hegemonic actor take on the quality of moral violations. True wisdom lies in really appreciating (as opposed to merely stating it) a fact stated by President Carter in one of his press conferences: 'The countries [Europe and the USA] are different . . . they have different perspectives and different forms of government.' One might add that they have different interests and that they stand at different points in the world system. The myth of trilateralism (perhaps like the myth of pan-Arabism) tries to shackle the freedom of different actors. By imposing a fake consensus, it backfires. It often forces some players to go to great lengths to assert their independence and uniqueness.

Some of the European-American disagreements have nothing to do with European 'cravenness' or cynicism. They reflect differing political and intellectual sensibilities. The fear of (seemingly) revolutionary nationalism that haunts the USA and triggers conditioned reflexes is not as pronounced in Europe. The Europeans fought Third World nationalism and know it up close. They know that revolutionary movements get betrayed, that they settle down, that it is quite different to live in a nationalist world than to imagine it, that the bright dreams of first-generation nationalists give way to foreign debts, to IMF guidelines and to the whole dreary business of governance.

I mention this view of nationalism, because it has a bearing on two Middle Eastern cases: Europe's attitude toward the Palestinians and toward the Iranian revolution. Some of the European sympathy for the Palestinians no doubt reflects the Europeans' reading of their own interests – and are not such pursuits the very stuff of international politics? – but there is also the impact of the political sensibility we have just described. 'It would be grossly unfair', writes a West German analyst, 'to ascribe specific European policies to boot-licking the oil princes. The EEC's stand on the Palestinian question rests on the merit of the case; it is not the result of Arab pressure'.

The other recent case was the Iranian revolution. For whatever it is worth, many of the principals of the Iranian revolution (including President Bani-Sadr) lived and agitated in France. The story of France's role in the Iranian revolution is a fascinating story whose details need not detain us long. But as Neauphle de Château (Khomeini's residence) became 'le coeur battan d'Iran', the French displayed greater receptivity to the aspirations of the Iranian revolutionaries than did the USA. The distinguished French intellectual, Michel Foucault, explained it as a yearning for spirituality in politics. To be sure, the French must have expected to gain where the Americans were going to falter, but again there was a different political culture at work. France's turbulent history left the French more prepared to understand the Iranian drama. For one, the French knew far in advance of the USA that the shah was doomed. In the 'facile geopolitical theorems' popular in US official circles, Iran was not even in a prerevolutionary situation – recall the 'island of stability' toast by President Carter. The French did not have the gift of prophesy, but perhaps their own revolutionary history helped them realize that the pomp and glitter of the monarchy would collapse before revolutionary turmoil.

The advocates of Pax Americana overlook the wild shifts in the USA's political behavior, each of which is presented to the Europeans as a *fait accompli*, as the latest piece of wisdom. In the early 1970s, when the French were in the throes of an agonizing reassessment of Marxism and of the USSR, triggered in part by Alexander Solzhenitsyn's revelations, the USA was fully committed to détente, wanted none of these 'sentimental' concerns to be raised. A few years later, the USA had experienced a change of mind. Now it wanted to enlist Europe in a crusade against the USSR. The men who peddled détente in the early 1970s had become its harshest critics – witness Kissinger. The men who came to power with promises of 'new politics' and human rights sermons became super-hawks – witness the Carter trilateralists. We cannot expect others to march to such erratic drumbeats. There is concern, says an unsentimental European critic, of Washington always falling 'prey to facile geopolitical theorems'.

Europe is vulnerable to the might and concerns of the superpower from the east and to the claims and anguish of the south. In Europe's vulnerability, in her skepticism about the utility of military force and about those 'facile geopolitical theorems' may lie greater wisdom than is apparent to those anxious to dispatch the gunboats, teach the hitherto quiescent a lesson, and take us back into the dreary days of the cold war.

10 Egypt and the Western Alliance: The Politics of Westomania?

IBRAHIM KARAWAN

INTRODUCTION

During most of the 1970s, the West elicited feelings of ambivalence in many Arab states and resentment among the Palestinians. Sadat's Egypt, on the other hand, was enthralled by the West. A careful look at Cairo's 'national' newspapers, shopping centers and military parades validates such a conclusion, particularly during the last years of the decade. The newspapers endlessly repeated President Sadat's claim that Washington held 99 percent of the cards in the game of the Middle East settlement. The shopping centers carried all the latest brands of Western luxury. And the military parades became the target dates for the arrival of American Phantoms or French Mirages.

In these three interrelated issue areas – the settlement process; economic liberalization and arms supplies – the central theme in the thinking of the ruling elite has been primary reliance on the West, which meant basically the USA. Hence, the Egyptian policy since 1975 could be accused of anything but lack of internal consistency. Despite minor zigzags, it has shown a clear sense of its objectives, toward the achievement of which it proceeded at times cautiously, at other times hastily, but always without a change of basic assumptions or direction.

Contrary to the images held by many in the USA and perhaps Sadat's own wishes, Egypt has not exactly been a 'one-man show'. While on the mass level during the 1970s there has been no considerable opposition to the decisionmaker's choices – with the sole exception of their socio-economic aspects – the Egyptian elite has indulged in notable criticism of Sadat's policies. In part, this development was made possible by the limited relaxation of restrictions on political activity and expression that prevailed in the Nasserist era. However, when the elite's criticism became rather biting and threatened to influence the mass of Egyptian society, the regime responded – through quick referendums – by making its main policies virtually above discussion. Still, Sadat's approach remains on trial. While the government calls for more time and promises stable peace, imminent prosperity and military strength, its critics advocate a change of policies which in their judgment represent nothing but an exercise in futility. The 1980s await to provide the final word.

It is the objective of this chapter to analyze the development of Egypt's relations with the Western Alliance, with particular emphasis on the second half of the 1970s. The role of the West, particularly that of the USA, as 'the architect of peace', 'the supplier of arms' and 'the financier of infitah' will be explored in the following pages. Although the analysis will focus on the ruling elite's perspective, attention will also be given to alternative and opposite Egyptian viewpoints. It should be obvious that equal attention cannot be given to Egypt's policies toward each member of the Western Alliance. In this chapter, primary emphasis will be placed on Egyptian-US, followed by Egyptian-European, relations. Finally, economic factors will be examined only within the broader sociopolitical context.

'THE ARCHITECT OF PEACE'

The turning-point for Egypt's shift at the level of a global alignment was the October War of 1973. For some – not including the Soviets, who suspected Sadat's policies from the beginning – it seemed puzzling that Egypt could launch a call for Pax Americana, while the barrels of its Soviet weapons were still warm. However, there is ample evidence to indicate that Anwar Sadat's aim in October 1973 was a war of Tahrik (activation of the political aspects of the Arab-Israeli conflict) and not a war of Tahrir (liberation of the occupied lands). Even prior to the war, he concluded that limited Soviet military aid to Arabs always led to greater US arms shipments to Israel. He also realized that negotiating with the USA through the USSR, as in 1970–2, led nowhere – either because of Moscow's primary interest in détente and 'military relaxation', or because the Americans wanted to demonstrate the futility of Arab reliance on the Soviets.[1]

More than a year before the October War, Sadat's intuitive judgment suggested the practical steps to be followed. In July 1972 he expelled Soviet experts from Egypt in order to end the country's image as a Soviet client, to please the Saudis, and to signal the USA his readiness for a new departure. In February 1973 he sent his national security adviser, Hafiz Ismail, for talks with his more famous counterpart, Henry Kissinger. The effort did not achieve any progress not only because Kissinger was busy with other global issues, but because he was not in the habit of dealing with cold or frozen crises. Moreover, as Kissinger informed Ismail, the Arabs, although defeated, were raising demands as if they had won the war in 1967. A more practical perspective would have been either accepting the *status quo*, or changing it. Both entailed various degrees of risk. To Sadat, breaking the stalemate was better than doing nothing.[2]

The experience of the October War reinforced Sadat's earlier conclusions. The massive US airlift to Israel and the subsequent virtual encirclement of the Egyptian Third Army were the primary factors behind Sadat's sudden pursuit of a ceasefire, despite his earlier resistance to Soviet demands for an end to the fighting. In the wake of the 22 October ceasefire, Sadat set his eyes on Washington and the Arab oil embargo. By then, he believed, the USA had gained a strong incentive to activate its role in search of a negotiated Arab-Israeli settlement. More importantly, Sadat knew well that the Soviets lacked any direct leverage over Israel. In Sadat's operational code, Israel was 'America's step-daughter' and Washington served as 'the source of the river of life carrying everything – from a loaf of bread to Phantom fighter bombers to dollars to meet the budget deficit'.[3] After all, Sadat calculated, when Eisenhower exerted pressure for a withdrawal from Sinai in the aftermath of the Suez War, Israel could not but comply. And when Johnson and Nixon did not pressure Israel after 1967, Israel ignored the rest of the world's demands that it withdraw from occupied Arab lands. So, why should not the premium be placed on establishing the US connection, while confining the Soviet's role to the signing ceremony?

A positive answer to that question was rendered easier by Sadat's deep mistrust of the Soviets: he was quite convinced that Moscow had favored his rivals in the domestic power struggle of May 1971 (that is, Aly Sabry and his group whom Sadat to this day calls Soviet agents). Sadat was fully aware of the Soviet anger over his role in frustrating the attempted coup of July 1971 in Sudan, in the aftermath of which hundreds of Sudanese Communist Party members were executed or imprisoned. Moreover, the Soviets did not provide Egypt with the weapons necessary to launch a limited war against Israel in 1971, and thus helped make Sadat's 'year of decision' a first-class political farce. As he repeated frequently, Sadat believed that the Soviets could not forgive or forget his humiliating decision to expel 20,000 of their military personnel from Egypt in 1972. Under the circumstances Sadat concluded that the Soviets had a vested interest in the perpetuation of an Arab-Israeli stalemate that would, in turn, secure Cairo's dependency upon Moscow. He saw little hope for Soviet help in furthering a settlement that promised to render their influence in the area negligible.[4]

Against this background, one may more easily understand – without necessarily accepting – Sadat's famous dictum that the USA possessed 99 percent of the cards at play in the chancy pursuit of an Arab-Israeli settlement. Only one month after the end of the October War, Sadat restored diplomatic relations with the USA and gave his strongest support to the US effort to reach a settlement. 'Dear Henry's' shuttle diplomacy had Sadat's unconditional blessing. Through it Egypt reached two disengagement agreements with Israel, supported another one on the Syrian front in May 1974 and tried unsuccessfully in July 1974 to set the stage for a similar disengagement agreement on the Jordanian front. However, the 'step-by-step' approach soon faltered. In part, this was due to the strategy's conceptual shortcomings; in part, it was the consequence of several developments, including Watergate, the Lebanese civil war and the Rabat Arab summit resolutions naming the PLO as the sole legitimate representative of the Palestinian people.

In January 1977 two important developments took place. The first was what has become known as the 'food riots' in Egypt. Since he assumed power in September 1970, Sadat's regime had not faced a more serious challenge than that posed by the 'riots'. A popular upheaval spread through all major Egyptian cities.The demonstrators attacked the symbols of the open-door policy, denounced the prevailing corruption and called for Sadat's resignation. The situation went beyond the government's control, warranting the army's intervention to stop the riots in which hundreds were killed or injured and hundreds were arrested. In the following months, the debate between Sadat and the opposition about whether what happened was a subversion led by Moscow agents or a popular uprising did not overshadow the significance of 18–19 January as reflecting the intensity of the socioeconomic crisis and the urgency of seeking an outlet. The explosiveness of this crisis and the resultant political instability set the parameters for Sadat's drive to move faster in disengaging Egypt from the Arab-Israeli conflict and, thus, to provide a prerequisite for the functioning of the open-door policy.

The second important development was the ascendance of the new Carter administration to power in the USA, which declared its commitment to seek a comprehensive settlement to the Arab-Israeli conflict, as opposed to Kissinger's incremental policy which Sadat had strongly blessed. Being a pragmatist, President Sadat was more than forthcoming in offering his total support of the efforts of 'dear Jimmy'. Since by that time he had become somewhat more familiar with the complexity of the US political system and the various constraints on the president's choices, Sadat intensified his public relations campaign in the USA through the mass media. He also did his best to receive and charm every senator or congressman – no matter how junior – who visited Egypt and to encourage more visits. And apparently on the assumption that nothing gets done without a deadline, he declared 1977 to be the year of a peaceful settlement and the 'turning-point toward prosperity'.

By now, it seems that Sadat thought the new administration had a reasonable chance to exert effective pressure on Israel for various reasons. On the US side, the new administration was still fresh, vigorous and relatively insulated against the pressures that usually accompany the pre-election period. On the Israeli side, the new prime minister, with his notorious positions about the 'liberated territories', risked widening the gap between the Israeli and US positions. And above all, the third and final year of the implementation of the Sinai agreement was about to begin. Any US administration, and especially that of Carter, was not likely to allow the collapse of the fragile structure of peace made possible by the Nixon–Ford administrations.

By the time the Carter administration began to pressure Israel in mid-1977, that country had a new ruling coalition of 'hawkish generals and doctrinaire rabbis' which did not yield to US pressure.[5] When, in mid-September 1977, Washington suggested the idea of a single Arab delegation to the Geneva conference, including Palestinian representatives, Dayan insisted that only non-PLO Palestinians may take part in a Jordanian delegation. In a statement released on 25 September, the Israeli Cabinet emphasized that no negotiations would be conducted with a united Arab delegation.[6] When Washington reached an agreement with Moscow about the points that appeared in their joint communiqué of 1 October 1977, Israel and its supporters in Congress and the mass media reacted strongly. As a result, the administration retreated five days later and reached an agreement with Israel on a working paper which defined the question of Palestinian representation and the nature of the committees at the proposed Geneva conference. Not surprisingly, most of the Arab states promptly rejected the American-Israeli agreement as favoring the Israeli position.

In mid-October 1977 Sadat sent a letter to Carter, asking for amendments to the US-Israeli working paper that might allow PLO representatives to take part in a unified Arab delegation. Carter's reply clearly demonstrated the constraints under which the new president worked. The handwritten reply was not delivered through the normal diplomatic channels. According to both Al Tohamy and Ghali,[7] the US president expressed his belief that the situation had reached a 'blind alley'; he could do nothing to bridge the gap between the two sides. In Carter's view, the disagreements among the Arabs themselves were often greater than those between them and Israel, and he felt that only an imaginative and unprecedented step was needed to break the deadlock. Whether Carter – who might have been aware of the Egyptian-Israeli secret contacts a month before in Morocco – was alluding to direct negotiations, can still not be verified. But according to the statements of the Egyptian president and the assessment of his top aides, Carter's personal letter played a very important role in accelerating Sadat's decision to go to Jerusalem.

Sadat's reading of the USA's performance was rather grim: Carter's meetings with Israeli and Arab leaders in April and May 1977 had led nowhere. Vance's shuttle diplomacy in the region in August left the major problems unsolved. Carter's and Vance's subsequent meetings with the Israeli and Arab foreign ministers in September 1977 did not produce results. Carter's attempt to find common grounds with the Soviets, in October, only antagonized the Israelis and their supporters in the USA, while his agreement with Israel on 5 October antagonized both the Arabs and the USSR. The failure of Carter's efforts sparked Sadat to undertake his risky initiative and to follow a different scenario played out on the world stage.

Obviously, Sadat did not drop the US card. On the contrary, he thought that by embarking on his 'imaginative and unprecedented action', he would increase the value of his US connection. By going to Israel and offering peace in his television diplomacy, Sadat aimed at changing the attitudes of the US public, Congress and the USA's Jewish community. The centrality of this objective in Sadat's strategic thinking is widely conceded by now.

What if this did not happen? According to Sadat's perspective, he was taking a rather calculated risk. If after the visit Israel did not respond positively, the 'worst-case scenario' that she always raised would clearly be revealed as an excuse for keeping Arab lands. In that case Israel's policy would be condemned and she would be further isolated on the international level. But more importantly, Sadat expected the 'Israeli-US connection' to weaken, thereby facilitating stronger US pressure on Israel. He further assumed that this would ensure his reacceptance among Arab ranks as the master tactician who achieved the unthinkable: the political disengagement between Israel and the USA.

No wonder, then, that since his trip to Jerusalem, Sadat has consistently insisted that Washington be a 'full partner' in the Egyptian-Israeli talks. Given the option of staying on the USA's good side or returning to the Arab coalition just before the Camp David conference, the Egyptian decisionmaker opted for the former, signed the Camp David framework and declared his faith that Carter would continue the peace process toward the achievement of a comprehensive settlement. Although underwhelmed by Reagan's victory in November 1980, and the new administration's 'Jordanian option', Sadat has continued emphasizing that the Egyptian-US connection is a strategic relationship, not a tactical move and that 99 percent of the cards of the game are in Washington's hands regardless of who occupies the White House.

After the continuing stalemate of the autonomy talks beyond their target date for completion in May 1980, the European Venice declaration in June 1980 and – most importantly – Carter's defeat in the presidential elections, Sadat showed some interest in exploring a West European role in pursuing a comprehensive settlement in the Middle East. Europe's interest in assuming such a role first became evident after Camp David and the subsequent Egyptian-Israeli peace treaty which were greeted in Europe with implicit criticism and unmistakable reservations. Some Arab countries, like Jordan and Saudi Arabia, tried to capitalize on those reactions and encouraged a European initiative. Their purpose was to persuade Europe to offer its own framework for a settlement in order to change the rules of the game as put down in Camp David.

The June 1980 Venice declaration stopped short of achieving that objective, even though it called for the recognition of the Palestinians' right of self-determination and the association of the PLO with the peace process. Nevertheless, President Sadat remained skeptical of the value of these moves in light of what he refers to as Arafat's inability to make decisions. It is likely that until April 1982 when Egypt is scheduled to regain control over all of Sinai, Sadat will be disinclined to broaden the framework of the peace process or to change the Camp David agreements or the UN Resolution 242 significantly.

The US administration fully shared Sadat's interest in checking an independent European role regarding the peace process. It is interesting to note that, while Washington encouraged the Europeans to replace the USSR as arms suppliers to Egypt, it discouraged them from playing an active role in the settlement process. This is not surprising in light of the fact that Washington obviously considered the former European role as beneficial and the latter as disadvantageous to US interests.

While the new Reagan administration was still formulating its policy toward the complicated Middle East problems. Sadat seized the opportunity in February 1981 to address the European Parliament and improve the low-key Egyptian-French relationship. In Luxembourg and Paris the essence of Sadat's message was that Europe should play its role in co-ordination with that of the USA and not in competition with it. He called on Europe to help bring about a mutual Israeli-Palestinian recognition and to agree on the guarantees it can offer in the final peace agreements. In his view, a triangular relationship involving Europe, the Middle East and Africa promised to yield great economic, strategic and cultural dividends. Sadat also took the opportunity to warn the West Europeans, especially the French, against Colonel Qaddafi's intrusive adventures in Africa – as exemplified in Chad recently.

Not unexpectedly, Sadat's policy of total reliance on the USA has had its domestic critics some of whom, like Heikal, had previously criticized

Egypt's total reliance on the USSR. These critics – naturally – have varied ideological and political stands, and thus lack a coherent platform. None the less, at the risk of oversimplification, I will briefly highlight their major arguments.[8]

First, although the USA is an important actor, putting every proverbial egg in the US basket is a grave mistake. Because the USA is not a direct party to the conflict, its role really cannot be that of a negotiator; and because the USA is not neutral, its role is far from being that of a mediator. Verbal articulations like 'full partner' do not solve the problem. The USA has significant interests in the Middle East and could exert leverage on Israel. However, this does not justify that Washington be assigned the role of the one and only architect of political settlement in the Middle East. Even US decisionmakers did not share President Sadat's estimates of what the US government can do.

Secondly, the exclusion of the USSR from the peace process was another mistake. It may be true that the Soviets gave Egypt less arms than Cairo needed, but it remains very true that the crossing of the canal was achieved by Egyptians using sophisticated Soviet arms against Israelis carrying US arms. The issue is not the moral one, of turning suddenly to your erstwhile chief supporter's main rival. The real issue is that the exclusion of the Soviets weakens the bargaining power of the Arab side as a whole.

Thirdly, Sadat overestimated what this 'honest' president or that clever secretary of state could do to promote a comprehensive settlement. Contrary to the political systems in the Arab world which are generally very personalized, the US system is marked by a high degree of institutionalization, if not fragmentation, of powers. There are immense societal pressures that often constrain the ability of the US administration to pursue certain courses of action, regardless of the administration's preferences. Carter's experience in the few days following the Soviet-US communiqué epitomizes this point.

Fourthly, while Soviet military aid to the Arabs was insignificant to permit a military victory over Israel, it was not the only or the most important factor in the Arabs' failure to defeat Israel. On the other hand, the USA's effort proved unable to reach a comprehensive settlement that meets the minimum irreducible Arab demands. It succeeded only in arranging a separate treaty between Egypt and Israel that rules out the Arab military option in the short run. This treaty contributed further to the weakening of the overall Arab position, since it isolated Egypt from the Arabs. Assuming 'rationality', it is unreasonable to expect Israel to be forthcoming in the 'autonomy talks' which have been dragging on between a party that has not been willing to give, and a party that has not been authorized to negotiate!

'THE SUPPLIER OF ARMS'

In the aftermath of the Egyptian-US exclusion of the USSR from the peace process, the Soviet arms transactions to Egypt have slowed down significantly. Consequently, after Sinai II the Egyptian army was facing serious problems resulting from the shortage of functional equipment and much-needed spare-parts. In response, President Sadat embarked on the policy of 'diversification of sources of arms'. With Riyadh footing the bill, Egypt was able to place orders on British and French jet fighters, helicopters and air-to-surface missiles. But maybe of equal importance to the Saudi financial support was the USA's political backing. As a matter of fact, both the financier and the broker did not leave any doubt about their blessing of Sadat's reorientation of Egyptian policy in the direction of the West. Undoubtedly they perceived a joint interest in breaking the USSR's monopoly as arms supplier to Egypt which had traditionally played a central role on the regional level.[9]

The beginnings of US arms transfer relationship with Egypt could also be traced back to Sinai II. At that time Kissinger aimed at establishing a 'quasi-military' relationship between Cairo and Washington on a symbolic level. Only six C-130 transport airplanes were delivered as a signal of support for Sadat, who was facing a campaign of criticism in the Arab world because of his acceptance of 'unilateral and partial solutions'. In the summer of 1977, in the midst of its attempts to reconvene the Geneva conference, the Carter administration agreed to sell Egypt fourteen additional C-130s to enhance Egypt's 'logistical flexibility' and to induce Cairo to proceed with US diplomacy in pursuit of a negotiated settlement. That was also the time of the much-reported Soviet and Cuban activities in Africa that extended from Angola to Ethiopia and Zaire. It was in the latter's famous Sheba I that the Egyptian president had decided to intervene and beef up the forces of the pro-Western Mobuto against radical guerrillas. The Egyptian leadership had hoped that such intervention would highlight to the USA and Western Europe the value of augmenting Egypt's military capabilities.[10]

Apparently more conditions had to be met by Egypt in order to set the stage for a full-fledged military relationship with the USA. Two of these were to materialize during the second half of 1977. First, by the end of the summer of 1977 Egypt's relationship with the USSR reached the point of rupture. The Soviets, still embittered by Egyptian behavior after the war, imposed a total arms embargo on Egypt and refused to meet Cairo's demands for the rescheduling of debts. In retaliation, Sadat abrogated the treaty of friendship and cooperation between Cairo and Moscow. Furthermore, he terminated the naval and air facilities previously given to the Soviets, and declared a unilateral moratorium on the repayment of military debts to the USSR for ten years.[11]

Secondly, the Egyptian policy toward America's 'special ally' in the Middle East, Israel, witnessed a dramatic and unconditional recognition through President Sadat's visit to Jerusalem in November 1977, which was preceded by negotiations between Egypt and Israel in Morocco during the third week of September 1977. On the one hand, Sadat's peace initiative enabled the USA to offer Egypt military assistance without jeopardizing its commitments to Israel. On the other hand, the growing isolation of Egypt in the Arab world led to a primary reliance on the USA for military assistance, economic aid as well as diplomatic backing. As a result, the military sales from the USA to Egypt jumped from $68·4 million in 1976 to $937·3 million in 1978.[12]

On 14 February 1978 Secretary of State Vance announced the administration's decision to sell Cairo fifty F-5Es in the context of a package-deal of $5 billion worth of arms to Israel, Saudi Arabia and Egypt. Despite his satisfaction with the package formula as a demonstration of a change in the USA's policy toward the area, Sadat was not quite pleased with the US offer of F-5Es, which he once described as a tenth-rate airplane. However, after the signing of the Camp David agreements, the transaction of these fifty airplanes was among the casualties of a major Saudi-Egyptian political rift and severe war of words, as a result of which the Saudis decided to suspend their financing of Egypt's share of the package deal.

But the Egyptian-US arms relationship was soon to gain a strong momentum after the collapse of the shah's regime in Iran, the signing of the Egyptian-Israeli peace treaty, and the Soviet intervention in Afghanistan – all of which, within less than a year, created an atmosphere conducive to further leaps in the emerging Egyptian-US connection. While the first and the third developments increased the US need for regional allies, the second was among the reasons for perceiving Egypt as an acceptable candidate. In the aftermath of the Egyptian-Israeli peace treaty, Egypt was offered £1·5 billion in military credits from the USA. Instead of the F-5E, Egypt placed orders for thirty-five of the more advanced F-4 aircraft, 800 M-113 armed personnel carriers (APC) and eleven improved Hawk anti-aircraft missile batteries.[13] For the fiscal year 1981–2 Egypt obtained additional US credits to purchase 244 M-60 A3 tanks in addition to forty F-16 jet fighters, 550 APCs and one additional Hawk surface-to-air battery.[14] In July 1980 the administration asked Congress to approve the sale of sixty-seven additional M-60 A3 tanks to Egypt. And in early September it was announced that Washington would sell Egypt 52 TOW anti-tank missiles in addition to their carriers and twelve 65-foot patrol boats.[15]

The military relationship between Egypt and the USA has been extended to include the transfer of military technology, licensing and coproduction of arms. Egypt's need for US assistance in these areas emerged after Saudi Arabia, the United Arab Emirates and Qatar withdrew their financial backing of the Arab Military Industries Organization (AMIO) in accordance with the resolution of the Baghdad summit conference. The organization had been predicated on a partnership among Gulf petrodollars, West European military technology and Egyptian infrastructure and workforce. Reportedly, France and Britain were reluctant to proceed with arrangements for licensing and coproduction of their weapons in Egypt in light of Cairo's inability to cover the expenses and for fear of offending a more lucrative customer, Saudi Arabia.[16] From Sadat's vantage-point, given the non-existence of a Soviet option and the evaporation of the Euro-Arab option, the USA was the only remaining alternative.

After some technical examination of existing Egyptian capabilities,[17] specific agreements were reached. On 21 October 1979 the two countries signed an agreement to cooperate in manufacturing and assembling armored vehicles and electronic equipment. Egyptian officials subsequently revealed that negotiations had already taken place with the USA for a licence to manufacture the F-5 jet, TOW anti-tank missiles and spare-parts of other equipment.[18]

To demonstrate that the growing strategic relationship with Washington was a two-way street, President Sadat offered the USA access to Egyptian military facilities 'to help any Arab or Islamic country that asks for such help, and to rescue the American hostages in Iran as well as to project more military power in the Middle East'.[19] Deputy Prime Minister and Foreign Minister Kamal Hassan Ali explained the offer in detail. The proffered facilities included: refueling rights, transit in airspace and movement of US military forces across Egyptian territory.[20] In fact, the US-Egyptian military relationship that developed was much more extensive.

Among the most important aspects of that evolving relationship was the deployment of two airborne warning and control systems (AWACS) to Egypt (in December 1979–January 1980) to improve US intelligence-gathering in the area and practise combat operations. Three months later, Qena Airbase in Upper Egypt was reportedly among the staging sites for the unsuccessful American rescue attempt in Iran. During July–October 1980 twelve USAF F-4Es were sent to Egypt for training in weather and desert conditions similar to those of the Gulf.[21] Late in August 1980 Pentagon officials announced a plan to construct a staging facility for the Rapid Deployment Force (RDF) near Ras Banes on the Red Sea.[22] Finally, in November 1980 about 1,400 of the RDF engaged in a two-week exercise in Egypt in the first action involving US ground combat units in the Middle East for more than two decades. Problems of aircraft logistics, maintenance, communication and camouflage for ground troops in desert conditions were emphasized during the exercise.[23]

It would be impossible to understand the growing Egyptian-US military strategic relationship adequately without examining the setting in which it developed. For the purpose of this chapter, the emphasis will be on the situational analysis from the Egyptian perspective. One should take into account, however, the high degree of convergence of perceptions and interests of Egyptian and US central decisionmakers, particularly since 1977. Having that in mind, we confront the question: why did Sadat pursue the aforementioned military relationship with the USA?

Most important in Sadat's calculations was to make it clear to the pro-Western oilproducing countries in the Gulf that Egypt could become the linchpin of US strategy in the Middle East. Through maintaining the inflow of US arms and military technology, and granting facilities to the US RDF, Sadat was actually sending a message to 'the ruling families of the sheik-doms and principalities in the Gulf' that they had no alternative to Egypt's role, if they were to reduce their vulnerabilities.[24] He wanted to prove to them that their arms embargo and economic boycott would not increase his vulnerability, but could increase theirs. After the end of the RDF training exercise in the Egyptian desert, Sadat put his message in these public words: 'I do not need the Saudis . . . They are the ones who need me. The American can come to Egypt to defend Saudi Arabia and return back to Egyptian territory.'[25]

In a number of instances of transfer of military equipment by the USA to Egypt, Sadat and his aides made it very clear to the US officials that the agreed-upon items had to arrive in Egypt before the nationally televised military parade on the 6 October. It has been reported that President Sadat took the time to plan even the most minute details of the annual parade himself to demonstrate Egypt's military strength to its neighbors. Given Sadat's repeated offers of assistance to the conservative Arab regimes, a demonstration of Egypt's military vitality would give credibility to his rhetoric. Also, Sadat's insistence on receiving US pledges to provide Egypt's air force with 'the prestige weapon', F-15s, has similar symbolic significance. When the USA conveyed to Egypt its agreement in principle, Kamal Hassan Ali was quick to describe that decision as 'a step that put Egypt and Israel for the first time on equal footing in access to sophisticated American weapons'.[26]

Such demonstrations of the dividends of a close alignment with the USA and peace with Israel may serve Sadat's objectives with one central actor in his domestic constituency, namely, the military. No sound analysis of this dimension can afford to ignore or play down the centrality of the military in the whole legacy of the regime, and the maintenance of its stability. One of the 'six principles' of the military takeover in July 1952 was to build a strong army. After that the military establishment continued to be the main power base of the regime. Under Nasser, the army enjoyed a disproportionate share of political power. Under Sadat, it served to a lesser degree as a pool of political recruitment (Hosni Mubarak, Kamal Hassan Ali) and as a last resort in 'restoring law and order' (the 'food riots' in January 1977).

Due to the gradual Soviet arms embargo since mid-1974 and the halt in the Arab finance of Egypt's military purchases from the West since mid-1978, the army's preparedness was significantly jeopardized. The inflow of US weapons and spare-parts as well as joint training with US troops may have aimed, among other things, at enhancing Sadat's political credibility among the military and demonstrating his regime's efforts at upgrading the preparedness of the Egyptian armed forces.[27]

On Egypt's part, Sadat's offer of access to military facilities for the USA could be viewed as one means of 'proving himself to the Americans', and enhancing his credibility as an ally of the USA to make up for the loss of Iran. Moreover, from Sadat's vantage-point, such an offer was a gesture in response to the economic and military aid given by the USA in support of his regime after the Camp David agreements, which he obviously sought to maintain in the future. Moreover, the Egyptian leader may have expected that the USA would have additional incentives to bring about a rapprochement between Egypt and Washington's friends in the Gulf. Needless to say, if such an effort – which according to Egypt's Defence Minister Abu Gazalla, has been in progress[28] – succeeds, Cairo's Arab isolation would be broken, paving the way for more economic and military dividends. If it does not succeed, the USA would have no other realistic alternative but to continue its assistance to Egypt, at least at the present levels.

While stressing that Egypt can play an active regional role to contain any potential instability in pro-Western countries, the public statements of US officials emphasized the need to keep this role limited. Former Secretary of Defense Brown gave examples only of 'logistical support and technical training'.[29] Harold Saunders repeatedly pointed out that the Egyptian military role could be useful not on a large scale, 'but rather particular units in a situation playing a role in Zaire or closer by in Oman or in Yemen if there was a conflict in these areas. Egypt should have the capability to play a modest role of that kind'.[30]

On Egypt's part, there have been repeated warnings against increasing Soviet presence in surrounding countries, like Libya, Ethiopia and South Yemen. President Sadat urged the USA to adopt a more assertive policy and get rid of the 'Vietnam complex'. According to his assessment, the USA should further bolster Egypt's military capability and gain access to facilities in the area. If the USA does not do that, the Soviets and their clients would try to outflank Egypt, strike at the Sudan and threaten the oil-rich Arabian Peninsula and the Gulf.[31]

Also, the enormous Libyan military acquisitions of advanced Soviet arms have been a distinct source of concern for the Egyptian political and military leadership. That concern did not stem from a belief that Libyan forces pose a threat to Egypt. Rather, it stemmed from the anticipation that the Soviets, Cubans, or East Germans – or their Libyan trainees – may use the stored arms against the Sudan, or to spread their influence through operations like that in Chad in late 1980. The Soviet presence and storage of arms in Ethiopia and South Yemen have been perceived by the Egyptian leadership as a potentially destabilizing factor to Sadat's allies: the Sudan, Somalia and Oman, as well as to North Yemen and possibly Saudi Arabia.[32]

In short, President Sadat's message to the West, and to the USA in particular, is that the sudden inflow of the oil wealth, the accumulation of military equipment, the rise of Islamic fundamentalism and the Soviet policy are bound to further instability in the Middle East during the 1980s. According to Sadat's assessment, the battle for the Gulf oil and the control of the oil sealanes has begun, and the West has no realistic option but to check its adversaries through projecting more military muscle and political resolve. Sadat seems to entertain great designs about Egypt's possible regional caretaker role in checking this looming instability.

The Egyptian leadership feels Egypt has a number of qualifications for that role. The first is Egypt's identity as an Arab and Islamic country which may legitimate its performance of that role in a way not available to any regional power which is non-Arab (like Iran under the shah), or non-Arab and non-Muslim (like Israel). The second is Egypt's central geopolitical location, which increases its strategic significance regarding a host of regional conflicts (namely, the Gulf and the Horn). The third is Egypt's political stability and reliability as an ally emanating from the homogeneity of its population, its long history of strong central control and its generally tame religious establishment. The last one is Egypt's military strength relative to the surrounding Arab and African states. Egypt's development of a large military infrastructure should enable her forces to convert quickly any significant arms acquisitions into usable military power.

Sadat's critics, on the other hand, have voiced several reservations about Egypt's assumption of the role of a regional policeman. In their view, Sadat pursued a course of action *vis-à-vis* the USSR as a supplier of arms that was bound – at least for a decade – to weaken the military preparedness of the Egyptian army. Diversification of arms may be a neat objective, but in implementation it has been faced with enormous problems of replacement and standardization. Despite the declared arms agreements with the USA – which are due to be fulfilled by the end of 1983 – the level of Egyptian armament will be less than what it was on the eve of the October War of 1973. Even more time will be needed before the new weapon systems and force structure are absorbed adequately by the Egyptian armed forces.

Secondly, the evolving Egyptian-US military quasi-alliance and the use of Egyptian territory as a launching-pad for US intervention in the Gulf raises legitimate questions about Egypt's proclaimed non-alignment. It does put Egypt totally on the side of the West in the midst of a growing cold war atmosphere. However, an Egyptian confrontation with the USSR is neither justifiable, nor feasible.

Thirdly, the overadvertisement of Egypt's readiness to act as an interventionary regional force may reveal a certain lack of touch with the Egyptian people at the present juncture. On the domestic level, there is a strong inward-looking attitude, rising expectations of prosperity around the corner, but not readiness for more painful sacrifices in fighting anybody, including the so-called Soviet surrogates. It would certainly look paradoxical to advocate Egyptian disengagement from the Arab-Israeli conflict and be willing at the same time to engage her in Arab domestic, inter-Arab, or African conflicts.[33]

Moreover, on the regional level, the other Arabs, especially in the Gulf, whom Sadat is offering Egyptian help, are not likely to seek it. The greatest destabilizing factor in their judgment is the continuation of the Palestinian problem. There are sizeable Palestinian communities in these countries and the Gulf rulers are afraid of the unwelcome demographic, political and social changes their presence implies. Sadat's peace – and normalization – with Israel, in the absence of a settlement to the Palestinian problem, makes any close association with his regime a net liability for those rulers both on the domestic, and inter-Arab levels.[34]

Lastly, on the global level, after the Iranian experience the USA could not afford to act once again on the basis of the Nixon Doctrine. In spite of the peculiarly American factors that 'mitigate against the functioning of an affective learning process' based on 'institutional memory',[35] the US trauma of the 'loss of Iran' and its products and byproducts (like the hostage crisis) was too sudden, too painful and too recent to be ignored during the next few years.[36] In addition, US policymakers may feel concerned about the possibility that enhancing Egypt's interventionary capability could tempt President Sadat to get involved in a military action against Libya. Such an action would aggravate regional instability, providing a more favorable atmosphere for increased Soviet presence and creating a situation of superpower involvement by proxy in another regional conflict, in an area already loaded with such conflicts.[37]

'THE FINANCIER OF INFITAH'

The discussion of the open-door policy (Infitah) brings us to the socio-economic setting of the political decisions that we have dealt with before. Obviously, this policy has not been studied in sufficient depth so far. As a result, a number of basic questions about it remain. One of these questions relates to the relationship between Egypt and the West. Where does Infitah fit within the policy package that the Egyptian regime adopted after 1973? Was the dismantling of Nasser's 'socialist' legacy considered a prerequisite in order to persuade the USA and its allies to sponsor Cairo's scenario in settling the Arab-Israeli conflict? Or was Infitah the ultimate objective, with the settlement of the Arab-Israeli conflict serving as a necessary condition for its realization? Or was it both?

Despite the scarcity of research, the available literature so far provides some suggestions. In his study of the 'Implications of Infitah for US-Egyptian relations', John Waterbury talks about the subordination of Egyptian domestic policy to the exigencies of maneuvering in the international arena. The essence of his argument is that, although Infitah and the turn to the West constitute a 'package deal', the first is a dependent variable while the second is the independent one. For Sadat's regime the central challenge was the restoration of Egypt's occupied territories. Once a decision was made in the immediate aftermath of the 1973 war, that only the USA can help Egypt regain Sinai, other decisions on the domestic front, including that of 'economic liberalization' were to follow quickly.[38]

Other students of Egypt emphasize the primacy of domestic structure. Kahiza and Cooper[39] argue that the roots of economic liberalization go back to the second half of the 1960s. Hence, Infitah preceded and even precipitated the turn toward the West and, after 1967, the search for a settlement of the Arab-Israeli conflict. According to this school, to understand the political economy of Egypt in the 1970s, it is necessary to follow its antecedents in the final year of Nasser's regime in spite of noticeable quantitative differences. The stagnation of 'state capitalism' and the growth of a consumer-oriented middle class led to greater pressures for economic liberalization and closer relations with the West, particularly the USA.

Both interpretations are partly lacking. The first treats President Sadat virtually in isolation of his social environment. The main decisions which have shaped Egyptian society are seen as the product of his style of thinking, way of reasoning and personal idiosyncrasies. On the other hand, the second interpretation, in its extreme form reduces the decisionmaker to a puppet in the hands of a certain class without specifying the way its hold over the decisionmaker is operationalized. Moreover, this argument overlooks the facts that in reality every policy has its antecedents and significant quantitative changes often lead to qualitative ones.

I would, thus, like to suggest that although the roots of Infitah go back to the post-1967 war period, Sadat's perception of his environment after 1973 led to the conclusion that full-fledged economic liberalization represented an objective to be sought both in its own right, and as a means to achieve other ends. Needless to say, Egypt's economic situation in the aftermath of the October War reached a critical point with a number of serious bottlenecks imposing stagnation. The most important of these bottlenecks resulted from a shortage of funds. The inflow of foreign funds was deemed the only outlet, given Egypt's meager and exhausted domestic resources, and the rising expectation of the Egyptian masses, for an immediate improvement in their standard of living.[40]

Initially, Egypt turned to its wealthy neighbors in the Gulf who had accumulated tremendous amounts of petrodollars after 1973. Cairo calculated that the Egyptian role and sacrifices in the war provided her with both the moral right, and the political leverage, for seeking large financial support from the Arab oilproducing countries. Besides, as Malcolm Kerr has rightly pointed out, the element of complementarity was very important in Sadat's high expectations from the Arab 'haves'. Egypt had a significant industrial base and the largest pool of skilled and unskilled manpower in the Arab world. The Gulf states, on the other hand, only had enormous wealth. Both sides lacked what the other had in abundance, so there existed a base for partnership.[41]

In addition, there were two important sociopolitical factors at work. The first was Sadat's complete reorientation of Egyptian foreign policy in a way that fit the interests of the conservative Arabs. He dropped the classification of Arab states into progressive and reactionary and adopted an active anti-Soviet policy in the area. The second was a 'new realism' which the war of 1973 generated in the Arab world as a whole. Haikal, in one of his shrewd insights, refers to the increased influence of a new breed of powerbrokers, middlemen, wealthy merchants, ambitious technocrats and arms dealers like Kamal Adham, Mahdi al Tager, Adnan Khashoggi and, one could add, Osman Ahmed Osman. This coalition had a vested interest in dismantling the machinery and symbols of the Nasserist era. The time was ripe, especially since that era did not end on a particularly positive note, and the fortunes of the Arab conservatives were in the ascendance. The era of the *thawra* (revolution) seemed to be over, while the era of the *tharwa* (wealth) was beginning.[42]

It was in such a context that the open-door policy was officially proclaimed in 1974. The essence of the policy was to create the conditions conducive for a trilateral approach in dealing with Egypt's economic malaise. According to this approach, Arab petrodollars and Western technology would be combined with Egypt's manpower and industrial and agricultural potential in a new Marshall Plan. In June 1974 law 43 was passed, opening the door for foreign investments, the establishment of free zones and the operation of market mechanisms in many areas of economic life.[43]

The implementation of Infitah left a lot to be desired. Foreign investments in productive areas of the economy have been seriously lacking. The ability to absorb the agreed-upon commitments of capital transactions has been hampered, among other reasons, by the problems of bureaucracy and the lack of serious feasibility studies. The free zones have become centers for the importation of Western luxury items, flooding the domestic market. This, in turn, posed a threat to certain domestic industries, nourished awkward consumption patterns, and triggered strong inflationary pressures that swept the whole economy. Disparities in income distribution have significantly increased.[44] Not surprisingly, social tensions continued to grow by leaps and bounds, reaching explosive proportions as in January 1977.

Faced with mounting political instability and attacks on the open-door policy, the regime's response was to pursue greater economic liberalization, to allow less political liberalization and to seek vehemently a settlement of the Arab-Israeli conflict, so that a more favorable atmosphere could be created for Infitah. It was expected that the termination of the state of war and subsequent regional stabilities would encourage potential foreign investors to inject capital into Egypt's economy. It is significant to recall here that the Egyptian-US Business Council in its report to President Sadat and the Egyptian government, in January 1977, emphasized that one major negative factor on foreign, and particularly US, investment in Egypt was the concern over the possibility of a resumed armed conflict with Israel.[45]

The developments that have followed since 1977 have been well publicized. Particularly after Camp David, Egypt could not maintain access to both Arab and Western financial resources. American economic aid was largely contingent upon pursuing a USA-sponsored peace with Israel. Arab aid, on the other hand, was made contingent upon Egypt's return to the Arab coalition and its pursuit of a comprehensive settlement. The choice between the two seems to have been made more on political rather than economic grounds. The first offered the Egyptian regime an immediate end to the state of war and entailed an increase of Western support. The second meant a return to an 'uneasy' coalition that was bound to run into a familiar stalemate. Moreover, there are indications that President Sadat either expected, or was made to expect, a speedy rapprochement with the pro-Western 'oil regimes' in the Gulf. Since this expectation did not materialize, the West has become the main 'financier' of the Infitah, with the USA assuming the largest share, followed by Western Europe and Japan.[46]

CONCLUSION

As the 1980s started, Egypt's dependence on the West as an 'architect of peace', 'supplier of arms' and 'financier of Infitah' has reached unprecedented levels in her recent history. To the Egyptian decisionmaker, the West had come increasingly to mean the USA, which assumed the key role in the above-mentioned issue areas. During the 1970s, there have been two discernible turning-points in Egypt's US connection. The first was the October War in 1973. The second was the peace initiative in 1977. After the former, Cairo's reliance on Washington has been at the expense of her relations with Moscow. Since the latter, Egypt developed a special relationship with the USA, while her relations with her fellow Arabs have been broken. These developments did not go uncontested in Egypt. The critics of President Sadat's policy package argued that there were other options, and that the net effect of the package has been extremely harmful. In response Sadat and his supporters argued that such a package was not only inevitable, but that it would eventually prove beneficial. The argument as to whether other – and perhaps better – options were available to Sadat in the 1970s can never be settled conclusively. However, the 1980s are likely to provide the balance sheet for the policies that Sadat has followed in the last decade.

NOTES: CHAPTER 10

This chapter is based on two projects in progress about 'Sadat's Jerusalem Decision', and 'US arms transfers and Egypt's regional role in the 1980s'. I owe a special debt of thanks to Professor Roman Kolkowicz for his encouragement and support of the first project. I am also indebted to UCLA's Center for International and Strategic Affairs and the Von Grunebaum Center for their financial support. I wish to thank Professors Malcolm Kerr, Paul Jabber and Ali Dessouki for their wise counsel and stimulating recommendations. However, I would like to absolve all the above-mentioned, as well as Dr Necla Tschirgi, who contributed many insightful editorial remarks, of any responsibility for what follows.

1 Presentation by Ambassador Tahseen Bashir, CISA Conference on the Middle East and the Western Alliance, Los Angeles, 21 February 1980.

2 Bahgat Korany, 'Absence of alternatives and crisis behavior: Egypt's war decision, October 1973', paper presented to the World Congress of the International Political Science Association, Moscow, 12–18 August 1979, pp. 23–9.

3 Anwar El Sadat, *In Search of an Identity* (New York: Harper & Row, 1978), pp. 295–6.

4 *al-Ahram*, 27 November 1977. For more details on the Egyptian-Soviet relations, see: Mohammed Heikal, *The Sphinx and the Commissar* (New York: Harper & Row, 1978); Alvin Rubinstein, *Red Star on the Nile* (Princeton, NJ: Princeton University Press, 1977); Uri Raanan, 'The Soviet-Egyptian rift', *Commentary* vol. 61, no. 6 (June 1976); and Pedro Ramet, *Sadat and the Kremlin*, California Seminar on Arms Control and Foreign Policy, Los Angeles, USA, February 1980.

5 For more details, see: Avi Shlaim and Avner Yaniv, 'Domestic politics and foreign policy in Israel', *International Affairs* (London), vol. 56, no. 2 (Spring 1980), pp. 242–62; Dan Morowitz, 'More than a change of government', *Jerusalem Quarterly* no. 5 (Fall 1977), pp. 13–19; Mattityahu Peled, 'The year of Sadat's initiative', in Milton Leitenberg and Gabriel Sheffer (eds), *Great Power Intervention in the Middle East* (New York: Pergamon Press, 1979), pp. 301–12.

6 *Jerusalem Post*, 28 September 1977.

7 Interviews with the Deputy Prime Minister Hassan Al Tohamy in the presidential headquarters in Cairo, 23 September 1977, and with Dr Butros Ghali, the Minister of State for Foreign Affairs in Cairo, 26 September 1977; see also Sadat's autobiography, op. cit., p. 302.

8 For more details, see Mohammed Heikal, *Hadith Al Mobadara* (The Talk of the Initiative) (Beirut: Dar al-Qadaya, 1978) (in Arabic); Mohammed Sid Ahmed, *Is an Egyptian-Israeli Peace Treaty Conducive to an Overall Middle East Peace?*, ACIS Working Paper No. 24, UCLA, May 1980; magazine of the Moslem Brothers, *al-Dawa*; the 1980 issues of the Labor Socialist Party newspaper, *al-Shaab*; and the series of articles written by the former Deputy Prime Minister and Foreign Minister Ismail Fahmy that were published weekly in the Arabic journal, *al-Mustaqbal*, February–April 1978.

9 Caesar Sereseres, 'US military assistance to non-industrial nations', in Stephanie Neuman and Robert Harkavy (eds), *Arms Transfer in the Modern World* (New York: Praeger, 1979), pp. 220–1.

10 See Joe Stark, 'The Carter doctrine and the US bases', *MERIP Reports*, no. 90 (September 1980), p. 7.

11 *Middle East Monitor*, 1 October 1977 p. 4.

12 *Foreign Assistance and Related Programs: Appropriations for 1980*. Hearings before the Committee on Appropriations, US Congress, House of Representatives, 96th Congress, 2nd session, pt 4, April 1980, p. 139.

13 ibid., p. 130. See *New York Times*, 11 July 1980, p. 3.

14 *Washington Post*, 26 July 1980, p. 6; *Baltimore Sun*, 9 September 1980, p. 1.

15 George Wilson, 'US will help Egypt revitalize weapons output', *Washington Post* 9 August 1979, p. 2; for more details about AMIO, see: Jake Wein,

Saudi-Egyptian Relations: The Political and Military Dimensions of Saudi Financial Flows to Egypt, RAND Corporation, Santa Monica, California (January 1980), p. 6327; and Raime Vayregnen, 'The Arab organization of industrialization: a case study in the multinational production of arms', *Current Research on Peace and Violence*, vol. II, no. 2 (1979), pp. 66–79.

16   *Washington Post*, 9 August 1979, p. 1.

17   *New York Times*, 22 October 1979, p. 13.

18   See *Washington Post*, 14 February 1980, p. 1; *Boston Globe*, 27 February 1980 p. 3; *al-Ahram*, 12 November 1980, 19 November 1980, p. 1.

19   *The Christian Science Monitor*, 14 July 1980.

20   *Washington Post*, 8 January 1980, p. 14.

21   ibid., 14 November 1980, p. 19.

22   See *Washington Star*, 7 September 1980, p. 3; *al-Ahram*, 14 December 1980, p. 1.

23   See *Washington Post*, 8 November 1980, p. 14; *New York Times*, 13 November 1980, p. 17.

24   *Christian Science Monitor*, 14 July 1980.

25   *al-Ahram*, 25 November 1980, p. 7.

26   *Washington Post*, 24 February 1980 p. 17.

27   For similar ideas, see: *Aviation Week and Space Technology*, 23 June 1980, p. 20; *New York Times*, 9 July 1980, p. 7; *Baltimore Sun*, 11 July 1980, p. 4.

28   According to General Abu Ghazalla. General David Jones, Chairman of the US Joint Chiefs of Staff, acting in 1980 as an intermediary between Egypt and Saudi Arabia, *Washington Post*, 4 November 1980.

29   *Supplemental 1979 Middle East Package for Israel and Egypt*. Hearings before the Committee on Foreign Affairs and its Subcommittee on International Security and Scientific Affairs, 96th Congress, 1st session, April–May 1979, p. 129.

30   *FY 1981 Foreign Assistance Legislation*. Hearings before the Committee on Foreign Affairs, US Senate, 96th Congress, 1st session, pt 1, March–April 1980, pp. 248–9.

31   *New York Times*, 9 December 1980, p. 8; *al-Ahram*, 28 December 1980, p. 1.

32   For more details, see Joseph Kraft, 'As Sadat sees his neighbors', *Washington Post*, 3 April 1980, p. 19; *al-Akhbar*, 14 February 1980 p. 1; and *al-Ahram*, 1 January 1980, p. 1.

33   A similar idea was expressed by Mohammed Hassanein Heikal in a personal interview, Cairo, 21 February 1981.

34   Lutfi Al Kholi, interview, Cairo, 22 February 1981. For a similar idea, see Herman Eilts, 'Security considerations in the Persian Gulf', *International Security*, vol. 5, no. 2 (Fall 1980), pp. 79–113.

35   See Paul Jabber, 'US interests and regional security in the Middle East', *Daedalus* vol. 109, no. 4 (Fall 1980), p. 71.

, 36   According to the *New York Times*, a secret Foreign Relations Committee report urged caution in any large-scale arms deliveries to Egypt. In the subsequent discussion a number of senators, including Joseph Biden, Jr, of Delaware and Paul Sarbens of Maryland, pointed out that the USA could not run the risk of duplicating its mistakes in Iran. See *New York Times*, 7 December 1979, p. 18. A similar viewpoint was advocated by the former Chairman of the Senate Foreign Relations Committee, Senator Frank Church, in the *Washington Post*, 19 February 1980, as well as in the testimonies of Harold Brown and Harold Saunders before Congress. For more information on the debate in the US about the lessons of the 'Iranian experience', see: Anthony Lewis, 'Who lost Iran?', *New York Times*, 1 January 1979; George Ball, 'Letter to the editor of *The Economist*', reprinted in the *Baltimore Sun* 26 February 1979, p. 13; Richard Burt, 'Iranian turmoil impels US aides to question effects of arms sales', *New York Times*, 6 February 1979; David Schoenbaum, 'Passing the buck(s)', *Foreign Policy*, no. 34 (Spring 1979), pp. 14–20; George Lenczowski, 'The arc of crisis', *Foreign Affairs*, vol. 57, no. 4 (Spring 1979); pp. 796–820; and Leslie M. Pryor, 'Arms and the shah', *Foreign Policy*, no. 31 (Summer 1978) pp. 56–71.

37 This viewpoint could also be found in US sources; for example, see *Aviation Week and Space Technology*, 23 June 1980, p. 20; and for a similar viewpoint, see William Quandt, 'The United States and the Middle East', a paper presented to Conference on the Middle East and the Western Alliance, UCLA Center for International and Strategic Studies, Los Angeles, 21–22 February 1980, p. 7.

38 John Waterbury, 'The implications of Infitah for US-Egyptian relations', in Haim Shaked and Itamar Rabinovich (eds), *The Middle East and the United States* (New York: Transaction Books, 1980), pp. 348–50.

39 See Walid Kaziha, *Palestine in the Arab Dilemma* (New York: Barnes & Noble 1979), ch. 4; and Mark Cooper, 'Egyptian state capitalism in crisis economic policies and political interests, 1967–1971', *International Journal of Middle East Studies*, vol. 10, no. 4 (1979), pp. 517–31.

40 Mohammed Hassanein Heikal, 'Egyptian foreign policy', *Foreign Affairs*, vol. 56, no. 4 (July 1978), p. 724.

41 Malcolm Kerr, 'Egypt in the shadow of the Gulf', in M. Kerr (ed.), op. cit.

42 Quoted in Ali Dessouki, 'The new Arab regional order', in ibid.

43 For more details, see Nazih Ayubi, 'Implementation capability and political feasibility of the open door policy in Egypt' in ibid.; and for a Marxist critique of the open door policy, see N. Kamel, 'Scenario of capitulation', *World Marxist Review*, no. 22 (March 1979), pp. 135–42.

44 Waterbury, op. cit., pp. 358–64.

45 *New York Times*, 1 December 1979.

46 For more details, see *Economic Support Fund Programs in the Middle East*, Report of a staff study to the Committee on Foreign Affairs, US House of Representatives, Washington, April 1979, pp. 2–35.

11 Palestinians and the Western Alliance: A Palestinian Perspective

TAWFIC E. FARAH

INTRODUCTION

The Palestinians have come a long way since the late Mrs Meir made her famous statement: 'There is no such thing as Palestinians.' The Palestinians are here, and they are here to stay. As Tawfiq Zayyad, the poet from Nazareth, says in 'Baqun' ('We shall remain'):

> Here – we have a past
> a present
> and a future
> Our roots are entrenched
> Deep in the earth
> Like twenty impossibles
> We shall remain.[1]

The Palestinians have constructed a political identity and a will of their own. They have done that in their *ghurba*, or exile, despite being geographically dispersed and fragmented and without their own territory.

The history of the past forty years shows that the Palestinians have grown politically despite repression by 'brother' and 'foe'. Their attachment to Palestine has not diminished. Short of complete obliteration, as Edward Said puts it, the Palestinians will continue to exist, and they will continue to have their own ideas about who represents them, where they want to settle, what they want to do with their national and political future.[2]

Their case revolves around a fundamental human right – the right to self-determination, which means that

> no human being should be threatened with 'transfer' out of his or her home or land; no human being should be discriminated against because he or she is not of an X or a Y religion; no human being should be stripped of his or her land, national identity, or culture, no matter the cause.[3]

Many nations have recognized the Palestinian right to self-determination, including countries of the Western Alliance. This analysis will examine the relationship between Palestinian leadership, the PLO and two groups in the alliance – the Common Market countries, and the USA. Two factors in the relationship of the PLO and the West will be underscored: the question of the PLO's legitimacy and what Fouad Ajami calls the 'lure of the West' – the complex psychological factors in the love–hate relationship Palestinians have with the West.

EUROPE AND THE PLO

The leaders of nine European Common Market countries issued a statement in Venice, Italy, on 13 June 1980:

> A just solution must finally be found to the Palestinian problem which is not simply one of refugees. The Palestinian people, which is conscious of existing as such, must be placed in a position, by an appropriate process defined within the framework of the comprehensive peace settlement, to exercise fully its right to self-determination.
>
> The achievement of these objectives requires the involvement and support of all the parties concerned in the peace settlement which the nine are endeavouring to promote in keeping with the principles formulated in the declaration . . . These principles apply to all the parties concerned, and thus the Palestinian people, and to the PLO which will have to be associated with the negotiations.[4]

At the same time, the nine governments said that 'they will not accept any unilateral initiative designed to change the status of Jerusalem' and charged the Israelis with creating 'a serious obstacle to the peace process' with their policy of expanding their settlements on the occupied West Bank of the Jordan River. French President Valéry Giscard d'Estaing, one of the prime-movers behind a Common Market stand on the Middle East, called the statement 'a clear text that does not evade the issues but offers a just and balanced point of view'.[5]

While the nine governments were making this statement, the US Secretary of State Edmund Muskie was expressing his divergent views. The EEC countries' declaration does not amount to a confrontation with the USA's position, but it does establish a distinct and clear European policy on the Middle East.[6]

The policies of the EEC and the USA have been divergent since 1973. In November of that year the EEC stated, 'In the establishment of a just and lasting peace, account must be taken of *the legitimate rights of the Palestinians*'. In June 1977 the EEC declared and stressed 'the need for *a homeland* for the Palestinian people'. This evolution was foreshadowed by a series of statements issued by the individual EEC governments since 1974.

Then, in 1974, the German, Hans Deitrich Genscher, spoke of 'allowance for the right of self-determination of the Palestinian people, including the right to establish state authority'. Mr Van Der Stoel, foreign minister of The Netherlands, used the term 'national identity' in referring to the vague 'just solution' to the refugee problem, and Mr de Guiringuad of France spoke of the 'recognition of the Palestinian right to a homeland which at the proper time could be given structures of statehood [*structures étatiques*]'.

At least on the Palestinian issue, the Europeans do not see eye to eye with the USA. There are differences in perception and approach, and varying interests in the region. These differences are not a function of 'stooping for oil', or 'licking anybody's boots'. Neither are they, as Henry Kissinger would have us believe, 'a gap between America's global interests and Europe's regional ones'.

The relationship between Europe and the Palestinians has not always been smooth (the battle over West German rearmament and the Gulf crises). But while this alliance has been dominated by the power of the USA, the situation has begun to change. America's predominance has declined, while Western Europe's has ascended: West Germany has moved into a dominant financial position in the European Community; Britain has moved from its special relations with Washington to a contentious membership in the EEC; France has moved beyond De Gaulle's obsession with independence from Washington to a policy of military autonomy with collaboration with NATO. France's good relationships with Iraq, Algeria and Saudi Arabia are part of a coherent French energy policy. (France imports about 70 percent of its oil from the Middle East.)

Although its predominance in Europe has declined, the USA has become preeminent in the Middle East, especially since the October 1973 war. The USA is now a full 'partner', 'insurer' and benefactor to a host of regimes in the area, including those of Egypt and Israel. Unlike its Western allies, the USA made a formal commitment to refrain from recognizing and/or negotiating with the PLO, until the PLO recognizes Israel's right to exist and accepts UN resolutions 242 and 338. Yet the PLO has dealt with the USA for reasons that will be discussed later. Although this relationship has not been good – at times one wonders if it will ever improve given the realities of US presidential politics. There are indications that both parties are becoming more sensitive to each other's position and limitations. Two factors, however, seem to escape US decisionmakers in their relationship with the PLO. They are the legitimacy of the PLO and the other factor referred to here as the 'lure of the West'.

LEGITIMACY OF THE PLO

The question of legitimacy is a crucial political variable in an area of the world where, as Michael Hudson suggests, the central problem of government is political legitimacy.

In the last fifteen years, the Palestinian resistance movement has developed from an embryo to a government in process that has been recognized on the regional and international levels.[7] The PLO Charter and its fundamental law modeled PLO institutions after those of established governments. The Palestine National Council serves as the 'Palestine parliament' with supreme legislative authorities. The Executive

Committtee is the 'Palestine Cabinet' with various departments and agencies directing Palestinian affairs. Its political department serves as the Ministry of Foreign Affairs with PLO offices in various countries operating as 'embassies'. The military department acts as a Ministry of Defense and is in charge of all military operations, including regular troops, guerrillas, *ashbal* (tiger cubs). The Palestine National Fund serves as a Ministry of Finance and National Economy. The Department of Information is in charge of the PLO's newspapers, radio stations and the official news agency, WAFA. There are other departments for education, social affairs, research and planning, health and occupied territories. The PLO has established its judiciary system. In the 6th Session of the National Council, held in 1969, a 'revolutionary court' was created. By Legislative Ordnance No. 5 of 1 January 1979, the Chairman of the PLO Executive Committee enacted the Revolutionary Penal Code, the Revolutionary Code of Criminal Procedures and the Revolutionary Rehabilitation Code. These codes are applied to all resistance groups as well as 'to all sectors of the Palestine people'. A court system has been established, manned by a judicial body that is independent except for administrative procedures. The judicial branch has been functioning and violators are tried and punished.

Table 11.1   *Support for the Chairman (in Percentages) by Age and Grade in School*

			Grades	
		1st (N = 82) (%)	2nd and 3rd (N = 155) (%)	4th (N = 73) (%)
I	Is the chairman of the PLO hard-working?			
	Always	89	91	90
	Sometimes	5	6	5
	Never	3	3	—
	Don't know	3	1	—
II	Does the chairman of the PLO do good work?			
	Always	90	90	95
	Sometimes	8	8	—
	Never	2	—	5
	Don't know	—	2	—
III	Does the chairman of the PLO help the people?			
	Always	85	91	93
	Sometimes	10	8	3
	Never	5	1	4
	Don't know	—	—	—

Note: For all three questions, the model response of each group is 'always'. Conversely, the proportion of 'never' responses is extremely low.

Structuring the PLO after a modern established government is not sufficient to justify it as representative of the Palestine people. I think it is more important to look at how the Palestinians themselves feel about the PLO and its leadership. Is it politically legitimate to them? To answer this question, I will review the findings of a 1978 study of Palestinian adolescents in Kuwait.[8] It provides data that substantiate the PLO's claim to legitimacy among a segment of the Palestinians in diaspora non-refugee camp dwellers.

Support for Arafat

Participants in the study were asked, 'Who is the most important person in the Palestine revolution?' The overwhelming majority named Yassir Arafat. The students were also asked to identify the chairman of the PLO. One hundred percent were able to do so.

The distribution of responses to the support questions is shown in Table 11.1. No relationship between year in school, age and the level of support for the chairman is ascertained. A possible explanation for the level of Arafat's support is that it reflects a Palestinian child's reverence for authority figures in general, and *Fedayeen* in particular. But even when support for the chairman of the PLO was empirically disentangled from reverence for authority in general, it was apparent that support for Arafat was not a particular manifestation of childhood deference for authority figures in general. The mean support scores for each authority figure are presented in Figure 11.1.

Figure 11.1   *Mean support scores for the chairman and five other authority figures*

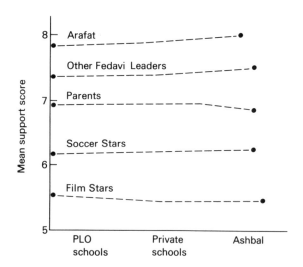

Sources of the Support for Arafat

Because Yassir Arafat is a leader of *Fateh* in addition to his other roles, it is surprising that political indoctrination did not have any impact on his support. *Fateh's Ashbal* (tiger cubs, who undergo political indoctrination and who were used in this study as a control group) were not significantly more supportive of the chairman than the others. The mean support score was 7·9 for the non-*Ashbal* and 8·0 for *Ashbal.* The chairman's support is not confined to the *Ashbal.* Exposure to political indoctrination barely influenced support for the chairman. Formal schooling also did not seem to have any effect on the chairman's support. Table 11.1 indicates that the students' grade in school is virtually independent of the level of support.

The study explored the family's role in generalizing support for the chairman. The findings underscored the importance, if not the reverence, that a Palestinian child has for his mother and father. Yet when the children were asked to make a choice (if they had to) between family and country, they invariably chose the country over the family, as shown in Table 11.2.

Table 11.2   *'There is Nothing Lower than the Person who does not feel deep Love, Respect, and Concern for His Parents.'*

	Agree (%)	Disagree (%)
PLO schools ($N=100$)	78	22
Private schools ($N=100$)	76	24
Ashbal ($N=40$)	64	36

$\chi^2=6\cdot321$; $P<0\cdot05$.

Table 11.3   *'When I Have a Problem, I seek the Advice of my Mother and Father*

	Agree (%)	Disagree (%)
PLO schools ($N=100$)	73	27
Private schools ($N=100$)	80	20
Ashbal ($N=40$)	66	34

$\chi^2=6\cdot321$; $P<0\cdot05$.

The following question substituted the word parents for family: 'If you had to choose between your parents and your country, which would you choose?' Again, the overwhelming choice was country, as is evident in Table 11.3. Palestinian parents teach their children to support Arafat and the PLO. The family seems to be the most important agency of political socialization among the children, as shown in Table 11.4. This relationship is maintained even when the political indoctrination variable is controlled.

Table 11.4   *Choice between Family and Country*

	Agree (%)	Disagree (%)
PLO students ($N=100$)	11	89
Private schools ($N=100$)	9	91
Ashbal ($N=40$)	—	100

$\chi^2=4.555$; $P<0.05$.

When the sex variable was controlled, no noticeable difference between the answers of the boys and the girls was evident. A Palestinian girl is apparently no more attached to her family than a Palestinian boy. Both boys and girls would give up their families for their country, if they had to. Socioeconomic standings are also independent of the support index, even after controlling for other variables. Arafat is equally esteemed by children of high and low socioeconomic groups.

Relationship between Support for the Chairman and Trust in the PLO

The relationship between support for the chairman and trust in the PLO was examined. It was difficult to analyze this relationship vigorously, because the data were not longitudinal. The relationship is positive and quasi-linear: a unit increase in support results in an increase of 0·41 of the index of trust. Support for Arafat is apparently an important stimulant for trust in the PLO.

What is significant about these findings, is that the PLO has widespread support among a segment of the Palestinian population, although it has not liberated one inch of Palestinian soil. It has given Palestinians an independent will and an independent identity; it has liberated them from many patronizing relationships. The weapons of the PLO have always defended these gains.

Moreover, Palestinian politics is not a spectator sport. Palestinians at all levels of the social ladder get involved. Few are the Palestinian homes that do not have a member of the immediate household, a relative, or a friend involved in the resistance movement, *al-Muqawama*. The politics of the Palestinian question, or *al-Qadia*, is an obsession for children, adolescents, women, men, the rich, the poor, the educated and the illiterate. At meetings of the Palestinian national council, the leadership is usually subjected to critical scrutiny. This occurs in very few Arab states. The Palestinian leadership has a seasoned and critical constituency scrutinizing its actions at all times. As a group, the Palestinians are highly politicized and, relative to other Arabs, they are highly educated. They boast the highest number of university graduates per capita among all Arab states.[9]

LURE OF THE WEST

As used by Fouad Ajami, the lure of the West refers to the complex love–hate relationship Arabs have with the West in general, and with the USA in particular. Ajami aptly described this complex phenomenon in his superb piece, 'The struggle for Egypt's soul'. He states: 'At the heart of the crisis lay the explosive problem of cultural dualism between an oriental interior and a modern wrapping.' [10] Modern wrappings are only that – wrappings. The core, or the interior, is and has always been an oriental and a traditional one.[11] This basic fact seems to elude many social scientists and Middle East experts, who have been weaned on Lerner's *The Passing of Traditional Society*, in which he assured us that 'traditional society is passing from the Middle East because relatively few Middle Easterners still want to live by its rules'.[12]

Lerner's assertion is shared by many US policymakers and academicians, who believe that whenever there is a contact between the 'old' ways of the interior and the 'modern' ways of the wrapping (or what Migdal refers to as culture contact theory), the 'new' will inevitably triumph – a variation of 'how are you gonna keep 'em down on the farm after they've seen Paree?' [13] Obviously, many people 'see Paree' and then return to the farm. Some even go to Paree but take the farm along. Anne Fuller in her study of the Lebanese village, *Buarij,* found this to be true. Despite yearly forays from the village to work in the city of Beirut, villagers did not change their attitudes, institutions and behavior.[14] Farah and al-Salem found that 'modern' individuals in Kuwait and Lebanon untie the modernization package and select the characteristics that suit them – modernization is not an either/or proposition.[15] Michael Hudson observed that in the Middle East 'modernization does not mean destroying the old but simply adding to the new'.[16] This phenomenon is often referred to as cultural dualism, 'bedoucracy', or cultural schizophrenia.

It should not surprise anyone to find that traditional society has not disappeared in the Middle East. It persists. Likewise, Islam has not returned. It has always been there – latent at times, but always there. Even devout Muslims have untied the modernization package. They have accepted the technology but rejected all other aspects of Western culture. Saad El din Ibrahim drew a sociological portrait of the typical member of *al-Takfir Wal-Hijra* (Repentance and holy flight) society, a fundamentalist Islamic group in Egypt. The profile that emerged from this original study is far removed from the image of the uneducated, fanatical individual some of us had imagined:

> The profile shows that the average member is in his 20s or early 30s, a university student or recent graduate. He is an achiever. His school grades have been better than average. He is interested in discussion, feels deeply about causes, is intolerant of conflicting opinions and is willing to use violence if necessary for ends he regards as noble. He wants Middle East oil wealth to benefit the people of the region. He views most cooperation with the West as neo-colonialism. He comes from the small landowning or middle class and likes to win at whatever he tries. Surprisingly he is more apt to have an engineering or a science

background than one in humanities. He isn't against modern technology but wants control over its introduction so as to avoid violating Islamic principles.[17]

Palestinian elites, decisionmakers in the PLO, including those who are US educated, are traditional people despite their modern wrappings. They deal with the West with caution, if not suspicion. Obviously, part of this caution and suspicion is related to the Arabs' experience with the West, namely, colonialism. Even when there are attempts at dialogue with the West and the USA, they are kept at a safe and respectable distance. Arab leadership, including the leadership of the PLO, that moves closer risks alienating itself from its own constituency.

THE PLO AND THE USA: PROSPECTS FOR THE FUTURE

Recognition of the PLO on the regional and international levels has come at a price. The PLO has had to give up the idea of a *purely* military solution to the Palestine question. As Edward Said puts it:

In 1974, however, the Palestinian leadership came to an important conclusion. For once it was evident at the same time that Arab Palestine could not be restored, but that after the 1973 war, some combination of Arab military and political pressure could make inroads on Israeli hegemony. Moreover, the Rabat conference confirmed what had already been evident – the PLO was the only possible representative of all Palestinians. *Thus when Yassir Arafat came to the United Nations in November 1974, any idea of a purely military solution to the question of Palestine had been given up.*[18] (emphasis added)

On many occasions the PLO has stated its willingness to think what used to be unthinkable. It signaled its willingness to accept a Palestinian state in the West Bank and Gaza (as in the 1974 and 1977 National Council meetings) with an implicit recognition of Israel as a neighbor.

These signals to the USA continued. In Lebanon (1975–6), for example, the PLO made every effort to protect US citizens. In 1976 the PLO supported a Security Council resolution restating the provision that 'the Palestinian people should be enabled to exercise its inalienable right to self-determination, including the right to establish an independent state in Palestine in accordance with the character of the UN'.[19] The same resolution explicitly stated the right of all states in the area to live in peace, territorial integrity and independence – an obvious reference to Israel's right to exist. The USA vetoed the resolution. When President Carter made his Palestinian declarations in March 1977 at Clinton, Massachusetts, the PLO used Arafat's speech to the Palestinian National Council to respond with positive signs. In fact, Arafat persisted with these gestures. He affirmed Palestinian willingness to accept a state, to recognize Israel and to deal directly with the USA (traditionally an opponent of Palestinian aspiration) as long as impossible things were not asked of him.

But, in my opinion, impossible things were asked of him. One was to accept UN Resolution 242 that spoke of the Palestinians as refugees. For the PLO to accept the resolution, would mean redefining the Palestine question in terms of refugees – in effect, conceding all its political gains. Another impossible thing was demanded: recognize Israel in advance, amend the PLO covenant, give up your arms and disband the PLO without any assurance that the USA and Israel would deliver their part of the bargain.

However, I do not think Palestinian-US relations are at an impasse. Both parties need each other:

(1) The USA is a superpower with significant strategic interests in the Middle East. (These interests are obvious and will not be enumerated.) A corollary of this is that a superpower will sooner or later free itself from Henry Kissinger's commitment to Israel; namely, that the USA would not recognize the PLO as long as the PLO did not accept Security Council resolutions 242 and 338. A superpower cannot be expected to be permanently bound by this commitment. I am not saying that the USA will abandon Israel. The USA will guarantee Israel's existence but not necessarily all of Israel's conquests.[20]

(2) A recognition that even though the USA does not hold 99 percent of the cards to a Middle Eastern settlement, it is capable of influencing a client-state. This client-state (where inflation runs at a rate approaching 100 percent) lives on an annual US subsidy of about $5,550 to every five Israelis. These subsidies are destined to increase before the USA finishes paying for the Sinai real-estate deal known as Sinai II.[21]

(3) The USA has a close relationship (some claim it is a patron–client relationship) with a number of Arab regimes. Some of these regimes subsidize the PLO. Many need to deliver some 'goods' domestically and regionally. They are hopeful that the USA will be able to come up with an equitable solution to the Palestinian question. The credibility of the USA (or, as Quandt referred to it, the *Misdaqiyat*) is at stake, and US strategic planners know how valuable these regimes are to US interests in the area. Performance on the Palestinian issue would enhance prestige considerably – domestically and regionally.

(4) Many ardent supporters of Israel are exasperated by the Begin government and its policy of settlements on the West Bank. Recently Senator Adlai E. Stevenson III of Illinois made this statement:

> The actions of the Begin government on the West Bank conflict with the policy of the United States, the policy embodied in UN Security Council Resolution 242, the Geneva Convention and the opinion of all other nations on earth. The policies of Mr Begin, as distinguished from those of his predecessors and the views of most of his countrymen, contemplate territorial aggrandizement, not the dreams of peace and justice upon which Israel was founded and for which it has been generously supported.[22]

On 15 June 1980 a statement signed by ninety prominent American Jews, among them some of the most conservative scholars and leaders in the USA's Jewish community, called on the Begin government to stop all further settlements on the West Bank and 'to conduct negotiations with any Palestinian body that renounces terrorism and accepts the path of peaceful negotiations as the only way to solve the conflict with Israel'. Such negotiations, the statement continued, 'should confirm each side in its national right, including Israel's right to exist as a Jewish state in secure and recognized borders and the Palestinians' right to a national entity.

A week later a similar statement, signed by another group of Jewish leaders – many of them young liberals – condemned Middle East bloodshed. It said, 'Peace is being held hostage by extremists on both sides. Their absolutism binds them to the tragic nature of the conflict – a conflict of right against right, of one just claim against another. 'The statement called upon 'all those concerned to work together publicly in search of a peaceful solution', commencing with an affirmation of 'the fundamental right to survival of a secure state of Israel and the fundamental right to national self-determination of the Palestinian people'.

On 1 July 1980, more than fifty influential Jewish leaders in the USA publicly expressed dissatisfaction with Prime Minister Begin's policies and signed a statement denouncing extremism within the Israel government. This statement represented the first major public split between the Israeli government and leading members of the US Jewish community, which has traditionally backed Israeli policy. The Americans added their names to a statement drafted by the Israeli leftist Peace Now movement already signed by 250 Israelis, including five former generals. In signing the statement, the US Jewish leaders said Israel could achieve 'peace and security through territorial compromise on the occupied West Bank'.

Jacob Talmon, an eminent Israeli historian, died in Jerusalem. His last article was an open letter to Prime Minister Begin. The danger of Palestinian self-determination, Talmon said, was a good deal less than the danger of Israeli domination of a hostile population. 'The chauvinism and sectarianism which your government encourages will not only hold the Jews of the world together but will alienate them from Judaism and Israel.' [23]

(5) The idea of a Palestinian state in the West Bank and Gaza has many influential supporters within the PLO and among many Arabs. As Walid Khalidi says: 'It is a matter of time, many Palestinians feel, before they have their own state.' [24] 'What worries me', a Palestinian professor confided, 'is what will we do with our state after we get it'.

NOTES: CHAPTER 11

This paper was presented at the Conference on the Middle East and the Western Alliance, University of California, Los Angeles, USA, 21–22 February 1980.

I am deeply grateful to Fouad Ajami, Faisal Al-Salem, and Fowzi Farah for their helpful comments, insights and discussion of the issues presented in this paper.
1 Zayyad in Naseer Aruri and Admond Ghareeb (eds), *Enemy of the Sun: Poetry of Palestinian Resistance* (Washington, DC: Drum and Spear Press, 1970), p. 66.

2 Edward W. Said, *The Question of Palestine* (New York: Times Books, 1979), p. x.

3 ibid, p. xiv.

4 Quoted in *Los Angeles Times*, 14 June 1980.

5 ibid.

6 ibid.

7 See Anis Kassim, 'The Palestine Liberation Organization's claim to status: a juridical analysis under international law', unpublished ms.

8 Most research on socialization has focused on socialization in existing political systems. This study explored the socialization of adolescents into the supportive values and attitudes of a state which does not yet exist. It investigated the acquisition of supportive attitudes toward the Palestinian Liberation Organization (PLO) among Palestinian adolescents in Kuwait. While other studies have focused on the children of the refugee camps, this study considered the socialization process among non-camp dwellers. See Tawfic E. Farah, 'Learning to support the PLO: political socialization of Palestinian children in Kuwait', *Comparative Political Studies*, vol. 12, no. 4, (January 1980), pp. 470–84.

9 See Nabell Shaath, 'Palestinian high level manpower', *Journal of Palestine Studies*, vol. 1, no. 1 (Winter 1972), pp. 80–95. On the question of politicized Palestinians, see Tawfic E. Farah, 'Group affiliations of university students in the Arab Middle East (Kuwait)', *Journal of Social Psychology*, no. 106, (1978), pp. 161–5.

10 Fouad Ajami, 'The struggle for Egypt's soul', *Foreign Policy*, vol. 35 no. 3 (Summer 1979), p. 21.

11 In looking at these psychological factors, I seek to emulate and borrow from the works of some very sensitive students of Arab society such as Al-Salem, Ajami, Al-Azem, Sharabi, Rumaihi, Ammar, Melikian and Diab. Most of these works will be found in Tawfic E. Farah and Faisal Al-Salem, *Politics in the Arab States: A Social-Psychological Approach* (London: Routledge & Kegan Paul, 1982).

12 Daniel Lerner, *The Passing of the Traditional Society: Modernizing the Middle East* (New York: The Free Press, 1958), p. 399.

13 Joel Migdal, 'Why change? Toward a theory of change among individuals in the process of modernization' *World Politics*, vol. XXVI, no. 2 (January 1974), p. 190.

14 Ann Fuller, *Buarij: Portrait of a Lebanese Moslem Village* (Cambridge, Mass.: Harvard University Press, 1961).

15 Tawfic E. Farah and Faisal Al-Salem, 'The traditionalism and modernization dichotomy: the cases of Lebanon and Kuwait', *Journal of the Social Sciences*, vol. 4, no. 2 (April 1976), pp. 38–52.

16 Michael Hudson, 'Democracy and social mobilization in Lebanese politics', *Comparative Politics*, vol. 1, no. 2 (January 1979), p. 255.

17 Roy Vicker, *Wall Street Journal*, 11 February 1980.

18 Said, op. cit. p. 224.

19 For a complete description of these developments, see ibid., pp. 224–38.

20 See, for example, George Ball, 'Crisis in Israeli-American relations', *Foreign Affairs*, vol. 58, no. 2 (Winter 1979–80), pp. 231–56.

21 See Ann Crittenden, 'Israel's economic plight', *Foreign Affairs*, vol. 57, no. 5 (Summer 1979), pp. 1005–16.

22 Quoted in the *Fresno Bee*, 1 July 1980.

23 Quoted in Arthur Schlesinger Jr, 'Middle Eastern quandries', *Wall Street Journal*, Thursday 3 July 1980.

24 Walik Khalidi, 'Thinking the unthinkable: a sovereign Palestinian state', *Foreign Affairs*, vol. 56, no. 4 (July 1978), p. 713.

Part Five

The Major Non-Arab Middle-East States
and the Western Alliance

12 Israel and the Western Alliance

ITAMAR RABINOVITCH

The late 1970s were years of profound change in Israel. The transfer of power from the Labor Party to the Likud alignment in May 1977, and the signing of the peace treaty with Egypt in March 1979, were the two most salient developments that have recently affected the country's domestic scene and external environment. Israel's relationship with the Western Alliance has been part of this development in two respects – as an aspect of the process of change, and due to its centrality, a catalyst of further change.

The term Western Alliance as used in this context carries with it some ambiguity. It denotes, in the first place, the increasingly loose group of the USA and its major allies. But from the Israeli point of view, it refers also to past and present efforts to organize formal and informal blocs of Middle Eastern states friendly to the USA or the West. Nor is there a single Israeli approach to these issues. The policies analyzed below are those pursued by successive Israeli governments, but the attitudes referred to are those articulated in the political and public debate over foreign and defense policies.

THE HISTORICAL RECORD [1]

Of the various factors that have shaped and characterized Israel's foreign policy since the establishment of the state, three are of particular import for the present analysis:

(a) *The Arab-Israeli conflict*. The Arab refusal to accept the state of Israel, the challenge to its legitimacy, the political and economic warfare, the permanent danger of war and its periodic eruption have been the fundamental facts of Israeli foreign and defense policies. Transitions from one phase of the conflict to another and differences of attitude among the Arab actors had, until the 1970s, limited importance in terms of the opportunities they provided for Israeli policy in the conflict.

(b) *An almost-exclusive Israeli orientation toward the Western powers*. Following a brief period of cooperation with the USSR and apparent neutrality, Israel placed itself squarely in the Western camp.[2] Despite periods of active and successful efforts in the Third World, the authors of Israel's foreign policy have been preoccupied with Israel's relations with Western powers. Since 1967, Israel's relationship with the USA has overshadowed all other aspects of the country's foreign policy both because of its own cardinal importance, and as a result of the waning of other relationships. It is interesting that except for a brief period during the 1950s this orientation has been supported by a broad consensus and has not been the subject of a serious public debate.

(c) *An ambivalent Western attitude.* It is one of the chief ironies of Israel's brief history, that a state which has been perceived by the Arab world as a Western outpost in its midst and has, indeed, identified itself enthusiastically with the West has also been confronted with the need to explain and affirm its value and usefulness to the Western camp. Even during periods of close cooperation based on a community of interests and a joint strategy, Israel had to contend with persistent arguments that the Western commitment to Israel was based on moral grounds or domestic pressures rather than on national interests; that the real interests of the West were in the Arab world; that the Arab-Israeli conflict was destabilizing the Middle East and maligning the Arab world's relationship with the Western world.

The dichotomy between this approach and Israel's outlook was particularly stark in the early 1950s when the USA and Britain were seeking to organize a bloc of Arab states tied to the West. Israel wanted a comparable treaty relationship, first, with Britain, and then with the USA that would consolidate the existence and legitimacy of the state, provide it with a security guarantee and guarantee the flow of necessary economic and military aid. But the USA was not interested in such a treaty while she was seeking to organize her Arab allies, nor did she become interested when Egypt was moving into the Soviet orbit. In August 1955 the Israeli prime minister could offer a telling and disillusioned analysis of the US outlook:

> I analysed the situation regarding the essentials of the defence treaty. The United States is waiting until Egypt is ready to make contact – without a parallel treaty with an Arab country it will not sign any treaty with Israel – whereas Egypt is moving farther and farther away from any tendency to contact with the West . . . At the same time the United States claims that a defence treaty with Israel is an impossibility as long as there is tension between Israel and the Arab states. It is necessary to lay the groundwork for an easing of this tension and it is America's intention to offer suggestions to this end. It is clear that these suggestions will only be a stumbling bloc to us – Dulles himself is announcing . . . that 'at first glance' we will probably not be pleased with them. We can only conclude, that there is no hope of a defence treaty in the near future.[3]

While all notions of and attempts at creating formal ties between Israel and the Western Alliance in the 1950s and early 1960s had no results, significant informal cooperation developed in a variety of ways. A virtual French-Israeli alliance existed from the mid-1950s to the early 1960s. In the late 1950s when the Middle East was polarized between the Western Alliance and its conservative supporters on the one hand, and the Soviet Union and its radical allies on the other, Israel adapted itself skillfully to the new situation. It was instrumental in helping the pro-Western regimes of Jordan and Lebanon to weather the crisis of 1958. Later it developed the 'policy of the periphery', close cooperation with three pro-Western states in the region that shared Israel's opposition to the USSR and radical pan-Arab nationalism – Iran, Turkey and Ethiopia.[4]

Israel's relationship with the USA continued to improve and develop during the 1960s. In 1962 the USA agreed for the first time to provide Israel with a major weapon system – the Hawk missiles. In the following years, as the superpower rivalry in the Middle East was exacerbated and US-Egyptian relations deteriorated, the sense of a US-Israeli partnership was strengthened.

THE IMPACT OF THE SIX DAY WAR

As in so many other respects, the war of June 1967 was a watershed in Israel's relationship with the Western Alliance. Further impetus was given to the process which drew Israel toward the USA and away from France and eventually Britain and other West European countries. To the US-Israeli relationship, several new and incongruous elements were added. Washingtton and Jerusalem shared a fundamental premiss – that Israel should not withdraw from the territories captured in June 1967 without a settlement of the Arab-Israeli conflict. They did not fully agree, though, on the nature of that settlement and the extent of Israel's eventual withdrawal.

Israel's control over Egyptian and Syrian territory and the growing realization that the USA alone could influence Israel to withdraw from them provided the USA with a new and significant leverage over these Soviet clients. American politicians and analysts realized the potential importance of this development, but at several points between 1969–72 they also felt that these potential long-term benefits were not worth the short-term losses they tended to ascribe to Washington's support of the Israeli position.[5]

It was in this context that the terms in which the idea of a US-Israeli defense treaty were being discussed underwent a profound change. While in the 1950s, and as late as 1963, it was an Israeli idea that the USA was reluctant to accept,[6] after 1967 the idea was being raised by Senator Fullbright and other Americans. They realized that with the escalation of the Arab-Israeli conflict, it was unrealistic to ask Israel to return to the pre-1967 borders without an adequate security guarantee and were willing to offer it in the form of a treaty with the USA. Opinion in Israel was divided on this issue and the treaty's advocates found Senator Fullbright's support to be counterproductive.[7]

Still, US-Israeli cooperation and coordination developed and expanded without formalization. The USA became Israel's chief arms supplier, replacing France and Britain, and providing the economic help needed for participating in a Middle Eastern arms race on a hitherto unknown scale. As Soviet involvement in the Arab world and in the Arab-Israeli conflict became deeper, US-Israeli relations come to be increasingly affected by novel considerations. The deep-raid bombings in Egypt in early 1970, and the joint US-Israeli effort to save the Jordanian monarchy in September 1970, were from an Israeli point of view, the best examples of US-Israeli strategic cooperation in the Middle East. They inaugurated a three-year period (September 1970–September 1973), which in many respects was the golden age of US-Israeli relations.[8]

CHANGES IN THE EARLY 1970s

Israel's sense of success and security in the early 1970s was gradually becoming unwarranted by a series of changes which developed imperceptibly then and surfaced in 1973. Chief among these were the rise in the collective power of the Arab world and the ensuing shift in the balance of power between it and Israel. This change derived from two unrelated developments. The relationship between the oilproducing countries of the Middle East, the oil companies and the oilconsuming industrial nations began to change in the late 1960s. By 1972 the 'energy crisis' was a fact of international life, though its political ramifications had yet to be determined. The Arab world's ability to translate these developments into political power was greatly enhanced by a transition which had occurred in inter-Arab relations. The quest for unity was replaced by the far more practical goal of Arab cooperation. One immediate outcome was the emergence of the Saudi-Egyptian axis, whose formation affected Israel's relationship with the USA and other members of the Western Alliance in several ways.

Egypt's change of orientation in 1972–3 altered the equation which prevailed in the Middle East since the late 1950s of the USA supporting both the conservative Arab regimes, and Israel, against Egypt, Syria and Iraq, who sided with the USSR. Egypt and Saudi Arabia now became Washington's chief friends in the Arab world, and Israel had to adapt to a situation colored by an emerging political and military alliance between the USA and Egypt.

The Egyptian-Saudi axis also laid the ground for the October War, which accelerated some earlier processes and generated some new ones:

(a) A major assumption which underlay US-Israeli relations in the late 1960s and early 1970s – namely, that Israel was capable of handling all local military challenges and crises – collapsed as a result of Israel's military reverses during the initial stages of the war and the need to resort to a US airlift.

(b) American, West European and Japanese dependence on Arab oil supply and quest for Arab markets and investments increased dramatically following the oil embargo and price rises of 1973.

(c) Israel's dependence on US military supplies and economic aid grew considerably due to the new dimensions of the Middle Eastern arms race after 1973.

(d) The war led rather unexpectedly to the inauguration of the 'peace process' under the USA's auspices, which culminated in the Egyptian-Israeli peace of 1979. It had been claimed in the past – by Israelis as well – that the USA's influence over Israel, the fact that Washington could induce Israel to return Arab territories while Moscow could not – was an important advantage the USA had over Moscow in the Middle East. In the years 1973–5 the USA was, indeed, instrumental in effecting three Israeli withdrawals from Egyptian and Syrian territory both in order to promote the peace process, and to enhance its own influence in Cairo and Damascus at the expense of the USSR.

Like other pro-Western states in the Middle East, Israel was affected by the fluctuations of the US position and policies in the region during the 1970s and by the growing divergence of the respective policies pursued in the Middle East by the USA and its West European allies. In the mid-1970s the USA registered considerable achievements in the Middle East – having replaced the Soviets in Cairo and having made some inroads into their position in Damascus. But the tide was reversed in the second half of the 1970s, when the Soviets advanced in the outlying areas of the Middle East without encountering an effective US response. Unlike Saudi Arabia or prerevolutionary Iran, Israel did not feel that a projection of US weakness had an immediate bearing on its physical safety; but it did feel the effects of Washington's weakened international position, and furthermore, that Washington's weakness *vis-à-vis* its local (Arab) allies was being translated into an increasing political pressure on Israel.

Differences within the Western Alliance had a similar impact. As a rule, Western Europe and Japan were more dependent on Arab oil supply, interested in Arab markets and investments, ideologically more supportive of the Palestinian cause, less conscious of Israel's strategic value and only marginally concerned with pro-Israeli sentiments and lobbies. Furthermore, changing a traditional pro-Israeli line to a line critical of Israel and supportive of Arab demands was an important asset they possessed in their relationship with the Arab world. It was, therefore, hardly surprising that the EEC countries often chose to emphasize their distinctiveness from US policy in the Middle East over issues concerned with the Arab-Israeli conflict.

The trend which led to a narrowing of Israel's relationship with the Western Alliance to a relationship with the USA was reinforced by the final collapse of the 'periphery policy'. Israel's relations with Ethiopia and Iran were destroyed by the fall of their monarchies and their replacement by radical revolutionary regimes. Israel's formal diplomatic relationship with Turkey was retained, but the strategic cooperation of earlier decades was terminated.

RECENT AND CURRENT TRENDS

While these processes have all shaped Israel's foreign policy environment in the late 1970s, three developments have had a particular impact on Israel's foreign policy and her relationship with the Western Alliance as the decade of the 1970s drew to a close:

(a) *The 1977 parliamentary elections and the coming to power of the Likud Alignment.* For the first time in the history of the state the labor parties were out of power and the government dominated by a center-nationalist-right wing coalition. This meant that the ideology, electoral platform and, in several respects, the actual political program of the Israeli government became further removed from the US, not to say the West European, outlook on the Arab-Israeli conflict. This is not to suggest a proximity of outlook between the Carter administration and the ousted Labor government. In fact, President Carter's attempt to effect a comprehensive settlement of the Arab-Israeli conflict and to solve the Palestinian problem resulted in the spring of 1977 in severe disagreements and tension with the Rabin government.[9] It was indeed Mr Begin's argument at the time that the Labor Party's attempt to coordinate policies with the USA was based on an illusion in as much as neither the Labor, nor the Likud, position was acceptable to a US government bent on achieving a comprehensive Middle Eastern settlement. Accordingly, upon assuming office he changed his predecessor's policies and relinquished the effort to coordinate policies with Washington. It is diffifficult to tell by the fluctuations of US-Israeli relations in the period May–November 1977 what their trend of development would have been since the opening of a direct Israeli-Egyptian dialogue altered also the focus of the US-Israeli relationship.[10]

(b) *The Israeli-Egyptian negotiations and peace.*[11] Peace with the most important Arab state had been a main goal of Israel's foreign policy since independence, but from the limited perspective afforded by the present, the price of the peace treaty with Egypt has so far overshadowed its advantages. An overall assessment of the Egyptian-Israeli peace is outside the scope of this chapter, but several points which directly affect Israel's relationship with the Western Alliance should be mentioned.[12]

One of the most important contributions of the March 1979 peace treaty was the demonstration that a peaceful resolution of the Arab-Israeli conflict was possible, that it was not an endless and hopeless conflict. It also presented the USA in the desirable posture of a peacemaker in contradistinction to the USSR as the patron of those opposing the peace treaty. Whatever the long-term prospects of the treaty, it certainly reduced the danger of another Arab-Israeli war in the early 1980s and, thus, stabilized the situation in the Middle East. Furthermore, the two chief military powers in the core area of the Middle East, both friends of the USA, had moved from a phase of hostility to a new phase of potential dialogue and cooperation, thus laying the ground for new possibilities of cooperation among the pro-Western states in the region.

On the other side of the balance sheet, Israel had to pay the heavy price; it had to pay in terms of its public image in the USA and Western Europe during the lengthy and arduous negotiations which preceded and followed the signing of the peace treaty. When signed, the treaty was largely received in the West as a partial and separate settlement whose value was to remain limited unless it was to be followed soon by additional settlements, particularly one addressing the Palestinian issue. Thus, rather than reducing the pressure of the Arab-Israeli conflict on Israel's international posture, the peace treaty tended to aggravate it by telescoping the conflict and focusing it on the more awkward Palestinian issue.

The implementation of the treaty has so far vindicated the traditional argument, that in any settlement with the Arabs, Israel would be giving away tangible assets for intangible and uncertain gains. Israel gave away the Sinai oil and is investing heavily in building alternative airfields, but the new relationship with Egypt remains ambiguous and fragile. The October War may, indeed, be 'the last war', but in projecting the military balance for the 1980s, Israeli planners cannot assume that Egypt will not participate in another Arab-Israeli war. The 'price of peace' has, therefore, to be paid along with continued investment in military buildup. Israel is now spending 35 percent of its GNP in the purchase of oil and defense expenditure, and the degree of its dependence on the USA in these two respects is embarrassing.

The Israeli dilemma is best exemplified by Israel''s attitude toward the military dimension of the new US-Egyptian relationship. This has clearly been facilitated by the Egyptian-Israeli peace; and should that peace remain stable, Israel will have no reason to object to US military supplies to Egypt or to joint US-Egyptian maneuvers. However, in the present state of uncertainty and ambiguity Israel finds it awkward either to aggravate its delicate relations with Washington and Cairo, or to comply with the accumulation of weapons and knowhow which might one day be turned against it. Nor can some Israelis avoid the feeling that the development of US-Egyptian military relations might be done at the expense of the 'special' US-Israeli relationship.

Finally, the bilateral Egyptian-Israeli relationship does not stand of its own. It is formally and practically linked to other components of the Arab-Israeli conflict and, particularly in the present circumstances, to the progress that will or will fail to be made in the negotiations for the implementation of the autonomy plan in the West Bank and the Gaza Strip.

(*c*) *The Western Alliance and the Palestinian issue.* From an Israeli point of view, one of the less desirable consequences of the developments of the late 1970s has been the appearance of a linkage in many Western quarters between the security of Western interests in the Persian Gulf and a resolution of the Palestinian question. In the aftermath of the fall of the Iranian monarchy, the Ka'ba incident in Saudi Arabia and the USSR's invasion of Afghanistan, two major schools of thought have crystalized with regard to the necessary Western (or US) response. One argues that the chief concern of the conservative oilproducing regimes in the area is their survival and that the USA's failure to check Soviet advances in the region and to appear as a credible guarantor of friendly regimes is the major source of danger for the Western-US position in the Gulf area. That school of thought generally advocates a strengthening of the USA's military posture of the area, and a bolstering of US credibility. It tends to laud the Camp David agreement as a move which stabilized the core area of the Middle East and facilitated US-Egyptian military cooperation.

The other school of thought is critical of US diplomacy in the Arab-Israeli conflict and of the Camp David agreement. It regards the latter as a mistake which drove a wedge between Egypt and Saudi Arabia and added another irritant to Arab-US relations. From this point of view, it is argued that a comprehensive settlement of the Arab-Israeli conflict, and particularly a resolution of the Palestinian problem, is necessary in order to mollify conservative Arab and Islamic opinion and as a precondition for the formation of any effective organization of pro-Western states. In response to Israeli willingness and occasional eagerness to become part of a pro-Western system in the region this school argues, very much like its predecessors in the early 1950s, that Israel's contribution should be primarily manifested in the concessions it can make to Arab demands.[13]

This point of view is reinforced by the views and policies of Washington's European allies, who advocate a solution of the Palestinian problem for reasons that have little to do with the security of the Gulf, but are rather related to the pursuit of their particular interests. Thus, in June 1980, the EEC heads of state in their Venice meeting recommended that the PLO be 'associated' with the negotiations to solve the Middle East conflict. But, in early August, the Select Committee on Foreign Affairs of the British Parliament went further than that in the report it submitted with regard to the policy repercussions of the Soviet invasion of Afghanistan. Both the reasoning and the conclusions are revealing. As quoted by the British press, the report said that 'in the Middle East and the Gulf . . . the solution of the Palestinian problem is a key issue for stability in the whole area. It is recommended that the PLO should *participate* in negotiations as long as it respects Israel's right to existence and security'.[14] These developments – the need to implement the Palestinian component of the Egyptian-Israeli treaty, the telescoping of the Arab-Israeli conflict into a predominantly Israeli-Palestinian conflict, and the American and European pressure – all converged to narrow the dialogue between Israel and her Western friends into a debate on the Palestinian issue.

It has not been a constructive debate, for a number of reasons. There are enormous inherent difficulties which militate against progress on, not to say solution of, the Palestinian problem. The political circumstances of the past few years have only served to exacerbate them. Thus, all efforts to pursue the solution outlined in the framework for peace signed at Camp David failed. The partners to the Camp David accords failed to mobilize support for the 'autonomy plan' among the Palestinians, or to draw other Arab partners, particularly Jordan, to participate in its implementation.

This is hardly surprising in view of the fact that the three signatories of the Camp David accords are deeply divided over the interpretation of their Palestinian component. The USA and Egypt do not accept Mr Begin's position that the debate over the future of the West Bank and Gaza should have been suspended for at least five years as part of the return for Israel's concessions in the Sinai. The differences of view go beyond the interpretation of the letter and the spirit of the Camp David agreements and are grounded in a genuine disagreement about the desired solution for the Palestinian problem and the final disposition of the territory of the West Bank and the Gaza Strip.

The Carter administration has voiced, during the past years, its disagreement with Mr Begin's views and policies on the autonomy plan but has done little, particularly since the end of 1979, to promote its own approach. Nor have the half-hearted US attempts to explore alternative avenues for dealing with the Palestinian issue gone very far. One of these avenues was the dialogue between Washington's European allies and the PLO. This dialogue has contributed to the PLO's international diplomatic success, but added little to its actual position in the Middle East. But Europe's policy has had counterproductive effects in Israel. Thoughtful Israelis realize that the European position has more to it than just a quest for oil and petrodollars, but they cannot fail to notice that these elements are there together with a measure of political cynicism. These Israelis realize that West European governments still insist on the PLO's acceptance of Israel's fundamental rights; their complaint is that the European position, in its entirety, tends to strengthen the PLO leadership's feeling that there is no need to moderate and accommodate its position since time is on its side. The resolutions adopted in Damascus in June 1980 are cited as the most recent illustration of this process.

Israel's own policy appears as a mirror-image of the above. It is the Begin government's policy to hold and reinforce its actual control of the West Bank and Gaza, despite the escalating price it has been paying in terms of its international standing. Many in Israel disagree with this policy, with some of its aspects, or with the methods of its execution. But the question they ask is whether an alternative Israeli policy that does not amount to a renunciation of the Israeli national consensus has any prospects in view of the regional and international circumstances. The question is not theoretical, in that it has already emerged as a crucial issue in the campaign for the 1981 elections which actually began in the summer of 1980.

Nor has this focusing on the Palestinian issue been the only cause and symptom of the lack of a serious dialogue between Israel and the Western Alliance in the past few years. The lowered US profile, foreign policy styles of the Carter and Begin administrations and the personalities involved, all contributed to this development. The haphazard fashion in which such issues as the strategic deployment in the aftermath of the Iranian revolution and the notion of US bases or facilities in Israel were discussed are cases in point. What seems necessary is a strategy that would restore a dialogue between Israel and the Western Alliance based on the following elements: a definition of common interests· a flexible formula for formal and informal strategic cooperation· a restoration of European credibility in Israeli eyes· an Israeli formula to the Palestinian issue that would be acceptable at least to the USA, Western Europe and Egypt.

NOTES: CHAPTER 12

1 For general studies of Israeli foreign policy, see Michael Brecher, *The Foreign Policy System of Israel* (London: Oxford University Press, 1972), and *Decisions in Israel's Foreign Policy* (London: Oxford University Press, 1975); and Nadav Safran, *Israel, the Embattled Ally* (Cambridge, Mass.: The Balknap Press of Harvard University Press, 1978).

2 The deterioration of Soviet-Israeli relations in the early 1950s is analysed and documented in Y. Ro'i, *Soviet Decision Making in Practice* (New Brunswick, NJ: Transaction Books, 1980).

3 Moshe Sharett, *A Personal Diary* (Tel Aviv: Ma'ariv Library, 1978), p. 1122.

4 The development of Israel's 'policy of the periphery' is described in Michael Bar-Zohar, *Ben Gurion* (Tel Aviv: Am Oved, 1977), pp. 1325–39.

5 See, for instance, Yitzhaq Rabin, *A Service Diary* (Tel Aviv: Ma'ariv Library, 1979), p. 249.

6 In 1963 after the formation of the (short-lived) federation of Egypt, Syria and Iraq, Ben Gurion addressed letters to the heads of governments of all UN members and warned them of the danger this posed to Israel. Special pleas were made to presidents Kennedy and De Gaulle. In one of his letters to President Kennedy, Ben Gurion suggested that a 'bilateral defence treaty' be signed between the US and Israel. Kennedy declined. The whole episode was a symptom of Ben Gurion's imminent departure from power. See Bar-Zohar, op. cit., pp. 1550–4.

7 For two opposing Israeli views on this subject, see the essays by Yoram Dinstein and Yair Evron, in H. Shaked aand I. Rabinovich, *The Middle East and the US, Perceptions and Policies* (New Brunswick, NJ: Transaction Books, 1980).

8 See Bernard Reich, *Quest for Peace* (New Brunswick, NJ: Transaction Books, 1977), ch. 3.

9 For Rabin's version of this period, see Rabin, op. cit., pp. 507–19.

10 See Colin Legum (ed.), *Middle East Contemporary Survey*, Vol. 1 (New York: Halmes & Meier Publications, 1978), pp. 135–42.

11 For an extensive documentation of the Egyptian-Israeli negotiations, see the first three volumes of the *Middle East Contemporary Survey* (New York: Halmes & Meier Publications 1978, 1979 and 1980). See also E. Ya'ari, E. Haber and Z. Schiff, *The Year of the Dove* (Tel Aviv: Zmora, Bitan, Modan, 1980).

12 A fuller assessment can be found in my 'Israel: the impact of the peace treaty', *Current History*, vol. 79, no. 450 (January 1980), pp. 9–11, 37, 38.

13 These ideas were suggested in briefings by US officials and diplomats in Washington and Tel Aviv in January 1980.

14 *The Times* (London), 6 August 1980.

13 Iran and the Middle East

RICHARD W. COTTAM

'Who lost Iran?' That question, so commonly asked, is remarkably revealing of the place of Iran in the US world view. It implies that the Iran of Mohammad Reza Pahlavi, Aryamehr, Shah-in-Shah of Iran, with all its imperial splendor, was in fact, just as Iranian revolutionaries contend, America's Iran. It suggests as well that the USA 'lost' its Iran to someone else, and that someone must be the USA's strongest competitor, the USSR. And, indeed, those who ask the question believe the probabilities are high that the overthrow of the shah was at the very least the beginning of a process that will culminate in Iran's becoming a Soviet satellite. For them, the Iranian revolution was indeed a major catastrophe.

This description of the Iranian situation is prototypically 'cold war'. And the 'loss' of Iran in the view of persisting cold-warriors is a manifestation of a deadly pattern: a basically stable pro-American regime, inadequately supported by an administration in Washington that is fatally lacking in will-power, falling victim to the conspiratorial planning of the USSR. Was there, in fact, external involvement in the shah's overthrow? The case is impossible to make on the basis of overtly available evidence. It is true that both the government of the USA and the government of the People's Republic of China regarded imperial Iran as a virtual surrogate-power, blocking a Soviet *drang nach suden*. But it is also true that the shah until his last weeks in power was overtly on excellent terms with the USSR and Eastern Europe.[1] Indeed, the shah was on good terms with a most unlikely assortment of governments. Pakistan saw Iran as a close friend and potential ally in its region. But relations between the shah and the leaders of Pakistan's regional foes, Afghanistan and India, were close and friendly. Israelis perceived the the shah as their friend and collaborator, but the shah's relations with bitterly anti-Israeli Iraq were close right up to the day of his departure. The shah was a consummate practitioner of the art of diplomacy. The Iranian revolution had a small external cheering section, but there is no evidence of any really significant external support.

Nor is it difficult to make a case for internal stability. The shah could boast of an internal security apparatus that, until 1978, his people regarded as omniscient, omnipotent and omnipresent. His economic policies helped translate a huge oil income into a rate of growth that was among the highest in the world. To be sure, inflation was a serious problem in the last four years, but far weaker regimes have survived far more serious economic difficulties. Yes, there was widespread corruption, but participation in corrupt practices was so pervasive that few people could condemn corruption from a position of purity. The opportunity to achieve great wealth was, in fact, perceived by much of the middle class. Yet the regime did fall victim to a massively supported and largely non-violent opposition.

As the hostage crisis made undeniably clear, the USA was inextricably identified with the fallen imperial regime of Iran. And that identification was the consequence of the Iranian-US relationship in the cold war years. The cold war was an era characterized by superpower interventions in the domestic affairs of third states, and in particular Third World states. Iran was a classic example of a state in which the intervening power was the USA. And in my opinion the primary purpose of that intervention was typical of US cold war interventions: to establish and maintain in power a regime able and willing to resist Soviet efforts to gain controlling influence over the third state's domestic political affairs.[2] In the case of Iran, the intervention appeared to have achieved its objective admirably. The Iranian regime seemed to be prosperous and stable. Yet as events were to demonstrate dramatically, there was in the regime a fatal vulnerability. What was that vulnerability, and are other such regimes similarly vulnerable? Obviously, different answers can be given to these questions; the purpose of this chapter is to look at the answers that have emerged and the policy implications of the answers.

1951–3: TWO US VIEWS OF IRAN EMERGE

There were some fascinating episodes in the relations of Iran and the USA prior to World War II. But it was only during and, even more particularly, after World War II that the USA's interest in Iran developed an intensity sufficient to make Iran a major focus of US diplomatic activity. The basis of this interest was Iran's geopolitical position – sharing a 1,600-mile border with the USSR and separating the USSR from the Persian Gulf and the Indian Ocean – and Iran's great oilfields. As the somewhat reluctant leader of the Western world, the US government was determined to resist expected Soviet efforts to gain control of Iran – whether by direct military action, or by internal subversion. A particular concern was that Iran's oil would continue to flow to the West. Rhetorically, US policy was described as being dedicated to keeping Iran within the free world. America, therefore, appeared to have economic, ideological and security concerns.

In 1951 events in Iran created a situation that would force the US government to adopt a policy that would test the relative importance of these three general concerns. A political movement that was in thrust nationalist and Islamic, liberal and social-democratic, succeeded in compelling the nationalization of the Anglo-Iranian Oil Co. and the acceptance of its charismatic leader, Dr Mohammad Mossadeq, as prime minister. Iranian nationalists viewed contemporary Iranian history as a thus-far unsuccessful struggle to achieve full independence from the imperial designs of European forums, in particular Britain and Russia. True independence required gaining control over Iran's great oil resource and eliminating the subtle and indirect form of a century of British control in Iran – seen as exercised primarily through local agents of British policy. Suspicion of the USSR was no less intense; the favored policy hence was one of neutrality in world affairs. The advent of Dr Mossadeq's government, therefore, meant the replacement of a government that had cooperated with the West with one that was a self-proclaimed neutral in world affairs, and one that would seek to eliminate from political life long-standing friends of Britain and new-found friends of the USA. Furthermore, there were strong signs of regime instability. Strains quickly developed within the movement, particularly between Islamic and secular intellectual leaders. And Britain, in retaliation against the nationalization of the oil company, established an economic blockade of Iran. Iranian communists became vociferously assertive, and the USA was confronted with the shock of an angry 'Yankee go home' campaign.

American decisionmakers concerned with Iran in this period shared a fear of and a determination to resist any Soviet move to take advantage of the Iranian situation. There was a common expectation that the most likely Soviet tactic would be that of political subversion. The Iranian situation had its parallel in much of the Third World. Nationalistic leaders, reacting to real or perceived Western colonial exploitation, were attempting to establish truly independent regimes. More frequently than not these leaders accepted much of Western liberal democratic tradition, but their anti-imperialism made non-alignment in world affairs the favored policy. Also, typically, the nationalist movement brought with it the instability that is likely to be associated with rapid change. And Western leaders feared the instability would provide a fertile field for Soviet subversion to exploit.

American estimates of the Iranian situation in 1951 differed sharply, and so inevitably did policy recommendations. American estimates of the situation in Iran fell into two general patterns, and these same two patterns can be seen in parallel situations throughout the Third World. The first pattern was essentially stereotypical. American viewing Iran this way placed Iranian leaders in two sharply defined categories. One category, typified by Mossadeq and his allies, was viewed as self-serving agitators, motivated by a desire for power and a willingness to pursue almost any tactic to achieve it. Despite their claim of neutrality, Mossadeq and his followers were in fact, wittingly or unwittingly, functional agents of the USSR. The Iranian mass was viewed as much too untutored politically to be able either to support, or indeed comprehend, liberal democracy. In fact, there was no real public opinion in a country so underdeveloped as Iran. The 'nationalist movement' therefore was engaged in a sham, pretending to lead a mass movement, when in fact, the Iranian mass was incapable of anything more than a brief response to a demagogic appeal.

In this view the second category of Iranian leaders was typified by traditional aristocrats, who strongly opposed the Mossadeq movement. They were 'moderate and responsible' men, who understood the real needs of the politically inert mass and could be counted on to oppose any communist subversion. For the good of Iran and the 'free world', this second group should receive the support it needed to return to the reins of government in Iran. Loy Henderson, appointed ambassador to Iran in 1951, and the Dulles brothers, Secretary of State John Foster and Director of Central Intelligence Allen, saw Iran in this pattern.[3]

The second pattern was far more complex and far less judgmental. Those who saw Iran in this pattern, saw an Iranian national movement that was a genuine popular force and was supported by a rapidly developing Iranian public opinion. Dr Mossadeq and his allies were accepted as philosophically Western and their popularity was considered genuine. At the same time, the instability of the Mossadeq regime was recognized and was seen to reflect in part an anti-British paranoia that, while understandable given the previous century's history, could provide the Soviet planners with a real opportunity. American policy thus had a dual objective of accepting and cooperating with Iranian nationalism – which was after all an irresistible sociopolitical force – while attempting at the same time to reduce the intensity of anti-British and anti-Western suspicions. Ambassador Henry Grady, who left Iran in 1951, and Secretary of State Dean Acheson saw Iran in this pattern.[4]

On 19 August 1953 the government of Dr Mohammad Mossadeq fell to a coup that was in large part directed, funded and logistically supported by the CIA.[5] Proponents of the first pattern had triumphed, and for the next twenty-five years they could reasonably claim that events had confirmed their view. There were moments of great difficulty, of course. General Fazlollah Zahedi, the Anglo-American choice for dictator of Iran in 1953, proved to be both incompetent as a leader and sensationally corrupt. But, much to the surprise and relief of the Anglo-Americans, Mohammad Reza Shah proved to be a leader of exceptional ability, and by 1955 was established as the unchallenged and unchallengeable dictator of Iran. American security and economic interests were equally well pleased with the shah's leadership. After a decade of consolidating power in Iran, the shah's military force began to gain the appearance, at least, of a truly formidable force. The shah's own contention that Iran would soon be on a par in terms of power with West Germany was taken seriously. And the shah's frequent remarks that Iran was a major military partner of the West were never questioned. Overlooked was the fact of relations with the USSR and its allies that were generally good to excellent and only occasionally uncomfortable. Even the purchase of Soviet military transport and artillery was accepted with equanimity. The image of the shah's Iran as a sincere and devoted ally against communist aggression was impenetrably solid.[6]

THE SHAH'S REGIME IN THE COLD WAR VIEW

As confidence in the shah's ability to remain in power in Iran grew, and as the strength of Iran's armed forces developed, US security interests in Iran began to take second place to economic interests. After 1963 the USA's financial, commercial and industrial relations with Iran developed in geometric progression: and when the price of oil, and hence Iranian oil income, sky-rocketed in 1974, the opportunities further multiplied. A great many Americans with economic interests visited or took up residence in Iran, and their Iranian contacts generally confirmed the view that they were predisposed to accept: a rapidly developing Iran, politically stable and genuinely devoted to the benevolent and progressive leadership of the shah. When there were undeniable manifestations of opposition to the government in the form of guerrilla activity inside Iran or large student demonstrations in the USA or Europe, the image of self-serving agitators who were dupes or agents of communism seemed appropriate. Iran, as a developing country, was by definition not yet ready for democracy. The 1953 cold war pattern was the image most concerned Americans in the 1970s accepted without amendment.

Another American interest in Iran developed and gained strength in the 1960s and 1970s. Reversing Mossadeq's clear policy of preference for and support of Arabs in the Arab-Israeli conflict, the shah moved toward a policy of increasing cooperation with Israel. Iran became the primary source of Israeli oil purchases. Economic interaction became increasingly vigorous on both a governmental and private entrepreneurial level. Cooperation also extended to military and internal security forces. American, Iranian and Israeli intelligence forces cooperated closely in encouraging Kurdish insurgency against an Iraq which, until the Iran–Iraq agreement of 1975, was viewed with parallel hostility by the three governments.[7] And Israeli involvement in the training of SAVAK, the Iranian intelligence and information service, was one of the world's worst-kept secrets. American Jews, deeply concerned with Israel's security, came to look on the shah's government with particular favor.[8] Thus, an ethnic interest was added to security and economic interests – all accepting essentially the same image of the shah's Iran.

Nor was there any real dissent from this view from ideological interests. Efforts by opposition Iranians to persuade liberal Americans to consider their case – a brutal and corrupt dictatorship imposed on their country by the USA – were consistently unsuccessful. Prior to the period of undeniable revolutionary ferment, only a few exceptional individuals such as I. F. Stone, and journals such as the *Nation*, were willing to challenge the prevailing image. A parade of the USA's social and intellectual leaders took happy advantage of the lavish hospitality of the shah's last ambassador to the USA, Ardeshir Zahedi, the son of Fazlollah Zahedi.

Within this generally favorable frame, however, there was among US governmental officials and business people a good deal of skepticism about some of the shah's policies. Defense Department specialists on Iran questioned the wisdom of the shah's military purchases and wondered aloud about the shah's real military purpose.[9] And when the last US ambassador to the shah's government, William Sullivan, was briefed by a group of US financial leaders in New York, he was given a pessimistic picture of Iran's economic prospects.[10] The group saw the shah's preoccupation with grandiose projects and fascination with the latest and most advanced technology deflecting him from a sound economic development path. Robert Graham's book, *Iran: The Illusion of Power*,[11] written in 1978, is a devastating critique of the shah's economic policies and his style of leadership generally. Graham had been a reporter in Tehran for the *Financial Times*, and his book can be viewed as the outer limit of criticism within the orthodox image frame. Graham could describe the vainglorious style of the shah's administration that made impossible decisional independence beneath him. He could dissect the multilayered internal security apparatus that provided what appeared to be an impenetrable shield protecting the shah from his people. But it did not occur to him to describe the political movements the shah needed protection from. The irony of Graham's book, in fact, is that it stands as the best analysis by a Western author of the overall malaise of the shah's administration, but although it was written during the very months in which the most massive popular rebellion of our era was well under way, in its first edition it failed even to take note of what was happening.[12]

Mossadeq and Khomeini, one the charismatic leader of the 1950s who symbolized Iran's quest for national dignity, the other the charismatic leader of the 1970s who symbolized Islamic Iran's quest for religionational dignity, were trivialized in the Graham book. The boundaries of the ·orthodox cold war image were not penetrated.

CARTER'S HUMAN RIGHTS POLICY: TWO VIEWS

Jimmy Carter's human rights program as applied to Iran becomes comprehensible within this context. The orthodox image of Iran accepted as fact the assumption that authoritarian control in Iran was necessary. As described above, it was premissed on the assumption that at its stage of development, Iran neded a long benevolently tutorial period. And, by this view, the shah was a more than acceptable leader. However, it could be argued that the shah was moving too slowly in the area of political rights and, hence, that some friendly prodding could do no harm. Indeed, if he followed advice the shah might even strengthen his position by broadening his base of support.

Within the context of the image of Iran that had prevailed since 1953, there was nothing wrong with this reasoning. Within that image the political leaders the USA had participated in overthrowing in 1953 were simply self-serving agitators without any real base of support from an Iranian public which lacked the maturity to grant sustained support to any political movement. Therefore, it followed that there was no need to concern oneself with those leaders or their successors in an Iran led by a progressive, responsible, moderate and pro-Western monarch. In fact any official contact – covert as well as overt – with Iranian opposition leaders was forbidden in 1967, and that prohibition was maintained and fortified during the era in which Henry Kissinger gave expression to the USA's policy.[13] Why should a US government gratuitously annoy the shah by making contact with individuals of utterly no political consequence? But, one could wonder, if the political opposition in Iran was of no importance, why must SAVAK and the other elements of the internal security system act with such brutality? One answer to that question, and the one given by those who were most uncritical in their acceptance of the orthodox image, was simply to deny the brutality assertion. But the evidence of brutality was too strong for others to disregard.[14] And it was from this group that support came for Carter's proddings on political rights. Put another way, for those observers who were receptive to the Robert Graham critique of the shah's government, the USA's efforts to push the shah in a direction of reform were **fully defensible**.

The application of Carter's human rights program to Iran was of course opposed by those, such as former Secretary of State Kissinger, who argued the case for total commitment to the shah and who asserted a highly favorable public assessment of the shah's rule. But less obvious was the fact that those who continued to see Iran outside the cold war stereotype were bemused, astonished and more than a little worried by the human rights application in Iran. Ambassador Grady had seen the Iranian national movement as an expression of a deeply felt desire on the part of a political elite with substantial mass support for true independence and dignity for the Iranian nation, and for an important section of the movement, for Islam. By opposing this movement the USA would follow exactly the path of the British of the previous three-quarters of a century, and would be viewed similarly by Iranian nationalists: the vanguard of the capitalist-imperialist West operating through Iranian agents to control Iran's resources and people. Grady feared that the USSR would take advantage of a US decision to oppose the national movement and would proclaim itself the champion of Iranian national aspirations.

After the overthrow of Dr Mossadeq with the blatant and undeniable assistance of the CIA, those who shared Grady's expectations saw their predictions half-fulfilled. Iranian nationalists and Islamic leaders did, indeed, classify the successor regime as the instrument of Western imperialism. When the shah seized and consolidated a personal dictatorial control of Iran, his continued close relations with the USA led to his becoming the symbolic manifestation of imperial control. Over the years, as the royal Iranian and Israeli relationship developed, the imperialism Iranian nationalists saw was amended as 'Western, capitalist and Zionist'. But, contrary to expectations, the Soviets inexplicably failed to take advantage of their opportunity. There was of course a strongly held historical fear of Russia in Iran, and a Soviet effort to ingratiate itself with Iranian nationalists would have required both subtlety and restraint. But there was no such effort. With only a few brief exceptions, Soviet relations with the shah were cooperative and friendly throughout the generation of royal dictatorship. Iranian Marxists – their number among the secular intellectual community steadily grew during the past generation – tended to scorn both Moscow and the Moscow-supported Tudeh Party.

In the view of those few Americans who persisted in seeing an Iranian opposition that was diverse but potentially of great importance, the Carter human rights program could not succeed in achieving its objectives because the assumptional underlay was wrong. Liberalization is a dangerous policy for one regarded by his opposition as the agent of a foreign government. Relaxing coercive control would not lead to a broadening of the shah's base of support. On the contrary, given the history of the shah's coming to power, the program was certain to be misinterpreted by the opposition. Since the opposition believed the shah was the active agent of US policy, the decisions of an American president to expand the scope of Iranian political freedom meant – the opposition would assume – that the Americans had decided to explore the possibility of allowing genuine Iranian political leaders to achieve power in Iran. There had to be US dissatisfaction with the shah. Since Iranians had believed that, prior to the decision to overthrow Mossadeq, the USA was the most sympathetic of external powers to Iranian national aspirations, a decision to return to its historical position was not out of the question. These Iranians believed there were signs that President Kennedy was toying with just such a decision before he died. Consequently, the Iranian opposition, in particular the liberal nationalists, were enormously encouraged by the Carter human rights pronouncements. Almost immediately they moved, at first cautiously and then far less so, to explore US intentions. Americans able to see an opposition feared that what would actually occur was that the opposition voices, long subdued, would be raised in the expectation that the USA would prevent their being punished for their temerity. But since the advocates of the program within the administration would not expect or understand the opposition activities, there would be no inclination to protect them. The shah, seeing no support from the US embassy for the opposition would quickly understand that, inadvertently, the administration's human rights policy would lead to the identification and persecution of Iranian liberal nationalist leaders.

Here again the expectations of those holding this view were half-fulfilled. The intensity and breadth of opposition activity in Iran, in 1977, both astonished and alarmed the Carter administration. Nor was it possible for members of that administration concerned with Iran to deny that the human rights program was a catalyst for opposition activities. Those engaged in these activities informed the administration through indirect channels of that fact.[15] But the Carter administration's support of the shah's regime was no less total than that of the Nixon–Ford administration. Some of the Carter policies toward Iran should have been and to some extent were perceived as negative signals by the opposition Iranians. The choice of William Sullivan as ambassador was interpreted symbolically. Sullivan, previously ambassador to Laos and the Philippines, presumably would be comfortable with and supportive of the shah. And the Carter administration's support of continued sales of highly sophisticated weaponry to the shah – weapons which the opposition saw as a waste of precious oil income and of use only to US strategic objectives in the area – was deeply disappointing to those beginning to take the risks of open opposition. But the Carter administration did not avail itself of the indirect channels that were present to signal oppositionists clearly that they could not count on US support should the shah persecute them because of activities they believed were encouraged by the USA's policy. This was not done, in all probability, because the administration could not really comprehend the importance granted the USA's role in Iran by the opposition. Lacking direct discouragement, the opposition continued to hope. The climactic moment for their activities came in December 1977. Carter had agreed to include Iran on his itinerary for a goodwill foreign trip over New Year's. Thereupon twenty-nine leading Iranian liberals inside Iran decided to make a major test of Carter's intent. They wrote a strongly but constructively phrased critique of the shah's government which they planned to make public in Iran on 23 December, one week before Carter's visit. But before publishing the statement, they made certain that the Carter administration knew of their plans and understood that this was a test of US intent. The optimal response they hoped for would be a veiled public expression by Carter of approval of their call for greater freedom and respect for the rule of law. What they expected minimally was a warning from Carter not to count on his support should they issue the statement. In fact Carter gave no such warning, and when he visited the shah issued statements of support that were so effusive that the shah could hardly have dared ask for more.[16] The test was a fair one and the results told the liberal nationalist center of the Iranian opposition that Carter's advocacy of human rights was sheer hypocrisy. This time there is strong evidence that the shah understood that Americans had spurned his Iranian critics. In the weeks that followed, the twenty-nine suffered various forms of harassment and persecutions. Some were jailed. Others had their homes or automobiles blown up. Later, on 8 September 1978, Iran's newest day of infamy known as 'Black Friday', when the shah's imperial guard fired on thousands of unarmed demonstrators, killing many – opposition estimates centered around the figure of 4,500 – Carter took time out from his Camp David discussions to assure the shah of US support. Just as those who saw Iran less stereotypically feared, the Carter human rights program toward Iran resulted in heightened opposition activity and led to greater, not less, dislike of the USA.[17]

THE SHAH'S VIEW OF THE USA

But those who saw Iran in this perspective did not have their expectations fulfilled in one important respect. They expected a severe, brutal and unrelenting crackdown on the opposition by the shah and his security forces as soon as Carter's lack of seriousness of purpose was clear. In fact, the one great mystery of the Iranian revolution was why the shah did not follow this course of action. It is, indeed, possible that part of the answer to this puzzle lies in the shah's interpretation of Carter's devotion to human rights. The belief in Iran that ultimate policy control lay with the USA government during the shah's regime was not held simply by the opposition. It was held by all but a tiny detached and sophisticated minority. And that did not include the shah. The shah's question to Henry Kissinger, in 1977, as to why the CIA was trying to overthrow him, tells volumes. So powerful and ubiquitous was the CIA that the very fact of a burgeoning opposition was seen as evidence that the USA was dissatisfied with the shah. Ayatollah Khomeini saw the great revolutionary movement as a reflection of God's will. There are signs that the shah and many of his supporters saw it as a reflection of CIA's will. With such a reality view, how was the shah to interpret Carter's repeated statements calling for a greater concern for human and political rights? Quite conceivably the shah believed that he must move in this direction or risk losing Carter's support. If so, Carter's strong signaling to the contrary could only confuse the shah and add to his indecision.

More likely, the shah's failure to suppress his opposition is to be explained in terms of the shah's own temperament. He appears to have been astonished, depressed and ultimately paralyzed by the extraordinary breadth of the revolutionary movement against him. In any case, his response was surely the worst possible. His acts of suppression against the opposition were sporadic, inconsistent and unnecessarily brutal. Iranians believe that as many as 65,000–70,000 men, women and children were shot down in anti-government demonstrations in the last fourteen months. The figure is surely too large, but it was and is broadly accepted. Photographs of dead children were circulated throughout the country, and with each report of violence taken against unarmed demonstrators, hatred grew. Particularly enraging were reports, some from the BBC, of tanks being driven back and forth over demonstrators in the Iranian cities of Mashad and Qazvin. But acts of brutality were alternated with efforts to appease the people. In the fall of 1978 the press, formerly one of the most tightly controlled in the world, was almost free. Prisoners were freed, and politicians thought to be respected by the people were pressed into government service. All these things tended to further encourage opposition activities, because they were seen as acts of weakness carried out by an unalterably brutal regime. Then finally, especially after the 18 February 1978 riots in Tabriz that the government had great difficulty bringing under control, the shah began to purge his security forces and his governmental officials – most of whom had served him loyally. In doing this, he damaged the morale of the people essential for his survival and reduced the public's fear of his internal security force. Contempt for SAVAK began to develop. Thus, deadly rhythm was being followed which led to an acceleration of opposition hopes and activities.

THE TWO VIEWS OF THE SHAH'S FALL

Much had changed in the world in the twenty-five years that separated the overthrow of Mossadeq and the development of an opposition tempo that would overthrow the shah. From the perspective of world view, the most important of the changes was the decline in intensity of Soviet-US hostility and competition. References to the late 1970s as 'post-cold war' and a period of détente reflected this changed assessment of the relationship. Yet my primary contention in this chapter thus far is that the view of Iran which proponents of Mossadeq's overthrow held, continued to prevail twenty-five years later. Opposition to the shah was either not perceived, or dismissed as of no significance. But by the fall of 1978 the fact of a major opposition could no longer be denied. The comfortable image of a progressive, responsible shah tutoring his accepting people could no longer be maintained. What image or images would take its place?

Just as in the 1950s, two sharply opposed images were advanced within the US government and the US media. Furthermore, they were remarkably parallel to the opposed image patterns of the 1950s. On 2 December 1978, the *New Republic* printed an article by Robert Moss entitled 'Who's meddling in Iran?' that neatly defines the stereotypical cold war view, 1978-style. The article was reprinted in the *Washington Post* and rumor has it that Zbigniew Brzezinski, the president's national security adviser, indicated his full agreement with the argument. Moss admits that 'The Soviets don't deserve all the credit for turmoil in Iran'; but the

'Shah's problems . . . certainly have been aggravated by covert warfare waged against him by the Soviet Union and proxy regimes like Libya'.[18] Most of his article discusses unverifiable assertions of Soviet subversive activity in Iran and the ability of the Soviets to exploit a chaotic situation. He contends that 'The Shah's own experiment in liberalization has helped release many pent up forces' and that 'The Shah confronted the classic dilemma of the reformer in a backward society accustomed to absolutism'.[19] The opposition is treated again as formless, easily manipulated, and naïvely vulnerable at best. The prescription: somehow to buoy up the shah despite 'the evident indecisiveness of the regime'. 'Iran without the Pahlavi regime probably would start out as a fanatical, Qaddafi-style Moslem regime that would give way after civil war to Marxist elements.'[20]

It is of course not possible to give as pointed a description of the alternate, non-stereotypical view. But there were certain commonalities in the complex image. Those holding it accepted the fundamental quality of a movement that could bring out as many as 8 million people on the holy day of Ashura, 10 December 1978, even though the demonstrators knew that thousands had died in earlier demonstrations. Clearly, this was not to any significant degree a movement stimulated by or orchestrated by the USSR or any other external force. In fact, those holding the more complex view in 1978 saw far less danger of Soviet activity than did their predecessors in 1953. But they also had a less clear view of the diverse elements within the movement. Given the fact that they had had no direct contact with opposition elements for the preceding ten years, governmental specialists on Iran could hardly quickly identify and qualitatively evaluate the component parts of the movement. It is not unfair to say that when the shah's last appointed prime minister, Shahpur Bakhtiar, fled Iran, there remained great uncertainty about the forces that would now give definition to a new and revolutionary regime. One point was well understood, however, and that was that the focus of the revolutionaries was on what they saw as Western imperialism acting through its agent, the shah. That Iranian belief coupled with the distress produced by severe inflation was, these people tended to believe, the source of fatal vulnerability for the shah's regime.

There is not much doubt that in the final critical months of the shah's regime US policy was still firmly in the hands of those who held the stereotypical cold war view. Critics of Carter's policy from the cold war perspective do have, this chapter is arguing, a case with respect to the human rights program. I believe it did contribute to the disintegration of the shah's regime – possibly even decisively so, if the shah did think he had to carry out his liberalization policies or lose Carter's support. But in the last twelve months of the shah's government, US support for the shah was unambiguous, with the exception of one statement made (and later reversed) by Carter. Few close observers doubt that the direction of US policy toward Iran in this period was in the hands of national security adviser Brzezinski, certainly the strongest administration proponent of the cold war stereotypical view.[21] But how could he hope to reverse the enormous revolutionary momentum that was developing in Iran? As the Moss article quoted above demonstrates, this was, for those who saw Iran as Moss did, a non-question. What revolutionary momentum? What was necessary was to help the shah take the kind of decisive action that could save him and his government.

A widespread Iranian belief is that the Americans were, toward the end, looking frantically for a transitional formula that would accept the shah's departure and would bring into a government leaders from the major revolutionary factions. Such a formula could keep the army from disintegrating and could provide a government with the strength to deal with extraordinary postrevolutionary problems – and incidentally curb the Left. Within Iran, liberal and left-of-center secular intellectuals, and liberal Muslim leaders as well, recognized clearly the fascist potential of the extraordinary mass involvement in the revolution, and were receptive to plans that would result in a government capable of keeping that fascist potential from materializing. Indeed, several transitional formulae were suggested by these people. Had they received US support in the form of placing pressure on the shah and his generals to accept such a formula, developments could have been much different in Iran. Had US policy been in the hands of those who saw Iran in complex terms, the compelling quality of this strategy might have been understood. But policy was in the hands of those who looked at Iran in stereotypical terms. Almost universally, Iranians believe that Shahpur Bakhtiar's selection as prime minister was part of a US scheme for a transitional government. But, as suggested above, it is most doubtful that those making US policy toward Iran had any clear notion of who Bakhtiar was. In any event, his selection lacked the ingredients of a serious transitional plan. Bakhtiar was unable to persuade any significant group connected with the revolution to join him. His own organization, the National Front, expelled him when he made his decision. It is far more likely that advisers of the shah, with implicit US approval, hoped to use Bakhtiar to divide the opposition.

One of the much-noted oddities of the Iranian revolution was the failure of so many of the shah's generals to flee Iran while there was still time to avoid inevitable revolutionary retribution. Obviously, these generals did not expect the revolution to succeed. Just as obviously, they expected that the force that would turn back the revolution would be decisive US action. Their behavior, in fact, is strong evidence for the thesis being developed here: the predominant US policymakers, because of the stereotypical image they held of Iran, and their Iranian counterparts failed until the last fatal moment to comprehend the momentous quality of the Iranian revolution. Within this context, the strange episode of the mission to Iran of General Robert Huyser is fully comprehensible. By January 1979, both US and Iranian policymakers had clearly accepted as fact that the shah was now incapable of functioning in a leadership capacity. Thus the shah's angry charge,[22] that the Carter administration acting through General Huyser invited him to leave Iran, is probably accurate. But the case developed by right-wing critics in the USA of the Carter policy, that Huyser was charged with bringing Khomeini into power is most improbable, indeed ludicrously so. Huyser's mission was almost certainly exactly what administration sources have since indicated it was. Huyser was sent to Iran to evaluate the Iranian military and to encourage the military leadership to stand firm, even if that entailed carrying out a coup d'état. There is no evidence that Huyser or his superiors understood that, by January 1979, the Iranian military rank and file were in the process of joining the revolution.

RETURN TO A MORE COMPLEX VIEW OF IRAN

The first attack on the US embassy, in February 1979, symbolized the situation for US policy. Overrun by as yet unidentified elements, the embassy was rescued by forces loyal to the new government. Iranians accustomed to think of the USA's omnipotence were now witnessing the USA's impotence. The magnificently equipped Iranian army, which figures so importantly in the USA's strategic thinking, was on the edge of disintegration. Major elements of the airforce had gone over to the revolution, and the supersophisticated aircraft sold the shah were largely grounded. What was to stop the USSR now? Not only was the 1,600-mile Soviet-Iranian border now virtually undefended, the Soviet ability to exploit ethnic minority restiveness was potentially unlimited.

But there was no Soviet move to weaken the Iranian government. On the contrary, Soviet efforts and those of the pro-Soviet Tudeh Party were clearly designed to establish close and good relations with Khomeini and the Mehdi Bazergan government. Two ethnic groups found in both Iran and the USSR, the Kurds and the Turkomen, did make strong bids for autonomy within a new Iran. There was some suspicion in Tehran of Soviet complicity in the two cases, but evidence supporting such suspicions was insufficient to sustain serious Iranian fears. This benevolent stance was taken by the Soviets, even though the Iranian government and Ayatollah Khomeini made clear their preference for Muslim challengers to the Soviet-supported government of Afghanistan. Furthermore, both Khomeini and the Bazergan government expressed their wariness of Soviet intentions in Iran and the Middle East. And Khomeini's hostility toward Iranian Marxists appeared to grow as the number of days in power lengthened.

There was little in these developments to' give confirmation to the diabolical enemy thesis advanced in the Robert Moss article. A strong trend did develop quickly toward a polarization of secular and religious forces that had been active in the revolution. But the split was uneven. Very early, much of the middle and upper-middle classes turned away from Khomeini. Indeed, as many people as could left the country. Those remaining were vastly outnumbered by the continuing massive support for Khomeini, especially from the Persian-speaking lower-middle class and lower class. Civil war, which Moss so clearly saw as part of Soviet calculations, was unlikely as long as the disparity in forces remained this great.

There was, in short, little that those holding the cold war stereotypical view could recognize in Iranian developments. The government was more fiercely anti-communist and less friendly toward the Soviets than the shah had been. There was governmental paralysis largely because of Khomeini's creation of a set of revolutionary institutions: a council, committees for each district of the country, a number of courts and guards.

These were set up to help the revolution consolidate power but remained long after that as a rival authority to the Khomeini-appointed prime minister and his Cabinet. Khomeini could act decisively and even brutally when dealing with those he saw as opposed to the revolution, mainly secular and ethnic elements. But confronted with conflict among people he saw as true Muslim and proponents of the revolution, he was maddeningly indecisive. Unemployment was high, but a continuing large oil income kept economic distress from undermining the new regime. For the time being, there was an uneasy stability.

The predominance of stereotypical thinking in foreign policy is likely to be crisis-associated, and in the first months following the revolution, there was no crisis in US-Iranian relations. American governmental policy toward Iran in that period suggests that those most influential in US decision-making had a complex, rather than a stereotypical, view of Iran. Some serious problems existed between the two governments as a consequence of Iran's drastically altered military-equipment policy. But by and large, US policy was carefully correct. Activities such as encouraging US firms to return to Iran and to renegotiate or activate contracts in fact led Iranians opposed to the new government to wonder if the Americans had after all really been opposed to the revolution. Indeed, Iran's second foreign minister, Ibrahim Yazdi, who had lived in the USA for sixteen years (always in strong opposition to the shah), was charged with being a CIA agent not only by proshah and pro-Bakhtiar exiles, but by the Left within Iran and by radical-Right religious leaders. The shah may have believed, as Moss tells us, that the revolution against him was Soviet-inspired. But the passivity of postrevolutionary Soviet policy plus the correct US-Iranian relations tended to convince Iranians in exile that the USA, not the USSR, continued to control Iran's destiny. Suspicions in this direction developed to the point that the Left and exile groups wondered if not only Yazdi, but Bazergan and even Khomeini, were functionally, at least, US agents. Robert Moss still has something to learn about conspiracy theories. Khomeini, for his part, said that he had come to believe that Iranian communists are US agents.[23]

Iranian imaginings of what the USA's policy in Iran is actually up to are very strange to US eyes. And they are not an unimportant factor in the diplomatic equation. For months and probably years in the future, US officials can expect to be confronted with pleas that the US government intervene on behalf of one group or another in Iran. Rather than thinking in terms of altering the situation in Iran by their own activities, Iranian groups will direct their energies to persuading the Americans to do so. This is the inevitable consequence of past US and other interventions.[24]

TWO VIEWS OF THE HOSTAGE ISSUE

Crisis in Iranian-US relations returned with a vengeance in November 1979 in the form of the hostage issue. But the two US world view patterns prevailing with respect to prerevolutionary Iran did not return. There were signs that they might. Speculation was common in Iran and the USA that the militants who seized the US embassy and took prisoner its occupants were dominated by Soviet-controlled Tudeh Party infiltrators. And, as a new twist, there was also speculation that the PLO exercised control and direction of the operation. The Iranian revolutionary view that Iran had been the victim of a Western, capitalist and Zionist conspiracy was balanced by a parallel US view that the Iranian revolution was being victimized by an Eastern, communist, PLO alliance. But evidence for this American view was too insubstantial to sustain the thesis.

Nevertheless two different views of Khomeini's Iran did begin to crystalize among Americans. And in one important respect there was a parallel with the earlier two views. One was neatly simplified, almost stereotypical; the other was far more complex. In the simplified view Ayatollah Khomeini was a devious, power-driven politician determined to establish in Iran a theocratic dictatorship. He and his fellow mullahs were viewed as a monolith seeking to institutionalize authoritarian control. This monolith was capable of orchestrating elaborate conspiracies. The taking of the hostages was an essential element of an overall strategy. It reversed a decline in popularity for Khomeini and, thereby, made acceptable the imposing of a theocratic dictatorship on the people. Those holding this view were strongly inclined to look for evidence of Tudeh/PLO infiltration and control. Evidence, such as the discovery that a few of the people holding the embassy had received PLO training, was seen as a conclusive indication of continuing PLO control.

For those holding this view, the policy prescription was inescapable. The USA must demonstrate, first of all, the willpower to impose its policy objective on the erring party. The Iranian regime must be subjected to a campaign of punishment that would demonstrate to Khomeini that he must release the hostages or suffer terribly. With such a strategy, the Iranian leaders understand that the costs of their policy are far greater than the benefits can possibly be. At the point of understanding, settlement is likely.

The opposing view had many variations. But on two basic points there was substantial agreement. First, Khomeini was taken more at face-value. Rather than seeing a clever and devious tactician seeking to impose a dictatorship of the mullahs, they saw a religious leader who was unconcerned with translating a vaguely articulated Islamic ideology into a program of action and even less concerned with strategy. He sanctioned the taking of the hostages in the belief that this action was an aspect of an unfolding, divinely guided plan with the objective of forcing the USA's policy away from its satanic course of oppressing Iran and Third World people. Furthermore, as the charismatic leader of the Iranian nation, his other-worldly views gave apparent definition to the nation he led.

Secondly, in the more complex view, the failure of Khomeini to give direction to the movement was compounded by his unwillingness to grant real authority to any set of governmental officials. He was fierce enough in his determination to oust all secularists from positions of authority. But he consistently refused to intervene in policy and power struggles among members of his own philosophically diverse entourage. The result was governmental paralysis. Khomeini's political associates consisted, at one pole, of individuals with considerable sophistication and an ability to give leadership in a technically demanding era. But there were, at the other pole, religiopolitical leaders who had only the vaguest understanding of how a modern government performs, but who were filled with a revolutionary zeal to bring Islamic values somehow to bear on every situation. Attitudes toward the hostages reflected these polar differences. At one end of the spectrum, taking the hostages was seen as a declaration of independence from great-power intervention.

Preferred strategy for Americans adhering to this picture of revolutionary Iran was to follow a course of action that would strengthen the internal bargaining position of Iranian decisionmakers who wished to release the hostages at the earliest possible moment. Such a strategy must be a subtle one. Any clear evidence of support for an Iranian faction could easily destroy that faction.

Carter administration policy in the hostage crisis reflected variously both views. Initially the strategy followed was a simple punishment strategy. But its application in November–December 1979 produced no movement toward settlement, even though the price Iran was paying was a severe one. This policy failure, however, did not lead to an examination of assumptions underlying that policy – assumptions of a power advantage. Rather, proponents of the strategy explained the failure as a consequence of allied timidity and unfaithfulness.

In January 1980 a strikingly different strategy was inaugurated – one that was far more in harmony with the thinking of those who saw a more complex picture of Iran. This shift appears to have had less to do with bureaucratic infighting, however, than to Iranian reaction to Soviet policy in Afghanistan. When the Soviets moved into Afghanistan, Sadeq Qotbzadeh, the Iranian foreign minister, was one of the first and strongest critics of Soviet policy. Since those who held cold war stereotypical views were likely also to see Khomeini's Iran stereotypically, this response was surprising to them. Briefly, at least, the Iranian crisis was obscured by the Afghanistan crisis and advocates of a tough line in Afghanistan were amenable to exploring a more conciliatory strategy toward Iran.

For more than three months, Washington followed the lead of Iranians such as President Abol Hussan Bani-Sadr and Foreign Minister Qotbzadeh who openly proclaimed their wish to terminate the hostage crisis. In essence, this phase of US policy was one of seeking to show that US-Iranian relations in the future, unlike the past, would be based on the principle of sovereign equality. Hopefully, Khomeini would see this as a move away from a satanic policy. But progress under this policy was excruciatingly slow, disappointments were frequent, and the suspicion grew that the USA was being played the fool. There followed, therefore, a return to a policy of punishment. Heavy pressure was placed on allied governments to join in economic boycott of Iran, and this pressure produced modest results. Administration rhetoric toward Iran became sharp and threatening. Presidential statements now explicated the possibility of escalating punishment to the military level. Indeed, this third phase of policy began to resemble a strategy of graduated compellence reminiscent of Vietnam. Little thought or consideration was given to the impact of such a policy on Iran's internal power struggle. But this attitude is in tune with the monolithic image of Iranian leadership of the stereotypical view of Khomeini's Iran.

The failed rescue mission and the shock of Secretary Cyrus Vance's resignation brought an end to this third phase. As this chapter is written, a fourth phase is still in effect that in terms of strategic objective resembles the second phase. In both cases the immediate objective was to strengthen, or at least not to weaken, those among the Iranian hydra-headed leadership who wished to release the hostages. Once again, progress is slow to the point of being imperceptible, and open warfare betwen Iran and Iraq threatens to slow the process even more.

American policy toward Iran in the hostage case thus has alternated from simple punishment, reflecting the stereotypical view, to complicated efforts to strengthen the hands of Iranian leaders known to wish to release the hostages. Neither strategy was successful. But from the point of stereotypical theory, the case is most interesting. Two crises in US foreign policy intersect in Iran. The one relating to the hostages, is essentially a prestige crisis. The other, relating to perceived Soviet aggressiveness in the area, is a serious security crisis. Since the security crisis is by far the more important, logic argues that it should dictate overall American response in the region. And in the process of doing so, the view of Iran should be brought into congruence with the cold war stereotypical view. Khomeini's intense dislike of communism and of the USSR has, on occasion, led US policymakers to assume that both the USA and Iran would be well served by rapid reconciliation. But whenever such an effort is made, Khomeini quickly disabuses optimistic Americans of their illusions. His determination to ally with neither of the great oppressor powers, the great satans, apparently is fierce and deeply sincere.

CONCLUSION

The tendency of a people involved in great crises to see their opponents in stereotypical terms, appears to be a natural one. By simplifying reality in this way, a terrible threat or a wonderful oportunity can be dealt with without debilitating ambivalence. A diabolical enemy deserving no sympathy, or a childlike people who for their own good need the benevolence of the tutorial services of a more advanced state, are two common examples of stereotypes of the cold war period. Americans inclined to stereotype saw the USSR and Iran respectively in these patterns. Strategies advocated will, of course, be congruent with the particular stereotypical image that is perceived, and for the generation and a half of the shah's dictatorship in Iran, US strategy toward Iran appeared to be remarkably successful. By establishing and supporting the shah as the tutorial ruler of Iran, US policy of containing the Soviet enemy was well supported. But there was no room in this stereotypical view for an Iranian opposition to the shah that was not simply an agent of the Soviet enemy. When evidence of such an opposition became undeniable in the course of the Iranian revolution, however, there was an effort to accommodate perceptually a new anti-communist regime in Iran to US containment strategy. But Iranians of the Khomeini persuasion saw not only the USSR, but the USA, Western Europe and Japan in an anti-imperialist variant of the diabolical enemy stereotype. Iranian strategy is congruent with that view, and has led to diplomatic isolation to a degree that is almost without parallel.

This chapter suggests, though, that the tendency to stereotype is highly variable and that many individuals of decisional importance are able to resist its full force. Such individuals persist in seeing other international actors, even threatening ones, in complex terms, and the strategies they prefer are likely to differ profoundly from those advocated by decision-makers who view primary actors in stereotypical terms. Tension between the two is apparent in US policy toward Iran for the last generation and a half. For most of that period the USA's policy reflected the stereotypical view, but since the Iranian revolution US policy has been more often in tune with a complex view. In revolutionary Iran, however, an anti-imperialist stereotype is giving full definition to Iranian policy toward the USA and its allies and to the USSR as well. So long as this tendency persists, US-Iranian relations are unlikely to improve.

NOTES: CHAPTER 13

1   The reader is invited to examine the treatment of the Iranian situation in the Soviet media prior to the revolution in Iran. A particularly valuable source for this in English is the Foreign Radio Broadcasts for the period.

2   The *US Foreign Relations* series is published through 1950 and contains much evidence of an evolving cold war view relating to Iran. Ambassador John Wiley was an early articulator of the cold war views. See, for example, his statement in *US Foreign Relations*, vol. 5 (1950), pp. 459–64.

3   For a contemporary account of the coup that expresses this view, see Kermit Roosevelt, *Countercoup: The Bloody Struggle for Control in Iran* (New York: McGraw Hill, 1979).

4   See the interview of Henry Grady in *US News and World Report*, 19 October 1951, pp. 13–17.

5   Roosevelt, op. cit.

6   For an account of Iranian-Soviet relations see Shahram Chubin and Sepehr Zabih, *The Foreign Relations of Iran* (Berkeley, Calif.: University of California Press, 1974), and Rouhallah Ramazani, *Iran's Foreign Policy, 1941–1973* (Charlottesville, Va: University Press of Virginia, 1975).

7   For the documentary evidence for this case, see *Village Voice*, 16 February 1976, p. 85. This is the text of the Pike Committee report.

8   See Herman Nickels, 'The US failure in Iran', *Fortune*, 12 March 1979.

9   *New York Times*, 2 August 1976, 1:5.

10   *New York Times* 30 May 1977, 24:2.

11   Robert Graham, *Iran, The Illusion of Power* (New York: St Martin's Press, 1978).

12   Graham added a chapter on the opposition in his 1979 paper edition.

13   Nickels, op. cit.

14   See, for example, the report of the International Committee of Jurists which, though mild, could not be dismissed easily, 'Human rights and the legal system in Iran' (Geneva, 1976).

15   I participated personally in this process.

16   For the text, see *Kayhan International*, 7 January 1978.

17   For a full account of this episode, see Richard W. Cottam, 'Arms sales and

human rights: the case of Iran', in Peter G. Brown and Douglas MacLean (eds), *Human Rights and Foreign Policy* (Lexington, Mass.: D. C. Heath/ Lexington Books, 1979).

18 See Robert Moss 'Who's meddling in Iran', *New Republic*, 2 December 1978, pp. 15–18.

19 ibid.

20 ibid.

21 See William Sullivan's statement to the effect that Brzezinski did have Carter's ear at this time. See *New York Times*, 22 June 1980, 3:1. He further elaborated on that theme in 'Dateline Iran: the road not taken', *Foreign Policy*, no. 40 (Fall 1980), pp. 175–86.

22 *New York Times*, 2 December 1979, 5:1. See also Mohammad Reza Pahlavi, *Answer to History* (New York: Stein & Day, 1980), p. 172.

23 See Oriana Fallaci interview with Ayatollah Ruhollah Khomeini, *New York Times Magazine*, 7 October 1979.

24 The strength of this Iranian tendency is well illustrated by one particularly pervasive conspiracy picture that gained currency after the US embassy, 'The Nest of Spies', was overrun for the second time and hostages taken. According to this picture both Khomeini and Carter were low in the polls in the Fall of 1979. Both rose to new heights of popularity because of the hostage issue. It follows, therefore, that there was collusion. Those accepting this logic would remark wisely that the hostages would be released right after the American election.

14 Turkey in Crisis: Implications for the Atlantic Alliance

CIRO ELLIOTT ZOPPO

The Iranian revolution and the Soviet invasion of Afghanistan have re-focused NATO's attention on the Middle East and its adjacent seas: the Persian Gulf and the Mediterranean. Historically, Turkey has been at the crossroads between East and West in this region as the guardian of the strategic Dardanelles against Russian hegemonic encroachments. Turkey was the first independent power in the Middle East to embrace Westernization as the vehicle for modernization and economic and political development. Turkey was, therefore, the precursor to Westerniza-tion and secularization in the Middle Eastern region,[1] and the only Middle Eastern country with a Muslim heritage to become a member of the Atlantic Alliance.

As we enter the 1980s the role of Turkey in the Middle East, in Mediterranean Europe, and particularly within the Atlantic Alliance, invites reexamination, as NATO attempts to relate to the foreboding revolutionary and international changes in the Persian Gulf. The changing technological and geopolitical context of the US-Soviet rivalry, the revo-lutionary relevance of Islam's political legacy, the viability of the Western political and economic models of development for the Middle East; and especially the capacity of the Atlantic Alliance to cope with threats to its political cohesion and its military effectiveness, arising from the West's unavoidable dependence on Arab oil, converge in Turkey's domestic and foreign policy crisis. The implications of this crisis reveal the nature of the dilemmas faced by the Atlantic Alliance when it must reckon with threats to its members' vital national interests emanating from areas and issues outside the treaty's purview. Because no other member of the alliance combines, as Turkey does, a Middle Eastern Muslim heritage with a Western political vocation, straddling Europe and the Middle East in more than geographic terms, Turkey's role has no parallel in the complex of relations between the Middle East and Europe. At issue in Turkey's national crisis are the future shape of Turkey's bilateral relations with the USA and the USSR, Turkish rela-tions with Western Europe and the Arab countries, and Turkey's political and economic system – the most significant contemporary aspect of that country's vocation to the West.

THE ANATOMY OF THE TURKISH CRISIS

Turkey is in its worst crisis since joining NATO, in 1952, and one of the most severe in the history of modern Turkey. Because of Turkey's military and political role in NATO, this crisis compounds the difficulties besetting the alliance's southern flank. The crisis currently investing Turkey extends to all sectors of the Turkish polity: the political system, the economy, foreign policy and national security. Although the import of Turkey's crisis for European security, Mediterranean and Middle East politics has not been sufficiently appreciated by politicians in either the USA, or Western Europe, the nature of the factors that have led to the crisis in Turkey could make it a major turning-point in the future relations between NATO and the Middle East. A crucial aspect of the present situation in Turkey is psychological and regards Turkey's national identity as a modern democratic nation, which is at the core of Turkey's European and Western vocation.[2] The possible consequences for Turkey's foreign policy of this crisis in national identity could have serious repercussions for East–West relations in the Mediterranean and the Middle East. The shifting nature of Turkey's relations with the USSR and Eastern Europe, and with the Arab states of the Middle East and the Maghreb, are directly linked with the crisis of national identity. Should the military, who have taken power, fail to return Turkey to a viable parliamentary government, radical changes in Turkey's domestic political system would intensify trends and could bring into question or emasculate Turkey's participation in NATO. The resulting situation would create a geopolitical imbalance in the Eastern Mediterranean and the Middle East not capable of being compensated for by Greece's military reintegration into NATO, nor by strengthening the security policies of other countries in the Mediterranean, members of the Atlantic Alliance or allied with the West.

The factors that have generated the national identity crisis are to be found in the generally chastizing US and West European responses to Turkish actions in regard to the various Cyprus crises, particularly the 1974 conflict that led to the invasion of the island republic by the Turkish armed forces. However, it was the coincidence of the 1974 Cyprus crisis with the far-reaching economic and political consequences of the OPEC oil embargo and the Left–Right radical polarization in Turkish domestic politics – underway before the energy crisis but accelerated by it – that intensified the identity crisis to the point where it has become the catalyst for questioning the very tenets of modern Turkey. These tenets are contained in the legacy of Ataturk. Bernard Lewis has labeled this legacy 'the Turkish nationalist revolution', and has succinctly described it as a great transformation to be defined not merely in terms of the Westernization of the economy or society or government, but of civilization. The Turks have renounced a large part of their Islamic heritage, turned to Europe and made sustained and determined efforts to adopt and apply the European way of life in government, society and culture.[3]

Opinions may differ as to the measure of success achieved in this attempt to Westernize contemporary Turkey. But there can be no doubt that in all important areas of the public life of Turkey – in the political system, the economy, national defense and foreign policy – the 'Westernizing revolution' has been accomplished, and may be irreversible. Nevertheless, Turkey is the only member of NATO whose political, cultural and social-historical antecedents are not European. Her commitment to the

West is, therefore, more demanding psychologically and politically, and ultimately contingent. Given her geographical location, Turkey is also the only member of the alliance in the Mediterranean exposed to a direct Soviet military threat by conventional warfare. The Soviet takeover of Afghanistan, and Iran's fragile non-alignment has weakened Turkish defense, already hobbled by the US arms embargo. The attitudes and the policies of Turkey's European and US allies toward the Turkish crisis are, therefore, uniquely crucial. They will have psychological impact of the greatest relevance for the political options available to Turkey in her domestic and foreign policies.

The Westernizing and modernizing legacy of Ataturk no longer rests on the personal experience of the majority of the Turkish nation. This is not only a consequence of generational changes, but also the result of trends in young-to-old ratios in the population. In addition, the politicization of Turkish workers in Western Europe seems to have resulted in strongly leftist, sometimes radically Marxist tendencies which have eroded loyalties to Ataturk's traditions. It is important to remember that these traditions represent more than the legacy of Ataturk bequested in the creation of modern Turkey after World War I. They are also the product of the process which shaped the content of that legacy, dating back to the Tanzimat in 1839.[4] Westernization has been the matrix of this historical process.

Shifts in the East–West balance of power that radically alter the military equilibrium and the political alignment between NATO and the Warsaw Pact are seen as dangerous to European security by most West European governments. They are believed to be threats to détente by practically all the parties of the political Left in Western Europe as well. Turkey is not likely, at this time, to return to a neutralist foreign policy, which given the disparities in military and economic power between the USSR and Turkey, would have to be 'Finlandized' in important respects. Nevertheless, significant changes in Turkey's relations with the USSR and Eastern Europe, with her Middle East neighbors, with Western European countries, and especially the USA, are underway. Indeed, under present crisis circumstances, the Turkish ruling elites must revise their foreign and defense policies, if they are to cope realistically with the pervasive effects of the crisis that exists in their national economy and their internal politics. Turkey, whose parliamentary democracy has been temporarily suspended by its military, faces the negative impact of the energy crisis and other restrictive changes in international economics experienced by her NATO allies, and is simultaneously beset by internal political instabilities, including widespread terrorism and economic difficulties that, in the aggregate, are more grave than in any country of the alliance.

An analysis that surmounts the political passions aroused by the Greek-Turkish conflict on Cyprus would become aware that Turkey does not have to secede from the Atlantic Alliance, or abandon its military organization, for the current Turkish crisis to result in conditions that upset the East–West conventional military balance – already subverted by the rapid increase in Warsaw Pact military strength – and fault political alignments in the Mediterranean; seriously undermining the already-endangered basis for détente in Europe. An agonizing search for foreign policy alternatives in economic, diplomatic and military relations epitomizes Turkey's current national crisis. Its common denominator has been a deep sense of alienation from Western Europe and the USA, widely shared by the Turkish political elites and their constituents. The policies of the USA are the most crucial referents in this search, because it has been the bilateral relationship between the USA and Turkey that has set the compass for Turkish foreign policy since World War II.[5]

THE US ROLE

In the postwar period, relations with the USA have been the pivot on which Turkey's continued Westernization has rested. It was the Truman Doctrine that set up the relationship. And on the basis of that bilateral relationship, Turkey joined NATO. Bilateral US-Turkish agreements continue to articulate Turkey's participation in NATO. The US-Turkish relationship will primarily and essentially shape what Turkish defense and foreign policy are and what they will become. The policies of the USSR and Western European countries – especially West Germany and Greece, each with opposing tendencies, the former cooperative and the latter conflictual – will be important. They cannot be as critical, however, short of an eventual acceptance of Turkey as a full member of the EEC.

In order to appreciate the decisiveness of US policies toward Turkey, and their role in Turkey's current crisis, the scope of US-Turkish relations must be evaluated. Since the USA has possessed the greater foreign policy resources in the security, political and economic spheres, it has crucially defined the limits and nature of Turkey's foreign policy options. This is likely to persist in the years ahead, though to a lesser but still crucial degree.

It is a fact that from the US perspective mutual security relations have been, and will continue to be, the crucial focus of US-Turkish relations. The political and economic aspects of these relations have been, and are, important, but they have been complementary and secondary. Consequently, the state of relations between the USA and the USSR, during the cold war and détente, have been instrumental in shaping the priorities accorded Turkey in US foreign policy.[6]

The NATO context of US-Turkish relations has broadened their scope by incorporating Turkey into the US policy outlook toward Western Europe without, however, diminishing the central importance of mutual defense concerns. The Cyprus conflict has acquired meaningful salience, in the minds of US policymakers, primarily in regard to the preservation of the political cohesion of the Atlantic Alliance so as not to weaken NATO defense.

The current emphasis in the USA's policy toward Turkey, which focuses on the use of Turkish facilities for assistance in the verification of the

Soviet military posture and the SALT agreements, the rehabilitation of Turkish defense and the promotion of Turkish political stability through Western economic assistance is, therefore, consistent with prior US policies. The latter have been global in perspective and anchored to the requirements of Soviet-US strategic deterrence and the East–West military balance.

Security against a potential military threat from the USSR was also a central concern for Turkey's leaders, following World War II, and best explains the rationales that led Turkey to look for an alignment with the USA before the creation of NATO.[7] The strategic significance of Turkey was perceived by the USA even earlier. President Roosevelt extended lend-lease assistance to Turkey in 1941, recognizing that the defense of a then neutral Turkey was related to the US national interest. However, US and Turkish foreign policies did not converge to establish a policy of common defense until Stalin's heavy-handed pressures against Turkey, at the Straits and on Turkey's eastern frontiers, led Turkish leaders to seek help from the USA. Turkey was one of the very first recipients of US assistance under the Truman Doctrine in 1947, and the USA, surmounting some West European objections, sponsored Turkey's entry into NATO in 1952.[8]

During the halcyon years of US-Turkish relations that ended with the 1964 Cyprus crisis, the mutual defense focus animated a harmony between US and Turkish foreign policies ruffled fleetingly only by the withdrawal of US Jupiter missiles in the wake of the 1962 Cuban missile confrontation. Throughout the 1950s, Turkey's foreign policy was in almost total harmony with US foreign policy positions. Turkey participated in the Korean War. It supported US policy on Suez and the US intervention in Lebanon. With US encouragement, Turkey was also a party, with Britain and Greece, to the 1959 agreements which set up an independent Cyprus. During the same period, the USA provided an unqalified strategic guarantee to Turkish security, a US military presence on Turkish soil for common defense purposes and over $6 billion in military and economic assistance to Turkey.

THE USA AND TURKEY OVER CYPRUS

The primacy of security considerations in US foreign policy toward Turkey best explains the thrust of US policy on the Cyprus conflict as well.[9] Although there is no question that ethnic congressional politics played a critically detrimental role in US relations with Turkey after the 1974 Cyprus crisis, the basic rationales for US actions toward the Cyprus conflict have focused primarily on the damage political and military conflict between Greece and Turkey can inflict on NATO cohesion, weakening deterrence and defense in the alliance's southern flank.

At the same time, the difficulties that have beset the formulation and especially the implementation of US policies toward Turkey since the 1974 Cyprus crisis are a prime illustration of the severe curtailment of executive power in US foreign policy that followed Vietnam and Watergate, compounded by ethnic politics. Prioor to Watergate the policy actions undertaken by the three successive presidents on behalf of Turkey would not have been frustrated by Congress as they have been repeatedly since 1974. However, the watershed in US-Turkish relations, though related directly to the Cyprus conflict, precedes the consequences of Vietnam and Watergate and troubled executive-Congressional relations. The letter sent by President Johnson to Premier Inönü during the 1964 crisis, marks the beginning of the deterioration in US-Turkish relations.[10] The Johnson letter qualified the US security guarantee, if Turkish actions connected with the Cyprus crisis led to Soviet involvement. In retrospect, it may be seen that the qualifications voiced about the US security guarantee, in that letter, were overdrawn. American executives have not been cavalier about the security and independence of Turkey. Equally misleading would be to conclude from the policies of the US government toward the Cyprus conflict – the more recent constraints of ethnic politics on presidential will notwithstanding – that the USA has taken sides. To the contrary, it has attempted to mediate between Greece and Turkey, and except for 1974, to manage the conflicts arisen as a result of Greek-Turkish differences over Cyprus. The USA had been generally successful until 1974. Because of its responsibilities as a global power facing the USSR, and because it is the guarantor of strategic security for the Atlantic Alliance, the USA has given priority however to the East–West military balance of power and the political cohesion of NATO.

The crisis-manager role has not been without political costs for the USA. The 1964 Cyprus crisis marks the beginning of the deterioration in US-Turkish relations, later so palpably evident. Starting with 1970, US-Greek relations also deteriorated, seriously enough to cause Greece, in 1974, to withdraw from NATO. American base rights and operations, in both Greece and Turkey, have been increasingly curtailed and suspended, for considerable lengths of time. The first Cyprus crisis occurred in 1960. The USA played a role. But the significance of the US role as crisis manager is most clearly seen in the 1964, 1969 and 1974 crises, because in each of these crises Turkey had reached the decision to invade Cyprus. At the height of the 1964 crisis, Turkish troops had embarked in Mersin ready to invade. The USA unilaterally prevented the invasion by interposing the US Sixth Fleet between the Turkish forces and Cyprus, and by informing Turkey that should a Turkish invasion create the opportunity for Soviet intervention, the USA could not be expected to automatically come to the aid of Turkey. This was a tough position to take in as much as it related directly to article V, the most important commitment of the NATO treaty. The confidential letter from President Johnson to Premier Inönü, detailing the US position, was made public by Inönü and marks a watershed in US-Turkish relations.

In the 1969 Cyprus crisis the USA again intervened directly, this time as mediator. Former Secretary of State Cyrus Vance became a special emissary from the US president to resolve the crisis. Again the USA acted to prevent a Turkish invasion of Cyprus. Mr Vance had, at first, a difficult time in gaining access to Turkish leaders. By means of shuttle diplomacy between Athens and Ankara, he succeeded nevertheless, in averting a Turkish invasion. This time, however, it was the Greek side that had to make the concessions. Foremost among them, the withdrawal from Cyprus of 15,000 Greek troops stationed there by Athens after the 1964 crisis.

In 1974, partly because of the changed US outlook on involvement in local conflicts, following Vietnam and Watergate, and partly out of sheer diplomatic fatigue from the long, thankless involvement in the Cyprus conflict, the USA did not forcefully prevent military operations. The Turks successfully invaded Cyprus.

Deep-seated historical hatreds, intense nationalisms and the passions aroused by the violent conflicts on Cyprus have led the Turks and Greeks alike to accuse the USA of partisan bahavior. However, only Turkey has been concretely chastized through the application of punitive measures by the US Congress. This has led to a commonly shared feeling of betrayal among the Turkish political elites and the Turkish masses. Only a handful among the Turkish ruling elites and high-level civil servants fully comprehend the vagaries of US ethnic politics and the foreign policy constraints they impose on US presidents. Even they share, however, the emotions of their countrymen, being convinced that the West discriminates against Turkey, because it is the only non-Christian nation in the Atlantic Alliance. This feeling has obvious political relevance in light of the current situation in the Middle East and Persian Gulf area, and Turkey's national identity crisis.

It has been argued that in an era of détente, the extent and nature of a Soviet security threat is unduly emphasized if the USA makes a potential Soviet threat the focal point of US policies toward Turkey. But, in the wake of the Soviet invasion of Afghanistan, this conclusion would be tenable only if it could be shown that the USSR does not value the relationship between military power and political goals and that, in an era of nuclear weapons, no effective relationship exists between military power and foreign policy objectives. This is a doubtful proposition, especially in the nuclear age when the potential threat, rather than the actual use of force, is the cutting-edge of the foreign policies of the major powers.

The political consequences of military power are fully appreciated by Soviet decisionmakers and their advisers. Military power is seen by them as one of the most important instruments of foreign policy. Its role and effectiveness are believed to be dependent upon the particular international political situation and upon the specific balance of forces developing in the world in a particular region. They believe, however, that international relations can be greatly influenced by conventional armed forces, used either independently or even in combination with nuclear forces. In their view, both forms of military power can be used not only in the process of military operations to establish a military presence, but also for applying direct and indirect pressure during the course of negotiations to achieve political goals.[11] Turkey as a regional power must always act in the shadow of outside forces, especially the neighboring Soviet military presence.

FOREIGN POLICY LINKAGES: THE USA, NATO
AND TURKISH DOMESTIC POLITICS

Although security considerations have been uppermost in US-Turkish relations, and are the primary focus in NATO for all members, concerns about Turkey's economy and Turkey's political system have also been part of the USA and NATO policy outlook toward Turkey. American policies, especially those that have addressed the economic and political aspects of the mutual relationship, have been rationalized in terms of the USA helping Turkey to develop a viable economy that could sustain the Turkish parliamentary system. This was the principal justification for US aid to Turkey under the Truman Doctrine, and once Turkey joined NATO, US military grant assistance was believed necessary to relieve the Turkish economy from the demands of military expenditures, since Turkey must procure all major weapons abroad. In 1961, for example, the amount given by the USA in military grant aid to Turkey was equal to the positive balance in Turkey's external balance of payments.[12] Buying military equipment abroad, represents a drain on foreign exchange reserves. For Turkey, a developing country, defense expenditures diverted from civilian to military use also tend to bring about larger negative economic effects. This is different from industrialized countries.[13]

Thus the importance of the bilateral US-Turkish relationship to Turkey's participation in NATO is also explainable by the relative economic weakness of Turkey as a member of the alliance. This is not surprising, since most burdensharing occurs in NATO through bilateral channels. Notwithstanding the diplomatic malaise besetting US-Turkish relations, resulting from the impact of domestic ethnic politics on US foreign policy, and in spite of the negative US foreign exchange balances occasioned by the energy crisis and the reordering of the international economic system, the USA remains the largest single contributor of short-range economic aid to Turkey. For example, at the 30 May 1979 session of the multilateral assistance program, the USA pledged $198 million, plus about $50 million in Eximbank credits. This was the largest contribution (West Germany was second with $200 million, and France next at $70 million). If the $350 million in various forms assigned by the US executive for military assistance to Turkey for the fiscal year 1980 is added, it becomes clear that the USA continues to be a source of major economic assistance to Turkey.[14]

In Turkey military and civilian sectors expenses are especially fungible. The problem is, however, that Turkey's economic crisis is of such massive proportions that the USA would have to make Turkey one of the highest priorities in US foreign policy to justify the level of economic aid required to alter dramatically the present condition of the Turkish economy. Turkey is currently struggling under the weight of about $17 billion in foreign debt and a $2 billion annual payments deficit. The rapid increase in crude-oil prices has hurt Turkey's economy, especially. In 1979 the value of imported crude oil, and byproducts, practically equalled Turkey's total export revenue.[15] At the very least, US direct economic aid to Turkey would have to be comparable to the several billion dollars given to Israel and Egypt together, following the Camp David agreement. However, the inflationary trends, the other adverse effects in the monetary and trade fields on the US economy, together with ethnic constraints on US foreign policy, make such a US posture toward Turkey unlikely; short of exceedingly successful presidential leadership, sustained by revisions in US foreign policy priorities under the Carter Doctrine, or the guidelines of a subsequent US administration.

Of the other members of the Atlantic Alliance, only West Germany is in a position to offer economic aid to Turkey in useful amounts, yet not sufficiently to decisively correct Turkey's economic situation. Actually, recent and projected decreases in the number of Turkish workers in Germany will adversely affect Turkey's economy by increasing unemployment and reducing foreign income. The other European members of NATO do not have strong enough economies to aid Turkey significantly. To the contrary, some like Italy and Portugal particularly, are in need of major economic assistance themselves.

In any case, NATO is not set up to deal with economic problems beyond encouraging economic cooperation for purposes of the common defense. The necessity for some form of economic cooperation among NATO members has been made explicit in article II of the treaty. However, whenever the NATO Council has considered economic cooperation within the NATO framework, it has almost always concluded that economic problems besetting members of the alliance should be resolved through other international organizations, such as the OECD and IMF, or on a bilateral basis. When Greece and Turkey requested special economic support, NATO ministers recommended, for example, in 1962 the establishment of a Turkish Aid Consortium, outside NATO. Recent requests by Turkey for economic assistance are also being implemented outside NATO. The aid to Turkey decided upon by leaders of the alliance at the 1979 Guadeloupe meeting is being channeled through an OECD-sponsored consortium.[16]

Turkey's international economic policies will of necessity reach out to the international system, and in particular toward those countries which can serve specific Turkish economic needs. The USSR, Romania and the oil countries of the Middle East are among them. In terms of foreign trade, the EEC occupies the most important place in Turkish economic policies. The USA has never been a major trading partner for Turkey. Only about 5 percent of Turkey's exports go to the USA, and US foreign trade to Turkey has been overwhelmingly for purposes of mutual defense. The share of the EEC in Turkey's foreign trade, on the other hand, has increased steadily, so that it now represents over 40 percent of Turkey's total volume of trade. Clearly, NATO will not be the vehicle for solving Turkey's severe economic crisis any more than will the USA alone.

THE SOVIET-TURKISH RAPPROCHEMENT

Except for indirect support to Turkish terrorists of the radical-Left, the USSR has played no significant role in precipitating Turkey's crisis, but has been deriving foreign policy benefits from its consequences and would make the most gains in the region, if Turkey's effective participation in NATO were further undermined; and Turkish relations with the Muslim countries of the Middle East further alienated Turkey from the West.

Russian aspirations toward the Straits and the Mediterranean bridge tsarist and communist regimes. Even the Soviet naval presence in the Mediterranean has many historical antecedents. In 1770 a Russian flotilla of forty vessels was dispatched to the Mediterranean to aid the Greeks in revolt against the Ottomans. It remained until 1774, when the Treaty of Kuchuk Kainarji reestablished normal relations between Russia and Turkey. Russian warships returned to the Mediterranean in 1798 against Napoleon, in 1806 to fight against Turkey and France and, in 1807, to attempt a passage through the Dardanelles. Russian efforts to control the Straits have involved war and diplomacy for centuries, punctuated by numerous treaties that secured Russian passage. Most notable were the treaties of Unkiar-Skelessi in 1833; Paris in 1854; Berlin in 1878; and the 1936 Montreaux Convention, which still governs passage through the Straits.[17]

During World War I, Russia extracted a commitment from the Allies for Russian control of the Dardanelles. The fall of the tsar brought repudiation by the Bolsheviks of all tsarist agreements. However, a Soviet secret understanding with Nazi Germany would have achieved the same goal had Hitler not invaded the USSR.[18] The objective remained compelling. In 1946 Stalin strongly, but unsuccessfully, pressured Turkey to revise the Montreaux Convention so as to allow the stationing of Soviet troops on the Bosporus, coinciding with Soviet attempts to get United Nations trusteeship over Rhodes and the Dodecanese, and Cyrenaica.

In recent years, the Soviet government has repeatedly underscored the legitimacy of its naval presence in the Mediterranean and the importance of this region to Soviet national interest. As the military power of the USSR increases its global reach, and as it continues to develop technological sophistication, Soviet hegemonical tendencies are likely to be strengthened especially in peripheral areas like the Persian Gulf and the Mediterranean. The costly, and at times risky, investment of Soviet political and military resources in the Arab East attests to the USSR's commitment to the goal of expanding Soviet influence in the Middle East and Mediterranean region. The Afghanistan invasion confirms it. Since these hegemonical tendencies are not simply a matter of ideology but also derive from the global scope of the Soviet superpower's national interests, which in the near-future will include reliance on Middle Eastern oil, these tendencies are likely to intensify if circumstances permit.[19] Turkey's severe crisis is providing new opportunities for Soviet diplomacy; in the first instance, through economic aid; secondly, by dovetailing with the impact of the Iranian crisis on Turkish foreign policy.

In the decade immediately following the founding of the Turkish Republic, credits advanced to Turkey by the Soviet regime – itself hardly installed in power – played a significant role in Turkey's industrialization. Soviet economic assistance to Turkey is again playing an important role in Turkish industrialization. Turkish projects for the development of heavy industries and the expansion in raw-materials manufacture subsidized by Soviet loans and aid generally fulfil a genuine need for the Turkish economy. Soviet aid and credit projects will in the near term exceed credits received from any single country, including the USA and West Germany. Because payments for these loans are generally made by Turkey through barter arrangements, they are easier to repay than loans from Western countries. This is likely to lead to further expansion in Soviet-Turkish trade.[20] An example is the Turkish-Soviet trade protocol for 1980. It stipulates a reciprocal trade volume of $600 million, reflecting a projected 40 percent increase in trade volume over 1979. In addition, the USSR will also increase the volume of electricity it furnishes to Turkey.[21] A similar trend has developed in Turkish economic relations with Eastern Europe, notably Romania.[22]

Therefore, Soviet economic assistance to Turkey has greatly increased during recent years and is of the kind that strengthens public-sector tendencies while filling some of the gaps in Turkish industrial development created by Western reluctance to invest resources in areas viewed as either too risky, or of dubious value for surmounting Turkey's economic problems. Hence, their impact has been also political, and helpful to Soviet relations with Turkey. The erosion of cold war attitudes, the USSR's benign change of policy toward Turkey, but above all the cooling of political relations between Turkey and the USA, starting with the 1964 Cyprus crisis and climaxing with the US arms embargo in 1974, generated the conditions that made possible a rapprochement in the political and economic relations between Turkey and the USSR. Turkish governments, whether led by the socialist People's Republican Party or the conservative Justice Party, have expressed their determination to expand economic relations between Turkey and the USSR. The military leaders, who took the reins of government in September 1980, have made no sustantial changes in this respect.

The USSR and Eastern Europe cannot replace the USA and Western Europe as major sources of economic assistance, technology transfer and commercial partnership. However, to the degree that Turkey is forced to become dependent for economic and development aid on the USSR, because of Western reluctance to help sufficiently, to that degree Turkish foreign policy will have to accommodate to the diplomatic positions of its powerful neighbor. Soviet diplomacy is engaged in an all-out effort to exploit Turkey's increasing sense of alienation from her Western allies by the promise of additional economic aid, especially development assistance to more than forty projects, and by structuring its economic aid to boost Turkish political forces favoring a predominantly public-sector economy. This would further hobble Western aid efforts which are geared to a major role for private enterprise and the market economy.

Since the late 1960s, efforts to develop the private sector of the Turkish economy – championed by the Adalet Partisi (Justice Party) – have met with stubborn resistance from the other opposite mass party, the Cumhuriyet Halk Partisi (People's Republican Party), whose historical *étatisme* and present socialist tendencies favor development of the public sector instead. The PRP, whether in power or in opposition, is highly influential in the policies Turkey pursues domestically and abroad. Within its ranks and among the party's sympathizers are found the majority of Turkish bureaucrats, technocrats, journalists and a good number of the military.[23] Soviet economic policies toward Turkey strengthen, therefore, public-sector influence, creating vested interests in continued and expanding Turkish economic relations with the USSR.

There is no doubt that the intensification of Turkish relations with the USSR and the countries of Eastern Europe are one manifestation of the deterioration in Turkey's relationship with the USA and of a search for less political dependence on the American superpower, and greater independence and flexibility in the pursuit of Turkish foreign policy. Sparked by the Cyprus conflict, this search for new foreign policy options has been rationalized also in terms of détente.[24] A fortnight before Soviet troops violated Afghan territory, the newly elected Justice Party government led by Demirel answered Brezhnev's message by emphasizing the Turkish foreign policy commitment to détente.[25] After the Soviet invasion, Turkey roundly condemned the invasion and supported all United Nations actions, but informed the USA that it would not join in active measures against the USSR.[26] Although the Afghan events did facilitate the conclusion on 10 January 1980 of the negotiations for a renewed US-Turkish defense cooperation agreement, a careful reading of its provisions suggests that the acceptance by the USA of almost all major Turkish positions may have been even more responsible for their successful outcome. Since the military takeover, Turkey's approach has not materially changed. At the October 1980 military parade in Moscow, Turkish and Norwegian diplomats were the only Western diplomats not to boycott the ceremony, for example.

TURKEY AND THE ARABS

Turkey's Middle East policy also illustrates the search for a more independent foreign policy and the increased awareness of her Muslim heritage. The sources of Turkey's increasing involvement in the Arab East have been the oil crisis and the felt need to find support for Turkey's policy on Cyprus. While they have converged in Turkish diplomacy, the former has been the more important. Turkey as a developing country without oil has been severely hit by the rapid increase in crude-oil prices that followed the 1973 Arab embargo. As Turkey's alienation from her Western allies has increased, the search for a meaningful Muslim legacy has converged with other requirements to focus Turkey on Middle East politics. The economic policy pursued by Turkey toward the Middle East is characterized by the Turkish government's proposal, in 1978, to 'combine Arab capital, European technology, and Turkish labor'.[27]

The results achieved by Turkey's diplomatic efforts to forge closer political ties with the Arabs, and to create much-needed economic exchanges, have been mixed and only moderately successful. The legacy of a shared history, while serving as a positive link with the Arab countries of the Maghreb, has remained a source of mistrust for Turkey's relations with the Arab countries of the Mashrek. Although Turkey is Middle Eastern as much as European, her historic choice of the West as a political model and her imperial past have isolated Turkey politically and economically from the Arabs. Turkey's participation in NATO, her aspiration to full membership in the European Community and her dogged pursuit of a pluralist democratic system are visible signs of her commitment to the West and they have been viewed with suspicion by many Arab governments. As Turkey's relations with the West increased in the postwar period, her relations with the Arab countries deteriorated.[28]

Turkey's role as a geopolitical buffer against the USSR, which has permitted the socialist Arab states of the Middle East to cooperate with the USSR for their security interests without risking a possible application of the Brezhnev Doctrine, has neither been noticed nor appreciated. It remains to be seen to what extent, and in what ways germane to Turkish-Arab relations, the events of Afghanistan will change this.

It is paradoxical, therefore, that the two Arab countries with which Turkey has succeeded in developing the most intense economic exchanges and generally cordial political relations are Iraq and Libya – two of the more radical Arab countries and, in the case of Libya, the most Soviet-leaning of Arab countries. In the case of Libya, too, a partial explanation derives from a shared Turkish-Libyan experience recent enough in their historical conscience to have policy relevance. The imperial Ottoman hand rested lightly on the shoulders of the Arab emirates of the Maghreb. Thus, Libya was relatively free of Ottoman control. More important, Turkish soldiers fought side by side with Libyan tribesmen in the unsuccessful attempt to repel Italy's colonial takeover of Libya, just before World War I, and then fought against Italy and the Allies during the war. This shared historical experience must help bridge the suspicions that arise as a consequence of the great difference in their political systems and in their foreign policies *vis-à-vis* the USA, the USSR and Europe.[29] The successful relations with Iraq may be explained, in part, by Turkey's and Iraq's common Kurdish problem,[30] and Iraq's more recent cooling of relations with Moscow.

The share of the Arab countries in Turkey's foreign trade has doubled during the last decade, from 6·69 percent in 1968 to 12·19 percent in 1977. Starting with 1978, Turkey has intensified attempts to develop economic relations with Arab countries, with some success. New economic agreements were achieved with Iran, Iraq, Libya, Jordan and Tunisia. However, the most important economic relations have remained those with Iraq, Turkey's major supplier of oil, and Libya in particular. The share of these countries' oil exports in Turkey's oil imports has become very high, and is expected to increase.[31] The significance of this Turkish dependence on Iraq and Libya may be inferred from the fact that the value of Turkish exports is now about equal to the amount Turkey spends for importing oil. An example of this increased cooperation is the joint Turkish-Iraqi oil pipeline project, completed in the 1973–7 period. It brings oil from Iraqi oilfields to Turkey's Mediterranean shore for shipment by sea. Another is the Arab-Turkish Bank, established with the participation of Turkey, Libya and Kuwait.[32]

Besides trade relations and banking activities, there has been a significant growth in joint Turkish projects with Iraq and Libya in ship construction and sea transport, and in the activity of Turkish construction companies. Again, the volume of these activities has been larger in Libya. The majority of the 50,000 Turkish workers in the Arab countries is at work in Libya building roads, harbors, irrigation systems and housing. Turkey has limited opportunities to export industrial goods to developed countries, but in the Arab countries, instead, there is a market for Turkish vehicles and spare automotive parts, electrical appliances, cables and wires, manufactured construction materials and plastic goods. This is the reverse of the kinds of goods Turkey can export to Europe. Turkey's exports to Europe are almost all agricultural products. As such, now that Greece has joined the EEC, and especially if Spain is admitted, Turkish agricultural exports to Europe will face tougher competition than ever before. Together with the necessity to increase export revenue to pay for the substantial increases in the price of crude oil, this increased competition in Turkey's sales to Western Europe is the reason why Turkey is trying to create an export market for its products in the Arab countries.

A rapprochement between Turkish and radical Arab foreign policies toward the USA and the USSR could have consequences for Western European policies and for the security of the Mediterranean. One factor that could accelerate this foreign policy convergence is the increasing number of Turkish technicians and workers in Iraq, and especially Libya. The mixture of 'Muslim' politics, leftist ideology and nationalism already at work in Turkish internal politics is bound to be reinforced, with the consequent impact on Turkey's 'foreign' policy. One recent result has been the official recognition by the Turkish government of the Palestine Liberation Organization, reinforced by a Turkish policy of opening up to revolutionary Iran for economic and diplomatic reasons.

Eventually more profound in its impact is Turkey's crucial dependence on Libya and Iraq for oil, in the context of an acute economic crisis that is unlikely to be quickly resolved, or resolved solely through Western assistance. Turkey, obviously, has not been alone in realigning its policy on the Arab-Israeli conflict to support the Arab cause. Her European allies have done the same. Like Turkey, they have also denied the USA the use of their territories during the Arab-Israeli conflicts. However, Turkey's geographic position and its dire economic situation make her more vulnerable to direct Soviet pressures, and would make her also more vulnerable to Soviet pressures indirectly applied through Arab states.

Turkish relations with some Arab states go beyond economic and diplomatic ties. Turkish officers are in Libya helping to reorganize the country's armed forces. Libyan naval and ground forces cadets have been training in Turkish academies. And starting this year, the Turkish airforce school will train Libyan air cadets. Libya has pledged financial assistance to the Turkish armaments industry.[33] Talks have been underway also between Turkey and Iraq on the possibility of training Iraqi gendarmerie officers and NCOs.[34]

Already, during the last Arab-Israeli conflicts, Turkey has allowed Soviet aircraft to overfly her territory. Although this can be rationalized in terms of Turkish support for the Arab cause, it is difficult to explain Turkey's refusal to allow U-2 flights to verify SALT II without Soviet consent, except as evidence of Turkey's need to accommodate to the USSR's positions. Closer relations between Turkey and radical Arab states can complicate further the US-Turkish relationship, and even Turkish relations with some of the moderate Arab states. The former has been strained for years by the Greek-Turkish conflict on Cyprus, and by the consequent 1974–8 US arms embargo against Turkey in particular. The US-Turkish relationship is pivotal to Turkey's effective participation in NATO, with Turkey's membership in NATO being an essential shield against Soviet hegemonical tendencies toward Turkey, the Mediterranean and Pakistan and Iran.

It remains to be seen how Turkey's alienation from the USA and Western Europe will affect her relations with other Mediterranean countries. It may be symptomatic that as Turkey has become more involved with Libya and Iraq, Turkish relations with Egypt have deteriorated. Turkey has also sought to participate actively in the Islamic politics of the Third World, hosting the Islamic Conference in Istanbul in 1976. One result was the establishment of the Economic and Social Research Institute of the Islamic countries in Ankara.

In the long run, because Turkey is undergoing a national identity crisis as well as an economic-political one, involvement in Islamic politics would weaken Turkey's secular Western vocation, further alienating Turkey from the West. The competition that is likely to arise between Turkey and her West European NATO allies as Turkey attempts to create a market for her manufactured goods in Arab countries can also increase Turkish friction with Europe and the USA, ultimately affecting the Turkish foreign policy outlook.

The southern shores of the Mediterranean are politically as fluid – and from a Western viewpoint almost as precarious a region – as the Persian Gulf but more critical to the East–West military and political equilibrium that sustains the détente in Europe. The mutually reinforcing factors created by the severe economic and political crisis in Turkey, Turkey's increasing political alienation from the West, and the search by Turkish diplomacy to compensate in the Arab East, creates opportunities for the USSR that could lead to Turkish acquiescence to developments undermining Mediterranean stability.[35]

Already there has been some direct impact on US-Turkish relations. During the final phases of the negotiations for renewing the use of US bases in Turkey, there were complaints by the Arab rejectionist states to Turkey that information gathered from US bases in Turkey about military movements in Syria, Iraq and other neighboring Arab states found its way to the Israeli general staff. This reportedly led Turkey to define NATO functions more restrictively, in the arrangements concerning US operations in Turkey. High-level military and civilian Turkish officials have presumably reassured Libya on that score.[36]

IN LIEU OF CONCLUSIONS

The trauma of the US arms embargo has unprecedentedly eroded the US-Turkish alilance relationship. And Turkey's precarious economic situation has forced the Turkish government to ask NATO to exempt Turkey from meeting the 3 percent annual increase in defense expenditures and the requirements of NATO's long-range program. Turkey's arms are, in addition, obsolescent. More worrisome still, is the eventual upshot of this on the relations between Turkey and the USSR.

A Turkey that feels politically isolated from Western Europe and in economic competition with her European allies in the Middle East, that believes the US security guarantee to be strongly qualified by the conflictual relationship with Greece, and that must rely for critical oil supplies on the most politically radical, pro-Soviet Arab states, is likely to accommodate Soviet policies toward the Mediterranean and the Middle East. A consequence of Turkey's effective participation in NATO might be the intensification of the already-serious erosion in the Turkish relationship with the USA.

An underrated aspect of Turkey's participation in NATO is Turkey's parliamentary democracy. Turkey is the only Muslim country of the Middle East that has been long committed to a West European model of parliamentary democracy. Until September 1980, there had been two short-lived military takeovers of the government – intended not to overthrow the democratic system. The third occurred in September 1980, and continues. Like the preceding ones, it is intended to rescue the country from political chaos. The Turkish crisis has raised, in the minds of Turkish political leaders and especially the youthful electorate, some serious doubts about the future of Turkish democracy. The major cause for these Turkish attitudes has been Turkey's alienation from Western Europe and the USA. But a contributing prior cause is to be found in the political Left–Right radicalization and polarization of Turkish domestic politics that has taken place following the 1960 military takeover. The 1964, 1969 and 1974 Cyprus crises and the extended and aggravated economic crisis have both contributed to this phenomenon and brought it to the surface. A crucial, additional factor has been the massive terrorism that has issued from the political polarization.

The safeguards against revolution and dictatorship inherent in the Turkish political system – foremost among them the Turkish armed forces' patriotic cohesiveness, discipline and commitment to public order and parliamentary democracy – can lead to the cautious conclusion that Turkey will not follow Iran's example. In light of the developments discussed above, however, Turkey's Western system of politics acquires essential importance for Turkey's relations with her NATO allies.

The common political ideology has been an important asset in the relations between Turkey, the USA and Western Europe. Without unduly oversimplifying, it may be said that shared political values have greatly aided in making it possible for the USA and Turkey to remain allies in face of the acute policy differences that have afflicted their relations since 1964. Obversely, they have provided a buffer against Soviet influence in

Turkey's internal politics. Turkey's democratic system has not only functioned in a positive way in Turkish-US relations, it has also facilitated Turkey's political, economic and military relations with the democracies of Western Europe, especially West Germany.[37] How critical the commitment to parliamentary politics is in the relations with members of the EEC, has been illustrated by the experience of Spain, Portugal and Greece. The continued maintenance of a parliamentary democracy in spite of the vicissitudes Turkey has been experiencing since it joined NATO, is a tribute to Turkey's commitment to Western democracy. If democracy should fail in Turkey, the negative political repercussions for NATO and the West will reach beyond Turkey's frontiers to the Middle East, the Mediterranean and Europe.

The USA and Turkey have barely finalized the agreements that are to guide their relations in the security area for the next five years. This is the second major reviision of the bilateral base agreements since Turkey joined NATO. A problem that has beset such negotiations in the past, and continues to complicate current US-Turkish relations results from differing US and Turkish perceptions in regard to Turkey's role in the security of the USA, and the definition of the security threat against Turkey. What is meant by the strategic significance of Turkey is at the heart of the matter.

At the beginning of the US-Turkish alliance in the 1950s, the differences were hardly worth considering. In the words of Nuri Eren, 'Unlike many of the Western European members of the alliance, Turkey, by virtue of its geography, is endowed with major significance in the alliance's global military and ideological strategy which goes beyond the limits of her status as a middle power.'[38]Setting aside ideological aspects, there is no question that this Turkish view continues to be widely held among Turkey's leaders. Until nuclear, ballistic intercontinental missiles, and related technology like satellites, became the mainstay of US and Soviet strategic forces, US leaders could have accepted the statement without reservations. Currently, and even more in the future, the statement requires several important qualifications.

Turkish territory is not needed to target the USSR either for nuclear warfighting, or nuclear deterrent purposes. For the USA, strategic equates with nuclear and global. The global reach of nuclear weapon systems, deployed and to be deployed in the 1980s, makes reliance on foreign territory and even the oceans, except for adjacent seas, not as crucial as before. For the USSR, this means the Baltic and the Norwegian Sea, in particular; for the USA, the North Pacific. In terms of strategic weapon systems, Turkey cannot be said to discharge a global, strategic function – any more than West Germany does – for US national security. An important caveat is warranted. For the years immediately ahead, particularly because of the recent loss of US intelligence facilities in Iran, intelligence installations in Turkey could perform a useful service for US deterrence of the USSR and for NATO by helping to verify SALT and monitor Soviet tests of strategic weapons. That these facilities are inadequate to achieve this alone, is suggested by American efforts to seek Turkey's permission for the resumption of U-2 flights. Technology will help decrease US reliance on the use of foreign territory for strategic verification in a few years. It is difficult without the use of evidence not in the public domain to ascertain how critical the U-2 flights would be to verification of SALT II, or to monitor Soviet tests. A major controversy over the requirements for verifying SALT II was a feature of the aborted ratification debate in Washington. Reconnaissance satellites are believed to be generally adequate to monitor deployments. By inference, what U-2s, based in Cyprus on a British installation and overlying Turkish airspace in the Black Sea area and along the Turkish-Soviet border, would furnish is data on Soviet testing of strategic weapon systems. Turkey's refusal to allow these flights without Soviet consent was eloquent testimony to the changes that have occurred in US-Turkish and Turkish-Soviet relations.

The Turkish definition of the strategic importance of Turkey, quoted above, remains valid at the regional, non-nuclear, or conventional level. But even in this context, it is somewhat qualified in terms of European security From the US viewpoint, the keystone of Western European security is NATO's central front, or the defense of West Germany. The linchpins of the defense of Europe are the US nuclear guarantee and adequate allied conventional forces. The East–West military balance in the Mediterranean has always been less clear and less stable because of the political as much as the physical geography of the region.

What is, then, the military importance of Turkey to the Atlantic Alliance and the USA? In the nuclear era, particularly for the Atlantic region which includes Western Europe and NATO's southern flank, deterrence of East–West conflict is the only rational policy option. This is the case of conventional and regional, as well as strategic, nuclear and global levels. In fact, an Atlantic Alliance–Warsaw Pact conventional conflict that did not risk early escalation to nuclear war in the European theater, and between the USA and USSR intercontinentally, is believed by most experts to be unlikely. Nevertheless, deevlopments in recent years in the US-Soviet strategic balance and in the Eurostrategic balance have caused concern in the alliance and have refocused the importance of the East–West conventional military balance. With or without SALT II, the military and political risks for Western Europe appear to be increasing. Turkey is the forward and key location for NATO southern-flank defense. Greece is not fully defensible without a Turkish forward defense in Thrace, for example. The continued emasculation of Turkey's defense capability would shift the NATO defense line to Italy and the 'choke points' between Sicily and North Africa. Not only would the western Mediterranean be more exposed to more direct Soviet pressure, but the US position in the Middle East and the Persian Gulf would also be undercut. A militarily strong and politically cohesive Turkey, not disaffected from NATO, would reinforce deterrence, at the conventional level, and help maintain the East–West political equilibrium in Europe. It would also help sustain the unaligned stance of Yugoslavia at a time when its future independence may be threatened by a succession crisis in its leadership. The stakes for NATO in Turkey's present crisis are high politically and militarily. A solution of the Turkish crisis is problematic at best. Western European and US policies may be well intentioned, but they remain inadequate. Time and circumstances are tilting against the West.

NOTES: CHAPTER 14

1 An historical analysis of this process is in Niyazi Berkes, *The Development of Secularism in Turkey* (Montreal: McGill University Press, 1964).
2 Seyfi Taşhan, 'Turkey and the West', *Dış Politika* (Foreign Policy) (Ankara), (May 1978), and *Dış Politika* (October 1979).
3 Bernard Lewis, *The Emergence of Modern Turkey* (London and New York: Oxford University Press, 1961), p. 479. See also Suna Kili, *Türk Devrim Tarihi* (History of the Turkish Revolution) (Istanbul: Boğaziçi U., 1980). Also Nuri Eren, *Turkey Today and Tomorrow: An Experiment in Westernization* (New York: Praeger, 1963).
4 'Tanzimat' means reorganization and was launched by the Imperial Edict of Gulhane, followed by another, Hatt-i Hunayun or illustrious rescript, of 1856. The latter had significant secularizing aspects. This came in the wake of Russia's defeat in the Crimea and the Treaty of Paris which ended the war and formally admitted the Ottoman Empire into the European community of great powers: J. C. Hurewitz, *Diplomacy in the Near and Middle East: A Documentary Record*, vol. 1 (Princeton, NJ: Van Nostrand, 1956), pp. 105–6.
5 Seyfi Taşhan, 'Turkey's relations with the USA and possible future developments', *Dış Politika* (July 1979).
6 A comprehensive analysis of the US-Turkish relationship in the postwar period is in George S. Harris, *The Troubled Alliance: Problems in Historical Perspective, 1945–1971* (Washington, DC: American Enterprise Institute and Hoover Institute, 1972).
7 Muharrem Birgi, 'Developments within the Atlantic community and Turkey', *Dış Politika* (December 1973).
8 Ferenc A. Vali, *Bridge Across the Bosporus: The Foreign Policy of Turkey* (Baltimore, Md: Johns Hopkins University Press, 1971), pp. 118, 125–6.
9 Useful references to the Cyprus conflict are Stephen G. Xydis, *Cyprus: Conflict and Conciliation, 1954–58* (Columbus, Ohio: Ohio State University Press, 1967); Lawrence Durrell, *Bitter Lemons* (Harmondsworth, Mddx: Penguin, 1959): Linda B. Miller, *Cyprus: The Law and Politics of Civil Strife* (Cambridge, Mass.: Harvard Center for International Affairs, 1968); and T. W. Adams and Alvin J. Cottrell, *Cyprus Between East and West* (Baltimore, Md: Johns Hopkins University Press, 1968).
10 A full text of President Johnson's letter and of Premier İnönü's reply are in *Middle East Journal*, vol. 20, no. 3 (Summer 1966), pp. 386–93. A Turkish analysis of the Johnson letter's impact on US-Turkish relations is in Mehmet Günlübol, *Dış Politika* (December 1971).
11 These Soviet views are best summarized in the concluding chapter of V. M. Kulish, *Military Power and International Relations* (Moscow: Soviet Academy of Sciences, 1972).
12 William Johnson and Ciro Zoppo, *Issues in US-Turkish Relations* (Santa Monica, Calif.: Rand , November 1970).
13 Osman Okyar, *Economic Cooperation Within NATO* (Ankara: Hacettepe University Press, 1979).
14 US Department of State, *Foreign Economic Trends and Their Implications for the United States: Turkey*, March 1979.
15 Erol Manisali, *Turkey's Place and Possible Developments in International Economic Relations* (Istanbul: Istanbul University Press, 1979).
16 Osman Okyar *Economic Cooperation Within NATO*, op. cit.
17 Nicholas V. Riasanovsky, *A History of Russia* (New York: Oxford University Press, 1963).
18 R. J. Sontag and J. S. Beddie, *Nazi-Soviet Relations, 1939-1941*, US Department of State, Publication 2023, Washington, DC, 1948.
19 An analysis of Soviet policy that is pertinent is Shahram Chubin, *Soviet Policy towards Iran and the Gulf*, Adelphi Paper 157, International Institute for Strategic Studies, London, 1980; see pp. 42–5 especially. Of interest also is Bradford Dismuker and James McConnell, *Soviet Naval Diplomacy* (New York: Pergamon Press, 1979).

20 Mukerrem Hiç, *Turkey's International Economic Relations* (Istanbul: Istanbul University Press, September 1979).
21 *The Pulse*, Ankara, 6 December 1979.
22 Details are in Önder Ari, *Turkey's Political and Economic Relations with the USSR and Eastern Bloc Countries* (Istanbul: Istanbul University Press, June 1979).
23 For a description of the recent developments that have occurred in the makeup and policies of the RPP, see Suna Kili, *1960–1975 Döneminde Cumhuriyet Halk Partisinde Gelişmeler* (Developments in the Republican People's Party 1960–1975) (Istanbul: Boğazici University Press, 1975). Of particular interest are the party membership lists and related data on pp. 465–521.
24 See, for example, Seyfi Taşhan, *Détente, Helsinki Son Seneti Ve Belgrad Konferansi* (Détente, the Helsinki Act and the Belgrade Conference) (Ankara: Foreign Policy Institute, July 1977); Ölgün Cidar, 'Foreign policy issues in the general elections', *Dış Politika* (July 1978); Osman Olcay, 'Turkey's foreign policy', *Dış Politika* (June 1971); and Ali Karaosmanoğlu, 'Paradoxes in the three conferences on détente', *Dış Politika* (March 1974).
25 *Tercuman* (Istanbul), 6 December 1979.
26 *Diplomat* (Ankara), 30 January 1980.
27 Esat Cam, *The Economic and Political Relationships of Turkey with the Middle Eastern Countries* (Istanbul: Istanbul University Press, June 1979), p. 7.
28 Ömer Kürkcüoglu, 'Recent developments in Turkey's Middle East policy', *Dış Politika* (June 1971).
29 A succinct summary of Libya's foreign policy orientation, obviously at odds with the basis of Turkey's foreign policy, are Qaddafi's statements during an interview with Youssef Ibrahim in the *New York Times*, 10 December 1979.
30 A history of the Kurdish problem, from a Kurdish viewpoint, is in Gérard Chaliand *et al., Les Kurdes et le Kurdistan* (The Kurds and Kurdistan) (Paris: François Maspero, 1978). The discussions on Turkey and Iraq are on pp. 69–151 and 225–303.
31 Erol Manisali, op. cit.
32 Escat Cam, op. cit.
33 *Diplomat*, 5 September 1979.
34 *Pulse*, 3 October 1979.
35 In December 1979, when the USA asked Ankara for the use of the US-operated Incirlik airfield to evacuate Americans from Iran, permission was refused. See *Diplomat*, 12 December 1979.
36 *Diplomat*, 21 January 1980.
37 A summary account of the nature of Turkish-West German relations is Oğuz Gökman's 'Turkish-German relations', *Dış Politika* (March 1977).
38 *Turkey, NATO and Europe: A Deteriorating Relationship?*, Atlantic Papers, No. 34, December 1977, p. 54.

NOTE ON CONTRIBUTORS

Fouad Ajami is a professor and director of Middle Eastern studies at the School of Advanced International Studies at the Johns Hopkins University. He is the author of the *Arab Predicament: Arab Political Thought and Practice since 1967* and other works. He contributes to *Foreign Affairs* and *Foreign Policy* as well as other forums.

Richard Cottam is a professor of political science at the University of Pittsburgh and a long-time consultant to the State Department. He is the author of *Nationalism in Iran, Competitive Interference and Twentieth Century Diplomacy* and *Foreign Policy Motivation: A General Theory and a Case Study*.

Tawfic E. Farah is president of the Middle East Research Group, Inc. of Fresno, California, and editor of the *Journal of Arab Affairs*.

Francis Fukuyama is currently a member of the State Department policy planning staff. Previously, he was a member of the Social Science Department of the RAND Corporation, specializing in Soviet foreign policy and Middle Eastern affairs. His most recent publication is *The Soviet Union and Iraq since 1968*.

Joan Garratt is a doctoral candidate in political science at Harvard University and a graduate associate of the Center for International Affairs at Harvard University.

Ibrahim Karawan is a doctoral candidate in political science and a research fellow with the Von Grunebaum Center for Near Eastern Studies at the University of California, Los Angeles. He is also a member of the Al Ahram Center for Political and Strategic Studies and has written in Arabic on Middle Eastern affairs.

James R. Kurth is a professor of political science at Swarthmore College and has written widely on such topics as the industrial sectors, military policy and American foreign policy. His recent articles have appeared in *International Organization* and in *The New Authoritarianism in Latin America*, edited by David Collier.

Robert J. Lieber is a professor of political science at the University of California, Davis. He was a fellow of the Woodrow Wilson Center's international security studies program at the Smithsonian Institution, Washington, DC, during 1980–1. His publications include *British Politics and European Unity, Theory and World Politics*, and *Oil and the Middle East War: Europe in the Energy Crisis*. His articles have appeared in many American and European journals.

Dominique Moisi is an associate professor at the University of Paris X Nanterre and assistant director of the Institut Français des Relations Internationales.

William B. Quandt is a senior fellow at the Brookings Institution. In 1977–9 he was on the staff of the National Security Council with responsibility for Middle Eastern affairs. His publications include *Decade of Decisions: American Policy Toward the Arab-Israeli Conflict, 1967–1976*.

Itamar Rabinovitch is head of the Shiloah Center for Middle Eastern and African Studies and associate professor of Middle Eastern history at Tel Aviv University. He is the author of *Syria under the Ba'th, 1963–1966* and co-editor of *From June to October* and *The Middle East and the United States*.

Masahiro Sasagawa is Middle East editor of the Japanese daily *Asahi Shimbun*.

He has published widely in Japan on Middle Eastern affairs. He was a research associate at the University of Jordan in Amman during 1980–1.

Steven L. Spiegel is an associate professor of political science at the University of California, Los Angeles, and the author of the forthcoming volume, *The War for Washington: The Other Arab-Israeli Conflict*. In addition to numerous articles on international affairs and American foreign policy, he is the author of *Dominance and Diversity: The International Hierarchy*, and co-author of *The International Politics of Regions: A Comparative Approach*.

Janice Gross Stein is a member of the Political Science Department at McGill University. She is the co-author of the just-published *Rational Decision Making: Israel's Security Choices, 1967* and has written recently for the *Journal of Strategic Studies* and *International Journal*.

Ciro Elliott Zoppo is an associate professor of international relations at the University of California, Los Angeles. He is a consultant at the RAND Corporation, a member of the International Institute for Strategic Affairs and of the Centre d'Études Politiques de Defense at the Sorbonne. A specialist in foreign policy, security and arms control, he is the author of many studies and articles published in the USA and Europe.

Index

Afghanistan: Gulf, security of, and role of USA and Europe 28, 31; Japan, and opinion of Soviet invasion of 41; USA foreign policy after invasion of 12, 13; USSR, and influence in 122–4, 130, 137, 138–41

Algeria: Egypt, and relationship with 157; French policy towards (1957) US criticism of 10

Arab-Israeli dispute, and North Atlantic alliance 49–81; and Camp David talks 62–7; and division within alliance 51–4; and October 1973 war 54–7; and politics of alliance 68–72; and settlement terms 60–2; United Nations, voting at 57–60

Arab-Israeli wars: of 1967 and US support for Israel 10–11, 152; of 1973 (October War) and US problems with allies 10–11, 16, 54–7, *see also* oil crisis; *see also* Arab-Israeli dispute

Arab Military Industries Organization (AMIO) 171

Asia-Pacific Association of Japan 36

Camp David agreements (1978) 14–15, 31, 32, 62–7; attitude of Germany to 22; and Palestine issue 15–17, 167–8, 204

Canada, and problems of the Arab-Israeli dispute: oil production, increase of, after 1973 crisis 86; and support of Camp David talks 64; and Palestine issue 66–7; and affirmation of Resolution 242 51, 52, 54; and terms of settlement 60, 61; United Nations, and voting on Palestine issue 57, 58, 59

Compagne Française des Pétroles (CFP) 93

Conference on International Economic Cooperation (CIEC) 98

Conference on Security and Cooperation in Europe (CSCE) 90

Cyprus, crisis of, and role of US and Turkey 230–2

Denmark: and reaction to Camp David agreements 65; and October 1973 war, disagreement within EEC 55

détente, European interpretation of 31

Economic Research Institute for the Middle East (Japan) 36

Egypt: Arab League, exclusion from 27; arms transfer from USA 170–5; food

riots in (1977) 165–6; foreign policy, reorientation of 177; Infitah in 175–8; Israel, and peace treaty with 88–9, 202–3; Middle East, and position of in 155–8; and Palestine issue 15, 16, 152; Soviet experience in 129, 130, 131–2, 169, 170; and relationship with USA 119, 148, 163, 164–9, 176; and relationship with the West **163–78**

Egypt-Israel peace treaty 202–3; Japanese support for 40

Energy crises: and effects on alliance 109–12; Euro-American energy diplomacy in Middle East **82–101**; Euro-American political differences 87–91; Euro-American relations and IEA 99–101; and Iranian revolution 104, 107–9; multilateral energy diplomacy, failure of 91–7; International Energy Agency, creation of 97–9; oil crisis (1973) and effects on Atlantic alliance 82–7, **104–13**

Ente Nazionale Idrocarburi (ENI) 93

Europe **18–32**; and Afghan crisis 31; Euro-Arab dialogue, and economic orientation 26–8; Feedral Republic of Germany, and policies towards Middle East 22–3; France, and policies towards Middle East 19–22; Great Britain, and policies towards Middle East 23–4; and security of the Gulf 28–32; political cooperation within EEC 24–6, 27–8; *see also* individual countries

European Coal and Steel Community (ECSC), and regulation of energy policy 92

European Economic Community (EEC): and alliance politics on Arab-Israeli dispute 69, 70, 71; Arab-Israeli dispute, and terms of settlement 60–2; and reaction to Camp David talks 64–5; Middle East peace process, and statements of 25–6, 53–4, 110; multilateral energy diplomacy, failure of 93; October 1973 war, disagreements among 54–5, 56; oil crisis, and effects on 84–5, 86, 90–1, 105–6, 108–9, 110–11; and the Palestine issue 57, 58, 59, 60

European Political Cooperation (EPC) 90

France: Algeria, policy in (1957), US criticism of 10; and alliance politics on Arab-Israeli dispute 68; Arab-Israeli

Publications of the Center for International and Strategic Affairs, UCLA

William Potter (ed.), *Verification and SALT: The Challenge of Strategic Deception* (Westview, 1980).

Bennett Ramberg, *Destruction of Nuclear Energy Facilities in War: The Problem and Implications* (Lexington Books, 1980).

Paul Jabber, *Not by War Alone: The Politics of Arms Control in the Middle East* (University of California Press, 1981).

William Potter, *Nuclear Power and Nonproliferation: An Interdisciplinary Perspective* (Oelgeschlager, Gunn, & Hain, 1981).

Roman Kolkowicz and Andrzej Korbonski (eds), *Soldiers, Peasants, and Bureaucrats: Civil–Military Relations in Communist and Modernizing Societies* (Allen & Unwin, 1982).